VENICE
THE HINGE
OF EUROPE
1081–1797

William H. McNeill

VENICE

THE HINGE
OF EUROPE
1081-1797

THE UNIVERSITY
OF CHICAGO PRESS
CHICAGO AND LONDON

THE UNIVERSITY OF CHICAGO PRESS, CHICAGO 60637
THE UNIVERSITY OF CHICAGO PRESS, LTD., LONDON

LIBRARY OF CONGRESS CATALOG CARD NUMBER 73-84192
INTERNATIONAL STANDARD BOOK NUMBER 0-226-56149-6

TO MY FATHER
JOHN THOMAS McNEILL
WHOSE ECUMENICAL VIEW OF EUROPE'S
PAST NURTURED MY OWN,
AND
WHOSE LIFELONG DEDICATION TO
CHURCH HISTORY
MAY HERE PERHAPS DISCOVER ITS
MUTED COUNTERPART

On the Extinction of the Venetian Republic, 1802

Once did she hold the gorgeous east in fee;
And was the safeguard of the west: the worth
Of Venice did not fall below her birth,
Venice, the eldest Child of Liberty.
She was a maiden City, bright and free;
No guile seduced, no force could violate;
And, when she took unto herself a Mate,
She must espouse the everlasting Sea.
And what if she had seen those glories fade,
Those titles vanish, and that strength decay;
Yet shall some tribute of regret be paid
When her long life has reach'd its final day:
Men are we, and must grieve when even the Shade
Of that which once was great is pass'd away.

William Wordsworth

Contents

Preface

IN 1944 when I first set foot in Greece and visited the great fortresses of Nauplion and Acrocorinth, the sight of the Lion of Saint Mark carved into their battlements took me completely by surprise. Nothing in my schooling had prepared me for such tangible evidence of western Europe's first overseas empire. Years later, when visits by Americans to Russia were still unusual, an evening in a colleague's house spent watching slides of old Moscow, whence he had just returned, led me suddenly to realize that I was looking at architecture that betrayed Italian affinities. This, too, struck me as surprising. Later still, the task of writing an article for the *Encyclopedia Americana* on Crete, undertaken for entirely mercenary reasons, led to a third surprising encounter—my discovery of Cretan art and literature of the seventeenth century.

Such chance experiences scattered across more than twenty years provoked this book. As my investigations attained clearer focus and definition, the project grew into a twin and corrective supplement to my essay on *Europe's Steppe Frontier, 1500–1800* (Chicago, 1964). In that book I tried to describe interrelations among the Hapsburg, Ottoman, and Russian empires of eastern Europe. As that essay approached the regions in question overland, this book tries to come at the same regions by sea, considering interrelations that arose primarily through contacts generated and sustained by men traveling on shipboard.

This book took shape initially through a pair of courses offered in the Department of History, The University of Chicago, as part of my ordinary teaching duties. To try out em-

Preface

bryonic ideas on students and benefit from their reactions is one of the most precious aspects of University life; and in this case, my initial ignorance made the direct instruction I had from the three students—Robert Finlay, Andrea Martonffy, and Thomas Noonan—who in 1968 sat through my first effort to come to grips with the Venetian imperial experience far greater than is usual in such relationships.

The privileged leisure of a Guggenheim Fellowship permitted me to undertake final research in Venice, Athens, and Turkey in the autumn of 1971 and sustained the actual task of composition in the months that followed. When the manuscript had been completed the following distinguished scholars generously expended that most precious of all commodities, time, in checking over the text: Fernand Braudel, Eric Cochrane, T. Bentley Duncan, Deno Geanakoplos, John F. Guilmartin, Hilal Inalcik, Arcadius Kahan, Frederic C. Lane, Traian Stoianovich, Speros Vryonis, and Lynn White, Jr. Amongst them, they corrected many errors and suggested various modifications of my initial formulations. Two were especially helpful: Hilal Inalcik, whose readiness to forgive my multiple ignorances in matters Ottoman was only matched by the incisiveness of his suggestions for amendment, and John Guilmartin, whose insight into Mediterranean seamanship and naval technology of the sixteenth century added a new dimension to my understanding.

In addition, the staff of the Venezia e Oriente section of the Giorgio Cini Institute at Venice proved most cooperative; so was Frank Walton, the director of the Gennadion Library, Athens. The Turkish government also put me in its debt by treating me as an official visitor when I set out to view the cradleland of the Ottoman empire on either side of the Sea of Marmara. Finally, The University of Chicago in according me leave from ordinary duties while continuing to offer the resources of its libraries provided the human and institutional framework within which this book came to birth.

Flaws, some no doubt serious, surely remain, due both to ignorance and to my limited sensibilities and imperfect conceptualization. For all such defects I remain solely responsible;

Preface

my critics, each in his own way and degree, have only been able to reduce the frequency of my errors and, sometimes, to diminish their scope.

W. H. M.
January 1973

Introduction

THIS ESSAY attempts to describe the ebb and flow of styles and skills across southern and eastern Europe between the eleventh and the eighteenth centuries. The abrupt rise of Latin Europe after about A.D 1050 toward parity with, and in some fields superiority to, the more anciently skilled Greeks of the Byzantine empire defines the beginning date. The end drags on until Napoleon extinguished the Venetian Republic and empire in 1797, just seven hundred years after the First Crusade had initiated Latin Europe's imperial ventures in the Levant.

Speakers of Romance, Greek, Slavic, and Turkish languages are the protagonists of this history. Such diversity presents formidable obstacles to comprehension of processes that ran across so many linguistic frontiers. Moreover, existing historiography is recalcitrant to the scale of vision attempted here. In recent times most historians of southern and eastern Europe have principally interested themselves in seeking national origins or in celebrating the illustrious achievements of one or another of the nations that shared the territory with which this essay is concerned. In addition, religious antipathy between Orthodox and Latin Christians continues to affect (sometimes unconsciously) the attitudes of modern scholars. The heritage of Moslem-Christian fear, hatred, and misinformation is equally pervasive and far more apparent in historical writing about southern and eastern Europe. This is due to the fact that nineteenth-century nationalist movements among the Christian peoples of the Balkans reaffirmed and reinforced the long-standing religious antagonism between Christian and Moslem, whereas these same nationalist movements, insofar as they drew their intellectual inspiration from western Europe, tended to minimize the gap between Orthodox Christendom and its western counterparts.

It is not surprising therefore that historians have often overlooked or underestimated the scope and significance of cultural linkages running across southern and eastern Europe in late medieval and early modern times. This book seeks to correct these deficiencies, by using a model of acculturation and/or cultural repulsion to organize the somewhat sketchy data that can be derived from recent scholarly writing in a mere four languages. The pitfalls of such a procedure are obvious. It is easy to exaggerate by fastening too eagerly upon casual instances of cultural linkages across linguistic and religious boundaries. It is even more tempting to achieve coherence by generalizing from a priori notions of social process rather than from firm evidence. How well this essay escapes these pitfalls is for the reader to decide.

It might be argued that an effort at synthesis such as this is premature. Far more work with primary sources is necessary before the outlines of Ottoman cultural and economic history begin to emerge clearly; and the same may be said for many other themes. On the other hand, detailed monographic research gains significance in large part from being connected with some overall view of historical development. By proving or (more characteristically) by disproving the adequacy and accuracy of some general thesis, detailed investigation gains a precision and meaning it cannot attain when conducted in an intellectual vacuum.

In times past, rival nationalist ideals provided guidelines for most historians of eastern Europe, even though the multinational structure of both Byzantine and Ottoman society condemned strictly national histories to an obvious sectarianism. Marxism offers another, more comprehensive approach, even though the class structure and economic relationships of eastern and southern Europe do not conform exactly to generalizations made more than a century ago by Marx and Engels on the basis of their knowledge of patterns of socioeconomic development in northwestern Europe. In particular, capitalists who acted like western capitalists were mainly foreigners; and the socioeconomic role of officialdom and of privileged bodies of armed men was far greater in eastern and southern Europe than the Marxian doctrine of class struggle—at least in its simpler and more dogmatic form—allowed for. In addition, Marxian analysis does not cast much light upon the religious antagonisms which played such an important role in the history of southeastern Europe, and efforts to explain nationalism as a bourgeois device for deceiving the proletariat remain notoriously inadequate to the facts.

In view of these circumstances it seems legitimate to propose an alternative model for the history of southern and eastern Europe, which may direct investigations toward hitherto inadequately explored fields, or offer a basis for reassessing already familiar data. The fundamental assumption of what follows can be stated quite simply: when a group of men encounter a commodity, technique, or idea that seems superior to what they previously had known, they will try to acquire and make their own whatever they perceive to be superior, but only as long as this does not seem to endanger other values they hold dear.

Widely diverse reactions flow from encounters with new and superior cultural traits: successful borrowing or inventive adaptation within the receiving cultural context are relatively rare but of great historical importance because it is in such circumstances that additions to human skills and capacities are most likely to arise. Far more common, but historically less important, are the instances when men draw back, reaffirm their accustomed patterns of life, and reject the attractive novelty because it seems either unattainable or else threatening and dangerous. In such cases it may become necessary to reinforce accustomed ways in order to withstand the seductions inherent in exposure to what appears to be a superior foreign product. Cultural change, sometimes very far reaching, may thus paradoxically result from especially strenuous efforts to maintain the status quo.

Within time and space with which this essay is concerned, my general thesis implies that cultural interaction amongst the diverse peoples of southern and eastern Europe never ceased to provide the major motor power for historical change. In particular, the advance of Ottoman state power into the

Introduction

Balkans did not mean an end to significant encounters between Latin Christians and peoples of the Levant. To be sure, the consolidation of Turkish power did alter the terms of this interaction significantly, and for a while persuaded many Orthodox Christians of the superiority of Ottoman institutions and ideas to those of the Latin west. Equally, it is erroneous to suppose that Muscovite Russia emerged from the eastern mists with Peter the Great. Long before Peter's time, Russians sought expertise where it was to be found: whether in Byzantium, the Moslem world, northern Italy, or, after 1650, in northwestern Europe. The well-known pattern whereby Italian renaissance techniques and ideas percolated north of the Alps in the sixteenth century had its analogue in the Orthodox world, where the reception of Italian renaissance skills was, however, somewhat slower (it came mainly in the seventeenth century) and affected smaller numbers of men than was the case in northwestern Europe.

The Republic of Venice played a key role in these processes. In the Middle Ages, since they depended on trade, Venetians were among the most inveterate go-betweens connecting the Latin with the Greek, Slavic, and Turkish communities. (Their activity in Arab lands will be neglected in this essay.) Even when Venetians ceased to engage regularly in trading ventures abroad, Greek and Jewish communities established themselves in the city of the lagoons. These groups created new links between east and west through their commercial and other activities. In addition, Venice became an imperial power soon after the First Crusade, and continued to govern Orthodox populations overseas until the final collapse of the Venetian state in 1797. Venetian Crete became particularly fertile ground for interaction between Italian and Greek forms of high culture. The eminence of the University of Padua (under Venetian jurisdiction from 1405) gave that institution remarkable pulling power in the Orthodox world during the sixteenth and seventeenth centuries. Until about 1630 Venetian policy was often antipapal, and the University of Padua vigorously resisted Roman Catholic efforts to enforce religious conformity. These circumstances made study at Padua particularly attractive to Orthodox students, who pursued courses in medicine and philosophy in substantial numbers. Last but not least, the geographical position of Venice at the head of the Adriatic made it marginal to the world of Latin Christendom and a major locus of interregional trade until about 1600. Such a city, where strangers came and went incessantly, was foreordained to play a leading role in the cultural interchanges within the area with which this book is concerned.

It seems therefore appropriate to focus attention especially upon Venice and Venetians as principal mediators and links between the Adriatic, Aegean, and Black Sea regions. Yet it is the process of cultural interaction as a whole that matters; and when some other Italian power, e.g., Genoa or the papacy, took the lead in challenging eastern peoples with western skills or ideas, as happened on some occasions, then a wider scope seems called for. On the other hand, the roles of France, Spain, England, Holland, Poland, and the Germanies have been treated as background rather than in their own right, not because they were unimportant in connection with Aegean and Black Sea history, but because it seemed better to focus upon Levantine relations with Italy, which were, at least until about 1700, more intense and significant than other paths of interaction between the eastern and western portions of Christendom.

ONE

The Frankish Thrust into the Levant, 1081-1282

STRANGERS FROM the west began to intrude upon the Greeks, Slavs, Turks, and Arabs of the Levant in growing numbers and in unaccustomed roles after about 1050. The most conspicuous of the newcomers were knights, professional fighting men, coming mainly from the region of northwestern Europe that lies between the Loire and the Rhine. They called themselves Franks, and their preferred style of combat was to encase themselves in armor and then charge the foe on horseback, shield on one arm, spear tucked firmly under the other. At the moment of impact, they leaned far forward over their horse's neck with feet held firm by heavy stirrups against the shock of collision.

These tactics had been invented at the Carolingian court about A.D. 732.[1] The effect was to concentrate overwhelming force at the spearpoint of the charging knight, for the momentum of a galloping horse and rider lay behind each spearthrust. No existing military formation could stand against such a concentrated force. Just like the heavy tanks of the 1940s, even a few score of armored knights could turn the tide of battle, so long as fighting took place in terrain open enough to permit a mounted charge. A few hundred such men became capable of conquering a whole country,[2] as the knights who followed Robert Guiscard (mostly, like their leader, from Normandy) demonstrated by grabbing southern Italy from the Greeks between 1059 and 1071. Robert took and sacked Rome in 1084; between 1081 and 1085 he waged war in the Balkans, seeking to do the same to Constantinople, the second Rome and capital of the still mighty Byzantine Empire. Guiscard's death from a fever—not defeat in the field—ended this venture. Twelve to fourteen years later (1097–99), his son, Bohemund, with other redoubtable men-at-arms, pushed Frankish fame as far as Antioch and Jerusalem in the course of the First Crusade.

Despite occasional setbacks in battle, such as those administered by Saladin (reigned 1173–93) in the Holy Land or by Italian pikemen at Legnano (1176), knights equipped and trained in the Frankish manner remained masters of European and Mediterranean battlefields until about the end of the thirteenth century. The Sicilian Vespers (1282), when plans nurtured by Charles of Anjou for conquering the Byzantine state collapsed in the face of Sicilian rebellion and the invading forces of the king of Aragon, conveniently marks the end of knightly dominance in the Mediterranean. For the Aragonese troops included a formidable contingent of crossbowmen, whose weapons were capable of piercing a knight's armor at a considerable distance. Even the most skilled and determined cavalry attack thereby became vulnerable; but it required a new and more complicated art of war—combining light field defenses (to channel and impede the knightly charge), carefully drilled and systematically deployed pikemen(for close-in defense), and improved missile weapons (crossbows in the Mediterranean, longbows in England)—before the battlefield supremacy of the knight was finally and forever overthrown. This occurred in the course of the fourteenth century in western Europe; knightly supremacy lasted about a century longer in the Baltic and in the middle Danube regions.

For almost exactly two hundred years before their thunderous, helter-skelter charge became tactically obsolete—i.e., between Robert Guiscard's first assault upon the Byzantine Empire in 1081 and the collapse of Charles of Anjou's efforts to do the same in 1282—Frankish knights occupied the most conspicuous and honorific positions in encounters between Latin Christendom and the peoples of the Levant.

But there was a second and more enduring dimension to the

Frankish outreach. For precisely at the time when western knighthood was demonstrating its superiority to alternative styles of combat on innumerable battlefields, a handful of Italian cities established naval and mercantile dominion over the waters of the Mediterranean. The rise of Italian sea power was closely connected with the successive phases of knightly aggression. Robert Guiscard depended on shipping scraped up along the south Italian and Dalmatian coasts for his invasion of the Balkans, 1081–85. Although the target of the Norman attack, Emperor Alexius I Comnenus (reigned 1081–1118), lacked a fleet capable of operating as far away as the Straits of Otranto, he realized that to harass or cut off Guiscard's access to supplies and reinforcements coming from Italy was of the highest strategic importance. Alexius met this situation by concluding an agreement with the Venetians, whose ships had already made the Adriatic their special preserve.

The Byzantine emperor's need for help against the Normans matched Venetian self-interest. A ruler like Robert Guiscard, once firmly in command of both shores of the Straits of Otranto, would be in a position to bottle up Venetian vessels inside the Adriatic or hold them to ransom on entering and leaving its narrow waters. For more than a century, Venetians had made voyages to Egypt and Constantinople,[3] glimpsing the gains that might accrue from long-distance trade. Such possibilities obviously depended on free movement in and out of the Adriatic; Guiscard's ambition therefore constituted a critical threat to Venetian mercantile interests.

But, like shrewd merchants, the Venetians put a high price on their naval aid to the Emperor Alexius; and he, being in no position to bargain, paid it to the full. By a chrysobull of 1082 he granted the Venetians full exemption from all ordinary excise taxes payable on entering and leaving Constantinople and most of the empire's Aegean and Mediterranean trade centers.[4] This grant of tax immunity resembled numerous grants by which Alexius and his predecessors had freed local landed magnates in Anatolia and the Balkans from the ordinary jurisdiction of public officials. Venice was, from the Byzantine point of view, an integral part of the empire; in form if not in fact the privileges conferred upon the Venetians therefore were accorded to subjects rather than to foreigners.[5] This was, nevertheless, a fiction. Governed by an elective doge, Venice was in practice fully independent, linguistically distinct from the Greeks of Byzantium, and religiously closer to the pope than to the patriarch of Constantinople, if only because Latin was the local liturgical language.[6]

Hence Alexius' grant of 1082 was fundamentally different from tax immunity granted to territorial magnates in return for military or some other form of state service. Venetians acted like foreigners in Constantinople; the local inhabitants viewed them as such, and soon came to hate them for their wealth and privileged status. But in the short run, Alexius got the help he so badly needed. The Venetians sent a fleet against the Normans and fought a number of engagements, with varying success, against Guiscard's ships. The Normans' withdrawal from the Balkans in 1085 was certainly influenced by the precarious naval position in which they found themselves. Venice thus contributed effectively to Alexius' first great military success.

But the commercial privileges of 1082 did not lapse with the end of the fighting. In the following years, the Venetians' immunity from excise taxes gave them a crushing trade advantage in Byzantine ports. As a result, most of the seaborne trade between Constantinople and the Aegean and Mediterranean coasts rapidly gravitated into Venetian hands. Simultaneously, their trade with Egypt expanded. Venetians were able to sell increasing quantities of spices and other luxury goods imported via Egypt from India and the southern seas to the wealthy classes of north Italy and trans-Alpine Europe. They also found it possible to gather cargoes of European timber, metals, and other coarse goods. These found ready market in Egypt and partially paid for the spices brought from the east. In this fashion, a pattern of trade that endured for more than four hundred years came sharply into focus during three to four decades following the chrysobull of 1082. Venetians became the principal commercial middlemen between Latin Christendom and the Levant—a role they continued to play with few interruptions until after the middle of the sixteenth century.

Naturally, such lucrative trade attracted rivals—in particular Pisa and Genoa from the western side of the Italian peninsula. The Genoese naval and mercantile presence in the eastern Mediterranean was coeval with the First Crusade, for that city sent a fleet to assist the crusaders in their siege of Antioch (1097–98). Pisan ships followed closely behind (1099). Thereafter these two Italian cities acquired a series of territorial strongholds along the Syrian coast, taking possession of portions of ports the crusaders seized to secure their initial inland bases at Antioch and Jerusalem (captured 1099). After the crusade had reached its goal, in 1100, a Venetian fleet put in an appearance along the Palestinian coast and assisted the crusaders in taking Haifa, where the Venetians secured trading rights and jurisdiction over one-third of the town, just as the Genoese and Pisans had done in the places they helped to capture.

The Venetians were, however, unable to follow up this venture. Danger much nearer home soon required all available forces. On the one hand, the Hungarian monarch, having annexed the crown of Croatia in 1102, began to make good his new claims to Dalmatia by sending troops to occupy Spalato, Zara, and other key points along the coast. This was a direct and serious challenge to Venetian control of the Adriatic, upon which the city's commercial eminence fundamentally rested.

Simultaneously, Venice faced serious difficulties in Italy itself. A fight broke out with Padua (1107) over control of the Brenta River; even more vital were complex armed struggles for access to the Po. Yet another kind of crisis descended upon the Venetians when severe floods damaged their old center at Malamocco, necessitating relocation on the (presumably higher) ground of the Rialto.[7]

The transfer of the center of government and trade to the Rialto must, in itself, have shaken Venetian habits and behavior loose from customary patterns, facilitating radical response to the problems they faced. Certain it is, at any rate, that in the next fifteen years the citizens of Venice found ways of asserting their power on an unprecedented scale, not only within the Adriatic but in the Levant as well.

One key to their success was the establishment of the famous Arsenal in 1104. Modeled on Byzantine precedents, the

Arsenal was a shipyard under public management that specialized in the construction of galleys for use in war. In later times, mass production of ships of a standard design became the hallmark of the Venetian Arsenal. Workmen developed unusual skill and efficiency as a result of specialization; standardized replaceable parts made repairs easy; stockpiling such parts allowed the state to maintain a cadre of skilled men always available, who, in case of need, could direct the efforts of a suddenly enlarged work force such as might be required for building a new fleet in a hurry.[8] Indeed, the efficiency and predictability associated with modern factory assembly lines were, to some extent, realized by the Venetian Arsenal. In its heyday, the Arsenal was capable of assembling a completely equipped galley in less than an hour.[9]

Obviously these advantages and economies were not attained all at once. Nevertheless, in the years after 1104, the size and formidability of the Venetian navy increased enormously. Instead of relying on vessels scraped together from whatever was already available (as in the campaigns of 1081–85 against the Normans), the Venetians became able to call on the services of ships designed for war; and they could make them available in numbers calculated in accordance with the strategic needs of the occasion, within limits set by the city's financial, material, and manpower capabilities. Obviously such radical rationality vastly magnified Venetian sea power.

As a result, the city was able first to reassert its vital trading rights on the Brenta and the Po. Then, from 1115, naval expeditions set energetically about the task of rolling Hungarian power back from the Dalmatian coast. By 1118 the Venetians had been sufficiently successful (despite the doge's death in battle) to conclude a truce with Hungary and turn attention to the urgent problem of restoring their trading position in the Levant. By this time, the Genoese and Pisans were well established in Palestine and Syria, and the latter had also secured the right to trade in Constantinople (1111), though on terms notably less generous than those which the Venetians enjoyed.[10] This was bad enough from a Venetian point of view, but the situation became really critical when the Emperor

Alexius died and his successor, John I Comnenus (reigned 1118–43), refused to renew the Venetian trade privileges of 1082.

Accordingly, in 1122 the Venetians launched themselves upon an altogether extraordinary effort. They assembled a fleet of more than one hundred warships, together with many other vessels (a total force of perhaps as many as 15,000 men),[11] and then proceeded to Palestine, where an Egyptian invasion was threatening the kingdom of Jerusalem with disaster.

The situation in the eastern Mediterranean had altered sharply with the success of the First Crusade. Commerce with Egypt had been disrupted. The much prized spices from India and beyond were rerouted to Syrian ports, where Pisans and Genoese merchants purchased them for distribution in Europe. Venetian trade at Haifa had not flourished, perhaps because the city's resources had been engaged too heavily elsewhere. One of the main purposes that inspired the Venetians to assemble such an enormous fleet in 1122 must have been the wish to re-establish their participation in the spice trade on a grand scale.

On their arrival, the Venetians easily drove the Egyptian fleet from the sea. This compelled the invading land forces to withdraw, since they required supplies that could only be delivered by sea. After harassing the retreating Moslems, the Venetians passed over to the offensive and assisted the crusaders in besieging and capturing Tyre (1124). The king of Jerusalem, as had become customary, transferred to the Venetians sovereignty over a portion of the town they had helped to conquer, and accorded them tax-free trading rights there. This concession, more genuinely than the almost abortive grant of similar rights in Haifa (1100), marked the beginning of the Venetian overseas empire.[12]

Having done what was needed in Palestine to secure their position, the Venetian fleet then invaded the Aegean as a means of bringing pressure on the Byzantine emperor to renew the broken-off trade privileges. Finally, en route home, the victorious expedition recaptured Spalato from the Hungarians (1125), who had taken advantage of the Venetian absence to take possession of that city once more. In view of such a convincing demonstration of Venetian naval power, in the next year (1126) the Emperor John I Comnenus reopened the markets of Constantinople and other Byzantine ports to Venetian trade on the same privileged terms as before.

The dramatic upsurge of Venetian naval and mercantile resources between 1082 and 1126 did not mean that the Adriatic city had won permanent and secure preponderance on the sea. Aside from the ever-present rivalry of Pisa and Genoa, whose naval power also grew very rapidly in these years, it remained true that whenever the government at Constantinople judged it necessary and was therefore willing to assign suitable resources for the purpose, a formidable Byzantine navy sprang into existence. Thus Emperor Alexius I was able to create a navy of his own, commanded by Greek officers and manned by hired crews recruited from among both Greeks and Latins, during the war against the Normans at the beginning of his reign; and on several subsequent occasions he built additional ships and organized important naval operations along the Balkan and Anatolian coasts. In the tenth century, similar fleets had seized naval supremacy from the Moslems and as late as the time of Emperor Manuel I Comnenus (reigned 1143–80) Byzantine naval forces attacked both Egypt and Apulia, though without enduring success.[13]

But Byzantine fleets were economically passive and, after 1082, did not even have the indirect fiscal value of protecting commerce that could be taxed by the Byzantine government. The imperial navy was designed specifically for war. Resources so employed subtracted from Greek manpower and materials available for ordinary mercantile activity by sea; the more so since the Byzantine officers in command of the fleet were not commercially minded. They had to please superiors within a bureaucratic hierarchy that habitually disdained commerce and did not build a navy to engage in trade.

Italian warships, on the other hand, exchanged goods as eagerly as blows with whomever they encountered. Captains and crew shared in any booty that might be seized; in addition they traded as opportunity might offer. Opportunity was not lacking, for a well-equipped galley, with its large crew of rowers-cum-soldiers and its easy maneuverability even in the face of unfavorable winds, offered a relatively safe means of transport for precious cargoes that bulked small in proportion to their value.

Thus between booty and trading profits, Italian naval enterprises often paid for themselves, or came close to doing so. Bureaucratically managed Byzantine fleets, on the contrary, constituted a heavy charge on the central government's financial resources, so that whenever pressing need relaxed, the authorities in Constantinople were liable to disband the fleet as an economy measure. In such cases, naturally, at least some of the crews and vessels that had been in the empire's pay turned to piracy as a means of using their skills for the improvement of their own livelihood.[14] This did nothing to help Byzantine trade and prosperity, though coastal dwellers may have found it hard to tell whether official taxes and forced labor for support of a war fleet or the ravages of free-lance pirates were harder to bear.

At any rate, Byzantine state policy and Italian enterprise combined to put almost all of the empire's long-distance, seaborne commerce into Italian hands within less than a century from the time when the Venetians first began to enter and leave Byzantine ports without paying taxes (1082). Whatever success Greeks may have had in maintaining commerce on the Black Sea (and information here is exceedingly scarce)[15] clearly failed to counterbalance the extraordinary expansion of Italian shipping.

The practical base for the spectacular expansion of Frankish knighthood is clear and remained relatively simple. The same cannot yet be said for the parallel expansion of Italian seapower and trade. To be sure, northern Italy had some obvious geographical advantages. In the well-watered Alpine foothills, suitable ships' timbers were easy to find close to navigable water. This was a critical advantage as against the Moslem peoples of the southern shores of the Mediterranean, who, in the absence of local forests, had to depend on imported timber for ship construction. This was both expensive and precarious, since rival naval powers could cut off the transport of such a bulky commodity as ships' timbers with comparative ease. The collapse of Moslem shipping in the Mediterranean after about A.D. 1000 was probably very largely a result of this strategic weakness.[16] Vis à vis Byzantium, however, Italians had no such geographical advantage. The Byzantines seem never to have lacked either timber or skilled manpower to build and operate their ships,[17] and any differential in the cost of suitable ships' timber (which may have favored the Italians when they first began to use their forests for naval construction) seems an entirely inadequate explanation for what happened.

A more promising line of inquiry would be to investigate Italian ship-building methods. In ancient and early Byzantine times, ships' hulls were held together by innumerable mortice and tenon joints, binding board to board to make a rigid, watertight hull. Only after the hull had been built were ribs and interior braces inserted to strengthen the whole and support deck and superstructure.[18] In late medieval and modern times, shipwrights first constructed a rigid skeleton of keel and ribs and then nailed planks to the ribs. This obviated any need for careful joining, since cracks could be filled with a mixture of fiber and pitch to produce a watertight hull every bit as seaworthy as that created by the older cabinetmakers' methods. Obviously, rib and plank construction was enormously cheaper. It required less skilled carpentry, fewer man-hours overall, and allowed the use of oak in shipbuilding for the first time, a not unimportant advantage since oak forests were the climax vegetation in most of Europe.

Ship-builders who first learned how to make seaworthy craft on the rib and plank principle were clearly in a position to turn out a far larger number of vessels in less time and at far smaller cost than had been possible before. Circumstantial evidence suggests that this occurred in the eleventh century; and if this is so, it is almost certain that the pioneers of the newly cheapened methods were the Italian cities that achieved dominion of the Mediterranean so suddenly. But until studies based on underwater archeology comparable to those which have now been done for ancient shipbuilding are in hand, certainty is unattainable.

As a matter of fact, the transition from one method of ship construction to the other may have been a longer and more complicated process than the suddenness of Italian expansion into the Mediterranean might lead one to suppose. Rib and plank construction had been used for river craft in Roman times, and the adaptation of this cheap method of construction for use on open water must have required a good many improvements and considerable experimentation.[19] Venice, because of its location in protected lagoons, lying quite literally between rivers and open sea, was ideally situated to conduct such experimentation. In emergencies, vessels intended for river traffic must have often ventured beyond the quiet waters of the lagoons out into the open Adriatic. Such experience, in peace and war, would be very likely to stimulate the kind of technical development needed to make rib and plank construction sturdy enough to navigate open water as a matter of course.

Whether or not the rise of Italian sea power in the eleventh century was tied in with the shift to rib and plank construction, other factors came powerfully into play. Chief among them was the general growth of wealth and productivity in Latin Christendom, based fundamentally on a rapidly growing population and the efficiency of manorial agriculture. This was what assured a market for high-priced luxury goods brought from the east; this it was that sustained fat middlemen's profits from the sale of these exotic commodities—profits which were usually greater than what could be gained by dealing in coarser goods. Moreover, the location of Venice at the head of the Adriatic gave that city a great advantage for trade with the Levant, for it lay at the point where navigation by sea had to give way to river or overland traffic across the fertile plain of northern Italy, to the Alps and beyond. Genoa, too, lay close to the northernmost reach of the Tyrrhenian Sea, although its immediate hinterland was not nearly so rich nor so easily traversed as that of Venice. This handicap was to some degree compensated for by Genoa's closer proximity to the French-Netherlandish heartland of feudal and manorial Europe, where northwestern Europe's most fertile fields supported the most formidable fighting men of the age.

All the same, the rise of trans-Alpine Europe is not enough to explain how it was that Venice, Genoa, and other Italian cities took advantage of new possibilities so vigorously. As a matter of fact, their enterprise played no small part in the overall development of Europe's economic life. Regional specialization was forwarded and sustained by long-distance trade, much of it conducted by Italians. New crops and techniques, long established in the Levant, were transplanted westward wherever suitable geographical and socioeconomic conditions allowed; again, often by Italians. Mercantile traffic quickly accumulated relatively large capital sums in Italian hands; and for more than four centuries Italian bankers and investors played a large role throughout Europe in mobilizing men and materials on an ever-larger scale for carrying through all sorts of enterprises—military, religious, administrative, commercial, and industrial.

What gave Italians such long and variegated leadership? The question is not easy to answer because the phenomena to be explained are so multiform; but in the most general way one can assert that Venice, Pisa, and Genoa, together with a few inland Italian cities like Florence and Milan, were able to organize collective effort more quickly and on a larger scale and, before long, at a higher level of skill, than was true elsewhere in the European or Mediterranean area. This allowed Italian cities to outstrip weaker, less organized competitors. It even permitted a single city like Venice to match the strength of territorially far vaster powers, like the kingdom of Hungary, which remained unable to muster its potential resources smoothly enough to counterbalance the efficiency with which the comparatively tiny Venetian community was able to organize for war as well as for peace.

Three aspects of the Italian cities' achievement deserve special consideration. First and most obvious: the merchants of Venice along with their principal rivals, the Pisans and Genoese, were able to keep whatever they made on a profitable deal. This meant that the profits from one voyage could be used to swell the scale of the next venture. Hence in a single lifetime a lucky and clever man could amass a substantial amount of trading capital, expanding his operations year by year. The suddenness with which Italian merchants took over Mediterranean trade is only explicable in terms of this kind of rapid buildup of capital.

An alternative way of describing what took place is to say

that commercial capital quickly flowed to the places where return on investment was significantly greater than elsewhere; and the main reason why profits were greater in Italy after 1050 or so was because a smaller proportion of the gain from any given transaction had to be paid over in taxes or otherwise devoted to the cost of protection.

Italian merchants of the eleventh and twelfth centuries attended to their own protection and felt no need to hire large numbers of foreign specialists in violence. The city administrators of Venice, Pisa, and Genoa were mostly merchants or ex-merchants, and Venetian magistrates regularly invested their spare funds in trading ventures.[20] No great gap of outlook or class interest therefore separated political leaders from the mercantile and seafaring population as a whole, despite great variations in individual wealth which rapidly developed as some men prospered and others met with disaster on the seaways and in the market places of Europe and the Levant.

As a result, in the eleventh and twelfth centuries, when Italian merchants took over the Mediterranean trade routes, they operated within a political framework that allowed an almost unhampered accumulation of commercial capital, whereas other regions of the Mediterranean littoral did not enjoy this kind of liberty. Wherever a territorial lord exercised effective tax power over traders, he was tempted to seize all or most of the profits from trade. How damaging this could be to the process of capital accumulation is nicely illustrated by the career of Amalfi, a city in southern Italy which remained in the forefront of Italian commercial expansion into the Levant only until the Norman kingdom took full control of the town (1130), whereupon Amalfi's trade withered,[21] presumably because the resources of the town were harnessed to the ruler's needs, that is, primarily to military rather than to commercial purposes.

The inability of merchants heavily taxed by a territorial sovereign to compete on even terms with merchants who did not have to pay such a high price for protection had important implications. As trade profits gravitated into foreign hands, local rulers were tempted to maintain revenue by raising the rates of taxation on home commerce, thereby throttling the goose that laid the golden eggs. And without gold, the sinews of war available to support a ruler's territorial power decayed precipitously.[22]

On the other hand, concentrated capital resulting from the profits of trade made a tempting target for needy and greedy neighbors—whether within the city itself (class war and civil uprisings) or without. To guard against such dangers required expenditures of money and of time. This regularly threatened to upset the delicate balance between public and private enterprise in matters military, commercial, and industrial, needed to sustain long-term economic growth. Insofar as resources were diverted from trade to public uses—defense, social services, ritual display—costs rose so that the initial advantage Italian traders had enjoyed vis à vis other Mediterranean merchants lessened and eventually disappeared. But it took a while for the initial imbalance to correct itself. Until after 1282 it seems clear that both Venice and Genoa continued to enjoy what Frederic C. Lane has felicitously called a favorable "protection rent" as against all rivals.[23]

Nevertheless, low political-military overhead was not the only basis for the sudden upthrust of Italian commercial power in the Mediterranean. A second aspect of the way in which Italian trading cities mobilized resources between 1082 and 1282 was of even greater and more enduring importance. Briefly, the Italians were able to create ad hoc corporations capable of coordinating important aspects of the routine activities of indefinite numbers of men across barriers of both time and space. Such corporations ranged in size all the way from a simple two-man contract that was dissolved at the end of a particular voyage to the largest corporate body of all—the commune, or city government itself.

Ad hoc corporations had the effect of coordinating behavior beyond familial or other traditional limits. Strangers routinely entered into cooperative and relatively predictable relationships with one another through such corporate structures. These entirely familiar yet really quite extraordinary patterns of conduct had the effect of magnifying individual effort enormously by creating the conditions for mutually supportive or complementary activity on the part of individuals who might be separated by long distances or even remain entirely un-known to one another.

Another important characteristic of these corporations was that they did not command a man's entire time or control all aspects of his behavior. They were ad hoc: that is, created for carrying out some relatively precise purpose. A single in-dividual could with no sense of impropriety simultaneously function within many different corporations. Not all such corporations were economic in aim: military, religious, social, and convivial purposes could also be pursued through such arrangements. Guilds and fictional brotherhoods, military units, hospitals, schools, monastic and other pious founda-tions, together with voluntary associations for humanitarian or aesthetic purposes, as well as governmental bodies of almost every kind, all qualify as examples of ad hoc corporations. But in eleventh-century Venice as in twentieth-century America the most important type of ad hoc corporation was that directed toward economic goals. This was so because economic corpora-tions were very numerous and affected the behavior of more men more of the time than did any other sort of corporation.

All complex societies develop ad hoc corporations. What was unusual about the Italian trading cities of the eleventh century (and northwestern Europe generally after about 1000) was the number and effectiveness of such arrangements. As compared to other peoples, the inhabitants of this hitherto rather back-ward portion of the globe proved strikingly capable of tran-scending kinship groupings and cooperating smoothly with persons who were not blood relatives but were recognized as belonging to some sort of wider in-group—whether that in-group comprised the inhabitants of a village, the citizens of a town, the speakers of a common mother tongue, or even the bearers of a common tradition of high culture, i.e., the culture of Latin Christendom. These broader groupings rarely came into play; the operationally important transfamilial in-groups for medieval Europe were the inhabitants of a village and the citizens of a town.

The basis of this special aptitude for operating within the framework of ad hoc corporations may have been technologi-cal. In the Po Valley and in the plains of trans-Alpine Europe, in the centuries just before 1000, tillage had been fundamentally reorganized as a result of the introduction of heavy moldboard plows. To pull such a ponderous instrument through the soil required four, six, or even eight oxen (later horses). This meant that no ordinary peasant household could put a plow team in the field on the basis of its own resources. Pooling available animals from several households was the only way enough animal power could be got together to pull the plow. This in turn required some kind of agreement as to how to divide the work and the proceeds of the common enterprise. Any man who failed to do his fair share or who otherwise tried to cheat his fellows faced immediate and drastic retaliation. He and his ox could be excluded from the next season's plow team, for who would care to work with, and depend upon, a lazy scoundrel? Anyone unable to find others willing to work with him in cultivating the soil therefore faced irremediable disaster: quite simply, unless he cooperated with his neighbors, he could not expect to eat. Under such compulsion, habits and attitudes conducive to effective cooperation beyond the limits of the biological family must have been impressed upon the vast majority of the population wherever the moldboard plow established itself.[24]

Human beings shaped by such work experience (and medieval three-field agriculture made plowing an almost year-round activity) must have been unusually ready to enter into extrafamilial cooperative relationships, even after they had left the land and migrated into town to pursue any of the myriad occupations that burgeoning town life allowed in the eleventh and subsequent centuries. This, I suggest, underlay the unusual facility with which the "Franks" (to use the Levantine term) were able to form ad hoc corporations, coordinating the efforts of comparatively large numbers of men across time and space with altogether exceptional efficiency. Insofar as Europeans whose rural base rested upon moldboard tillage had a palpable superiority in coordinating social behavior beyond the limits established by kinship ties, the sudden commercial dominance achieved by the Italian mercantile republics in the Levant in the eleventh century becomes more readily understandable.[25]

The legal forms of business cooperation used in Venice and

other Italian trading cities began by being essentially the same as those used elsewhere in the Mediterranean. The capital cost of a ship (unless it was constructed with public funds in the state Arsenal) was divided up into a number of shares (usually twenty-four), each of which might be further subdivided indefinitely, usually by quarterings.[26] Owners of shares in ships expected to recover their investment and make a profit by charging whatever the market would bear for carrying goods and passengers from port to port.

Overseas trading ventures were usually conducted through partnerships. Some partnerships were familial and lasted a lifetime. Others were arranged for a single voyage. The dominant form of such a contract until the thirteenth century or after was known in Venice as *colleganza* and elsewhere in Italy as *commenda*. According to this type of contract, a silent partner contributed two-thirds of the initial trading capital, while the remaining third came from the active partner who accompanied the goods and conducted appropriate transactions at whatever ports the ship might put in. Within thirty days of his return from a voyage, the active partner was legally bound to present his associate with an accounting of all transactions made on their joint account, together with a record of travel and other expenses. They then divided the proceeds of the venture equally. As commercial capital became more abundant in Venice, a variation of this arrangement became common, whereby the traveling merchant (or agent) contributed no capital of his own, but secured only one-quarter of the profit.[27]

Obviously, when one of the contracting parties owned no personal share in the trading capital, the community of interest between the partners was less apparent than in the older arrangement. Inflated expense accounts became a standing temptation. Moreover, as the scale of trade grew, it was not easy to find suitable quantities of scarce goods on hand at the time a fleet of ships put into port. Similarly, selling an entire shipload of imported goods all at once tended to depress local prices. It therefore became common during the fourteenth century for merchants of Venice and other Italian cities to station agents at important trading places all year round, where they stockpiled suitable goods in anticipation of each ship's arrival and sold commodities imported on their principal's account whenever prices seemed best at any time of year. In return, such agents were entitled to a percentage of the value of the goods they turned over on behalf of the merchant or firm back home. A single agent could act for several principals; a single firm might entrust different transactions to different agents.

Such an arrangement called for accurate records, attested by some reliable, neutral authority. Public notaries served this purpose, recording and certifying sales and purchases made by the local agent on someone else's account. Payment could often be arranged by letters of credit, balancing off one transaction in Italy against another in Constantinople, Alexandria, Flanders, or somewhere in between. From this it was an easy step to issuing bills of exchange in anticipation of future payments secured either by a merchant's reputation and expected profit from future transactions or by other kinds of income-producing property—land, mining rights, taxes, and tolls.

These practices were well known to Jewish and Moslem traders long before Italian merchants became important. But Venice and other Italian cities[28] began to leave Levantine precedent behind in the latter part of the twelfth century by inventing ways of mobilizing private capital for public uses. Initially, a few wealthy Venetian families invested in the ship of state as they were accustomed to invest in ordinary wooden ships. That is, they supplied needed funds to the city's magistrates by dividing the required amount into twelve shares (one man took two). Such sums were repaid with suitable interest from public revenues, i.e., mainly by receipts from excise taxes on goods moving in and out of the city. Fresh crises soon called for other and larger loans. Before long investment in state loans became compulsory; and between 1187 and 1208, magistrates developed methods for determining each family's share and assessing the exact sums due as subscription to each new loan. Then in 1262 all outstanding public debts were consolidated into a single account, and annual interest on the total was fixed at 5 percent. Regular payments of interest and principal on this public debt continued uninterruptedly until 1379.[29]

The development of the Venetian public debt was a remarkably rational way of meeting mounting political overhead costs. The financial crises confronting the Republic were mainly military; effective response required money for hiring soldiers and equipping fleets, often in large amounts and at short notice. Loans and a tax base that allowed repayment between emergencies evened out the incidence of such costs over time. Even more important, mobilization became more effective, since the men and the materials required for sudden military exertion could be marshaled on a voluntary (or at least semivoluntary) basis by paying for them.

Yet in proportion as such costs mounted, Venetian traders began to lose part of the advantage they had enjoyed vis à vis Byzantine subjects in the eleventh century. In other words, the margin in their "protection rent" began to narrow in the course of the twelfth and thirteenth centuries. The costs of defending Venetian commerce and colonies grew as ships and men engaged in trade ceased to be able to protect their wealth through their own action. Professional soldiers and specialized warships, more numerous than could be advantageously used for transporting precious commodities, became an increasingly important supplement to the military force inherent in the trading communities themselves.

The rather rapid increase in the cost of Venice's political overhead between 1082 and 1282 is an example of how an equilibrium upset by an initial imbalance between different segments of the Mediterranean littoral righted itself. Yet Venetian methods of meeting their mounting protection costs were skillfully designed to minimize inhibitory effects upon capital accumulation and the expansion of trade. This was what permitted Venice to survive for so many centuries as a major trade center and important political power.

Each of these arrangements, from the simplest *colleganza* to the administrative complexity of Venice's consolidated public debt, enhanced the city's capacity to mobilize men and goods in larger quantities and in shorter periods of time for the pursuit of consciously framed goals. Even young and poor men with little or no personal capital could enter into *colleganze* with richer and older persons, or with widows and orphans who were glad to share profits with a vigorous man on the make. In this fashion a career open to talent became readily available to anyone shrewd and lucky enough to do well in trade. As a result, all ranks of Venetian society could find a place and take active part in the processes whereby the relatively tiny population of the city learned how to exercise economic and other forms of power over much vaster populations scattered throughout the Levant and most of Europe. For everyone who bought or sold, produced or consumed, any part of the growing volume of goods which Venetians chose to carry from one market to another contributed to the mounting wealth and power of the organizing center of the entire system, the city of Venice.

As the trading network became more closely woven, things previously impossible ceased to be so. Ordinary emergencies like that created by local crop failure could be countervailed by deliberately arranging to import grain from afar. Thousands of eager and ingenious men circulated throughout the Levant and western Europe, looking for goods they knew could be sold at a profit elsewhere. Not infrequently they coaxed new wealth into existence by developing local skills and resources for the supply of some distant market of which the inhabitants had previously never dreamed.

The most massive response to these new opportunities came in northern Italy itself, closely followed by developments in the Low Countries and adjacent regions of northwestern Europe. The response in the Mediterranean lands was somewhat weaker, but still very great by all ordinary standards. But it was only after the end of the thirteenth century that the parts of Europe draining into the Baltic and Black seas began to react very noticeably to the economic impulses generated by the market system centering in northern Italy. Stimuli felt further afield, e.g., in India and the spice islands of Indonesia, must have been real too; but information is almost nil about how the spices destined for European consumption were produced and started on their way to European markets.

In reflecting upon the remarkable manner in which Italian businessmen integrated such far-flung human activities from the eleventh century onward, it is worth reemphasizing the centrality of mutual trust and cooperation among persons who were not blood relatives. Here, more than in the essentially transient advantage of a more favorable "protection rent," lay the long-range basis of western power. Voluntary coordination of effort in the framework of what I have called ad hoc corporations made for a level of efficiency seldom attainable by compulsion. Other societies found (and continue to find) it very difficult to attain the necessary level of mutual trust beyond the family circle. This is illustrated by the fact that Greeks, Jews, and Arabs had long known the *colleganza* type of contract, but found it hard to trust partners who were not also relatives. Similarly, buying and selling on commission was completely familiar to the Moslem and Jewish mercantile communities; but such agents, again, were most comfortably recruited from among relatives.[30] Italians, too, often preferred to entrust business to brothers, sons, and cousins; but it is also clear that from the eleventh century, when the scale of business began to expand very fast, Venetians and other Italians were quite ready to enter into *colleganze* with men who were merely fellow citizens.[31]

The third distinctive characteristic of the Italian mercantile cities as they emerged to power and wealth in the eleventh century—namely their bellicosity—is an aspect of the first and an application of the second of their more general advantages. A system of government that permitted merchants to retain their capital gains, maximizing their "protection rent," was sustained by the fact that the mercantile community was usually quite capable of its own defense, and indeed of undertaking offensive war. Similarly, the success that Italian merchants had in organizing violence was a special case of their general aptitude for creating and working within ad hoc corporations. Yet the military side of Italian expansion deserves separate attention, if only because trade, piracy, robbery, and war were intimately and inextricably intermingled in the Mediterranean area (as elsewhere) throughout the Middle Ages.

It was, after all, by virtue of their formidability in battle that the Venetians first secured special privileges in Byzantine ports in 1082. Similarly, Pisans and Genoese won their first footholds in the Levant by feats of arms. The military ethos that in other parts of Europe tended to be identified with the knightly class lodged firmly within city walls in Italy. Venetian nobles were traders. They could not trace their descent from any landed class, but felt themselves no less noble for that. In Genoa and other north Italian cities landed families migrated into town and took to trade as the most effective way to achieving fame and fortune; but in doing so they maintained the habits of violence and energetic self defense that had become the price of successful landholding in the lawless ninth and tenth centuries.

An extreme readiness to resort to violence often paid off handsomely. Escape from sudden depredation, whether on land or sea, was obviously essential for successful trade; and the crew that not only managed to protect its own trading goods but succeeded in seizing someone else's in addition came home with that much the more profit to show for its exertions. Fellow citizens were not usually regarded as fair game; and in dealing with others prudence often dictated peaceable haggling rather than high-handed seizure. Formal agreements usually defined the rights and obligations of foreign merchants come to trade. Yet these legal integuments were very fragile. Swift and sudden violence, whether in port or on the high seas, was a constant possibility, not least because merchants from different Italian cities were perpetually liable to attack one another.

At sea, the tasks of defense and offense were shared by all on board. Venetian state galleys carried arms and armor as prescribed by public authority; on private vessels arrangements varied, but for all lengthy voyages suitable stocks of weapons were quite as essential a part of the ship's equipment as were sails and spars. Ashore, successful trade called for arms, too. Terms of trade responded, among other things, to the armed strength of the parties as manifested on the spot. A judicious mix of threat and negotiation sometimes allowed a group of merchants to monopolize the available supply of a commodity, with enhanced gains as a result. Only by living with arms in hand, preferably within a fortified enclosure where goods might be stored safely, could foreign merchants obtain the best possible guarantee of security when operating far from home. Local sovereigns sometimes permitted or acquiesced in the erection of (to us) surprisingly elaborate fortifications for this purpose.[32]

The very intensity of organizational innovation that developed in the leading north Italian cities between 1082 and 1282 raised in unusually acute ways the perennial human question of where to draw the boundary of the cooperative ingroup, and where to identify the rival and at least potential enemy. After long struggle, Pisa went under as a major trading power, being unable simultaneously to combat Genoa by sea and Florence by land. Genoa eventually split apart into rival factions. Venice, on the contrary, maintained effective cohesion among the citizenry as a whole, in spite (or perhaps because) of sharp differentiation in wealth and hereditary distinctions of status that divided the population between nobles and commoners.

The cohesion achieved among the citizens of Venice in part reflected the isolated, insular location of their city. Until the fifteenth century, the troublesome mix of landed with urban interests that disturbed Genoa and Florence, for instance, had no analogue in the mercantile and industrial community that grew up on the islands of the Adriatic lagoon.

Details of the city's constitutional history need not detain us here. The dogeship had become unambiguously elective early in the eleventh century, though election procedures were not defined until later. In the course of the twelfth and thirteenth centuries public functions were increasingly taken over by councils and boards on which the richer families of the city were represented. A class of professional clerks, recruited from among commoners, also came into existence. They kept records and implemented the policies decided on by the more aristocratic councils and boards. But final definition of the Venetian constitution occurred only in the fourteenth century, and we can therefore reserve a more exact description until the next chapter.

Suffice it to say that the proliferation of public councils and boards that took place in Venice during the eleventh-thirteenth centuries offers another example of Venetian facility for forming ad hoc corporations. Their effectiveness in organizing public action to meet felt needs—whether it was a question of paving Saint Mark's Square or of capturing Constantinople—provided many spectacular instances of the success such patterns of organization could bring.

Most assuredly, the Venetians had need for skillful deployment of their resources. In the twelfth century, the city found itself boxed in between potentially threatening and comparatively vast territorial monarchies. To the south lay the formidable Norman kingdom of Italy and Sicily and its eastern rival, the Byzantine Empire. To the north lay the German empire of the Hohenstaufen (with traditional claims to sovereignty over north Italy) and the kingdom of Hungary (united with Croatia after 1102, and thereby inheriting claims to the Dalmatian coast of the Adriatic.)

Venetian policy was affected by the fact that the prosperity of the city required commercial access to the territories controlled by each of these monarchies. Neutrality, buttressed by treaties defining Venetian trading rights and privileges, was the policy that best accorded with this circumstance. A brisk flow of trade also offered advantages to the rulers of these great states in the way of tax revenues and a supply of strategic and luxury goods required by their armies and courts. This meant that there were persuasive reasons to induce even powerful rulers to come to terms with the Venetians.

It is a very striking fact that the Byzantine emperors, who, unlike the other territorial rulers with whom the Venetians dealt, derived no direct tax revenues from Venetian trade, nevertheless continued to allow the Venetians to do business in their ports during most of the twelfth century. The policy was intensely unpopular among the inhabitants of Constantinople; but efforts to withdraw Venetian tax exemptions (1118, 1171) were always broken off after a few years.

Losses inflicted by marauding Venetian fleets perhaps had something to do with the Byzantine emperor's decisions to come to terms; but need for a better supply of critical materials —metals, arms, and the like—was probably an even more compelling consideration. Venice was well situated to act as middleman between the mining districts of central Germany, the armament shops of Milan, and the eastern markets for such commodities. And in an age when well-equipped knights were a tremendous asset on any battlefield, an adequate supply of arms and armor, or of the metal from which to manufacture these indispensable elements of the knight's equipment, was essential to the security of every state.[33]

But even if it constituted a kind of norm, neutrality buttressed by trade treaties did not always prevail. As the breaks in trade relations with Byzantium illustrate, circumstances sometimes arose which provoked the Venetians to intervene, arms in hand, to affect the balance of contending forces in their own interest. Generally speaking, Venetian policy opposed territorial extension toward the Adriatic on the part of any and all of the four powerful neighbors with which the Republic had to deal. In the twelfth century the most stubborn contest was with the Hungarians for control of Istria and the Dalmatian coast. Hungarian support for local elements that were eager to overthrow Venetian control of that coast thrice led to wars; each time the Venetians, with the advantage of superior mobility that command of the sea gave them, were able to reestablish their authority.

Venetians did not seek to administer the Istrian and Dalmatian coastlands directly. Local counts, bishops, and other traditional rulers continued to govern; but Venetian nobles were regularly insinuated into such posts, thus increasing the likelihood that Venetian interests would be carefully looked after. Treaties defined the relations between the various coastal administrative authorities and the dominant city. Usually these provided for some sort of ceremonial tribute—often trifling in amount—plus help in war, e.g., provision of a galley or two. In addition, Venetian ships were assured the right to put into port without let or hindrance, whether for trade or to take refuge from storm or from some pursuing foe. Venice also tried to enforce the rule that all ships leaving Adriatic ports had to call at Venice and offer their goods there for sale before going elsewhere.[34]

Such a pattern of dependency obviously hampered Dalmatian and Istrian trade, and deprived cities like Zara and Spalato of potential port revenues. (Ragusa, further to the south, remained beyond the Venetian sphere of influence most of the time, as did Ancona on the Italian side of the Adriatic.) This means that when even quite small Hungarian forces penetrated to the coast, they were easily able to fan smoldering discontent into open defiance of Venetian power. But since the Hungarians were unable to maintain large forces in the field for any length of time, the resulting conflicts remained well within Venetian capacities. Control of the Adriatic coast, from below the Po mouth on the Italian side to as far south as Zara on the Dalmatian side, was so important to Venice that the city was always ready to put forth the necessary effort to force rebellious communities to submit.

A much more threatening situation for Venice began to develop when the German emperor, Frederick Barbarossa (reigned 1152–90), set out to consolidate his imperial power in Italy. Venice, in alliance with Byzantium and the Norman kingdom in the south, played an active part in bringing the association of north Italian cities known as the Lombard League into being (1167); and it was this coalition that eventually defeated Frederick's army in the battle of Legnano (1176) and compelled him to abandon his efforts at exacting anything more than ceremonial deference from northern Italy.

But before Barbarossa's failure had become clear, Venice pulled away from the Lombard League and even joined forces with one of Frederick's agents in besieging Ancona for a few months in 1173. The reason for such inconstancy was a sudden collision with the Byzantines that flared up between 1166 and 1172.[35] The Emperor Manuel I Comnenus, like Barbarossa, saw himself as a Roman emperor and dreamed of fastening his control upon Italy, as a proper Roman emperor ought to do. In 1157 his forces occupied Ancona, encouraging revolt against the Normans on the part of the still partly Greek-speaking population of southern Italy, and threatening Venetian egress from the Adriatic. Then, as the Venetian collision with Barbarossa developed in northern Italy, Manuel thought he saw a favorable opportunity to throw off the haughty foreigners' trade dominance. Accordingly, in 1172, he planned and executed a sudden coup, seizing Venetian men and goods in every port of his dominions.[36]

26

Venice responded to this affront by sending a mighty armament eastward, which, however, accomplished nothing because plague broke out among the crews. Important constitutional changes ensued at home. Recriminations over the failure climaxed in the murder of the doge; and new election procedures were then defined (1172, and again in 1178) which had the effect of sharpening the distinction between noble and nonnoble classes on the one hand and of increasing the collective responsibility of the noble class for the management of public affairs on the other. The authority of the doge and of the common people suffered a corresponding erosion. These changes, made in time of extraordinary crisis, when acute collision with both the Byzantine and the German imperial power threatened the survival of Venetian prosperity and independence, gave the Venetian state a distinctive character. Important decisions were made by councils of varying size, voting privately. Behind such collegiate decisions stood the pride, wealth, and collective self-consciousness of the Venetian nobility as a whole, a group of a few hundred businessmen for whom the affairs of state were no more (and no less) than the affairs of the biggest and most important company in which they could participate.

The closer involvement of the noble class in the management of the Venetian state paid off handsomely. The crisis period of the 1170s was the time when initial experiments in public debt management magnified the power of the Venetian state enormously, making a large proportion of what had before been private resources available for public purposes on demand. Enhanced resources, nevertheless, were used with caution. The Venetians preferred diplomacy to war, and in the crisis of the 1170s allowed others to do the heavy fighting. In Italy, the Lombard League proved capable of defeating Emperor Frederick Barbarossa's knights without any help from Venice in 1176. In the same year, the Seljuk Turks defeated the Byzantine armies at the battle of Myriocephalon in Asia Minor. Thereupon, the Emperor Manuel found himself dangerously exposed to an attack from Italy which was being planned by the Normans in conjunction with Venice. He accordingly decided to split the alliance by coming to terms with Venice.

This meant freeing the prisoners he had held since 1172, renewing the old trading privileges, and promising to pay back the value of all the goods he had confiscated from the Venetian traders.[37]

This triumph in the east was fully matched in the west. The equivocal role Venice had played in the last stages of the struggle between Frederick Barbarossa and the Italian states made the city of Saint Mark's a logical place for peace negotiations. Accordingly, in 1177, the defeated emperor shared the doge's hospitality with Pope Alexander III (reigned 1159–81), who had become the organizer of victory against the Germans. A vast number of other dignitaries of church and state were also on hand for the peace conference. The doge's role as host and peacemaker, acting as a mediating third power between the twin and rival heads of Latin Christendom, mightily flattered Venetian self-esteem, both at the time and subsequently. But pomp and ceremony did not distract Venetian attention from the art at which they excelled: driving a hard bargain. In return for their lavish hospitality, Frederick granted the Venetians full exemption from imperial tolls throughout his dominions, thus putting the trade policy of the Holy Roman Empire of the German nation vis à vis Venice on a par with that of the Roman Empire of the east. Pope Alexander III, for his part, assigned jurisdiction over Dalmatia to the patriarch of Grado. This powerfully reinforced Venetian dominance in the Adriatic by assigning ecclesiastical control of its eastern shore to a prelate who could be counted on to look after Venetian interests.

These gains were reinforced and given lasting significance by the rapid decay of both Byzantine and Hohenstaufen imperial power in the decades that followed. Manuel Comnenus in the east and Frederick Barbarossa in the west had been rivals, each aspiring to give substance to their proud and ancient title of Roman emperor by reuniting that empire's provinces, severed since the fourth century, on a Mediterranean-wide basis. But such dreams overstrained administrative and economic resources available to either of them. Hence, after the death of Manuel in 1180 and of Frederick in 1190, the empires over which they had presided rapidly lost cohesion.

As the central administration decayed, local magnates and (in the west) city communes achieved effective autonomy.

Under these political circumstances, the trade net, pioneered so successfully by Venice and other north Italian cities, flourished mightily. Local rulers, controlling only small bits of territory, were not in a position to siphon off very much of the profits from interregional trade for their own purposes. Any effort to tax merchants heavily drove them away to some neighboring, rival place; and rulers needed what merchants brought in the way of luxury and strategic goods so badly that they could not long afford to let rivals benefit from traders' presence. Hence the profits of trade tended to accumulate in the hands of merchants and merchant-bankers rather than in the coffers of kings and lesser territorial lords. Townsmen and capitalists were often inclined to reinvest their gains in new economic enterprises, aimed at increasing the volume of commerce and expanding their profits. In this way, new mines were opened up, and credit advances to weavers and other craftsmen induced (or allowed) them to produce a larger supply of goods designed for distant markets. In addition, improvements of urban facilities—walls, warehouses, pavements, public buildings, and private dwellings alike—both expressed and reinforced the wealth and power of the merchant class.

In the Levant, this sort of self-sustaining capital accumulation failed to occur. Byzantine tax collectors on the one hand, and bands of robbers and pirates on the other, put crippling obstacles in the way of private or corporate accumulation of commercial wealth in the hands of the empire's subjects. Byzantine officials' efforts to treat the Latin merchants as ruthlessly as they were accustomed to treating their Greek subjects always proved self-defeating. For example, when the Emperor Andronicus I Comnenus (ruled (1183–85) unleashed the Greeks' pent-up rage against privileged foreigners, he provoked a general massacre of all "Franks" who happened to be within reach of the mobs of Constantinople and some other towns; but this merely led to economic paralysis, military weakness, and a squalid series of political coups and counter-coups.

One—The Frankish Thrust into the Levant

Loss of trade revenues was not the sole factor weakening the Byzantine state. In addition, the peasant base upon which all other elements of society rested suffered sharp erosion, both in the eastern Balkans and in Asia Minor. Here a key factor was the increased frequency and severity of nomad raids. Turkish-speaking raiders descended upon the Balkans from the steppe lands north of the Black Sea; similar bands afflicted the cultivators of Asia Minor even more severely, for there they actually took possession of the central plateau. Open grasslands spread as cultivators were carried off as slaves, or fled.[38]

The weakening of the Byzantine state had gone so far by the beginning of the thirteenth century that native Byzantine elements were no longer able to stave off Latin aggression. This became clear during the Fourth Crusade when Venetian ships and crews, in alliance with a few thousand knights coming mainly from northern France, captured Constantinople and put the city to sack (1204).

It is not at all certain that the Venetians were the prime movers in diverting the knights of the Fourth Crusade to Constantinople. Others, notably the commander-in-chief, Boniface of Montferrat, had personal and familial interests that may have led him to prefer Constantinople to Jerusalem as an immediate target.[39] Yet whoever was mainly responsible, it is clear that the Venetians did not hang back, for their trade had suffered since 1171 and still more since 1183. The hatred exhibited by the Greek public for Venice was fully reciprocated.

By the terms of agreement reached among the leaders of the crusade at the time they decided to storm Constantinople, Venice was to secure "a quarter and a half of a quarter" (i.e., three-eighths) of the booty and lands that might accrue to the victors. Initial grandiose plans for the partition of the conquered empire soon proved empty. Within a few years, a new-sprung Bulgarian empire dominated nearly all of the European hinterland close to Constantinople; on the Asiatic side a Greek "Empire of Nicaea" took control of northwestern Anatolia; and in the west another Greek prince ruling from

Arta in Epiros divided the western Balkans with Serbian župans.

Latin rule was successfully imposed in the Morea, Attica, and in most of the Aegean islands, including Negropont and Crete. Around Constantinople itself, only a very small region remained under Latin control after the loss of Salonika to the despot of Epiros in 1224. The supply of skilled fighters needed to sustain Latin power over wider territories was simply unavailable. Immediately after taking the city, most of the Crusaders, having collected a rich booty from the accumulated treasures of Constantinople, were eager to go home. For those who stayed, fiefs, however impressive on paper, proved difficult to get much revenue from. Only where Latin merchants were able to develop export trade to the west did Latin lords find it possible to make their lands yield a worthwhile income, a fact that confined them to regions of easy access to the sea. In the absence of a manorial regime like that of northwestern Europe in which moldboard cultivation both tied the peasants to the soil and permitted them to produce a substantial surplus without undue effort, the pattern which allowed knights to multiply so rapidly in Frankland, each subsisting on little more than the produce of a single village, simply could not establish itself. In the east knighthood remained exotic, requiring a comparatively wide-ranging commercial net for its support. This fact sharply limited its effective range, despite the fact that Frankish knights remained invincible in the field, or nearly so.[40]

The Venetians were in a better position than the other participants in the Fourth Crusade to hold what they had won; yet Venice, too, soon recoiled from the plans of the first few years. By far the most important territory that fell to Venice in the initial distribution of spoils was the portion of Constantinople assigned to their sovereignty. The leader of the crusade, Doge Henry Dandolo, remained in the city he had helped to conquer until his death (1205). Thereupon the local Venetian community chose a successor, who acted quite independently of the Venetian government in dealing with the Latin emperor and other foreign powers.

Until 1219 relations between the Venetian community in Constantinople and the public authorities in Venice remained ambiguous. The Venetians of Venice set out to extend a string of bases down the coast of Greece by occupying Durazzo, Corfu, Modon, Coron, and Cerigo between 1204 and 1207; only in 1211 did they begin to make serious efforts to take possession of Crete, although that island had been assigned to Venetian control in the aftermath of the conquest of Constantinople.[41]

Venetian efforts to cash in on territorial gains from the Fourth Crusade were hampered by war with Genoa, 1205–18. This arose out of trade policy. The conquest of Constantinople in 1204 seemed to the Venetians to offer a golden opportunity for them to assert a monopoly. At his coronation, the Latin emperor of Constantinople, in addition to opening all ports to the Venetians without payment of excise taxes, had promised to exclude the Genoese and Pisans completely from his lands. The enmity of both these powerful trading cities soon proved too much to withstand, so the Venetians decided in 1206 to admit the Pisans to trade; but until 1218 they maintained the prohibition against Genoese shipping. The Genoese did not submit meekly; large "piratical" fleets—i.e., privately financed war ventures—opposed the Venetians wherever they were vulnerable. Fighting concentrated around Corfu and on Crete, where Genoese fleets enjoyed valuable support from local Greek populations, for whom the Venetians represented a national-cultural oppressor. In 1213–14 the Venetians were in fact driven from Durazzo and Corfu by the newly founded Despotate of Epiros. This was something of a victory for the Genoese: although ambigously so, since the despot of Epiros promptly made terms with the Venetians, conceding trading rights. In Crete, however, the Venetians slowly prevailed, driving the Genoese from the island in 1216.

As long as the main effort of the Venetian state was engaged against these Genoese forces, the Venetians in Constantinople could expect relatively little support from their homeland. This allowed the Constantinopolitan community to pursue its own policies, acting with only loose regard for decisions made in Venice.[42] Basically, the Venetians in Constantinople tried to prop up the strength of the Latin empire as best they could. As feudatories of the emperor, Venetian citizens took control of strategic regions commanding the sea approaches to Constantinople. In particular, the Galipoli peninsula and the "archipelago," i.e., a cluster of Aegean islands around Naxos, passed into the hands of Venetian vassals of the emperor. But in 1205 the Bulgarians defeated and captured the newly crowned Latin emperor in a battle near Adrianople. This prevented the Venetians from taking possession of the landward approaches to Constantinople in Thrace, which had also been assigned to them. In the ensuing fifteen years, a series of military failures on the part of the Latin empire made it clear that the resources available to the Franks in Constantinople were not enough to keep the city safe without substantial support from Venice in the form of war galleys and manpower.

Adequate protection of Constantinople from Greek and Bulgarian attack required an end to the war with Genoa. Accordingly, the Venetians concluded peace in 1218, admitting their arch rivals to trade in Constantinople, though not on terms as advantageous as those enjoyed by Venetian citizens. In the next year, the Venetian government induced the community in Constantinople to recognize the supremacy of the home authorities in all political-military matters.[43] In return, Venetian warships started to patrol the approaches to Constantinople regularly, as they had long been accustomed to do in the Adriatic.

The much enlarged imperial territories that thus accrued to the Venetian state after 1204 had to be governed somehow. In Corfu briefly, and in Crete more permanently, the Venetians resorted to the form of military administration used by all the Latin crusading states. That is, the city granted fiefs to knights and serjeants who undertook to build castles and defend the land in return for the income to be derived from territories granted to them.[44]

Holders of these fiefs were all Venetian citizens; their lands came by confiscation from Greek magnates. This stirred bitter opposition among the native Greeks. So did the Venetian religious policy which transferred all ecclesiastical property and prelacies to Latins, and expected the Greeks to abandon their traditional form of Christianity and accept Latin rites and doctrines. As a result, revolt simmered in Crete throughout the thirteenth century, and the mountainous inland regions of the island were not brought under effective Venetian administration.

The real key to Venetian success in empire building did not rest on infeudation. Rather the remarkably long life of the Venetian empire rose from a judicious blend of centralized bureaucratic administration and institutional forms that encouraged local communities of Venetians resident overseas to participate in public affairs. A step in this direction had been taken in 1200 when a *bailo* was appointed to supervise Venetian affairs along the entire Syrian and Palestinian coast. But it was in Crete that lasting patterns of imperial administration were worked out. Basically, what was done was to export a simplified model of the Venetian home government to Crete. This allowed Venetian residents abroad to enjoy accustomed roles on governing boards and councils, while centralized control was assured by entrusting principal executive powers to officers appointed from Venice, usually for a term of two years.

This practice dated from 1208, before Crete had been conquered, when the Venetians appointed a doge of Candia (the main city of the island) to act as chief magistrate and military commander. As the title implied, his role was conceived as analogous to that of the doge of Venice, with the important difference that the office was not for life, as in Venice, but only for two years, renewable at the discretion of the Lesser Council or Senate, which made the appointment in the first place.[45]

The first doge of Candia, Giacomo Tiepolo, divided the island into six administrative areas and named them after the *sestiers* into which Venice itself was divided. Fief holders from the *sestiers* acted as members of a Greater Council, modeled on the *Maggior Consiglio* of Venice, to which all nobles belonged. Even if living permanently abroad and responsible for a share in local affairs, Venetian citizens retained full rights and obligations toward the home government, being required, for instance, to subscribe to compulsory state loans on the same basis as those actually resident in the city. As the Venetians developed more elaborate procedures for controlling magistrates at home, similar steps were taken to control and review the activity of the doge of Candia and other overseas administrators; but since the full elaboration of the system occurred in the fourteenth century, it seems best to put off further description until the next chapter.[46]

The gradual definition of legal forms of control over distant colonies was effective, thanks to the fact that Venetian shipping maintained frequent contacts between colonists overseas and their homeland. Venetian shipping, in turn, depended on trade; and as a rule the Venetian state was more interested in advantageous conditions for trade than in dominating territory. Accordingly, Venice concluded trade treaties even with such political rivals as the despot of Epiros (1216) and the Greek emperor of Nicaea (1219). As for the Latin rulers of the Levant, they all, like their nominal chief, the Latin emperor, depended upon communications and supplies provided by Venetian ships.[47]

A major consequence of the capture of Constantinople by the Latins in 1204 was that the previous isolation of the Black Sea from its connecting Aegean and Mediterranean waters came to an end. The Byzantine government jealously guarded access to the Black Sea and had normally compelled vessels passing through the Bosporus to unload at Constantinople and offer their wares for sale. This was aimed primarily at assuring an adequate food supply for the capital city, since whenever nomad harassment relaxed, the western and northern shores of the Black Sea were capable of producing large quantities of grain for export.[48]

After 1204, therefore, Venetians enjoyed free access to the Black Sea for the first time. Trade centered at Soldaia in the Crimea; but until the Mongol conquest established a single supreme authority (1242) throughout the western steppe lands, unstable political conditions around the shores of the Black Sea seem to have prevented commerce from assuming much importance. At any rate, Venetian records are very scant; and when the pace of Black Sea commerce did begin to quicken, in the second half of the thirteenth century, the Genoese rather than the Venetians played the principal role.

The remarkable upthrust of Black Sea trade in the second half of the thirteenth century appears to be a function of a general shift of Asian trade routes. Prior to about 1250, spices continued to arrive on the Mediterranean coast either via the Red Sea and Egypt or via the Persian Gulf and Syria-Palestine; overland caravan traffic from China was not of great importance. In 1253 a new war of major proportions broke out between Venice and Genoa for control of the Syrian spice outlets. By 1258 Venice proved the stronger; but the fruits of victory were largely nullified by the fact that in 1261 Genoa's ally, the Greek emperor of Nicaea, Michael VIII Paleologus (reigned 1259–82), seized Constantinople by *coup de main* at a time when the Venetian fleet happened to be absent on operations in the Black Sea. The Genoese promptly tried to exclude the Venetians from the trade of Constantinople completely. This provoked a new war, which came to an end only in 1270, after Michael VIII readmitted the Venetians to Constantinople's markets in order to escape too much dependence on the Genoese.

Nevertheless, from 1261 the Genoese displaced the Venetians as the primary representatives of Latin navigation in the Black Sea. In this new role the Genoese proved themselves formidable indeed. They vigorously set out to develop trade with the Crimea and all round the Black Sea coast. This accorded well with Mongol policy, which traditionally assigned high prestige and privilege to merchants.[49] As a result, caravan trade all the way from China, plus spices come from India overland to Trebizond (near the eastern end of the Black Sea), quickly attained considerable importance. This diverted valuable goods from the ports of Syria and Palestine, where trade decayed and the remnants of the crusading states faded rapidly toward extinction. The Christians lost their last stronghold in the Holy Land with the fall of Acre to the mamelukes of Egypt in 1291. The most conspicuous accomplishment of Frankish knighthood in the Levant was thus swept away.

In addition to the precious cargoes of distant origin that

enriched Black Sea ports, articles of local production (grain, salt, fish) together with furs, wax, and slaves coming from the Russian north and from the Caucasus area added significantly to the value of their trade. Genoese merchants profited greatly, possessing major fortified bases at Pera, across the Golden Horn from Constantinople, at Caffa in the Crimea, and enjoying almost equally favorable conditions at Trebizond as well.[50] Yet Genoa did not create an overseas empire like that Venice had begun to construct after 1204. Instead, the Genoese inhabitants of strongholds like Pera and Caffa set up local governments of their own, and sometimes followed policies that led to open conflict with the Genoese authorities at home.[51]

Between 1261 and 1282, Venice played an ambiguous role in the Levant. On the one hand, the Venetians curried favor with the Greek emperor, Michael VIII, who was eager to play them off against the Genoese. On the other hand, the Venetians could not easily reconcile themselves to the loss of their privileged position in Constantinople, and toyed with projects for restoring a Latin emperor by force. This possibility came to life after 1266 as a result of a fresh advance of French knighthood into southern Italy and Sicily.

In that year, at the pope's invitation, Charles of Anjou, brother of King Louis IX of France (Saint Louis), won control over the former Norman territories of the south. The pope wished to have a strong yet reliable ally on his southern flank, to replace the Hohenstaufens, who since 1194 had threatened to nip the papal territorial position in Italy between northern and southern pincers.[52] The death of Emperor Frederick II in 1250, swiftly followed by that of his son, Conrad IV (1254), gave the pope his chance. Conrad left no legitimate successor. In Germany disputed elections led to an interregnum that lasted until 1273, when a poor and obscure nobleman, Rudolf of Hapsburg, secured the imperial title largely because he was too weak to threaten anyone.

In Italy the popes took advantage of their traditional rights as suzerains of the kingdom of Sicily to confer possession on Charles of Anjou, who had to win his new kingdom by defeating Frederick II's bastard, Manfred of Hohenstaufen. Once firmly in control, Charles of Anjou sought to legitimize his new role by reviving old plans for the conquest of Byzantium —a Norman dream since the time of Robert Guiscard.[53]

Charles' plans provoked Emperor Michael VIII to embark upon elaborate counter moves, including a successful effort to deprive Charles of papal support by himself submitting, on behalf of the Greek church, to papal ecclesiastical supremacy at the Council of Lyons (1274).[54] Venice hesitated, for full realization of Charles' Balkan ambitions, like earlier Norman efforts to cross the Straits of Otranto, would have bottled Venice up inside the Adriatic. But eventually, in 1281, Venice lined up on the Angevin side just as events moved toward their climax.

In the next year, revolt broke out in Sicily, on the very eve of Charles' intended attack on Byzantium. King Pedro III of Aragon came to the rebels' aid, and his fleet drove the French forces from the island. Charles died in 1285 without being able to restore his power. With him died the supremacy of Frankish knighthood in the Mediterranean. Knights' superiority in battle and in society lingered on only in remote regions like Prussia (where the Teutonic Knights arrived from Palestine in 1229), Hungary (where Angevin rule brought an infusion of French culture in its train, 1310–86), and Cyprus (where an increasingly archaic style of French chivalry endured until near the end of the fourteenth century).

No doubt the ill-success that attended Saint Louis' crusades foreshadowed the overthrow of Frankish knighthood;[55] but it was the Aragonese victory in Sicily, won by infantrymen who were equipped with hitherto unparalleled numbers of crossbows, that sealed this important shift in military-political affairs. Crossbowmen could pierce the armor of a charging knight at a safe distance; they were even more deadly in sea fights. Bowmen stationed aloft in the crows' nest could shoot with almost perfect security from behind a sheltering parapet and rake enemy ships with their iron-tipped bolts. In particular, the crowded rowers of a war galley, laboring in the open, made an extremely vulnerable target for crossbowmen. This was demonstrated after 1282, when the Aragonese compensated for their inferior rowing skills in sea battles against

Charles of Anjou's forces by chaining their vessels together and relying upon crossbows to destroy the opposing crews that dared to come within range.[56] Transferred to land, massed crossbow fire proved almost equally effective. The extraordinary career of the Catalan company is evidence thereof, for after conquering Sicily these infantrymen first demonstrated an easy superiority over Turkish mounted archers in Asia Minor and then brushed the Latin chivalry of Greece aside to establish an ill-famed regime in Athens.[57]

The history of crossbow design and manufacture seems to be unknown,[58] but there is definite evidence that the number and importance of these weapons in sea warfare increased markedly in the years following 1282.[59] It looks as though the value of crossbows for land warfare assumed a new order of magnitude only after the weapons 1) began to be manufactured in comparatively vast quantities for use at sea, and 2) the skills for maintaining these relatively complicated instruments had spread among a few thousand increasingly professionalized bowmen-mariners.[60] Large-scale manufacture of these bows may have started in Genoa and/or Barcelona, perhaps in preparation for the campaign of 1282. Genoese crossbowmen, at any rate, became suddenly famous during the fourteenth century and rivaled English longbowmen, Flemish pikemen, and Swiss halberdiers in depriving the knight of his supremacy on his home ground: France.[61]

The Sicilian Vespers may therefore stand as a benchmark in the history of relations between the Latin west and the Greek and Moslem east. The alliance between Frankish knighthood and Italian shipping had reached a dead end. The new formidability of infantrymen, equipped with comparatively elaborate weapons that could only be produced by skilled artisans but were exceedingly easy to learn to use, gave the towns of Italy a chance to slough off the medieval carapace of knighthood, and assert their power, in all its manifold forms, independently. Doing so, they inaugurated a new era—the era of the renaissance.

Before taking up this second chapter of our story, however, something should be said about the cultural interactions provoked by the first phase of Latin expansion eastward. It was mainly knightly patterns of conduct, not those of Italian townsmen, that attracted attention in the Levant, affecting the battle style and perhaps the self-conception of Egyptian mamelukes as well as of Greek fighting men and rulers.

The interpenetration of Latin and Greek military methods and outlook went very far in the time of the Comneni. And with military technique went some of the trappings: tournaments and familiarity with French romances, for instance. The same remained true of the successor states to the Byzantine Empire after 1204. Even the anti-Latin rulers of Nicaea and Epiros continued to hire Latin knights to stiffen their armies;[62] conversely, the French court of the prince of Achaia spawned romances and historical poems written in Greek by men who shared the traditions and values of French chivalry to the full.[63]

Emperor Michael VIII Paleologus, like the Comneni before him, associated much with Latins and found a few Greek courtiers who, like himself, were willing to sacrifice the autonomy of the Greek church in return for papal support. But the immense majority of the Greeks hated the Latins and tried to have as little to do with them as possible, while cultivated men of learning, masters of pagan as well as of the Christian classics, looked down upon the "Franks" as barbarians.[64] Whatever reception Latin styles of life had in the Greek world therefore was confined to a very restricted circle of warriors and courtiers; and with the decay of knighthood, the appeal of western aristocratic culture came abruptly to an end.

The contrary movement whereby Latins assimilated Greek civilization was also inhibited by deep-seated antipathy. To be sure, western crusaders were much impressed by the fortifications of Constantinople and borrowed from Byzantine models when building their own castles, both in Palestine and in northwestern Europe. More elaborate and powerful siege engines may also have reached the west in part through the crusading encounter with Byzantium.[65] There are also several recorded instances of Frankish assimilation into Byzantine society. Some of the knightly mercenaries from the west married Greeks and founded distinguished families; and descendants of the French barons who conquered the Morea in

1205 began to merge into the Greek population of the peninsula within three generations.[66]

But such cases were exceptional; closer contacts between the Greek and Latin segments of Christendom generated mutual dislike and repugnance more often than anything else. These feelings were expressed, above all else, in theological controversy. In 1054 the pope and the œcumenical patriarch anathematized one another. Subsequent efforts to patch up the quarrel, like that of 1274, never proved viable. On both sides of the schism, the clergy armed themselves with arguments giving voice to the hostility each party came to feel toward the other. The existence of these watchful corporate guardians of doctrine made it difficult for anyone to occupy any sort of middle ground. Religious identity, manifested publicly by ritual acts, defined everyone's role as either Greek or Frank or Moslem. Even the children of mixed marriages (who were numerous enough to have a distinct name, *gasmules*, and at least an elementary corporate consciousness) had to choose one religious identity or the other.

In the Balkan hinterland, however, ecclesiastical lines were not so sharply drawn. Since the times of Saints Cyril (d. 869) and Methodios (d. 885), use of the Slavonic language in the liturgy and as a language of piety and learning distinguished the Slavic churches both from the Greeks and from the Latins. Lines of ecclesiastical jurisdiction responded, but often sluggishly, to changing political conditions. For example, when a revolt against the Byzantines in 1185 led to the establishment of a second Bulgarian empire in the eastern Balkans, the new rulers sought eagerly for ecclesiastical independence. The Greeks were loathe to agree to such an arrangement; but in 1204, after the fall of Constantinople to the Franks, the pope readily consented to recognize the full administrative autonomy of the Bulgarian church and the legitimacy of the Bulgarian monarch's sovereignty, sending a papal legate to crown Kaloyan (reigned 1197–1207) king. Similarly, in 1217 another papal legate crowned Stephen II Nemaya king of Serbia, and in 1253 Daniel, the Russian prince of Galicia and Volynia, also accepted a crown from the papacy in hope of securing western military aid against the Tatars. From Rome it surely looked as though the process which had brought many other outlying realms of Christendom under papal obedience (e.g., Hungary, Poland, Scandinavia) was well on its way in the Balkans.

Yet an awareness of deep cultural divergence was never far from the surface; and the closer to Rome geographically the more conscious the Balkan Slavs were of these differences. Thus in 1219, Saint Sava, brother of King Stephen II of Serbia, secured recognition of the autocephaly of the Serbian church from the Greek patriarch in Nicaea; and in 1222 he crowned his brother for a second time, to wash away the Latin taint that lingered from his first coronation. Among the Bulgars, antagonism to Rome was weaker, and jealousy of the Greeks was correspondingly greater. Nevertheless, in 1235 the Bulgarian monarch broke with the papacy, allied with the Greek emperor of Nicaea, and as part of the deal secured from the Greek patriarch full recognition of the independence of the Bulgarian church, under a new patriarch of Tirnovo. As for Daniel of Galicia, he sent a Russian monk to Nicaea about 1250 (before getting his crown from the pope) who came back duly consecrated as metropolitan of Kiev. From that time onward, until 1441, Russians alternated with Greeks in the metropolitinate of Kiev—aptly bodying forth the ambiguous autonomy the Greeks accorded to the Russian church.

Accommodation with the papacy at the beginning of the thirteenth century in Bulgaria, Serbia, and Galicia was not accompanied by any lasting cultural assimilation to the Latin west, though some Serbian church buildings do show Romanesque touches. This was far outweighed by the massive Byzantine artistic influence that came fllooding into Serbia during the second half of the century, assisted and sustained by the deliberate and conscious policy of Saint Sava and his successors, who looked to Mount Athos as the primary font of religious truth and guidance.[67]

The way in which Byzantine styles and skills spread into Serbia as soon as royal patronage created sufficient concentration of wealth to support a luxurious and costly art was only one of many demonstrations of the attractive force inherent in the eastern artistic tradition. Even the Latins were impressed by Byzantine art and luxury crafts; a few of them were also ready to take Greek learning seriously, especially in matters scientific. Both art and learning depended closely on the patronage of courts and the personal tastes of particular rulers. Thus, from about the mid-twelfth century until the death of Emperor Frederick II (1250), the Norman court of Sicily reflected the ambitions and personalities of its crowned heads in becoming the seat of a remarkable mingling of Greek, Latin, and Arabic styles of civilization. The Norman kings and their Hohenstaufen heirs aimed to equal or surpass the splendor of Byzantium and Cairo. This required art and learning as well as arms and money. For instance: astronomer-astrologists had long been valued experts at Arabic and Greek courts; the Norman kings wished to enjoy the same services. Having secured the text of Ptolemy's works from Constantinople, they therefore ordered them translated into Latin, along with some of Aristotle's treatises on natural science.[68] The study of medicine also benefited from the confluence of Arabic and Greek learning in the kingdom of Sicily. Salerno became the seat of the premier medical school of Latin Europe, where translations of Galen and Avicenna instructed doctors from all western Europe in the principles of their craft.

Sicilian translations were, however, less influential for the development of Latin learning as a whole than translations made in Spain from Arabic versions of Greek works. A factor in insulating the Sicilian court from other Latin centers of learning must have been the bitter and unremitting enmity between the popes and Frederick II, which stamped Frederick as a foul heretic in the eyes of most of Catholic Europe. Hence, like the spread of knightly manners into Byzantium, the spread of Byzantine learning into the west was limited by the narrow court circles through which alone these patterns of cultural borrowing passed.

Art and even luxury products were, by their nature, more public. Accordingly the imported objects and imitations of Byzantine art styles that found lodgment in Latin Europe played a considerable role in shaping the way western art developed in the eleventh to thirteenth centuries. The migration of art objects, and of artisans possessing high luxury skills, is hard to follow in detail. A few spectacular episodes, such as the

One—*The Frankish Thrust into the Levant*

arrival of table forks in Venice with a Greek princess who married the doge's son in 1005, or the forcible transplantation of silk workers from Thebes to Sicily by King Roger II in 1147, happen to have entered the literary record;[69] in addition, many features of Venetian public life, from the doge's formal costume to the design of war galleys and the idea of a state-managed arsenal, derived largely from Byzantium and may initially have required importation of Byzantine craftsmen.

This was certainly true of the most conspicuous aspect of Byzantine cultural diffusion: the spread of religious art forms and ideas that had their seat and most perfect development in Constantinople, yet were imitated, with varying degrees of proficiency and success, not only in Italy, but in Germany, Russia, France, and even in such distant regions as England and Sweden in the eleventh to thirteenth centuries.[70] Three phases of this process may be distinguished: before about 1050, a few individual craftsmen and isolated objects—illustrated church books, carved ivories, embroidered silks, and the like—reached western Europe, where they inspired inexpert imitations and adaptations to local taste.

From about 1050, a far more massive importation of Byzantine art occurred, centered in Venice on the one hand and in Sicily and south Italy on the other. When the Venetians set out to celebrate the grandeur of their state by erecting a splendid new chapel for the doge (1043) they looked to Byzantium for a model, and accordingly designed the Church of Saint Mark on the pattern of the Church of the Holy Apostles in Constantinople. The decoration of Saint Mark's was carried through piecemeal, and at first by mosaic artists imported from the Greek world. Consequently, many phases of the development of Byzantine style are represented within Saint Mark's walls.[71]

The Norman monarchs of Sicily, characteristically, commissioned bigger projects which were carried through on a single plan and in relatively short periods of time. A chief example is the cathedral at Monreale, built on a Latin plan but decorated with mosaics that were executed by Byzantine artists between 1174 and 1182. Sicily and Venice, both of which thus became seats of major artistic monuments conceived on Byzantine lines, acted as foyers whence iconographic and other aspects of this art then spread deeper into western Europe.[72]

A third phase of Latin-Byzantine artistic interaction set in after 1204, when a massive quantity of precious objects taken as booty flooded into Venice and other parts of Latin Europe. The Latin conquest of Constantinople also interrupted imperial patronage for Byzantine artists. This compelled them to travel away from old centers in Constantinople and Salonika in search of employment. The rise of high art in the western Balkans under the patronage of Serbian princes was one by-product of this development; reinforcement of Greek elements in the art of Italy, and through Italy in the rest of Latin Europe, was another.[73]

The interplay between stimuli imported from Byzantium and local classical survivals in the rise of the Romanesque and Gothic styles of art and architecture is a complex and disputed matter. Until the middle of the thirteenth century these developments remained distinctively French, with a colonial offshoot in England. Italy and Germany remained enthralled by the art of Byzantium, as locally modified and developed, until, almost at the moment when French knighthood lost its military supremacy, the Gothic art of France began to move onto Italian and German ground. Yet this acknowledgment of the aesthetic power that had accrued to French Gothic architecture also coincided with the initial emancipation of Italian painting from its older symbiosis with Byzantine styles, that is, with the announcement through art of the dawn of the renaissance.

Venice and Sicily played no part in this development; until long after the end of the thirteenth century their artistic connection with Byzantium remained unbroken. Yet Venice did take a leading part in economic and political affairs of Italy and of the Levant, where for about two centuries after 1282 the Venetians played the role of a Great Power. To trace the main lines of this development will be the aim of the next chapter.

·TWO·

Venice as a Great Power
1282-1481

BETWEEN ABOUT 1280 and 1330 Mediterranean ship design underwent another fundamental change. The Venetians made correspondingly drastic changes in the ways they organized navigation and trade; and the regulatory patterns they hit upon both supported and were supported by the city's peculiar constitutional structure. The Venetian constitution in fact froze in the form it attained early in the fourteenth century and survived externally unaltered until the demise of the Republic in 1797. By contrast, the new system of navigation, introduced in the early fourteenth century, lasted only about two hundred years.

Nevertheless, the end of the period treated in this chapter is defined not so much by technical and organizational changes in nautical matters as by the rise of vast territorial states—Turkey, Spain, France—each of which was able to assemble larger resources than Venice or any other mere city state could command. As a result, by the last two decades of the fifteenth century, Venice and the other Italian city states could no longer equal or outmatch the political giants impinging upon their spheres of operations. Venice, in other words, ceased to be a Great Power, but became instead a pacesetter in matters of high culture for much of Orthodox and part of Latin Christendom.

At the beginning of our period, the breakthrough toward full

46

autonomy for the relatively small Italian city states was facilitated by (and at the same time helped to bring about) the collapse of the rival imperial structures of the high Middle Ages. First to fall was the Byzantine Empire (1204). We have already said something about the alliance between Frankish knighthood and Venetian sea power that destroyed the Greek Empire of Byzantium. The Holy Roman Empire of the German nation collapsed half a century later, when the papacy succeeded in mobilizing Italian and trans-Alpine resources—spiritual as well as material—against Hohenstaufen efforts to give administrative reality to their imperial title. But papal government of Latin Christendom also proved fragile. Pope Boniface VIII (reigned 1292–1303) tried to bring the French monarchy to heel. Instead, the French came close to capturing the papacy during the so-called Babylonian captivity (1307–78); and initial efforts to return the pope to Rome merely created first two and then three rival pontiffs (1378–1415). When a united and restored papal government did return to Rome, the Italian city state pattern of life and politics demonstrated its new ascendancy by nearly capturing the papacy, just as the French monarchy had almost done in the previous century. For the popes, once back in Rome, became renaissance princes, and often seemed to act more as local rulers of an Italian city than as directors of Christendom as a whole.

The collapse of imperial and papal universalism was by no means the only factor permitting the cities of Italy to become Great Powers. The decay of knighthood was an essential precondition. Equally indispensable was the continued ability of Italian cities to mobilize men and resources over wider and wider regions, reaching further and further down the social scale. Prime movers and chief to profit from this continued process were the businessmen and artisans of a few north Italian and south German-Rhenish towns. As long as citizens (rather than officers and officials of territorial monarchs) remained in charge of mobilizing the human and material resources of Europe for consciously conceived purposes, so long and no longer did city state patterns of society continue to dominate Europe's life. This period ran from about 1280 to about 1480, or to seize upon two convenient signposts, from the Sicilian Vespers (1282) to the death of Mehmed the Conqueror (1481).

The power of European city states in these two centuries was sustained by the fact that at the beginning of the period the means and geographical range of economic mobilization within Europe underwent a mutation. Between 1280 and 1330, under the management of capitalists and entrepreneurs domiciled mainly in cities of northern Italy, a series of important inventions drastically cheapened transport. This allowed trade in articles of common consumption to attain previously unequaled volume. Geographical barriers were broken through; linkages were extended in space and simultaneously shortened in time.

The principal instrument of this revolution in Europe's economic organization was an improved seagoing ship. Beginning about 1280, bigger ships that navigated winter and summer as a matter of course carried more goods in greater safety and with shorter turnaround times than had been possible before. They did so not only in Mediterranean waters, but in the Black Sea and through the Straits of Gibraltar to North Sea ports as well. Sea carriage was, of course, enormously cheaper than portage overland;[1] and soon after 1300 it became easy and normal for merchant ships to travel from Genoa or some other Mediterranean port to Caffa in the Crimea in one direction, or to Bruges in Flanders in the other. As a result, regions of Europe that had previously existed independently of one another as far as goods of common consumption were concerned began to merge into a single, vastly enlarged, sea-linked market.

The key date for opening the Black Sea to Mediterranean commerce was 1204; but as we saw in the preceding chapter, really large-scale trade from Black Sea ports began to develop only after 1261. The key date for opening the Straits of Gibraltar was 1291, when a Genoese buccaneer and business man, Benedetto Zaccaria, crushed a Moroccan fleet that was attempting to maintain Moslem control over the straits.[2] Thereafter, Italian ships faced no serious political or military obstacle in passing freely from the Mediterranean to the North

VENETIAN SPHERE OF INFLUENCE IN EASTERN EUROPE

Sea. Within a generation, such voyages became matters of course.

These truly impressive extensions of the geographic range of Italian shipping went hand in hand with important changes in ship-building techniques and navigational methods. Perhaps the key improvement was the introduction of more powerful steering devices that used mechanical advantage—whether pulleys or levers—to exert force on a scale far transcending the limits of ordinary human muscles. In ancient and early medieval times, European seamen had steered their ships by means of an oar trailing from somewhere near the ship's stern. Such devices were limited by the strength of the men who manipulated them. Larger vessels required an adjustable steering surface affixed to the ship's frame by some sort of heavy, permanent hinge. The stern-post rudder, introduced first in northern seas during the thirteenth century, satisfied this requirement: it could be made as large as desired, and it was not difficult to invent linkages that gave a steersman enough mechanical advantage to keep the rudder at a desired setting even amidst heavy waves.[3]

With the invention of more powerful steering devices, ships could be greatly enlarged. This called for adjustments in the way sails, masts, and rigging were arranged. Square sails, like sternpost rudders a northern device, appeared in the Mediterranean shortly before 1300, and were combined in various ways with the old "lateen" rig. In addition, "castles" fore and aft rose high above the ship's waist. They provided better vantage points from which to defend the vessel, and also offered the crew enclosed living quarters, as was necessary for successful winter navigation. These changes were so substantial that a new name—rendered "cog" in English—came into use to distinguish the improved type of ship from its predecessors.

Simultaneously, advances in techniques of navigation made the new cogs safer and more useful. The compass came into use in the Mediterranean soon after 1270. It allowed direction-finding under cloudy skies, for by recording each change in a ship's compass bearings (and the time at which such changes took place)[4] a practiced navigator could make reasonably accurate guesses as to location, even after several days under clouded skies and out of sight of land. As this became practical, charts of the Mediterranean and adjacent coastlines were worked out—the so-called portolans—showing compass bearings between ports. Following the appropriate course as defined by such charts allowed ships to travel in winter almost as accurately toward the desired landfall as in summer, when clear skies (at least in the Mediterranean) allowed the captain to check his direction by sun and stars.[5]

The combined effect of a better defense (thanks to crossbows) and of the improvements in navigation and ship design that came to the Mediterranean in the period 1280–1330 cheapened transport and altered the conditions of maritime life in many different ways. Thus, for instance, since ships began to operate all year round, sailing became a fulltime occupation as never before. As a result, the citizen–sailor–soldier–trader–jack-of-all-trades who had first sustained Italian mercantile prowess throughout the Mediterranean began to disappear.[6] Resulting social differentiation, in turn, presented such cities as Genoa and Venice with critical problems of political management—how to handle an emerging marine proletariat. Their contrasting political fates in the fourteenth century were closely related to the different way the two governments reacted to this circumstance.

But if the rise of a marine proletariat strained the civic order of the leading maritime republics of Italy, simultaneously business boomed for those who owned ships and engaged in long-distance trade. Italian capital resources far exceeded those available to others within the geographic scope of the enlarged sea range that opened to European ships. Hence it was mainly in Genoa and Venice and related Italian financial centers—Siena, Florence, Milan—that the financial management and control of new interregional trade patterns concentrated.[7] Italian wealth and power expanded correspondingly. By shouldering its way to the forefront of these developments, a single city could draw upon the resources of distant regions, wherever Italian ships, and markets fed by those ships, began to transform local patterns of the production and consumption of goods.

The currents of trade that the Italians had established in the eleven and twelfth centuries supplied the lifeblood of this expanding economic structure. Timber, metals, weapons, and slaves from the northern shores of the Mediterranean and Black Sea coasts were exchanged for "spices"[8] in Egyptian, Syrian, and Black Sea ports. These spices came from afar— India, southeast Asia, China, or more rarely from Iran or the immediate hinterland of Levantine ports.

More important because more susceptible of growth was another very ancient trade: the movement of grain, wine, and salt within the Mediterranean and its adjacent waters. As urban populations grew, the importance of securing a substantial and dependable inflow of grain, year in and year out, increased. Climatic variations from season to season meant that the sources of surplus grain also varied, sometimes quite suddenly. But, in general, Sicily and Apulia in southern Italy were major exporters of grain in the thirteenth and fourteenth centuries. In addition, the Black Sea coasts began to supply Venice and other Italian cities.[9]

The geography of trade in salt and wine fluctuated more slowly, but remained very important. In fact the earliest basis of Venetian mercantile prosperity had been the distribution of salt throughout the Po valley.[10] Venetian salt initially came from salt pans along the Dalmatian coast and in the Venetian lagoons themselves; by the thirteenth and fourteenth centuries other sources of supply as far away as Cyprus supplemented local production; but the Venetian monoply of salt distribution in the Po valley and other parts of north Italy remained an important part of the city's economic role.

The evolution of the wine trade was intimately connected with the development of trade in wool and woolen textiles. What happened was this: a sweet dark wine with unusually high alcoholic content could be made from a special kind of grape that grew, initially, in Cyprus and the Morea. Northern Europeans delighted in this sort of wine, which came to be known in England as malmsey.[11] By carrying barrels of malmsey to England, therefore, Italian merchants had a commodity they could easily exchange for English wool, which was of unusually good quality for the manufacture of fine cloth. Skilled and highly specialized artisans in Flanders and Italy worked the raw English wool into finished goods, which were sold all over Europe and the Levant.

The expansion of high quality textile manufacture in western Europe, sustained by this interregional pattern of exchange, reacted in turn upon the spice trade. Previously, Italian merchants had often exported large quantities of coin or of uncoined silver, since other European goods of sufficient quality to command sale in the Levant had been in chronically short supply. But since European raw material, labor, and capital could all be brought to bear on an increasing scale without undue difficulty, it was possible to expand the amount of high quality woolen textiles put on the market to match any likely increase in the supply of spices from the east, where supplies of raw materials, labor, and capital were also, presumably, reasonably elastic. Hence all parties, and especially middlemen, were in a position to profit. The spice trade could grow without completely draining Europe of precious metals, whose use as a medium of exchange lubricated the growingly complex economic system.[12]

The far-flung integration of skills and resources that went into Europe's fourteenth-century textile trade was the single most important achievement of the Italian city state economy;[13] but many other, less massive but also impressive, developments went along with the rise of this interregional wool-wine-spice pattern of trade. An interesting example was the trade in alum. This mineral was mainly used as a mordant in dyeing. The best alum known to Europeans in the thirteenth to fifteenth centuries came from Asia Minor. The trade took on a new character after 1275, when Benedetto Zaccaria began to develop rich new alum mines at Phocaea, located on the mainland not far from the island of Chios.[14] In the years that followed, the Genoese set out to organize the distribution and sale of alum in Flanders on a mass scale. Having captured Chios in 1346, they used that island as an entrepôt, collecting the yield of all the mines of Asia Minor there. This assured a constant supply of adequate quantities of alum to fill the holds of vast, specialized ships that were built just for the alum trade. Some twenty such vessels, of a size greater than any wooden ship attained before or afterward, plied regularly between Chios and Bruges, winter and summer, stopping en route only at Cadiz to take on water and other supplies. This technical and financial organization cut transport costs per unit weight to a fraction of what competing carriers had to meet. As a result, the Genoese enjoyed a safe margin against all rivals in the alum trade for nearly two centuries.[15]

Another trade, that in slaves, played a far greater role than scholars recognized until recently. In spite of ecclesiastical rules against enslaving Christians, Genoese and Venetian merchants carried many thousands of at least nominally Christian slaves from Black Sea ports to Egypt and elsewhere in the Mediterranean. Most of these people had been captured by Tatar raiding parties that harassed the Russian lands incessantly. In addition, some of the peoples of the Caucasus had a custom of selling children to slave dealers. Numbers are hard to estimate, but according to one calculation, in the 1420s as many as two thousand persons were shipped from Caffa to Egypt annually.[16]

The careers open to these slaves varied. Some few, by joining slave armies like the corps of mamelukes who dominated Egypt, 1250–1798, or by being purchased by the Ottoman sultan to fill out the ranks of his slave household, emerged to positions of great wealth and power in the Moslem portions of the Mediterranean. Physically attractive women regularly became concubines to the Turkish upper classes and as such mothered sons of the reigning sultan as well as of lesser dignitaries of the Ottoman regime.[17] Other slaves were condemned to a miserable life of toil on sugar plantations in Cyprus or Crete. Most became household and personal servants to the upper classes both in Moslem and in Christian[18] cities, doubling, not infrequently, as bodyguards or concubines.

Until the Portugese rounded West Africa, slave raiding across other segments of the Moslem-Christian frontier did not develop so systematically, nor on so large a scale, as in the Black Sea region. But until the nineteenth century, forcible migration from one region to another as a result of enslavement never ceased to churn the coastal and seafaring populations of all the Mediterranean regions.

Massive exchange of staple commodities of low value in proportion to their bulk—wool, salt, grain, alum, cotton, timber—was the genuinely new element of this "renaissance" pattern of trade. It opened up all the advantages of specialization (which Adam Smith later analyzed so persuasively) to a larger proportion of the entire population of Europe than had been possible before cogs and associated advances in navigation cheapened long-distance transport so effectively. Both north and south of the central Mediterranean axis of this trade system an inflow of high value goods from more distant regions enriched the total pattern of exchange. Thus from sub-Saharan Africa came gold and ivory, arriving in North African ports by camel caravans managed by Moslem merchants.[19] Similarly, slaves and furs reached Black Sea ports from Lithuania and the Russian north, also largely through the hands of Moslem intermediaries.[20]

At the heart of the whole system lay a handful of commercial and industrial cities in northern Italy: Milan, Florence, Genoa, and Venice chief among them.[21] In the fourteenth century, before the German Hansa merchants had opened regular sea passage around Denmark between the Baltic and the North Sea, the cities of northern Italy were located near the midpoint of the interconnecting seaways that ran uninterruptedly from the Don mouth on the Sea of Azov in the northeast to the Elbe mouth on the North Sea in the northwest. This convenient location certainly contributed to their dominance, but did not assure it. This is proven by the fact that although Sicily was even better situated geographically, it nevertheless fell into economic decline at the end of the thirteenth century just as the straits at either end of the Mediterranean opened to Italian shipping.

To be sure, there were inherent instabilities in the pattern of interregional exchanges which Italian entrepreneurs of the thirteenth and fourteenth centuries organized. The spread of techniques and the discovery of sources of raw materials in new places sometimes obviated earlier need for long hauls. As northwestern Europe developed—and it did so very rapidly—skills and resources that once had to be imported from the east and south could be supplied locally. In proportion as this happened, Italian capitalists, artisans, and shippers were liable to lose their strategic advantage.

Thus, for example, the alum trade, so skillfully organized by the Genoese, broke down after 1460, partly because of the discovery of new mines in western Europe itself,[22] and partly because the Ottoman sultan chose to tax the alum exported from Asia Minor so heavily as to destroy the price advantage Genoese organization of the distribution system had formerly secured for the Levantine product. The wine trade also migrated geographically. The kind of vines that produced malmsey wine were transplanted not only to Crete, where they provided a basis for a thriving export in the fourteenth and later centuries, but also to southern Spain (early fourteenth century), Portugal (by the 1380s) and the Madeira Islands (1425). As port and madeira wine became available on the northern market, hauling malmsey from the Levant became uneconomic. That strand of trade therefore diminshed after 1400 and disappeared entirely some two centuries later.[23]

Other commodities—silk and sugar chief among them—also migrated from east to west during the centuries with which we are here concerned. Sugar plantations, starting from the Syrian coast in the eleventh century, spread their golden blight in both Cyprus and Crete,[24] before migrating to the Atlantic islands (Madeiras especially) en route to the New World.[25] And the complex of skills needed for growing and manufacturing silk, brought from the Balkans to southern Italy in the twelfth century, spread northward in Italy (where Lucca became a major center) and also into France.[26]

All the same, migration of economic skills to new regions often stimulated new trade patterns even while pinching off older ones. Thus the decay of silk importation from the east was at least partly compensated for by the rise of cotton production in the Levant. Supplies of raw cotton, raised primarily in Syria and Asia Minor, played a growing role in European textile manufacture in the fourteenth and fifteenth centuries. Cotton, indeed, became Venice's principal bulk import from the east.[27]

Another and more important instability in the city state

trade patterns showed itself clearly in the fourteenth century. Periodic financial crises and economic depressions on a pan-European scale began to manifest themselves from the 1330s. In the next decade, the demographic catastrophe of the Black Death (which, incidentally, penetrated western Europe via the Crimea) brought a far more enduring setback to Europe's wealth. In many places, including some important Italian cities, population did not equal the level attained before 1346 for centuries.[28] But the impact of the boom and bust cycle and of the Black Death differed from place to place. However costly, neither the one affliction nor the other sufficed to over-throw—or even to undermine—the power that the most active Italian cities exercised over Europe as a whole.[29]

This was not true, however, of a third sort of instability to which the Italian financial-mercantile-industrial complex remained vulnerable. The city inhabitants depended for their daily food on supplies brought from afar. As long as the financial and technical devices for concentrating enough grain to feed thousands and tens of thousands of men remained a monopoly of urban entrepreneurs, the supremacy of the major Italian city states could not be challenged effectively. When, however, territorial monarchs learned to use similar devices to concentrate food supplies sufficient to support large armies in the field for months at a time, the day of city states as great powers came to an end. In other words, when bureaucratic agents of kings and emperors learned to use the techniques of financial management and of transportation which had been first worked out by cities for their daily support,[30] then the inherent advantage of larger resources in manpower and ma-terial began to tell decisively against small states like those into which Italy (and part of Germany) had divided. With this, a new period of European history began: conveniently and tra-ditionally called "modern."

Taking the renaissance city state era as a whole, Genoa and Florence appear to have been the chief seats of innovation and creativity. Florence became the greatest center of textile manu-facture and of innovation in art and letters. Genoa nurtured the most active commercial entrepreneurs, both on the Black Sea frontier and in the western Mediterranean–North Sea areas. The persistent weakness of the commune of Genoa was, perversely, a strength: private groups had to organize on a more enduring basis and with larger resources to carry through everyday activities, such as the construction of a new ship. From this it proved feasible to organize entire fleets as private ventures; and a privately organized fleet that happened to capture valuable territory could transform itself into a territorial sovereign, operating largely or entirely with the aim of maximizing profits and minimizing costs for the shareholders who had financed the original venture, or for their heirs.

This, for instance, was the history of the remarkable Maona of 1346, which conquered Chios and established a government there that lasted until 1566. Organized initially as a way of financing a single fleet, the Maona was later reorganized into an enduring company, with shares apportioned among the original contributors to the enterprise. The shareholders not only organized a government for Chios, they also managed the island like a great estate, developing the specialized culture of mastic, and as we have just seen, also using the island as an entrepôt for a remarkably well organized alum trade.[31]

This institutional inventiveness, which anticipated in remarkable degree devices later employed by Dutch and English capitalists of the seventeenth century in their imperial ventures overseas,[32] was matched at home by the development of "albergos" and banks. "Albergos" were business-political groupings headed by a noble family and embracing an indefinite number of retainers and dependents. Genoese politics came to turn upon the rivalries of these corporate groupings, whose feuds constantly threatened civil war. More fertile for the future were large corporate banks, of which the most famous, the Bank of Saint George, ended up by taking over many functions from the bankrupt and helpless commune of Genoa, including the defense and management of distant colonies like Caffa in the Crimea.[33]

Venice by comparison lagged behind; yet it, too, responded effectively to the new opportunities and dangers inherent in trade rivalry with such restless neighbors as Genoa, Florence, and Milan. A series of setbacks in the last decades of the thirteenth century—precisely when Genoa's expansive, innovative energies reached their peak—showed the Venetians that important changes would have to be made to keep up with their rivals. Overseas, Genoese fleets proved superior to Venetian naval forces in a long and hard-fought war, 1293–99. Simultaneously, bad relations with the Greek emperor of Constantinople (resulting from Venice's alliance with Charles of Anjou in 1281) hampered trade; and from 1281–99 Crete, too, was in revolt.[34] Lastly, the fall of Acre in 1291 to the sultan of Egypt provoked papal efforts to organize a fresh crusade. In particular, the pope sought to compel Venice and other Christian communities to boycott Egypt, thus embarrassing the Venetians in still another way. These difficulties were matched by severe internal troubles, climaxing in a plot on the part of a few popular aristocrats to overthrow the constituted government. The executions and banishments that resulted from discovery of this "Tiepolo conspiracy" coincided with a sharp collision between the papacy and Venice over control of the city of Ferrara. The pope unleashed formal interdict (1309–13), which created further difficulties for the Venetians—ranging from revolt in Dalmatia (stirred up by the king of Hungary with papal encouragement) to difficulties in collecting monies due them in London.

But the severity of these crises provoked a series of responses that proved remarkably successful—so successful, indeed, that the Venetian constitution assumed a form that did not alter significantly thereafter until the final collapse of the Republic in 1797. The two principal innovations were the unambiguous definition of membership in the Great Council, accomplished 1296–97, and the establishment of an executive Board of Ten, charged with protection of the Republic from internal as well as external enemies. Instituted initially as an emergency measure in 1310 in the aftermath of the Tiepolo conspiracy, the Board of Ten was made permanent in 1334. The Ten soon became the most powerful of all the committees and councils that constituted the government of Venice, mainly because it met frequently, and could both decide and act swiftly when circumstances called for despatch.

The upshot was not only enhanced administrative efficiency, but consolidation of the noble class that supplied the magistrates and councillors responsible for directing the government of Venice. Only members of the Great Council were eligible for such roles; and by defining membership in that body as those whose fathers or grandfathers had in fact been members (the so-called closure of the Grand Council), a hereditary political caste was created. Initially, the effect was to widen the circle of men who mattered politically, since some of those whose rights were confirmed in 1296–97 had dropped out of politics, either from lack of interest or from lack of sufficient wealth to carry much weight in public affairs.[35] In the long run, however, the closure of the Great Council checked the adlection of new men to the political class and generated a pervasive traditionalism that eventually stifled the public life of Venice.

The consolidation of the Venetian noble class after the crises of the early fourteenth century was as much a matter of economics as of politics, however. Political offices were sometimes salaried; hence at least some of the impecunious noblemen (and there were always such in Venice) could maintain themselves by political activity. More important was the fact that public regulation and control of merchant fleets, worked out in the second and third decades of the fourteenth century, made it more difficult for any individual or private company to rake in windfall profits from some temporary and local monopolization of the market. Moreover, public and competitive bidding for command of the merchant galleys had the effect of adjusting bids to anticipated profitability, thus diverting a substantial proportion of trading profits to the state itself. This checked the processes of economic differentiation among noble families, though it did not eliminate wide differences in wealth.

Introduced as a kind of extraordinary measure in times of unusual uncertainty on the seas, the regulated voyage, or *muda*, became normal by the 1330s. The voyages continued, with only occasional interruption, until the 1530s.[36] The Venetion *muda* depended first of all on the development of a new kind of ship, the merchant galley. As the name implies, these were oared vessels, designed for carrying cargo by being made wider abeam and, usually, longer than war galleys.[37] Large crews of about two hundred men per ship were needed to pull the oars, though in open waters Venetian merchant galleys usually depended solely on their sails.[38] The Venetians experimented with vessels of this type from about 1294, but a standard pattern did not emerge until 1318 when the government undertook construction of new merchant galleys required for carrying freight to and from Flanders via the Straits of Gibraltar.[39] This was a new route, and a perilous one as far as Venetian navigation was concerned, having been pioneered by Venetian vessels just three years before, in 1315.[40]

Compared to cogs and other sailing ships, merchant galleys enjoyed greater security against both piracy and shipwreck. The galleys of the *muda* traveled in a convoy as a rule, and a properly armed crew could defend even a single galley against most forms of attack. Oars made maneuver and/or escape easier in battle; they also allowed the captain to find safe harbor and avoid rocks and shoals despite unfavorable winds. Against these advantages lay the massive fact that such vessels were expensive, since the large crew had to be fed and paid. Merchant galleys were, in short, only suited for carrying relatively precious goods for which extra security counterbalanced, and more than counterbalanced, higher freight charges. In their own way, therefore, the Venetian merchant galleys were as specialized a carrier as the vast Genoese alum ships of the fifteenth century, and never constituted more than a small part of the Venetian merchant marine.[41]

Yet they were of great importance, for once the *muda* system came fully into operation, merchant galleys, built in the Arsenal and owned by the state, enjoyed a legal monopoly for carrying spices and other precious goods to and from Venice by sea. The most lucrative branch of Venetian trade was thus confined by law to specialized, publicly owned vessels.[42] How very lucrative the galleys' trade was may be gathered from figures made public by Doge Tomasso Mocenigo in 1423. Even if inexact, their order of magnitude must match the facts fairly closely. The spice trade was a matter of major concern to all Venetians; and expert merchants studied quantities and prices with hawklike intensity, since their profits depended on these variables. Hence, the doge's assertion that ten million ducats were invested annually and produced a profit of four million ducats (however he may have calculated profit) cannot be too far from the truth.[43]

Management of the galley voyages was not left in the hands of public officials. Instead the state rented the galleys out to the highest bidder,[44] though not until appropriate public bodies had weighed available information about current economic and political conditions and then decided how many ships to send to which ports and what the sailing dates should be. The successful bidders obligated themselves to pay a sum of money to the state for the right to operate each galley on its projected trip. When prospects for a profitable voyage seemed bright, the sums bid on the galleys went up, thus making sure that private persons and companies did not reap all the benefits. When prospects were poor, the bidding price went down, and especially toward the end, the state sometimes had to offer a subsidy in order to persuade anyone to undertake the role of entrepreneur.[45]

Moreover, the successful bidder was not free to set his own freight prices. The Venetian government treated merchant galleys as the United States government treated railroads in the first half of the twentieth century, regulating rates for different commodities and requiring the galleys to accept goods offered for transport by any citizen at the same price all others paid. Sailing dates were calculated so as to facilitate speedy turnover of trade goods between the Levant, Venice, and North Sea ports.[46] With arrivals and departures defined months ahead, all concerned could make suitable arrangements for buying and selling, loading, unloading, storing, borrowing, lending, and in other ways making ready for maximally expeditious trade and profit-making. These advantages were great enough that Venetian authorities also sometimes defined legal loading periods for other commodities—mainly cotton —which were too bulky for the merchant galleys and were therefore carried on privately owned cogs instead.[47] In addition, from very early times Venice set up special boards charged with supervison of trade in grain and in salt. These authorities administered complex regulations aimed at assuring an adequate food supply for the city while simultaneously making money for the state.

But many sorts of goods remained exempt from official regulation; and within the Adriatic navigation was entirely unhampered (and unassisted) by *muda* restrictions. Ample scope therefore remained for private shipowners to operate within the framework of public regulation that assumed enduring form in the 1330s. For some two centuries thereafter, the basic rhythm and pattern of Venetian trade was dominated by the comings and going of the state-owned merchant galleys and by the *muda* regulations applied to privately owned cogs engaged in long-distance trade.

The system was designed, consciously, in such a way that really big private business could not prosper in Venice. Small traders, being guaranteed access to the galleys and equal freight rates with even the largest shipper, could compete on even terms with anybody. Most benefits that might come from doing business on a big scale were eaten up by difficulties of efficient management at a distance. Moreover, any specially lucrative new shipping venture, after it had been pioneered by private companies, attracted the attention of public authorities, who regularly acted to open such fields of commerce to the general trading community by organizing a *muda*, available on the usual terms to all who wished to share in the venture.[48]

The Venetian state made the big investments—in ships, and in the protection of trade by means of diplomatic and warlike enterprise. This left day-to-day transactions open to any citizen who had a bit of capital to venture, or who could borrow capital from someone else. Under these conditions, private persons continued to be able to build up a considerable fortune within a lifetime, given suitable luck and prudent attention to business. Correspondingly, bad investments or bad luck could wipe out a man's trading capital very suddenly. Merchants continued to form numerous partnerships and other kinds of business associations with many different individuals, breaking off or renewing such relations voyage by voyage or after a longer period of years, according to their pleasure.[49] This atomistic, unspecialized sort of mercantile organization accorded well with the *muda* framework; the *muda* in turn preserved it into the sixteenth century—the age of the Medici and

Fuggers—when Venetian business organization began to wear an increasingly archaic aspect.

It is impossible to say how large a number of Venetians engaged actively in trade. Venetians alone were entitled to consign goods to the galleys;[50] only nobles could bid for command over them. As aforetime, the rowers and bowmen of the quarterdeck who sailed on the merchant galleys were entitled to trade in a small way on their own account. But many Venetians were too poor or profligate to be able to engage in trade, and public officials stationed overseas were legally forbidden to do so, presumably because it was feared that they would abuse their public powers if allowed to buy and sell on their own account.

Yet for all the statistical uncertainty that surrounds the matter, it seems clear that the legal framework for long-distance trade as defined in the 1330s maintained a broad enough distribution of wealth within the Venetian polity to sustain a vivid patriotic consciousness up and down the social scale.[51] This in turn strengthened the constitutional arrangements worked out in the same critical decades at the beginning of the fourteenth century.

As these patterns of economic and political conduct took hold, even wealthy nobles found enough reward in at least occasional state service that they could not well afford to spend all their lives in merely private efforts to increase their personal fortunes. As for the poor nobles, they found officeholding a way to relieve poverty and reinforce prestige. The only way to office was to secure the respect and confidence of fellow members of the ruling caste. This required conformity to a norm of behavior which was set, for the most part, by very elderly men who, having served year after year on various boards, in councils and as magistrates, emerged at the top of the political heap and occupied the most influential and honorific posts.[52] It was a norm of conduct that emphasized prudence, anonymity, and deliberation in service of the state. Penalties for infringement of the aristocratic code of behavior were severe. Capital punishment was ruthlessly meted out to men suspected of trying to overthrow the noble caste's political monopoly or of entering into treasonous relations with foreign rulers. No one was exempt. The execution of Doge Marino Faliero (1355) for plotting to restore long vanished dogal powers was only the most dramatic of many similar episodes.[53]

The rigor of the mold into which Venetian aristocrats were thus compelled to fit made the monopoly of political office which the nobility had arrogated to itself more or less tolerable to other classes. Flagrant abuses of power were likely to be punished; political office was not often used for naked self-aggrandizement; the same laws applied to rich and poor, noble and commoner, cleric and layman. Few Venetian businessmen became as rich and powerful as the most successful Genoese and Florentine entrepreneurs; furthermore, private associations remained far too weak to threaten the Venetian state in the way Florentine guilds and Genoese "albergos" (not to mention Genoa's private fleets) often did. Venice's resultant political stability gave the city important advantages, both economic and political. In the fourteenth and fifteenth centuries, the city's unique political-economic structure was strong enough to act as a Great Power on a European and Mediterranean-wide basis; only after the period with which we are here concerned did the constitution become the object of such idolatry as to inhibit really effective response to changed circumstances.

This eventual failure is understandable just because of the extraordinary success that accrued to the Venetians after they were able to mesh all these new technical, socioeconomic and political patterns together. The years from about 1320 to 1346, when the Black Death struck, were among the most prosperous in all of Venice's long commercial history. At the beginning of this period, the Genoese were handicapped by a decade of bitter strife between Genoa and their colony on the Bosporus, Pera. This made it easy for the Venetians to establish themselves in the Black Sea trade in a big way, side by side with their rivals.[54] In the same way, Venice's Flanders galleys broke in upon what had previously been a Genoese preserve and prospered greatly by cheapening transport for spices between the Levant and North Sea ports.

The old overland routes from northern Italy to Flanders withered in face of the new competition from Genoese and Venetian ships. The fairs of Champagne, so prominent in earlier medieval economic life, dwindled to insignificance. But the new sea route did not affect overland exchanges with lands further east, mainly in Germanic Europe, where a galaxy of towns situated along the upwaters of the Danube and Elbe rivers—Nuremberg, Augsburg, Ulm, Vienna, and Prague— developed an increasingly active trade with Venice. In 1318 Venetians constructed the first *Fondaco dei Tedeschi* to house German merchants come to purchase spices and other luxuries for distribution north of the Alps. Metals from the Harz and Bohemian mountains—later also from the Carpathians and Bosnia—were the most important commodity these merchants offered in exchange for Venetian spices. The Venetians in turn distributed the German metals up the Po and throughout the Mediterranean coastlands.

Another product that became available in increasing quantity was the sweet strong wine of Crete. Between 1299 and 1363 relative peace prevailed in that island, allowing cultivation of the much prized grapes to increase. Cretan wine commanded ready sale not only in England and Flanders, but in Venice itself and in regions around the Black Sea. An increasing demand for Black Sea grain, for English wool, and for Flemish cloth meant that local magnates and entrepreneurs in each of these regions could afford to buy increasing quantities of imported spices, wine, and other luxuries. As for the Venetians, they came to depend on grain brought in from the Black Sea ports, not simply in time of emergency as in the thirteenth century, but on a year-in, year-out basis.[55]

This swelling pattern of long-range interregional exchange met sharp setback when the Black Death spread its ravages throughout Europe and the Mediterranean world (1346–49). For Venice this crisis was followed by a long series of disastrous military defeats. King Louis the Great of Hungary (reigned 1342–82) forced Venice to surrender Dalmatia (1356) after a long struggle. At the same time, Hungary, together with the duchy of Austria, began to intervene in Italian political-military affairs in a way calculated to weaken Venice. Even more important were conflicts with Genoa, stimulated, perhaps, by the shrinkage of trade volume from the Black Sea ports. A hard-fought war, 1350–55, ended in Genoese victory.

Venice agreed to abandon all Black Sea ports except for Caffa, where the Genoese were in command and able to dictate conditions to Venetian visitors.

This disaster was swiftly followed by a revolt in Crete, 1363–66, provoked by efforts to squeeze more taxes from the island to help pay for imperial defense. Venetian fief holders and Greek magnates fought side by side against the home forces in this war, and were defeated only when Venice sent mercenary troops to the scene. Thereafter, Crete and other key points in the Venetian chain of imperial possessions in the Levant were garrisoned by a standing force of professional soldiers, paid in cash from imperial revenues. The older fiefs remained, but the backbone of local defense no longer consisted of enfeoffed knights and serjeants. Local ties arising from a growing interpenetration between Venetian landholders and the Greek magnate class made these forces no longer fully reliable from a Venetian point of view.[56]

While insurrection in Crete was in progress, civil war broke out in the territories of the Golden Horde; and as that state broke apart into warring fragments the caravan routes became unsafe. The spice trade thereupon reverted to more southerly termini in Syria and Egypt. Cyprus became the preferred Christian base and entrepôt for this rerouted trade, and that island entered upon a period of unexampled prosperity while Black Sea commerce dwindled.[57]

Connections eastward from Black Sea ports were permanently severed as a result of Tamerlane's victorious career (reigned 1370–1405) in Central Asia and the western steppelands. He utterly destroyed the cities of the Volga (1391, 1395) by forcibly removing to Transoxania the artisans and merchants who had survived his initial slaughters. The result was to knock out essential staging points for the caravan route connecting the Black Sea region with China and India. The caravans were never restored.[58] On the other hand, the Grand Duchy of Lithuania (from 1386 associated with Poland) and the kingdom of Hungary extended their power southward and eastward onto the steppe. This advance gave new life to trade routes traversing Moldavia towards Lvov and crossing the Carpathians into Transylvania. But this trade was, on the whole, a poor substitute for the Asian riches that had formerly flowed into Black Sea ports.[59]

As Black Sea trade and profits thus decayed, the struggle to monopolize what remained intensified. In 1378 Venice secured control of the island of Tenedos, at the mouth of the Dardanelles. This provoked a renewed war with Genoa which soon turned into a life-and-death struggle. Venice found herself literally ringed around with enemies, for Hungary, Austria, Naples, Padua, and Aquileia all leagued together against the Republic of Saint Mark. The critical struggle was on the sea. After a series of naval victories in the Adriatic, an enormous Genoese fleet totaling some two hundred ships established a base of operations at Chioggia inside the lagoon, within eyesight of Venice itself.

In this supreme moment of crisis, the entire population of Venice rallied, despite tense encounters and bitter disagreements between rulers and ruled when news of the initial defeats reached the city. Every resource of money, goods, and manpower was mobilized; a new fleet was speedily fitted out; and through a series of risky actions, the access channels from the Adriatic into Chioggia were blocked. The besieging Genoese thus found themselves in their turn besieged. A Genoese relief expedition was unable to open the blocked channels; the Venetians eventually cut off all delivery of supplies to Chioggia from the mainland, and the Genoese were thus starved into surrender. It was an enormous victory for Venice, and left the city exhausted.

Peace was concluded in 1381. Venice abandoned Tenedos and the island was demilitarized; in addition, the Venetians gave up important positions on the Adriatic to Austria, Hungary, and the patriarch of Aquileia. But the important fact was that Venice retained her imperial and commercial position in the Levant, and was therefore able to make a very rapid recovery simply by diverting ships and manpower, already in hand, from warlike to commercial activities.[60] All the same, the war of Chioggia strained Venetian resources to the limit. Only because nobles and wealthy commoners had rallied to the public service in recklessly conspicuous ways had civic morale held and means been found to turn the tables on the besieging

Genoese. At the end of the war, thirty commoners were rewarded for their services to the Republic by admission to the Great Council, thus becoming officially noble.

Genoa never recovered from this defeat. Unbridled faction took over. In the next generation, Venice's other great rival and trade partner, Milan, also experienced an intestinal political crisis of the first magnitude following the death of Gian Galeazzo Visconti in 1402. Gian Galeazzo had set out to consolidate his power throughout northern Italy; his death, and the ensuing disorders within the Milanese dominions, persuaded the Venetians to undertake armed intervention in alliance with Florence. As a result, between 1405 and 1429 Venice conquered a substantial domain on *terra firma* and became one of the largest territorial powers of Italy. In addition, Dalmatia was recovered from Hungary, 1409–20; simultaneously, a forward policy in the Levant led to annexation of extensive new territories to the Venetian empire: Durazzo (1399), Corfu (1402), Argos and Nauplion (1388), Corinth (1422), Salonika (1423).

Obviously more than a change in Venetian policy lay behind such a series of aggrandizements. The central fact was that Venetian military, political, and economic institutions functioned better than those of any of their immediate neighbors and rivals; and the rise of more distant centers of power—in particular, the rise of the Ottomans—often presented lesser interstitial polities of the Levant with a choice between Venetion suzerainty and submission to the Turks. Faced with such a choice, rulers and the Balkan upper classes preferred the Venetians, who were therfore able to extend their power (however fleetingly) to such points as Salonika and Argos-Nauplion without any expenditure of effort on their part whatever.

The management of the Venetian commune became more and more professionalized and, on the whole, remarkably efficient. The development of ambassadorial diplomacy—whose earliest surviving records, especially dear to an older generation of historians, date from 1379[61]—is only one example of the kinds of changes that came to Venetian administration. Resort to a professionalized military establishment went hand in hand with professionalization of diplomacy; and although

Machiavelli (1469–1527) later blamed mercenary armies for Italy's collapse, Venetian experiences with *condottieri* were, on the whole, quite satisfactory. *Coup d'état* was never attempted; even disloyalty was dangerous, as the fate of a famous mercenary captain, Francesco Bussoni, Conte di Carmagnola, demonstrated. In 1432 the Venetian authorities suspected him of meditating a return to the Milanese service where he had previously won his fame. He was summarily tried and executed. This was no more than Venetian magistrates were prepared to do to one of their fellow nobles suspected of treason; and the fate of Carmagnola perhaps made other Venetian commanders more obedient, or at least more circumspect in dealings with the Republic's enemies.[62]

By paying well for services rendered, and by always maintaining skeleton forces on an active footing as garrisons at key points on *terra firma* and overseas, the Venetians found it possible to expand their armies in time of war and to diminish expenditure in time of peace without sacrificing either social stability or military effectiveness. The scale of operations Venice could sustain is suggested by the fact that in 1450, when the war of succession to the Visconti of Milan was in progress, Venice routinely kept 40,000 soldiers under arms, plus up to as many as one hundred galleys (ca. 20,000 men) at sea.[63] Such forces made Venice a great military power by the standards of the day.

The Venetians preferred to find their army commanders abroad, since a victorious (or even a defeated) general who was also eligible for membership on the councils and boards that ran the government constituted an obvious threat to the ruling clique. But the rank and file of Venetian armies came mainly from within Venetian territories, including territories overseas, where companies of *stradioti* (i.e., Orthodox Christian soldiery) were raised, as seemed necessary, at least as early as 1402.[64]

As a matter of fact, the Venetian military establishment of the fifteenth century was no more than a translation to land of arrangements that had become customary in naval matters. Rowers and bowmen who manned naval vessels were paid a fixed monthly wage; they were recruited for the most part from among the inhabitants of Venice, although Crete and other overseas possessions were also required to provide one or two galleys as called upon. These arrangements were in turn based on the standard custom and practice of merchant voyaging. Even in the fifteenth century a considerable overlap continued to exist between merchant marine and naval units, since the merchant galleys, so important in trade, were also useful as war vessels. Cogs, too, could serve as supply ships, and despite being privately owned were liable to conscription for state service in time of war or sudden emergency.

Naval command was entrusted to Venetian noblemen as a matter of course. Victorious admirals were not felt to be a threat to the constitution, perhaps because each galley in the navy was also under the command of a Venetian noble, and young noblemen frequently served on board as bowmen or in other subordinate capacities. Thus the network of personal and family relationships that sustained the aristocratic esprit de corps was sufficiently represented on board ship to make the navy an unlikely place for tyranny to sprout.[65]

Money paid to soldiers, sailors, administrators, and bureaucrats of various kinds was mostly spent within Venetian territories; hence the fiscal problem was to devise and administer a tax system capable of intercepting enough cash from everyday exchanges to permit reasonably prompt payment of the state salariat. This the Venetians were able to do without much difficulty, since the city's entrepôt economy made it easy to levy taxes on goods as they passed across the open quays, being loaded and unloaded.

In addition to excise taxes, the Venetians resorted to direct taxation from the time of the war of Chioggia (1378–81), when the old semivoluntary pattern of state loans broke down. After 1453 direct taxation was put on a permanent basis, and ceased to be an emergency measure; and in 1463, when a long and disastrous war against the Turks began, the administrative authorities carried through a cadastral survey of all real estate in the city together with estates on the mainland owned by Venetian citizens. This henceforward provided the basis for direct taxation, tax levies taking the form of a percentage of the annual yield from the property in question. The percentage figure could be adjusted up or down, depending on the financial needs of the government. In this way a flexible and relatively equable tax system was perfected. Excise taxes took care of ordinary expenses, more or less; direct levies on real estate took care of emergencies of all kinds. The old pattern of raising money by loans to the state was not given up; sale of certificates of indebtedness, subscribed to voluntarily, sometimes even by foreigners, added still further to the state's capacity to mobilize funds in time of need. But the cadastral survey, kept up to date year after year, provided a better source, if only because such taxes were not repayable.[66]

Direct and indirect taxes were also assessed in Venetian territories overseas; and governors and captains appointed to posts in each of the Venetian colonial possessions were required to keep accurate accounts of receipts and disbursements. Tax income was sent to Venice; even quite minor local expenses had to be approved by the appropriate central authorities.[67]

Efficient financial management was, in fact, the real secret of Venetian military and political power. By the fifteenth century, the Republic enjoyed an annual income larger than that of any of its Italian rivals, and larger in all probability than that of most of the kingdoms of Europe that bulked far bigger on the map.[68] Money paid for soldiers and for warships. It also paid for the supplies that made armies and navies effective, as well as the salaries of the men who administered the Venetian government, collected the taxes, and managed all the aspects of Venetian life that fell under the jurisdiction of public authorities. Venetian taxation was heavy and in the provinces it often seemed oppressive. Within the city itself, however, the tax patterns actually helped the poor—assuring relatively cheap food for instance; and insofar as Venetians enlisted in the armed services or held other jobs with the government, the tax system acted as a redistributor of income within the city.

What was remarkable was not the severity of taxation: other states equaled or surpassed Venice in this respect. Rather it was the niggling effectiveness of official bookkeeping. The state was run like a business firm,[69] with skilled clerks to keep the books, directed by magistrates who were themselves accustomed to working within limits set by debits and credits entered in a ledger. In effect, the Venetian nobility transferred to affairs of state the habits of management they were accustomed to exercise in course of everyday private buying and selling. The result was a relatively high level of rationality in distributing and redistributing state-managed resources, although strains and contradictions between reasons of state and sound business principles were never entirely lacking,[70] and Venetian magistrates often reacted more slowly to changed circumstances than a more autocratic regime might have done. Important decisions always had to pass through some sort of collegial process; but the requisite deliberation perhaps avoided as many mistakes as it provoked or permitted. Nothing, at least in principle, escaped the financial measuring stick. Every time fresh sums had to be approved for the maintenance of routine or the launching of new activities, there was occasion to reconsider, weigh, and deliberate as to whether the proposed allocation of money (and of the resources money commanded) was wise, necessary, desirable.[71]

Most of the states with which Venice had to deal were managed on very different principles. Genoa fell victim to its longstanding internal feuds in the years immediately after the war of Chioggia, and never again was able to challenge Venetian power in the eastern Mediterranean. Instead, the city of Genoa became a bone of contention between France and the Duchy of Milan, and Genoese capital and entrepreneurial skills speedily dispersed into multifarious private channels, becoming particularly active in Spain and Portugal as those countries rose to empire overseas.

Hungary, too, suffered severe internal disruption after the death of King Louis the Great in 1382. When the royal power settled into a more or less stable pattern again, the advance of the Ottoman Turks induced the Hungarians to yield to Venice in Dalmatia in order to confront the advancing Moslem tide more effectually. All Venice's other erstwhile enemies—Austria, Aquiliea, Naples, not to mention Padua (from 1405 brought under Venetian rule)—remained or became weak, at least by comparison with the forces Venice was capable of wielding against them. The tattered remnant of the Byzantine

Empire in Constantinople and the scarcely less tattered fragments of Greek and Latin principalities scattered through the Levant—from Cyprus in the east and Caffa in the north to the principality of Achaia in the south—were similarly helpless in comparison with the resources Venice regularly commanded. Only Milan to the west and the Ottoman Turks to the east—each a remarkable despotism, though on very different territorial scales—were left to dispute prestige and power with the Venetian Republic.

The clumsy organization of rival and neighboring polities gave Venice ample opportunity to consolidate her empire in the Levant during the fourteenth and early fifteenth centuries. This was facilitated by a gradual melioration of relationships between Orthodox and Latin Christians, due, in large part, to the steady advance of Islam. In particular, the advance of the Turks into the Balkans put special strains on the Greek rulers of Constantinople and Mistra.[72] They lacked the means to oppose the Turks in war without help from the Latin west; yet the price Latins exacted—apostacy from the creed of Orthodoxy—alienated the rank and file and excited no enthusiasm even among those who felt the price had to be paid. Toward the end of the fourteenth century, however, matters began to change. The confusion that beset the papacy during the Great Schism (1378–1417) required Latin Christians to revert to councils as a means of governing the church. This accorded well with Orthodox tradition and principles. Secondly, Latins as well as Orthodox Christians began to perceive the Ottoman Turks as a serious threat to Christendom, particularly after 1389, when Turkish power reached the Danube after defeating the Serbs at the battle of Kosovo. Finally, on both Greek Orthodox and Latin Catholic sides, leading churchmen and laymen found old certainties and dogmatic formulations less and less persuasive, and felt a need for new approaches to religious as well as other kinds of truth. Mystical piety that discounted abstract theological formulations was a powerful solvent of the medieval dogmatic collision between Greek and Latin branches of Christendom; so was the secularizing humanism that began to prevail in select circles among Greeks and Italians alike.

The result of these circumstances was to make it easier for

Greek and Latin Christians to respect one another and even to cooperate. Cultural consequences were important, as we shall see in chapter three. The political consequences were less significant because they were fleeting; but from 1388 when Argos and Nauplion passed peacefully under Venetian control, until 1423 when the Venetians moved into Salonika by invitation of the local Greek despot, Latin and Greek rulers in the Levant often turned to Venice as the best available guard against the Turks; and Venetian imperial policy reciprocated by relaxing earlier discrimination against the Orthodox clergy in territories under their control. In particular, Orthodox priests were permitted to conduct services freely and minister to their flocks so long as they did not submit to ecclesiastical discipline from abroad, i.e., from Constantinople.[73]

Old hostilities between Greeks and Latins in Venetian imperial territories diminished sharply under this regimen. Regular channels were established for forwarding complaints against officials stationed overseas; and these were available to Greeks as well as to Venetian citizens. In addition, special magistrates visited the colonies at intervals to check up on the performance of the city's official representatives. Fiscal pressure upon the Orthodox inhabitants of the Venetian empire remained heavy; but no one was exempt, and the maintenance of internal peace in Crete after 1363, together with the general growth of commercial agriculture, made taxes bearable.[74] Modest prosperity set in, at least for some. Among the Greeks of Candia, the chief town of Crete, a small but strategically important commercial and professional class came into being just before the fall of Constantinople to the Turks in 1453.

The weakening of Genoese competition after 1381 and the improvement of Venetian relations with the Orthodox world at large made for a second period of Venetian commercial prosperity in the Levant, comparable to the prosperity that had prevailed in the decades before the Black Death. The Venetians' spice trade continued to flourish. In addition, mounting quantities of wine, grain, and other agricultural commodities came onto the market in Aegean and Dalmatian ports, at least partly because of the spread of large estates which were exempt or nearly exempt from imperial Byzantine (or any other kind of central government's) taxation. This, too, nourished Venetian trade.[75]

In addition, full-blown plantation agriculture increased the supply of sugar from Cyprus and, to a lesser extent, from Crete. Large-scale rationalization of sugar production began in Cyprus about 1368, when the financially embarrassed king of Cyprus, in return for a loan, granted Fredrico Cornaro, a Venetian merchant banker, extensive rights to the peninsula of Episcopi. Cornaro organized irrigation and imported a slave labor force; in addition he was responsible for improvements in methods for processing the cane. Massive capital investment in sugar mills, irrigation systems, and slaves paid off handsomely, for there was a vigorous demand for sugar in Europe and the Near East, and Cornaro's large-scale methods produced a cheaper as well as a better product. The Cornaro family soon became the richest in Venice, rising far above the level to which men whose business operations remained within the framework of the Venetian commune itself could ever attain.[76] Others imitated Cornaro's plantations, but nowhere on the same scale until cane was carried to the Madeiras in the latter fifteenth century. Cotton was a second new plantation crop of increasing importance; it later escaped the plantation production pattern and became a major peasant-produced cash crop in Syria, Anatolia, and the southeastern Balkans.

Another dimension of economic expansion was industrial. Venice developed the production of luxury goods—glassware, soap, silks, jewelry—for export as well as for sale within the city itself. Such commodities appealed especially to the landowners whose exactions from peasants of the Levant were what kept the grain trade in a flourishing condition, and allowed towns such as Venice to feed themselves. Older export patterns, whereby Venice acted as entrepôt for woolen cloth and metals coming from Germany, northern Italy, or Flanders, also remained vigorous.[77]

All the same, the economy was not so expansive as it had been in the first half of the fourteenth century. Venice prospered at least in part by taking over Levantine trade formerly carried in Genoese bottoms.[78] More important: rise to the status of a Great Power deprived Venice of the advantage of a favorable protection rent which earlier generations of Italian traders had enjoyed. Instead, mounting costs of defense and public administration cut into trading profit—and, incidentally, redistributed wealth within the Venetian community in an equalizing direction. To entrust defense to private hands and put no brake upon accumulation of private capital was suicidal, as the fate of Genoa clearly showed. Venice escaped this danger; but by multiplying public officials, clerks, committees, and boards the Venetians added enormously to their overhead costs.

At the same time, as recipients of public salaries and wages proliferated, the proportion of the total population that had a direct and palpable stake in the state also increased. Invitation to class war and public revolt of the kind that disturbed Genoa and other big towns of northern Italy in the fourteenth and fifteenth centuries diminished correspondingly.

The growth of the administrative machine also encouraged or at least went hand in hand with a mounting taste for display in matters public as well as private. This, too, diverted resources from economically remunerative to conspicuous, sometimes culturally significant, consumption. Increasingly elaborate and luxurious public ceremonials, of which there came to be a great many in the Venetian official calendar, expressed civic pride and enhanced sentiments of solidarity among rich and poor, nobles and citizens. Insofar as such ceremonies were financed from public funds, they represented yet another form of income redistribution through state action.[79]

Despite these triumphs of rationality and skill, Venetian state power was limited by its relatively narrow territorial base. This became evident in the later decades of the fourteenth century, when Venice had to face a new threat—the rising strength and territorial expansiveness of the Ottoman Turks. Within a century, by 1481, the Turks utterly outstripped Venetian strength on land and had also defeated them on the sea, thereby announcing the end of the city's right to rank as a Great Power in European affairs.

The rise of the Ottoman Empire has to be understood against the background of Byzantine and Seljuk decay. In the case of Byzantium, from the time of the Emperor Michael VIII

Paleologus (ruled 1259–82), landholders who had secured immunity from the ordinary administrative jurisdiction of public officials became so numerous and their estates became so extensive that the substance of the empire crumbled into a collection of private and all but autonomous lordships.[80] While this "feudalizing" process cut back the flow of resources into the hands of the central authorities, agricultural production for market continued or in some districts may even have increased in importance. Large landholders sold grain[81] and other products (often to Italian wholesalers), and with the money income they thus secured were able to buy luxury goods—often, again, delivered from afar by Italian ships. The profits of trade in Byzantine territories continued to gravitate into Genoese and Venetian hands. The central government was all but helpless because the most powerful element in Greek society, the landed aristocracy, found itself in intimate symbiosis with Italian merchants, whose buying and selling permitted the Byzantine landowners to maintain the increasingly urbane style of life to which they were pleased to accustom themselves.

Among the Greeks, the price was urban decay,[82] alienation of the peasantry, and radical weakness at the center. The Byzantine emperors were unable to tax the major trade flow[83] and, lacking cash, could not pay for an army or navy in the least equal to forces available to the Turkish, Serbian, and Italian neighbors with whom the Greek rulers had to contend. Nor could the emperor in Constantinople command an efficient feudal army. The well-to-do landholders of the Byzantine state were more adept at squeezing income from their peasants on the one hand and jockeying for court titles and perquisites of office on the other than at submitting to the hard and dangerous life of a soldier. The military ineffectiveness of the Byzantine aristocracy was reinforced by the way military technology developed. The fact is that the heavy-armored knight became an anachronism,[84] just as Byzantine institutions shifted toward the pattern of big estates that could, under other circumstances, have supported a formidable array of knights. Byzantine feudalism thus weakened Orthodox Christendom's power to resist attack from outside; whereas Latin feudalism, older by some three centuries, had had exactly the opposite effect!

A second weakness of the fourteenth- and fifteenth-century Byzantine society was the absence of any shared ideal. Some of the upper classes toyed with Hellenism, and looked back to pagan antiquity for models of personal and collective life. Faithful Christians could not feel comfortable with such pagan leanings: on the other hand, Orthodox leaders divided between those who felt some accommodation with the papacy was desirable and those who rejected all truck with Latin schism. Monkish hesychasts, whose mystical encounter with God put a distinctive mark upon Orthodoxy from the 1340s, were indifferent to worldly matters on principle; and their political champion, John VI Cantacuzenus (ruled 1347–54), had to rely on Turkish military help to attain the imperial office. The other popular movement of the 1340s—the Zealots, who took control of Salonika (1342–49) and launched a class war against the aristocracy—opposed hesychasm, but failed to tap any alternative doctrine upon which to found a successful polity.[85]

Byzantine weakness allowed a cluster of successor states to arise in the Balkan interior. Backwoods hardihood permitted both Bulgars and Serbs to create self-styled empires consciously modeled on the Byzantine pattern. Rumanian princes in Wallachia and Moldavia, and no less formidable war captains in Bosnia and Transylvania also established a series of local states, owning the shadowy suzerainty of the kingdom of Hungary. But any really substantial success, like that which came to the Serbian king Stephen Dushan (reigned 1331–55), simply incorporated Byzantine weaknesses into the conqueror's distended polity. Local ethnic solidarity could not support any genuinely imperial state. The Serbian version of feudalism therefore soon became almost as damaging to royal power as Byzantine feudalism was to the imperial power of Constantinople.[86]

The break-up of Seljuk administration in Asia Minor coincided chronologically with the evisceration of Byzantine government, but the fragments into which Turkish society disintegrated were significantly different from those of the

Balkans. First of all, tribal groupings were or became important. In-migration of nomadic groups—the so-called Turcomans—from lands to the east appears to have taken place on a considerable scale. The Turcomans were militarily formidable, and their advance tended to thrust back the limits of cultivation in many parts of the peninsula.[87]

Even more important for the future was the institutionalization of dervish communities among the Anatolian Turks. Distinctive rituals involving emotionally powerful music and dance invited the adept to mystic communion with God.[88] Men who had experienced such an encounter were not interested in details of theological doctrine, and blurred the line between Islam and Christianity to the point that the differences almost disappeared. The neophyte was, in fact, invited to explore a path to God that surpassed formal, official Islam just as much as it left formal, official Christianity behind. This made conversion to Islam exceedingly easy. Christians were not expected to repudiate their past, merely to transcend it.

The reach of dervish piety was enhanced by the proliferation of lay associations, the so-called *akhi*. These were groups of artisans and others—often young men—who set out to pursue holiness in association with dervish experts in the path to God. In many Anatolian towns, such organizations became so important that when Seljuk central authority faltered, they took over town government and local defense, at least in time of emergency.[89]

The Ottoman state linked these two distinctive elements of Seljuk disintegration into a new and powerful synthesis. Warriors schooled in the traditions of the nomad Turcomans shared in religious enthusiasm as generated among the dervishes, thereby sustaining the so-called *ghazi* (literally "holy war") spirit and discipline. The combination assured the Turks of a persistent advantage in battle against their Christian rivals.

The Ottomans had no monopoly on the ghazi role. From 1250 or so, ghazi raiders permeated the frontier zone that lay between Christian and Moslem state power in Asia Minor. In the next century, however, the Ottomans preempted the ghazi tradition, since other Turkish frontier rulers, having reached the sea, had nowhere to go; whereas the Ottomans, having crossed the Dardanelles into Europe (1346), were able to preserve the ghazi pattern by extending its range all the way across the Balkans.

The seed from which the Ottoman Empire grew planted itself in the northwest corner of Asia Minor, where the Anatolian plateau descends abruptly towards the Sea of Marmara. About 1291 a small band of ghazi warriors in that region accepted an obscure tribal leader named Osman as their captain. Success in raids on Byzantine territory attracted recruits from deep within the domain of Islam, particularly after 1301 when Osman won his first notable victory by ambushing a Byzantine force sent to relieve the beleaguered city of Nicaea [Turkish: Iznik] in Bithynia. A mere thirty-six years later, all of northwestern Anatolia had submitted to the Ottomans—as Osman's heirs are called—including the notable cities of Bursa, Iznik, and Izmit [Greek: Nicomedia]. Within a decade Turkish forces crossed into Europe; by 1354 they had occupied the fortified town of Galipoli and subdued wide regions of Thrace. In 1372 Emperor John V. Paleologus, along with the Bulgarian king, acknowledged Ottoman suzerainty; by 1387 all the Turkish states of Asia Minor had done the same; and in 1389 the Serbs were compelled to submit, thus extending Turkish power to the Danube.

Until the time of Beyazid I (reigned 1389–1403), the Ottoman community remained an association of ghazi warriors, gathered under chiefs and captains whose past successes in battle attracted the willing obedience of booty-hungry followers. Tribal structures underlay some of these groupings, but ghazi principles contravened traditional divisive tribalism. As a consequence, the bond of a common religious ideal, actuated through freely accepted personal ties of subordination to a ranks therefore remained indefinitely expansible. New recruits, chosen commander, outweighed and obscured traditional tribal patterns of organization among the Ottomans. Turkish including converts from Christianity, fitted in readily. Indeed religious conversion was not required. Christian rulers who submitted to Ottoman suzerainty served with their fighting forces in Ottoman ranks. Christians therefore constituted a substantial proportion of the sultan's field army as late as 1402, when Beyazid marched against Tamerlane. What held the federation together? First of all, the descendants of Osman, who often had to win their way to the succession by main force or by demonstrated success in the field, were all extremely competent men, successful generals and ghazis in their own right. They could therefore command the respect and loyalty of even the most hard-bitten veteran. Second, from the time of Orhkan (reigned 1325–62) the dervish enthusiasm (and religious heterodoxy) of ghazi warriors was systematically supplemented by Moslem law and learning, imported in an orthodox Sunni mold from the Arabic and Iranian heartlands of Islam. This provided the expanding Ottoman realm with a system of law and administration suitable for cities and regions behind the lines, shaped and sanctified by authoritative Moslem tradition. Third, from the time of Murad I (reigned 1362–89), and more conspicuously under his successor Beyazid (1389–1403), the sultan's slave household took over important functions of government. Many of the sultan's slaves were armed and trained as soldiers. The famous janissary corps was the largest and most important but not the only formation staffed by the sultan's slaves. Their number, equipment, and discipline sufficed to assure the sultan's preeminence over any other ghazi captain of the marches, should matters ever shape toward a military showdown. Thus it came to be true that the ghazis followed Ottoman standards not only because they wanted to, but also, increasingly, because they had to.

The victories that came to Turkish forces were sustained by two other circumstances. First of all, the Ottoman polity offered unusually wide scope to men of talent and ambition, regardless of social origin or religious upbringing. Turkish recruits from beyond Ottoman frontiers were always welcome; and the prospect of being able simultaneously to make a fortune and strike a blow for the faith of Muhammad attracted a continual flow of eager young warriors from the east as long as Ottoman armies continued to win battles and conquer new territories from the realm of Christendom.

This influx from the east commingled with a parallel influx

of warriors of Christian birth. They found the Ottoman service attractive not merely because of its material rewards, but also because consistent victory persuaded them that God was on the side of Islam. The Ottoman government and ruling class never discriminated against persons not of Turkish descent. The important role of the sultan's slave household made such discrimination all but impossible, for its members were recruited from outside Moslem ranks. Slaves entered the sultan's household mainly from Christian peasant households,[90] yet some of them rose to the topmost positions of command. These men were obviously uninterested in Turkish genealogies, and vigorously maintained the principle that rank went with office and achievement rather than according to any kind of hereditary pattern. The sultan's service therefore offered a career wide open to talent. Not only the sultans themselves but their principal servants and subordinate administrators tended to be men of unusual abilities, ambition, and vigor.

In the second place, at the opposite end of the social scale, the peasantry and poor townsmen of the Balkans had small reason to love their Christian masters, and acquiesced cheerfully enough in transfer of lordship to the Turks. Once the ravages of initial conquest had passed them by, the peasants of the Balkans usually found the exactions of their new masters less onerous than the dues and services Christian landlords had formerly demanded of them. As long as annual campaigns took the Turkish ruling class off to distant frontiers for war every summer, the peasants were left to themselves for much of the year. Moreover, the sultan's government tried to assure peace in the rear by regulating the rents and services that could legally be assessed against the peasants during the months when Turkish warriors did reside in or near the villages assigned for their maintenance.

Hence, even after Beyazid had been captured by Tamerlane (1402), and civil war broke out amongst his sons, the Ottoman Empire did not go up in smoke as at first seemed might happen. By 1413 one son, Mehmed I (d. 1421), made good his power over most of the lands Beyazid had controlled; and after another succession crisis, 1421–23, Sultan Murad II (reigned 1421–51) emerged as master of practically all of the Balkans

and of Anatolia. The empire finally acquired its natural capital in 1453, when Mehmed II, the Conqueror (reigned 1451–
81), captured Constantinople.[91]

Between them, Sultans Murad II and Mehmed II elaborated
the Ottoman administrative structure so that it proved capable of holding together even such a territorially vast state as
that which Turkish victories created in the course of the fifteenth century. The old marcher lords with their ghazi follow-
ings were reduced to the proportions of a frontier guard. The
interior of the state was parceled out into provinces, presided
over by officials who were mostly recruited from among the
sultan's slaves. Ordinary Turkish warriors were granted a fief,
or *timar*. The timariot's duties in war as well as the amount of
income he was entitled to draw from his holding were carefully prescribed.[92] Essential public services—education, religion, poor relief, water supply, etc.—were supported by a
different kind of land grant known as *waqf*. These were tax-
free, i.e., owed nothing to the state, and were administered for
the most part by experts in Moslem learning. By Mehmed the
Conqueror's time, the sultan's personal household became a
third element in the state, for it included some ten thousand
infantrymen—the famous janissaries—and a smaller number
of cavalry. In addition he controlled a powerful artillery park,
capable, once brought into position, of battering down any
existing defensive walls, even those of Constantinople, as he
proved in 1453.

Mehmed's regime therefore exhibited a complex, consciously contrived equipoise. Official Sunni Islam counterbalanced the variously heterodox versions of the faith that
dervishes continued to propagate. Similiarly, the militiary
force of Turkish cavalrymen supported by timars was counterbalanced by the standing force of the sultan's household
troops, supported by tax income and booty. Finally, to these
balances a third was added: that between the empire's cor-
porately organized Christian and Moslem communities. It is a
striking and fundamentally important fact that as organized,
official Sunni Islam took over everyday regulation of Moslem
conduct in the Ottoman state the frontier pattern of conversion
from Christianity came almost completely to a halt. The legal

precision of official Islam did not invite conversion. Only on frontiers where prolonged war gave renewed scope to the dervish-ghazi tradition did mass conversion to Islam occur after about 1400. Thus, for example, conversions took place in Albania as late as the eighteenth century because in that wild land social conditions perpetuated guerilla warfare between Moslem and Christian tribesmen of the sort that made the name of George Castriotis or Scanderbeg (active 1443–68) famous throughout Christendom.[93] Elsewhere in Ottoman lands, dervish religiosity became the preserve of those already Moslem, while a reorganized and reinvigorated Orthodox Christian church presided over the religious (and some of the secular) needs of the Christian portion of the population.

At the fulcrum of each of these balances stood the figure of the sultan. As long as that position was occupied by men as personally bold and competent as were Mehmed II the Conqueror and his predecessors, the system worked wonders. Under Mehmed, resources from the entire Balkan and Anatolian peninsulas were once again concentrated at the capital, as in the greatest days of Byzantium's past. Vast and formidable armies could be launched eastward against rival Moslem rulers or westward against the Christian foe, according to the sultan's will. Economic sovereignty was regained: the internal trade of the empire passed into Turkish, Greek, Jewish, and Armenian hands. Italian merchants were tolerated as trade partners only on conditions defined by the Turkish administration.

Taxation was heavy, and Mehmed was capable of mulcting everyone possessing ready cash by recalling the coinage and reissuing it in depreciated form. He also confiscated a large proportion of all the waqf land of the empire in order to increase the number of timariots available for military service. Such acts, enforced by a vigorous and ruthless administration, were certainly resented; but there were compensations. Internal peace conduced to prosperity, and in a rough and ready way the burdens of supporting the imperial armies and administration fell more or less equally on all regions and classes of the empire. Moreover, the system worked. Mehmed mobilized a wider spectrum of his subjects' resources for war and other imperial purposes—building up the splendor of Istanbul, for instance—than had ever been achieved before his time. His empire therefore became a power far greater than any that had preceded it on Balkan and Anatolian ground. Venice and other Christian states on Ottoman frontiers simply could not compete.[94]

As mentioned above, Venice reacted to the Turkish advance by gathering scattered Christian territories under the protection of the standard of Saint Mark. This policy led to relatively minor wars with the Turks in 1416, and again in 1425–30. In these clashes, Venetian supremacy on the sea was countered by Turkish superiority on land. As a result the sultan was able to achieve his central purpose in the second war against Venice by capturing Salonika in 1430. In 1444 the Venetians participated rather ineffectually in the crusade of Varna, which ended in Christian discomfiture; in 1453 a few Venetian ships and men helped to defend Constantinople, but in the very next year Sultan Mehmed concluded a treaty giving Venetians the right to trade freely in the Ottoman Empire in return for payment of a 2 percent *ad valorem* duty.[95]

This was not, however, a stable relationship. The Venetians yearned for the past, when they could dictate terms of trade to the peoples of the east; and the Turks were not willing to see the Latin mastery of the seas continue indefinitely. In 1460 Mehmed raised the tariff rate payable by Venetian ships to 5 percent; simultaneously he embarked upon a furious flirtation with the Florentines, and thereby successfully forestalled any retaliatory Venetian or Genoese trade boycott.[96] When to these hurts the Turks added direct military aggresion against territories under Venetian administration (they seized Argos by *coup de main in* 1462) the doge and his councillors decided on war.

Venice entered this struggle at the peak of her military prestige, having created a large (by Italian standards) state on *terra firma* by means of half a century of victorious war. Moreover, the city's coffers were full, and Venetian diplomacy was able to assemble a truly formidable array of allies for an attack on the Turks: Hungarians under Matthias Corvinus, Albanians under Scanderbeg, and most important of all, Uzun Hasan, of the White Sheep, ruler of Iran. The Venetians took the offensive by seizing all of the Morea, and aimed, also, at occupying the island of Lesbos. But Turkish land forces proved too strong. In particular, the Arsenal was unable to supply the Venetians with enough cannon for successful siege operations against Acrocorinth; and the Greek population of the peninsula soon became restless in the Venetian rear, after having greeted them at first as liberators.[97] In Albania, too, Venetian relations with the local population went sour, when new-fangled Venetian fiscality, old-fashioned tribal honor, and Byzantine patterns of infeudation fell foul of one another. But the really significant matter from the Venetian point of view was that even when fully engaged on land, the Ottoman government was able to build a navy equal and indeed superior (at least in numbers) to the Venetian fleet.[98] This was a fundamental turning point in Mediterranean affairs. For the first time since the eleventh century Italian sea power came to be outweighed by a fleet based in the Aegean and Black seas.

Turkish ships eventually drove the Venetians from the central Aegean. The key struggle was for the island of Negropont, conquered by the Turks in 1470. Thereafter, the Venetians attempted to make contact with Uzun Hasan along the southern coast of Asia Minor (having promised to supply his troops with gunpowder weapons); but the linkup never took place, owing to the fact that Mehmed defeated the Persian army in the interior of Asia Minor in 1473. Thereafter, the Venetians remained on the defensive, fighting the last years of the war in the Morea, Albania, and along the Dalmatian coast, where their best efforts failed to check the advance of the sultan's forces.

The long war, 1463–79, also brought decisive changes in the Black Sea region. Uzun Hasan had formed an alliance with Moldavia, Georgia, and a new-sprung "Gothic" state in the Crimea. After the Turks turned Uzan Hasan back, Mehmed determined to mop up the north shore of the Black Sea to forestall any similar threat in future. Accordingly, while expelling the Venetians and their allies from the south and west of the Balkan peninsula, Ottoman forces also captured Caffa (1475) and destroyed both the Italian trading colonies and the Gothic state in the Crimea. The Turks also reduced Moldavia and Georgia to tributary status, and established suzerainty over the Crim Tatars.[99] Thenceforward, until 1774, the Black Sea was an Ottoman lake, and Istanbul resumed the economic imperium over all the Pontic coastlands which Constantinople had lost in 1204.[100]

The Venetians concluded peace in 1479 on terms that made the Turkish victory unmistakable. They gave up Negropont and Lemnos, withdrew from Scutari in Albania, and agreed to pay an annual tribute of ten thousand ducats for the right to trade in Ottoman lands. The most valuable parts of their overseas empire remained: Crete and Corfu, together with three tiny handholds in the Morea at Coron, Modon, and Nauplion. But Venetian power and privilege in the Levant had been decisively and emphatically rolled back. The doge's annual marriage with the sea had become an empty boast: it was now the Turkish fleet that predominated along all the Mediterranean coasts.[101]

The changed maritime balance was paraded to the world in 1480 when the Ottoman fleet attacked Rhodes on one flank (garrisoned by the Knights of Saint John) and in the same year escorted a Turkish expeditionary force that successfully landed on Italian soil and laid siege to Otranto. Venice, embroiled with her Italian neighbors over Ferrara, was blamed for the Turkish advance; but in truth the Republic, exhausted by the long war just concluded, had little choice in the matter.[102] It was the death of Mehmed the Conquerer in 1481 (perhaps from poison), and the reaction this provoked within the Ottoman lands against his aggressive plans,[103] rather than any effective countermove on the part of Italians that induced the Ottomans to withdraw from Apulia without undertaking the conquest of the peninsula as Mehmed had intended.

Yet despite this withdrawal,[104] by 1481 the Ottoman empire had clearly become a power of a new order of magnitude. It was the most dramatic and for Venice the most threatening of several similar imperial consolidations that took place in course of the fifteenth century. In the north, for instance, Muscovy emerged as a formidable state by 1480, when Grand Duke Ivan III threw off even the pretense of subordination to the Tatars. In 1479 a united Spanish monarchy, resulting from the marriage of Ferdinand of Aragon with Isabella of Castille, brought most of the Iberian peninsula under one directing hand. In the next century, Safavid Iran, Mughal India, Manchu China, Hideyoshi's Japan, the Hapsburg monarchy of Europe, and the Spanish and Portuguese empires overseas all sprang into existence.

These states all had a common denominator: they were gunpowder empires, exercising local monopoly of powerful siege guns.[105] This worldwide technological revolution of warfare may be compared to the more local but still significant nautical revolution that took place in the Mediterranean, 1280–1330, which had sustained the upthrust of Italian city state wealth and power during the renaissance period. For just as the new ships and styles of sea fighting that came in at the end of the thirteenth century rewarded the Italians' urban skills and patterns of organization, so, too, the big siege guns that altered the balance between local defense and central authority so drastically in the century 1450–1550 acted just as emphatically against the interests of small states of any and every kind, including those that had flourished so mightily in northern Italy between 1282 and 1481.

States like Venice simply could not hope to mobilize resources on a scale to match what came within the grasp of a ruler like Mehmed II. Even if their skills remained distinctly inferior to levels attained in the narrow confines of the leading Italian city states, and even if the administrative articulation of means and ends remained relatively crude and wasteful by comparison with the fine controls Venice and similar cities had developed, it still remained the case that the big new gunpowder empires could exert far larger force than was available to any mere city state.

Venice and the other states of Italy therefore ceased to rank as great powers in their own right. Venice remained a force to be reckoned with; but after 1479 it was clear to all concerned that the Venetians could deal with the Ottoman Turks only if supported by powerful allies—whether Moslem like the Safavid Shah of Iran or Christian like the monarchs of Spain. These, with the sultan himself, had become the great powers of the modern age: Venice had sunk to secondary rank.

THREE

Cultural Interactions
1282-1481

VENICE'S ROLE in the cultural interactions among Latins, Greeks, Turks, and Slavs in the period of her greatest commercial and political power was of trifling importance. The city was not yet the seat of a powerful, distinctive high culture. Only after about 1450 did Gentile Bellini (ca. 1429–1507) and his brother Giovanni (ca. 1430–1516) inaugurate the Venetian school of renaissance painting by adapting to uses of their own the skills and artistic ideals that had been worked out in Florence a generation earlier. Similarly, although alliance with Florence in 1425 against Milan occasioned Venetian spokesmen to invoke the common defense of republican liberty as justification for the new departure in foreign policy,[1] humanism nonetheless retained a foreign, Florentine flavor in fifteenth-century Venice, extraneous to everyday concerns.

Classical models and examples seemed unnecessary for the conduct of public affairs. Venetian constitutional stability meant that neither upstart tyrant nor beleaguered republican freedom called for propagandistic defense at home; and the business of making money needed no sort of intellectual defense either, because immemorial custom sanctioned it fully. The further fact that Venice had no classical past to look back upon, and that the region of Italy which the city came to dominate had played a marginal and undistinguished part in pre-Christian times, meant that local pride provided no particular impetus to researches into Roman antiquity. In other respects, too, Venice remained slow to change its well-established ways. Costumes, for instance—often a sensitive indicator of cultural affinities and aspirations—remained in the Byzantine style—richly brocaded and hanging loose from the shoulders—long after the upper classes of other parts of northern Italy had turned to a tight-fitting, form-revealing mode.

Indeed, as long as Venetian institutions were working as well as they did between 1282 and 1481, there was little pressure toward change from within; as a result, Venetians encountered remarkably little outside their city that seemed worth imitating. They therefore remained laggard by comparison with cities of the Italian mainland in taking new winds of doctrine and styles of sensibility seriously. To be sure, in 1405 Venice annexed Padua, the seat of an important university, and Verona, erstwhile seat of a distinguished court culture.[2] The Venetian republic thus incorporated parts of the Italian mainland where major cultural innovations were beginning to stir; but until near the end of the fifteenth century, new currents of thought and feeling scarcely penetrated the islanded fastness of Venice itself. Given the firm texture of use and wont that defined and limited the behavior of the noble class who ruled the city, anything else would be surprising indeed. A thoroughly conservative taste befitted such a community; and, in general, so it remained. Only after a generation's time lapse, when mainland innovations in art and letters had become thoroughly safe and familiar, were they likely to win the approval of potential Venetian patrons, and so seep into the city itself.

Thus it is not really surprising that Gothic styles of architecture, brought to Venice initially by Dominican and Franciscan friars,[3] continued to govern the city's taste through the first half of the fifteenth century. The doge's palace (exterior completed 1424), like the Ca d'Oro (completed 1440), relied upon Gothic ornament to proclaim the public and private splendor of the city. In painting, a Byzantine conservatism prevailed until the mid-fourteenth century, when Gothic models from north of the Alps began to transform Venetian taste, as had already happened in architecture. Florentine painting, with the intellectual-technical delights of linear perspective, reached Venice in the 1440s, but Venetians did not take up the new style actively for another twenty years or so. Then in the late 1470s Pietro Lombardo (ca. 1435–1513) began to introduce classicizing architecture and sculpture to Venice so that shortly after 1481 Venetian art entered upon its florescence, enjoying both full familiarity with and effective independence of Florentine and other mainland models.[4]

Venetian art history is like a sensitive litmus paper, indicating the general tone and direction of the city's cultural development. Until after 1481, when Venice's imperial power was already entering on a downward path, the city remained a follower, not a pace-setter in matters cultural. This sort of lag between the apex of material power and the attainment of wide-ranging cultural influence is to be expected. Art and intellect are camp followers, parasites on practical success. Moreover, they often flourish best when the pinch of hard times requires men to take thought or seek solace because unconsidered routine behavior has ceased to bring the same satisfactory practical results as aforetime.

Nevertheless, Venice's cultural lag creates a certain awkwardness, since it seemed appropriate in chapter two to use the term "renaissance" as a label for the period of Venetian military and economic greatness. Thus the period under consideration in this chapter, though it corresponds chronologically to the renaissance city state dominion over Europe, analyzed above, ought to be described culturally as late medieval, or something of the sort. It was only in the period after 1481 that the full force of Florentine renaissance culture flooded into Venice itself, whereupon that city in turn began to act as a beacon and transmitter of aspects of renaissance culture to the Orthodox (and even to the Moslem) world of the Levant, as well as contributing its part to the propagation of Italian culture among the trans-Alpine nations of Latin Christendom.

The subsequent cultural importance of Venice was certainly enhanced by the fact that during the two centuries 1282–1481 the Republic remained marginal to Latin Christendom, though less completely so than in earlier times. The strenuous demands Venetian magistrates made on their citizens' loyalty left scant room for other ties. In particular, the Venetian clergy were strictly subordinated to secular authorities. The pope figured more often as a foreign power than as an ecclesiastical superior;[5] and the religious enthusiasm associated with the Dominican and Franciscan friars lapped up against the well-consolidated patterns of Venetian political and economic behavior without the one much affecting the other, so far at least as public events are concerned. A Venetian Savonarola never arose; religion remained always subject to civic and secular control. "Veneziani, poi Christiani! [Venetians, afterward Christians!]" accurately sums up the city's relationship to Latin Christendom, insofar as Latinity found its Christian expression in obedience to the pope.

The cultural activities at which Venetians excelled were all connected with celebrations of civic solidarity. Both solemn processions of state and riotous expression of rivalries between the city's different *sestiers* found a place in the round of the year's ceremonials; but the most distinctive of Venetian cultural traits was the institutionalized license of Carnival. The severe restraints imposed on public behavior by the code of Venetian noble life as consolidated in the first decades of the fourteenth century must have generated more than the usual amount of individual frustration and strain. Perhaps for this reason, the celebration of carnival in Venice began to assume unusual importance precisely at the time when Venetian political institutions froze into their final form.[6] The wearing of masks released everyone, rich and poor, high and low, from the constraints of normal social roles; and just because these roles came to be far more precisely defined in Venice than in most other communities, the catharsis experienced through a temporary shedding of ordinary restraints came to be unusually great.

Other factors contributed to the peculiar elaboration of carnival season in Venice. The city's wealth helped, and the rhythms of the *muda* permitted this population to suspend most ordinary business in the weeks before Lent without suffering much pecuniary loss. In addition, the patterns of family life that resulted from so many young men spending years overseas or serving on shipboard for prolonged periods of time must have introduced a special volatility into Venetian sexual behavior. The city was famous for its prostitutes, who could, if they cared, shed their identity (without necessarily altering their behavior very much) during carnival season. Among the nobility, strict seclusion of young women complemented the extensive exposure of young men to foreign customs and sexual mores. Yet from the end of the thirteenth century, to have legitimate heirs, a noble had to marry into another noble family or one of *cittadini* rank, i.e., take a young woman as wife who had previously left her father's home only to go to church with a chaperone. The grave demeanor, endless committee work, and personal anonymity dictated by the code of the Venetian nobility allowed no normal expression for the personal tensions such a family system must often have generated. No wonder rich as well as poor (for whom carnival also allowed at least indirect expression of social strains, class jealousy, etc.) let themselves go with special abandon at carnival time!

This sort of balance between normal constraint and a short season of license presumably contributed very greatly to the stability of Venetian public institutions. Its larger importance, however, came in the time of the Catholic reformation, when the boiling energies of religious conviction sought to impose far tighter limits on human conduct than had been common previously. In proportion as Catholic Europe experienced a real constriction of socially permitted behavior, the institutionalized release of a licentious carnival season, pioneered in Venice in the fourteenth and fifteenth centuries, took root and spread. Or so it would seem.[7]

In spite of the importance that Venetian carnival customs were later to have for other peoples, this and other civic rituals which Venice developed more lavishly and lovingly than was done elsewhere in Italy, remained unimportant beyond the city's own limits while Venice was still a Great Power. Thus, insofar as Venetian culture was distinctive it remained local, inapt for export because it was tied so closely to the unique institutional and occupational structures of Venetian society.

Yet the two centuries 1282–1481 were of great importance for the cultural landscape of Europe and set the stage for a subsequent age in which the export of what we are accustomed to describe as renaissance culture from Venice to a broad region of southern and eastern Europe did occur. It seems best, therefore, to attempt to characterize what took place during this period of time with no particular regard for Venice, but in the broadest sort of way and with special attention to the regions of Europe in which Venice was later to exert a significant cultural influence.

At the beginning of the period, three styles of high culture competed for the allegiance of the European upper classes: a "Gothic," a Byzantine and a less well consolidated Persano-Mongol-Turkic complex, enriched with a dash of Chinese art and technology, not to mention Indian mystical practices, all built upon an Islamic, Arabic base. The geographic focus of Gothic culture was northern France and the lower Rhinelands; Byzantine culture was at home primarily around the Sea of Marmara and in the Aegean basin; the Persano-Mongol-Turkic style of civilization centered in Iran with offshoots in Anatolia and along the Volga.

During the fourteenth century, all three of these styles of high culture continued to win converts along the periphery of their respective fields of force. The art, literature, music, and styles of sensibility associated with each of these civilizations offered palpable enrichment to European landowners and other men of wealth who could afford, with the general advance of commercial market relations, to be interested in such refinements. The widening of the European market economy, associated primarily with the enterprise of Italian city state capitalists and technicians, thus prepared the way for a geographically widened receptivity to each of the three competing styles of high culture. The privileged elites, who gathered to themselves most of the wealth created by local participation in interregional trade, constituted fertile ground for the reception of high culture, and, generally speaking, accepted whatever lay closest.

Best known is the spread of Gothic art and the associated forms of chivalric literature and courtly manners through Germany, Italy, Hungary, and Poland. In the fourteenth-fifteenth centuries, Gothic outposts reached eastward as far as Moldavia in the north and Cyprus in the south. This chivalric culture flourished in courts and camps of Latin Christendom for a full two centuries after the knight lost his dominance in battle. Indeed the end of a truly effective military role for such gentlemen freed them for the conquests of the boudoir—and of bureaucratic officeholding. In painting, the development climaxed in what art historians call the Gothic "international style"—pretty, delicate, delightful, but also just a bit effeminate. The term reflects the wide distribution attained by this courtly, aristocratic art, which nevertheless commanded wide acceptance in a city like Venice during the first decades of the fifteenth century. The Gothic complex extended of course to architecture and music; even the idea of writing poetry in the vernacular was trans-Alpine initially.

On the more strictly intellectual side, the establishment of theological faculties in Italian universities parallel to older schools of medicine and law may also be thought of as an aspect of the spread of "Gothic" culture. For Italian theological faculties were set up in the fourteenth century to teach the scholastic theology that had risen in Paris during the twelfth-thirteenth centuries, reaching its classic formulation with the work of Saint Thomas Aquinas (d. 1274).[8] In the latter part of the same century, an important group of Byzantine churchmen also fell under the spell of Aquinas' rational theology, partly because of its intrinsic charms, partly because of the Aristotelian (thus ultimately Greek) basis of Aquinas' demonstrations, and partly because the new rational theology offered a basis for rapprochement with the Latins, whose aid was all too obviously needed for defense of Orthodox Christendom against the Turks.[9]

As elements of Gothic culture traveled eastward, however, they affected fewer and fewer amongst the population at large, and became narrowly dependent on the patronage of local rulers. Thus Gothic churches built by Stephen the Great (ruled 1457–1504) in Moldavia,[10] as well as the Latinizing circle of Byzantine churchmen around the Paleologue emperors of the fourteenth-fifteenth centuries, were creatures of court policy, and testify to the military alliances with the Frankish west these rulers hoped for, more than to any broader assimilation of the "Gothic" style of civilization in these fringe areas of its expansion.

The fourteenth- and early fifteenth-century expansion of Byzantine styles of high culture is also familiar enough, insofar as it involved transfer of Greek learning to Italian humanist circles. Specialists have also long been aware of the contemporary, and in the long run no less important, consolidation of Orthodox ecclesiastical culture in the Balkan hinterlands and in distant Russia.

The fact is that Byzantine high culture developed a profound internal split early in the fourteenth-century. God-intoxicated mystics collided head on with secularizing, Latinizing, humanistic currents of thought. Debate opened in 1338 when a monk from Calabria named Barlaam[11] challenged the orthodoxy of hesychast doctrine; by 1351, victory within the hierarchy of the Orthodox church rested firmly with those for whom the mystical vision of God's "energies" was the supreme goal of religious life.[12]

The mystical ideal was peculiarly at home in monastic communities, invigorating, reforming, expanding, and intensifying the religious experience of thousands upon thousands of monks, who then, both in known and unknown instances, spread their faith far and wide—up and down the social scale, and into new regions of the Balkans and Russia. In the eastern Balkans, the key figure in this propaganda was a monk, Euthymios, who became patriarch of Tirnovo in 1375 after spending time on Mount Athos and becoming adept in hesychast exercises. Until deposed in 1393, he used his high office to forward hesychasm in Slavic lands. In particular, Patriarch Euthymios organized the translation of suitable texts of piety from Greek into a newly standardized Church Slavonic, and conducted a lively missionary correspondence as far afield as Wallachia and Kiev.[13] His work took root through the reform of old and the foundation of new monasteries, with the result that the Slavic- and Rumanian-speaking peoples of the eastern Balkans were effectively won over to this version of Orthodox high culture on the very eve of their conquest by the Turks. Christians who had seen God's emanation with their own eyes, or knew men who had themselves experienced such compelling encounter with the divine essence, were interested neither in Latin theology nor in the teachings of Moslem dervishes. With such an armor Orthodoxy was safe against the political-military disasters that came thick and fast in the fifteenth century. In the western Balkans, a similar monastic revival occurred. In some cases pious accounts of the deeds of missionary monks survive;[14] in many instances no record exists. But it is clear that just as the hesychast form of piety carried all before it even in the sophisticated circles of Constantinople, so too the force of the mystic experience prevailed at the court of the Serbian kings, where in alliance with the ancient Byzantine imperial tradition of art hesychast monks brought the western Balkans fully and firmly into the circle of Orthodoxy. Thereby they almost drowned out the siren song emanating from the Latin west, whose Gothic styles of culture had made some inroads into Serbia in the thirteenth century.[15]

In distant Muscovy, too, revivified piety in the hesychast pattern took root through the example of Saint Sergius of Radonezh (ca. 1314–1392), who founded the very influential Monastery of the Holy Trinity near Moscow in 1337. This institution became a nursery for saints and a model for other monastic foundations throughout the length and breadth of the Russian lands. Exactly how the mystical techniques of Mount Athos reached Russia is unclear, though one of Sergius' disciples is said to have come from Mount Athos; and in later time wandering Russian monks often came to the Holy Mountain to renew and refresh their faith at its font.[16]

Hesychast adepts won respect by the authentic holiness of their demeanor, magnified, in ordinary men's eyes, by their occasional lapses into eerie trance. From the time of Gregory Palamas (ca. 1296–1359) hesychasm also possessed a subtle and complex theoretical explanation of the mystical experience that could meet the arguments of Latin rational theology on even terms. Finally, for laymen unable or unwilling to opt for the monks' severer path, practical handbooks of devotion applied hesychast styles of piety to the sacraments of the church and the routines of ordinary life.[17] The result was a doctrine and practice that appealed to all ranks, high and low, sophisticated and simple. As a result, everything Byzantium lost politically was countered by the vigor of hesychast missionary activity which manifested itself particularly powerfully in the latter half of the fourteenth century.

The rise of richly endowed monasteries multiplied places at which the high traditions of Orthodox religious art could flourish. The development of the Bulgarian and then of the Serbian empire in the Balkans, of the Greek despotate of Mistra in the Morea, and the division of the Russian lands among a number of rival princes also multiplied potential art patrons. Moreover, the hesychast surge of religiosity accompanied a change in ritual practice which increased the market for the painters' art throughout the Orthodox world. The iconostasis, separating the main body of the church from the altar, was raised, so that the congregation ceased to be able to view the rituals of the eucharist, but feasted its eyes on row upon row of icons instead. Space, so created, had to be filled.

The result was a widespread and variegated flowering of religious art. In Constantinople itself the splendor of Byzantine mosaic reached a peak in the decoration of the monastic church of Chora (literally, "The Fields," commonly called by its Turkish name, Kariye Cami), completed in 1321. Like the wealthy bureaucrat, Theodore Metochites (1270–1332), who planned and paid for them, these mosaics and frescoes reflect the piety and sophistication of Byzantine high society. Hesychasm found less conspicuously opulent but artistically just as powerful expression in murals painted at Mount Athos, and throughout the Orthodox world, and in the art of icon painting, which represented the most characteristic as well as the most popular visual embodiment of the new styles of piety.

Art historians are not yet agreed upon how to classify schools or trace detailed relationships amongst the surviving examples of this art. Two observations suffice here. First, in Orthodox regions remote from Byzantium and Mount Athos— Crete, Muscovy, Serbia—professionally skilled and technically excellent works of art were produced in the fourteenth and fifteenth centuries. This was partly a result of a diaspora of professionally skilled artists from Constantinople itself (and icons from Constantinopolitan workshops); and partly the result of artistic professionalization within monastic communities, where painting became a holy and highly respected mode of fulfilling the requirement of manual labor prescribed for all monks. Thus in Russia, for instance, a supremely skilled Byzantine painter, Theophanes the Greek, arrived in Novgorod in 1378, and later transferred the scene of his activities to Moscow. There in 1405 he associated with a monk of Holy Trinity monastery, Andrei Rublev (ca. 1370–1430)—by common consent classed as the greatest of Russian icon painters—in decorating the walls of the Cathedral of the Annunciation.[18] Similar collaboration between émigrés from the centers of Byzantine culture—Constantinople, Salonika—and local, professionalized monkish painters produced the much-admired murals of Serbian churches;[19] and at a somewhat later date the Venetian island of Crete also became the seat of a powerful variant of the Byzantine art tradition through exactly the same sort of interaction.[20]

Second, Italy shared marginally in this extraordinary flowering of Byzantine art. To be sure, as remarked above, in the fourteenth century Gothic models appealed rather generally to innovative taste; but a conservative religious art continued to attract Italian attention, especially at the level of the common man. In Venice, where Byzantine cultural influences were always stronger than in Florence and western Italy, icon painters organized into a guild in 1271 and exported their wares to Italy, as well as throughout Orthodox Christendom. Many of these "madonneri" were Greeks from Crete or elsewhere who found the Venetian enrivonment congenial—or at least advantageous for the sale of their handiwork. But, like the Greeks, many Italians fully accepted the notion that tried and true "Roman" (i.e., Byzantine) portraits of saints, Christ, and the Virgin—the latter derived, according to common belief, from the hand of the Evangelist Luke himself—were the sole authentic ones. Systematic disregard of Tuscan novelties, so pronounced in Venice until after 1450, derived at least in part from such traditionalist convictions.[21]

Literary symbiosis and incipient interaction between Greek and Italian traditions was illustrated in the poetry of a Cretan merchant and man of affairs named Leonardo Dellaporta (ca.

1346–1420). As his name suggests, he was of Italian ancestry, but he wrote in Greek and depended mainly on Byzantine literary conventions. All the same there are traces of familiarity with Italian literature, not least in the fashion in which Dellaporta chose to write in the Cretan dialect, which, so far as anyone knows, had not previously been used for formal poetic composition.[22] His career illustrates the closer cooperation and widened sympathy between Venetians and Greeks that developed in the face of their common fear of the Turks; but the interpenetration of Greek and Italian literary tradition, evident in his poetry, is no more than an isolated harbinger of the more fruitful and famous literary cross-fertilization that took place in Crete during the seventeenth century.[23]

By comparison to the religious, artistic, and literary reinforcement of Byzantine civilization wrought by hesychasts during the politically disastrous fourteenth century, the infusion of Greek learning that enriched Italian humanism toward the end of that same century was a mere trifle, affecting only a tiny handful of scholars and gentlemen of leisure. An awareness of the riches of Greek literature had been dawning on Latins from at least the twelfth century; and a series of missionary-diplomatic efforts to revive the church union agreed to at the Council of Lyons (1274) kept communication open between Greek and Latin ecclesiastics throughout the fourteenth century. Rapprochement from the side of Byzantium on the part of figures like Demetrios Cydones, the translator of Aquinas, or the Emperor Manuel II Paleologus (reigned 1391–1425)[24] was matched by the eagerness of Latin conciliarists to authenticate their recipes for church government by gaining support from the Greeks. A key figure was the Byzantine aristocrat and diplomat, Manuel Chrysoloras, who excited widespread response when he began instruction in Greek at Florence in 1396. Chrysoloras played an active role in arranging for the Council of Constance, and was even viewed as a possible candidate for the papal dignity, but died before the council actually began its sessions.[25]

This confluence of Constantinopolitan and Italian humanism reached its high point at the Council of Ferrara-Florence, 1438–39. The Greek delegation, seven hundred strong, that attended this council included the leading prelates of the Orthodox church as well as Emperor John VIII Paleologus (reigned 1425–48) and distinguished laymen like Gemistus Pletho, a Platonist and would-be reformer both of thought and of society. Pletho's conversation with intellectually active laymen in the city of Florence ignited a powerful spark, from which the Florentine Academy eventually emerged, and with it a challenge to the reigning Aristotelianism of Scholastic philosophy.[26] A vogue for things Greek established itself amongst a small scholarly circle in Italy during and after the council. Since the central task of the council was to reconcile Orthodox with Catholic doctrine, the main business consisted of painstaking comparison of papal theology with doctrine as declared by the Greek Fathers and the seven Greek-speaking œcumenical councils whose authority both churches recognized. But in their spare time churchmen and laymen first at Ferrara and then at Florence evinced almost as lively an interest in collecting Greek manuscripts and discussing the merits of Greek pagan authors, many of whom had previously been only imperfectly known to Italian and other western scholars.[27]

For the first time, a command of the Greek language became critically important for western churchmen and ecclesiastical administrators. How else could one understand what the council was all about? Simultaneously, the delights of Greek classical literature opened before a select few from the west, who, having mastered Greek, found the pages of Plato, Plutarch, and other famous authors suddenly available to them. The effect was dazzling, as anyone who has turned from the Latin to the Greek classics will readily understand.

Because the Greek and the Latin representatives at the council of Ferrara-Florence had so much in common intellectually, the result was far more fertile than anything arising from the dictated settlement of Lyons a century and a half before. To be sure, just as at Lyons, papal headship and the Latin versions of disputed theological doctrines prevailed. Given the political helplessness of the Greeks, any other result would have been inconceivable. Some Greeks (including Pletho) who were unwilling to accept the simplistic formulae of concord so carefully hammered out at the council withdrew before the final ceremonies proclaiming union between the Greek and Latin churches took place in July 1439. Some of the signatories from the Greek side acted only reluctantly, in obedience to the emperor's command; but a handful of Greek ecclesiastics genuinely convinced themselves of the virtues and values of adhering to the principle of One Flock, One Shepherd, and believed that the doctrinal points previously separating the churches were either unimportant, or that the Latin phraseology could be reconciled with authenic biblical and patristic teachings. A small company of Greek Roman Catholics thus emerged from the council, of whom the two most distinguished representatives were the Cardinals Bessarion (d. 1472) and Isidore, metropolitan of Kiev (d. 1463). These men remained faithful to the union all their lives. When opinion among the Orthodox turned sharply against them, they withdrew to Italy, where they continued to promote reconciliation with Rome among the Orthodox and to propagate familiarity with Greek learning, both sacred and secular, among the Latins.[28]

Very soon after the council concluded its activity at Florence, the structure of Greek society which had allowed Byzantine humanistic scholarship to flourish disappeared, and the Italian milieu alone remained hospitable to this sort of literary activity. Sociologically, the privileged urban class that had nourished Byzantine classical scholarship in the Paleologue era was very much like the leisured upper class of Florence and other north Italian towns that had emerged by the 1430s; and it is clear that the values inherent in pagan literature, both Latin and Greek, answered to the felt needs of such men, whether or not they happened to wear clerical garb. A world view in which human action and judgment remained autonomous— under God, no doubt, but only at a comparatively vast remove —made room for self-conscious cultivation of personal and private abilities. This appealed strongly to a number of intellectually inclined Italians, though in Venice the collective ethos of the aristocracy never ceased to counteract such a spirit. Familiarity with Greek pagan authors did not create this frame of mind, but mastery of Greek learning, always, of course, confined to a few, did enlarge the erudition and broaden the intellectual choices before the minority of Italians who embraced the humanistic ideal. By facilitating the transfer of Platonism to Italian soil, the Council of Florence played no small part in achieving this result.[29]

Before considering the further evolution of relationships between the Latin and Greek segments of Christendom, something needs to be said here about the expansion of the third of the major high cultures which was competing with the Gothic and Byzantine styles of civilization for the allegiance of European peoples at the end of the thirteenth century: what I clumsily call the Persano-Mongol-Turkic tradition. Unfortunately, the facts are scarcely known, owing to the undeveloped state of Turkish studies. Nevertheless, there can be little doubt that a radiation of cultural elements from the Iranian heartland of this culture took place during the fourteenth century that bears comparison with the simultaneous expansion of both the Gothic and the Byzantine cultural styles.

Appreciation of what happened is hindered by the fact that the destruction wrought by Tamerlane's armies at the close of the fourteenth century checked the development of this form of high culture in the western steppelands.[30] This had the effect of obscuring what had been achieved before Tamerlane's time, both by damage to records and by making the steppe civilization of the fourteenth century negligible in later ages, because a different culture—that of Russia—occupied the same ground during the eighteenth century and erased nearly all surviving traces of earlier patterns of high culture.

Enough information is nonetheless available—even without the careful sifting of archives prerequisite to a proper scholarly reconstruction of events—to make it obvious that the broad steppelands of the lower Volga, Don, and Dnieper river valleys constituted a vast mission field for the Persano-Mongol-Turkic style of culture in the fourteenth century. After some tergiversation, the Tatar khans who ruled these lands settled on the courtly culture of Iran as their preferred model.[31] No one who has examined the paintings from the so-called Album of the Conqueror, which derives in all probability from some Timurid or Tatar court in the western steppes, will suppose that this style of court culture lacked a professionalized level of artistic skill comparable to that attained by Byzantine and Gothic painters.[32] Religious, literary, and musical aspects of Tatar culture of the western steppelands remain obscure; but there is strong reason to suppose that refined taste and eagerness for novelties, whether coming from Anatolia and Persia, from Byzantium and Armenia, or from the Latin lands of the Mediterranean,[33] prevailed, at least among a small circle of courtiers.

The Iranian center of this cultural style experienced something of a climacteric in the fourteenth century, similar to that which came to Byzantium. Political disarray accompanied a florescence of poetry that attained its zenith in the work of Hafiz (d. 1390). Simultaneously, Persian miniature painting achieved a new stylistic definition, though its finest expression came only in the next century.[34] The high culture of Mughal India as well as that of the Ottoman and Safavid empires of the sixteenth centuries derived in substantial measure from this fourteenth-century Iranian efflorescence.

To be sure, Ottoman high culture did not feed on Iranian elements alone. The institutions and culture of the Seljuk sultanate offered a useful model for Ottoman rulers in their early days. A stream of emigrants from Seljuk towns—poets, physicians, administrators, architects, as well as an array of religious experts—brought Seljuk urban culture to the rising frontier principality in the northwest immediately after the initial Ottoman conquests of Brusa and Nicaea (1326–31). Their arrival implied the reception of a significant Arabic element, thanks to the establishment of madrassas (that is, schools of Islamic studies) where the text of the Koran and the intricacies of the Sacred Law were the only approved subjects of study. In addition, Byzantine models were not without their importance for the Turks. This is particularly evident in the field of architecture, where before the end of the fourteenth century Ottoman designers were putting Byzantine (as well as Seljuk) masonry skills to work in constructing severely elegant mosques and other monumental structures—tombs, caravanserais, madrassas.[35]

Ottoman literature was created through massive translations and adaptations from Persian and, to a lesser extent, from

Arabic *belles lettres*. This appropriation of the Islamic literary heritage began to assume massive proportions under Sultan Murad II (reigned 1420–51), who was himself a poet and discriminating patron of letters.[36] Byzantine and Christian influence also found literary expression, as, for instance, in the immensely popular poem on Muhammad's birth and miracles, written by Suleiman Çelebi in 1409. This work supported the growth among Moslems of devotional practices analogous to those inculcated by Christian works of popular piety such as Nicholas Cabasilis' *Life in Jesus Christ*. In effect, Çelebi's work transferred Christian patterns of devotion to the person of the Prophet, insofar as this could be done without express idolatry.[37]

Enough was said in chapter two about the dervish orders and their musical-mystical tradition to make clear that the literary and artistic aspects of Ottoman civilization were supplemented by a vigorous and distinctive style of religion. Like hesychasm, dervish piety had strong popular roots and also commanded the adhesion of rulers and high officers of state. Yet an opposition party formed around the class of learned experts in the Sacred Law, who were entrusted with everyday jurisdiction over all of the empire's Moslems. In Byzantium, as the power of the secular government waned in the fourteenth and fifteenth centuries, the class of learned prelates and bureaucrats shrank back, leaving the field to monkish mystics. Quite the opposite occurred among the Turks, for as the Ottoman state went from strength to strength, the weight and importance of Moslem legal experts—or *ulema*, to give them their Arabic appellation—increased. Correspondingly, dervish religiosity receded toward a more marginal position in Ottoman society.

A severe crisis arose after the capture of Beyazid by Tamerlane in 1402. Rivalry among his sons allowed popular and dervish elements, especially in the European provinces of the empire, to rally behind Musa; whereas the more orthodox Islamic elements, dominant in Anatolia, adhered to Mehmed. In 1413 Mehmed won a crushing victory over Musa and reunited the empire; but this did not end the struggle. Three years later a close associate of Musa named Bedr ed-Din, and his brother Mustafa, provoked an armed revolt in the Ottoman heartlands of Thrace and northwestern Anatolia. Strains between nomadic herdsmen and settled populations entered into this rebellion. Rural *vs.* urban, rich *vs.* poor, ethnic Turk *vs.* convert to Islam were all also in some degree involved. The movement was suppressed by force, but discontents that had found expression in Bedr ed-Din's movement lingered on. Once having come to blows, it was difficult thereafter to establish or maintain any sort of mutual trust between the officers of state and the extreme, ecstatic wing of the dervish movement.[38]

This upshot in the Ottoman lands should be compared to events in Latin Christendom, where at almost exactly the same time the Council of Constance (1415–17) repaired the official hierarchy of the Roman church by choosing a pope who soon commanded general recognition as sole legitimate successor to Saint Peter. Thereafter, such disparate challenges to official religion as the Hussites of Bohemia and the Rhineland mystics —disciples of Meister Eckhart (d. 1327), Johannes Tauler (d. 1361), Gerard de Groot (d. 1384), and their ilk—were dealt with by a mixture of official repression and benign neglect.

The Ottoman authorities handled dervish heterodoxy in exactly the same way; whereas Byzantium, owing to the decay and breakup of the empire, went a different path, making the analogue of what in the two neighboring realms remained or became a marginal style of religion into the central practice and aspiration of Orthodox Christianity.

The antinomianism that lies deep within mystic religiosity presented Muscovy, the one great Orthodox state which began to emerge at the end of the fifteenth century, with peculiar difficulties and unique possibilities. After all, a church that could only be governed by men who felt themselves in some deep sense traitors to the true ideals of religion by the very fact of concerning themselves with administration and material matters was in no position to oppose the will of secular rulers by appeals to any kind of sacred law.[39]

The compromise between mystical piety and administrative predictability that emerged in the world of Latin Christendom had its weaknesses too, as Luther's Reformation attested. The same was true in Ottoman lands, where, particularly in Asia

Minor, an underground of religious dissent continued to trouble the Ottoman regime. Uzun Hasan's attack of the 1470s owed part of its force to the fact that the Horde of the White Sheep, which Uzun Hasan headed, preserved scope for simpler, less hidebound, and more emotionally vibrant forms of Islam.[40] His defeat in 1473 thus turned back an armed heterodox threat to the Ottoman regime for the second time. The supreme crisis came only after 1499, when attack from without, mounted by the perfervid followers of Shah Isma'il's religious revelation, triggered widespread revolt within Ottoman borders. This explosion was as important for Ottoman religious and social history as the almost contemporary Lutheran reform was for the history of Latin Christendom.

These comparisons, however, run beyond the chronological limits of this chapter. As long as Sultan Mehmed II the Conqueror sat on the Ottoman throne (1451–81), a bold and tolerant spirit prevailed in court circles at Constantinople. The sultan was not personally devout,[41] though he was superstitious. He diverted himself by staging debates between famous champions of rival Moslem schools of thought, and exhibited curiosity about details of Christian ritual and belief. Mehmed's intellectual curiosity extended also to mathematical astrology and other kinds of religiously suspect scientific learning. Ptolemy's *Geography*, for instance, attracted the Conqueror's attention, and he had a world map prepared for his information in 1465. His Greek biographer, Kritovoulos, also credits him with an interest in Stoic and Aristotelian philosophy.[42]

Unlike his predecessors, Mehmed affected the style of an absolute monarch, rejecting the simpler manners of a Turkish khan. Persian heretics and Christian converts to Islam played prominent roles in his personal entourage; and some of them were at small pains to hide their religious heterodoxy or indifferentism. Italian technical experts and adventurers served Mehmed throughout his reign;[43] from them and from the Greeks the sultan learned to compare himself with such ancient worthies as Alexander and Caesar. When it suited the situation, Mehmed allowed his Italian secretaries to claim Trojan ancestry[44] for the Turks; but Homer had a vastly smaller hold on him than the fourteenth-century Persian poets, whose style he imitated (with only indifferent success) in the eighty poems from his pen that are known to exist.[45] He was interested also in art, and immediately after concluding peace with Venice in 1479 officially requested the city to send him a skillful painter. Accordingly the Venetians dispatched Gentile Bellini to the sultan's court, where he executed several works, of which the familiar portrait of Mehmed alone survives.[46]

Needless to say, the atmosphere of Mehmed's court offended pious Moslems. Sober and educated members of the *ulema* agreed with ecstatic and uninstructed dervishes in finding the sultan and his entourage guilty of irreverence if not of sacrilege. Opposition grew during the long and difficult war, 1463–79, when properties that had been set aside for religious and charitable purposes were confiscated wholesale and re-granted as *timars*. Hence it is not surprising that with Mehmed's death a powerful reaction set in. After 1481 the Ottoman court deliberately turned its back on Italy, gave up Mehmed's plan for conquering Rome, and adopted a more rigorously pious tone. Until the nineteenth century the Turkish court was never again so open to novelties from every direction, including the Christian west, as it had been under Mehmed II.

This reaction was reinforced by a parallel revulsion against western entanglements that came over Greek Orthodoxy soon after the Council of Florence. The learned arguments and philosophical-theological agreements that had prevailed at Florence cut no ice among the rank and file of Orthodox Christians. News of the union was received joyfully in Italy; it seemed an enormous triumph for the papacy, capping the restoration of Latin unity achieved at Constance twenty-two years before by a no less significant reconciliation with the Greeks. But the hope of making the unity of Christendom a reality[47] soon met with irremediable disaster. The first definitive setback occurred in Moscow, where it only took the grand duke three days after official proclamation of the union (1441) to decide that the Council of Florence and the Orthodox prelates who had subscribed to the articles of union with the pope were in error.

Three—Cultural Interactions

The Russian church had been moving toward the assertion of a greater autonomy from Constantinople for some time, partly because the œcumenical patriarchs, by trying to steer a middle course between Muscovy on the one hand and Lithuania on the other, managed only to irritate both. As a result of the pattern of Russia's initial conversion to Christianity, the highest ranking prelate of the Russian church was the metropolitan of Kiev.[48] By the fourteenth century that city had ceased to be an important center of population; and Metropolitan Peter (in office 1308–26) transferred most of his activity to Moscow, which remained the usual seat of the "Metropolitans of Kiev and all the Russias" thereafter. A rival hierarchy arose in Lithuania, and when Kiev passed into Lithuanian hands, the nominal seat of the Muscovite metropolitan escaped his actual control. As between the rival claims of the Muscovite and Lithuanian hierarchies, the œcumenical patriarch tried to keep clear of controversy by endorsing neither, a policy that won few friends on either side.[49]

These jurisdictional complications were supplemented by a powerful current of religious culture coming from Tirnovo, the seat of the Bulgarian patriarchate. The Turkish conquest of Tirnovo in 1393 (an event that precipitated the deposition of the famous and influential Patriarch Euthymios, the propagator of hesychasm) provoked a diaspora of monks and some laymen into Rumanian and Russian lands. They brought with them Slavonic ritual books and a tradition of independence from and, indeed, suspicion of Constantinople.[50]

In 1437 the œcumenical patriarch nominated Isidore of Monemvasia, a Greek prelate of strong Latinizing tendencies, as metropolitan of Kiev. Isidore had scarcely arrived on the scene before departing for Florence, where he played a prominent role in bringing the union to fruition. Returning with the new dignity of the Roman cardinalate, awarded him by a grateful pope, Isidore proclaimed the union in Cracow and Kiev, but when he reached Moscow (1441) and proceeded to do the same, he was arrested, deposed, and then permitted to escape. The Russians thus emphatically repudiated what they viewed as wanton tampering with orthodox truth.[51]

The next fundamental setback to the papal cause came in

1444, when a Christian crusade met crushing defeat at Varna. No effective military aid for beleaguered Constantinople was forthcoming from Latin Christendom thereafter; and as this became clear, the major reason most Greeks had for accepting union with the papacy vanished into the realm of the might-have-been. As a matter of fact, the unbending hostility of the populace in Constantinople and of the monks of Athos had never been in doubt; and some of those who had acceded to union at Florence began to back away from the Latinizing position after getting back home. The most important such figure was George Scholarios. As a layman at Florence he had argued for the union on the ground that the Christian fathers, whether Greek or Latin, were inspired by the same Holy Spirit, and therefore could not really disagree, however much their words might seem to differ. Yet in 1444 after his return to Constantinople, he came out against the union and devoted himself to learned demonstration of, and popular agitation against, papal error in the matter of "Filioque." In 1450 he became a monk, and took the name of Gennadios.[52]

While matters were thus in doubt at Constantinople, the Russians remained aloof, tentatively seeking support from the œcumenical patriarchate for their defiance of the pope. In 1452, matters came to a head. Mehmed began his reign by blockading the Bosporus just north of Constantinople; attack on the city itself was clearly imminent. The pope decided that strong measures were called for. Fresh promises of military aid from the west[53] persuaded the reluctant patriarch and the helpless Greek emperor to come out openly for church union. Accordingly, in December 1452, Cardinal Isidore, late metropolitan of Kiev, had the satisfaction of presiding over a ceremony in Hagia Sofia at which the union was formally proclaimed. Six months later the city fell to the Turks and Justinian's great church, the scene of Isidore's triumph, became a mosque.

Russian reaction was predictable. In their eyes, Byzantium had paid the price of apostasy from God's truth. Muscovy alone remained faithful to Orthodox Christianity, having stalwartly resisted papal blandishments from the start. In 1459 a synod at Moscow officially proclaimed the autocephaly of the Russian church; and attempts to lure the Russians back to obedience having failed, the œcumenical patriarch reacted in 1469 by denouncing the metropolitan of Moscow as schismatic. Thus instead of reconciliation and union, the Council of Florence split the Christians of eastern Europe into three clearly defined and mutually hostile churches: the Roman, the Muscovite, and the Greek Orthodox. Only in the eastern parts of Poland-Lithuania were Orthodox populations of any size brought under papal obedience; and even there uniate success was slight.[54]

Repercussions of the Turkish capture of Constantinople were wide and deep, among Moslems as well as among Christians.[55] For the Turks, their great victory meant the attainment of a goal which had eluded the Umayyads in the glorious days of caliphal unity. No greater judgment of God in Sultan Mehmed's favor could be imagined; and this recollection must have done much to blunt the force of pious opposition to the sultan in the latter years of his reign.

The city itself quickly developed into a major center of Islamic high culture, overshadowing both of the empire's earlier capitals, Bursa in Asia and Edirne in Europe. Indeed, Istanbul, as the Turks called the city on the Bosporus, soon dominated the entire empire, thanks to its incomparable geographic position, where waterways from north and south allowed easy concentration of resources drawn from the entire Black Sea and Aegean basins. As a consequence, the center of gravity for the whole realm of Islam shifted perceptibly northwestward, toward Europe. The prestige of the sultan's government, which drew by far the larger part of its resources from its European provinces, reached a new high among Moslems everywhere. The Ottoman Empire became an heir to Rome and to the universalist aspirations associated with the Roman imperial tradition, without, of course, repudiating or weakening its Islamic identity. On the contrary, the spectacular military success that came to Turkish arms in 1453 simply confirmed the superiority of Islam over Christianity in the eyes of all the followers of Muhammad, however much they otherwise differed among themselves.

It was, however, among the Orthodox Christians that the

Turkish capture of Constantinople wrought the sharpest and most significant changes. Within a month of taking possession of the city, Sultan Mehmed sought out the monk Gennadios, redeemed him from the slavery that had fallen to his lot after the sack of Constantinople, and installed him as œcumenical patriarch. From the sultan's point of view, he thereby secured the services of an influential prelate who could be trusted to administer the Orthodox church in a sternly anti-Latin spirit.

There was nothing new in such a relation between Moslem Turks and Christian churchmen. Orthodox prelates had long been accustomed to conducting much of the worldly as well as the religious business of their flocks in territories under Turkish control. The Sacred Law of Islam required them to do so, since Moslem judges could not and would not decide cases arising between unbelievers; and the Koran expressly commanded the faithful to allow "People of the Book," i.e., Christians and Jews, to follow their own religious customs, so long as they recognized the superiority of the Moslem community by paying a head tax. No orthodox Moslem government could dream of contravening such an explicit command from Allah; and by 1453 the Ottoman state had become so distrustful of the enthusiastic dervish forms of Islam as to inhibit efforts at forcible or semiforcible conversion of the sort that Moslems, inspired by the ghazi spirit, had freely resorted to in the early days of Ottoman expansion.[56] The disappearance of Christian state officials—judges and tax collectors in particular—therefore automatically meant the transfer of their functions to ecclesiastical administrators, at least insofar as such functions were internal to the Orthodox community.

With Gennadios' appointment as patriarch, what had before been haphazard and local acquired an administrative capstone that made the entire Ottoman-Orthodox state and social structure considerably more commodious for both parties. First of all, Orthodox bishops under Turkish dominion escaped from their troublesomely ambiguous earlier loyalty to the Christian emperor of Byzantium. The patriarch took over the old imperial role as head of the Orthodox community, even flaunting the imperial double eagle among his insignia of office. Mehmed, recognizing how useful it was for the stability of his state to have Orthodox Christians governed by a firm hand, went out of his way to enhance the patriarch's prestige. Accordingly, the sultan personally invested Gennadios with the symbols of his office in a splendid public ceremony; and the new patriarch was accorded the right to ride a horse (forbidden all other Christians) and immunity from the jurisdiction of all Moslem authorities save that of the sultan himself. Patriarch and sultan, in fact, entered upon a close if ambivalent personal relationship, exploring the nature of religious truth as well as appropriate patterns of administration together.[57] Their collaboration symbolized and expressed the anti-Latin alliance of the Greek and Turkish peoples which the institutional arrangements of 1453 effectively consummated.

The Orthodox church both gained and lost from its tie-in with Turkish state power. On the one hand, the authority of the œcumenical patriarch increased greatly. The Turks found it convenient to have important matters affecting their Christian subjects settled in the capital; hence all such affairs tended to pass through the patriarchal office. To be sure, the formal structure of the Orthodox churches remained decentralized. Even after Turkish power extended to Syria, Palestine, and Egypt (1517), the three Orthodox patriarchates of Jerusalem, Antioch, and Alexandria retained a theoretically equal rank with the œcumenical patriarch of Constantinople; and the three autocephalous archbishops of Peć (Serbian), Ochrid (Bulgarian), and Cyprus remained administratively independent of the patriarchate, at least in theory.[58] But in practice, the patriarch in Constantinople and officials around him came to play a decisive part in the affairs of all these sister churches, primarily because important business conducted with the Turks had to pass through Constantinople, where advice from the œcumenical patriarchate often carried the force of a command.

All the same, the œcumenical patriarchs paid a high price for their enhanced authority. By canon law, vacant ecclesiastical positions were supposed to be filled by a double process: election locally, followed by approval from higher ecclesiastical authority. From the beginning, however, all episcopal and archepiscopal appointments had to be approved by the Turks.

From an Ottoman point of view, bishops were a special kind of state official, and as such were compelled to pay a fee at the time of their entry upon office, just as other high state appointees were required to do.[59] Since the grand vizier, as a good Moslem, had scant regard for the strictly religious qualification of candidates for such appointments, the effect was to put ecclesiastical office up for sale to the highest bidder. Under these conditions, ruthless fiscality became the *sine qua non* of a successful career in the Orthodox hierarchy. Piety and learning ceased to matter; accordingly, both decayed precipitously, at least among bishops and their immediate aides.

The spread of such a spirit among the higher Orthodox clergy did not prevent the continued cultivation of an intense mystical pattern of piety among monks and laymen. For spiritual athletes, affairs of this world were evil anyway, so that corruption and venality among high clergy was no more than what a religious man expected. Extreme asceticism and burning faith were thus not in the least incompatible with the most pervasive ecclesiastical involvement with Mammon. The Orthodox Church accommodated both extremes; and by administering justice among Christians, collecting taxes, and channeling the resources of the Orthodox community of the Ottoman Empire to their own and Turkish uses, the high officers of the church in fact became a very important and necessary complement to the Moslem administrators of the empire.

A profound ambiguity pervaded Orthodox attitudes toward the Turks. The Moslems were religiously (and perhaps also fiscally) less oppressive than the Latins. The oft-quoted phrase, "Better to see the turban of the Turk ruling in the midst of the city than the Latin miter,"[60] expressed a preference that was both widespread and well grounded among the Orthodox of the Balkan peninsula. Yet the Turks' conquest of 1453 also signified one more victory for anti-Christ portending the end of the world, which Orthodox scholars had fixed for 1491–92.[61] Gennadios subscribed to this opinion,[62] and presumably therefore thought it his duty to maintain the Orthodox community of true believers as nearly intact as possible during the brief interim before the skies should open and Christ appear in glory to judge the quick and the dead. Pending that climax, preservation of Christian truth from taint of Latin error was more important than anything else, since the salvation of souls depended on it. Administrative duties simply distracted the mind from really important matters; hence it is entirely in character that Patriarch Gennadios resigned his office in 1456 to retire to Mount Athos as a monk. Twice he was called back as patriarch; but exact chronology and the date of his death remain unknown.[63]

As the ecclesiastical and corporate life of Orthodox Christians within Turkish territories underwent this rapid redefinition of roles vis à vis Latins[64] on the one side and Moslems on the other, the cultivated Byzantine elite that had engaged on and off since the 1270s in a long flirtation with the "Franks" dispersed and disappeared. Many simply shifted their pattern of apostasy and became Moslems. Leakage from Orthodoxy at the top of the social pyramid did not cease and probably accelerated after the capture of Constantinople. But whereas before 1453 the high and mighty of Byzantine society had usually looked toward the Latin west, now they turned toward the Turks; and insofar as the mystical experience of Orthodox religiosity remained closed to them, such persons found no insuperable obstacle in becoming Moslem. Paths of conversion were always open; annual public ceremonies in all principal towns welcomed new recruits to the faith of Muhammad; and the penalty of death was meted out to anyone who, having accepted Islam, later backslid into Christian (or Jewish) error. But as long as Mehmed reigned there were no penalties for merely nominal conformity to Islam; and the upper echelons of the Turkish administration abounded with converts from Christianity whose indifference to the faith of their childhood carried over to the faith of their choice.[65]

A small number of the old elite of Byzantium emigrated to the west. Some arrived immediately after the fall of Constantinople; others came only after the Greek states of the Morea and Trebizond came under Turkish control (1460–61). Crete served as an important staging ground for some of these refugees, and the city of Candia, which had already begun to develop into a significant center of Greek learning and piety, profited notably from the emigration. The Cretan school of Byzantine art achieved an independent existence as a result of the influx of talent from the mainland, and literary activity also soon began to blossom on Cretan soil with unaccustomed vigor.[66]

A swarm of several hundred highly cultivated Greeks came to Italy, often via Venice, and there reinforced the familiarity with Greek classical authors that had been implanted in Italian intellectual circles at the time of the Council of Florence. Some of them filtered beyond the Alps into France, Germany, Spain, and England, where they were harbingers of the revival of Greek studies in those distant parts.[67] Among the more famous of these refugees was John Paleologus, brother of the last Byzantine emperor and father of Zoë Paleologus, who, in 1472, having grown up in Rome on the periphery of the papal court, married Ivan III, grand duke of Moscow, bringing with her to remotest Russia a strong whiff of Italian renaissance culture and the aura of the Christian Roman empire.

The absorption of the Byzantine elite into either Moslem or Latin ranks cost the Orthodox community dearly. As the purchase of office became normal, the men who rose to the top of the church hierarchy were seldom either pious or cultured in any deep sense. At the monkish, popular level, Orthodox mysticism remained vigorous; but the monks and mystics abandoned the culturally impressive expressions of their faith cheerfully enough, yielding to Moslem disapproval of all public manifestations of wealth, art, or ceremony connected with Christianity. Greek and Slavonic cultural activity in the Balkans therefore shrank back to the dimensions suited to peasant and monkish piety; and an unthinking, superstitious hostility to Latin Christendom soon supplanted the learned polemic against papal error that Gennadios and his generation of Orthodox champions had conducted.[68]

Amply protected by Turkish armies, Orthodoxy no longer needed to defend itself intellectually. Greeks simply ceased to listen to anything coming from Italy or other parts of the Latin world. Dialogue with Islam was equally sterile, because long-established principles allowed each side to neglect the other. Accordingly, theology withered away among the Orthodox, and even legal learning failed to flourish[69] in a situation where *bakshish* almost always prevailed over legal principle when it came to getting things done. Mysticism itself, the heart and soul of Orthodoxy since the early fourteenth century, froze to the patterns created by the early generation of hesychast adepts. This meant that mystical piety, reduced to ritualized repetition, risked becoming merely perfunctory too.[70]

All in all, by 1481 when Sultan Mehmed II died, a precipitate decay of all the higher manifestations of Orthodox Christian culture in the Balkans had become obvious. Nothing that others were interested in was happening among the Ottoman empire's Christian subjects. But the overthrow of Byzantium as a center of living Orthodox culture had an important side effect: it allowed the Muscovites to assert their new-found autonomy with much greater conviction and plausibility than could otherwise have been the case. What Orthodox Christianity lost in Byzantium was therefore counterbalanced, at least in part, by the upthrust of a significant new cultural center far to the north.

The essential facts are well known and need no elaboration here. In 1448, a Muscovite prelate, Jonas, accepted appointment as metropolitan of Kiev and all the Russias. The succession to the ill-fated Isidore was thus defined. Then before any formal recognition of Jonas' title had been secured from Byzantium, the Greeks submitted to union (1452) only to suffer God's punishment for their betrayal of Orthodoxy in the following spring. Thenceforward, as Russian churchmen saw it, a heavy responsibility rested on Muscovy, where alone in all the world the truths of Orthodoxy, untainted by Latin heresy, had been preserved. Even when a repentant œcumenical patriarch in 1484 formally denounced ties with Rome, the Russian church paid little attention. By that time the grand duke had begun to call himself Tsar (i.e., Caesar),[71] signifying that the Muscovite ruler had inherited the role in the divine order assigned by God, once and forever, to Constantine and his successors.

As Christian and Roman emperor, the tsar became responsible for defending the church and assuring its safety against enemies, whether within or without. The Muscovite church, in short, had become central to God's plan for the salvation of mankind; Moscow became the "Third Rome"[72] in succession to the cities on the Tiber and on the Bosporus; and the task of all right-thinking men was to guard Orthodoxy as divinely established in the Russian lands against innovation of any and every kind.

In Lithuanian lands, however, extreme religious confusion reigned. The Orthodox church at first recognized the Union of Florence, yet nevertheless accepted Metropolitan Jonas until his identification with Moscow's new religious pretensions became clear. The link with the papacy was then revived (1459) but foundered again in 1469 when the uniate metropolitan of "Kiev and all the Russias" asked and was granted communion with the œcumenical patriarch of Constantinople! Thereafter, there were two rival "Metropolitans of all the Russias," one in Moscow, the other in Kiev; one refusing to recognize the religious authority of the œcumenical patriarch, and one submitting, at least in form, to that obedience. In practice, nonetheless, the œcumenical patriarch's authority in Lithuanian territories was insignificant. The Roman Catholic grand duke appointed prelates to Orthodox and Catholic sees alike; and the men he appointed to the Orthodox hierarchy were usually lay nobles who submitted to clerical ordination without altering their style of life in any noticeable fashion. Religious leadership of Orthodox communities therefore devolved upon lay brotherhoods, in which townsmen played a prominent part.[73]

In Muscovy, by contrast, church and state were mutually supportive. To be sure, there were pious men who fled administrative duty and upheld a fundamentally anarchic, personal ideal of holiness in the hesychast tradition. But an opposing ideal of ritual splendor and moral rigor counterbalanced the mystical antinomianism of the saints, and accorded well with the court tradition of the grand dukes of Moscow. Under Ivan III (reigned 1462–1505) the ingathering of the Russian lands was carried almost to completion with the annexation of Novgorod (1478) and Tver (1485). Ivan also escaped even nominal subordination to the Tatar khans by assisting, militarily and diplomatically, in the definitive breakup of the Golden Horde into rival states (1480). Full political sovereignty was indeed prerequisite for taking on the world role of Orthodox Christian emperor, which Ivan III aspired to. Marriage with Zoë Paleologus in 1472 gave additional color to his imperial aspiration; for Zoë (who reverted to Orthodoxy and took the name of Sophia on leaving the pope's lands behind) was the daughter of the last Byzantine emperor's brother. Zoë also brought with her a taste for splendor and refinement as befitted an Italianized Greek of imperial rank. She arranged for a series of Italian architects and engineers to come to Russia, the first of whom, Ridolfo Fioravanti of Bologna, arrived in 1475.[74] He was entrusted with the task of rebuilding the most holy of Moscow churches, the Cathedral of the Assumption; but it is symptomatic of the attitude of the Russian court toward even the most talented strangers from the west that Fioravanti was instructed to make the new building conform to old Russian architectural styles. Distinctive Italian elements were restricted to the skills of stone-cutting, brickmaking, preparation of mortar, and to a few decorative details: the structure and main lines remained thoroughly autochthonous, as Ivan, and perhaps also his wife, clearly desired.[75]

In military architecture and such technical matters as guncasting, the Italians had a freer hand, for there it was performance that counted. Ivan III undertook a thorough going reconstruction of the Kremlin towers and walls, completed only in 1499; and employed several different Italian architects and engineers on this task. Palaces, too, and additional churches within the Kremlin walls were also entrusted to Italian experts, with the result that the oldest surviving structures of Moscow's citadel all betray, in greater or less degree, traces of the Italian taste and skill that entered into their creation.[76] Private houses in old Moscow also reflected something of the Italian architectural impact, through imitation of the court's example.

Yet the Italian elements in the culture of imperial Moscow were no more than embellishments upon native structures. A newly powerful Russian style of civilization was in process of defining itself in 1481, combining, as every important new cultural pattern must, diverse traits assembled from far and wide into a more or less coherent, aesthetically and intellectually attractive whole. Ritual, both of church and state, requiring rich garments and precious furniture of diverse sorts, was a side of Russian cultural development in these decades that should be noticed because it is little familiar and seldom valued much by western minds. Music, military organization and technology, techniques of river transport, as well as the well-known icon and fresco paintings were other distinctive aspects of Russian cultural development in these formative years.[77] No one examining the earliest surviving parts of the Kremlin will doubt that they express in brick, stone, and paint a very successful synthesis of Byzantine, Persian, Slavic, and west European elements. In doing so, the Kremlin structures make palpable to modern eyes the cultural achievement of Ivan III's Russia, where a new center of Orthodox civilization took root and began to grow at the very time when Balkan Orthodoxy, together with the Orthodox communities under Lithuanian sovereignty, was suffering precipitous decay.

The net effect, therefore, of the shifts of cultural alignments that followed hard on the heels of the Turkish capture of Constantinople in 1453 was to permit a new Ottoman and a new Muscovite style of civilization to come into focus, dividing nearly all of eastern Europe rather sharply between them. In addition, the cultural polarity between Latin Christendom, represented more powerfully by the renaissance culture of Italy than by any of its regional variants, and the two new-sprung civilizational styles of eastern Europe, was more clearly drawn, psychologically and geographically, than had been true in earlier times.

If we compare this situation with the cultural landscape at the beginning of the fourteenth century, it seems clear that fundamental realignments had taken place. Three metropolitan centers still disputed the loyalties of European peoples, but their character and complexion had altered substantially, while the geographic centers of cultural creativity had moved closer together in space. Instead of being strung out in line, as in 1300, from Iran-Anatolia via the Aegean-Black Sea regions to northern France and the Rhinelands, metropolitan cultural centers now formed a triangle, with north-central Italy and Moscow competing against the Ottoman style of civilization. The rise of two new cultural centers in eastern Europe was closely tied to the consolidation of imperial state structures that concentrated wealth and talent from far and wide in their respective capitals, Istanbul and Moscow. The west remained more diffuse and complex, for the Italian renaissance version of civilization was not the only form of high culture to command widespread attention in the period after 1481. Nevertheless, the rise of new political units mattered very much for western Europe's early modern cultural history too. It is therefore appropriate to turn our attention to politics and war once more in the next chapter, before returning in chapter five to a consideration of Europe's cultural interactions in the period 1481–1669, which will concern us in chapter six.

· FOUR ·

Venice as a Marginal Polity
1481-1669

The Long war, 1463–79, had proved that Venice was no match for the newly consolidated Ottoman Empire to the east. But within Italy Venice remained a Great Power until the end of the century, as the Republic of Saint Mark demonstrated in a successful war against Ferrara (1482–84) whereby the Venetians rounded out their holdings on *terra firma* by gaining complete control of the lower course of the Adige River. The greater goal, control of the mouth of the Po, eluded the Venetians' grasp, however, though it required action of all the other great powers of Italy—Milan, the papacy, Florence, and Naples—to assure that result.

This situation changed abruptly after 1494 when the French king, Charles VIII, invaded Italy with the intention of reasserting a claim to the crown of Naples derived from the time of Charles of Anjou. Charles VIII, like his Angevin namesake, dreamed of using Naples as a springboard for a great crusade against Constantinople; but his plans were cut short by a league of Italian and foreign powers that compelled him to withdraw in 1495 from the kingdom he had seized so easily at the beginning of that same year.

Thus within a few months, Italian balance-of-power statecraft, in which the Venetians played a prominent part, turned the French back. Yet things were not as before. French military superiority to the Italians had been unambiguously demonstrated. His lengthy and exposed line of communications, plus the intervention of Spanish forces, compelled Charles to withdraw from Naples; but even in retreat, the French army was able to repel Italian attacks. Moreover, the ease with which the French had marched the length of Italy whetted the appetites of two other ambitious territorial monarchs: the Hapsburg Maximilian (reigned 1493–1519) and the Spaniard Ferdinand (reigned 1479–1516). With the French, who returned to Italy only five years later by occupying the Duchy of Milan in 1499, these two foreign potentates disputed control of the Italian peninsula until their deaths, whereupon the struggle took a new form because Charles of Ghent, Maximilian's grandson, combined both the Spanish and the Hapsburg inheritances in a single vast sprawling structure. As Emperor Charles V (1519–58), his territories ringed France round; and after 1526 his forces (drawn mainly from Spain) dominated Italy by controlling both Milan in the north and Naples in the south. Not until 1559 did the French monarchy give up the ambition of breaking the ring and winning possession of at least part of Italy. As a result, throughout the period from 1494 to 1559 Italy remained the preferred field of battle for the French, German, and Spanish rulers of Latin Christendom. Italian cities and towns were rich and offered better booty than alternative battlefields; in addition, command of Italian skills and resources, mobilized through pre-existing city state administrative structures, offered far greater rewards to the victors than could be anticipated from seizure of territory in other parts of Europe.[1]

Milan (1499) and Naples (1503) were the first major Italian states to pass under foreign control. In 1508 it looked as though Venice's turn would be next. The League of Cambrai, formed in that year, planned a partition of Venetian possessions on *terra firma* among the pact's French, Hapsburg, Spanish, and papal signatories. The Hungarians were also invited to join in. Only the Turks were left out—which was not surprising, for the professed aim of the league was to prepare for a crusade against Constantinople after clearing away the Venetian obstacle! Obviously, Venetian resources were as much outclassed by such an array of enemies as they had been in struggles against the Turks. But the Republic's Christian foes were not united by anything but greed. As a result, after suffering initial defeats and seeing their armies driven from all of mainland Italy, Venetian statesmen proved capable of splitting the league. By allying first with Maximilian and the pope against the French and then with the French against the Hapsburgs, Venice actually emerged by 1517 with almost all its mainland territories intact.[2]

From one point of view this was an enormous Venetian success. Citizen morale held up even when prospects were at their bleakest. Moreover, Venice's mainland subjects remained loyal.[3] Recovery of the lost territories was greatly assisted by the fact that the local populations clearly and emphatically preferred Venetian taxation to erratic plundering at the hands of an ill-paid foreign soldiery. They therefore opened their gates to the Venetians whenever they had an opportunity. As a result, the Venetian state and empire survived; and after 1517 the lands of *terra firma* and Venetian possessions overseas continued to supply important resources—men, money, and manufactures—for upholding the strength of the Republic of Saint Mark.

All the same, the war of the League of Cambrai marked the end of Venice as a Great Power in Italy, just as the war of 1463–79 against the Turks had marked the end of Venice as a Great Power in the Mediterranean. Plans for expansion along the Adriatic coast all the way to Apulia and for the definitive control of the Po mouth—plans which had helped to provoke the alignment of 1508 against Venice—were given up; but only through some such consolidation of a larger territorial base within Italy (including, no doubt, the eventual annexation of Lombardy and Tuscany) could the Venetian Republic have hoped to remain a Great Power, able to compete on more or less even terms with the new-sprung giants that had begun to surround Italy, east, north, and west.

A program for uniting Italy against the "barbarians" was never clearly set forth by Venetian publicists. Even if they had done so, the predictable reaction in Florence, Rome, and elsewhere would have made such a program unlikely to succeed. After 1508 few Venetians even thought of it.[4] The task was to survive by following a rigorous conservative policy at home and a policy of cautious armed neutrality abroad. As a result, from 1517 onward until the final destruction of the Republic by Napoleon in 1797, Venice remained a marginal polity, balanced precariously between Ottoman east and Christian west, and caught no less precariously between the Austrian and Spanish centers of Hapsburg power, the one pressing down from the north, the other reaching up from the south.

This rather abrupt political transformation was reinforced by critical changes that came to Venetian economic life just when the military-political crisis was at its most acute stage. The success of Vasco da Gama's voyage to Calicut, 1497–99, upset the spice trade; by 1502 supplies of pepper and other condiments coming to the Mediterranean from the East Indies had been cut off. In 1509, the very year when Venetian fortunes in the war of the League of Cambrai were at their nadir, the Portuguese fastened their political-military control over the Arabian Sea through a decisive naval victory off the port of Diu. Portuguese chances of monopolizing the spice trade with Europe never seemed better than in this initial period of their imperial expansion. Acute dismay reigned in Venice, Alexandria, and Beirut; for more than a decade the flow of spices to these ports became sporadic and substantially smaller than before the Portuguese began to interfere with traffic on the Indian Ocean.

At the very beginning of the century, Venetian trade with the Ottoman Empire had suffered disruption owing to a bout of renewed warfare, 1499–1503. Peace terms deprived Venice of Modon and Coron, useful way stations and fortresses on the southwesternmost part of mainland Greece. After 1500, Turkish forces controlled the coastline as far north as the Gulf of Corinth. Trade was resumed with the peace, but Venetian economic roles in the east had changed. The slave trade and other thriving branches of Levantine commerce—e.g., the trade in wine and furs—passed almost entirely from Italian hands. What remained was mainly sale of articles of western manufacture, especially woolen textiles and metals, in exchange for Ottoman manufactures—carpets and cotton and silk cloth, for example—and agricultural commodities like currants, mastic, and grain. For a while, the sultan continued to allow Venetian and other western ships to enter the Black Sea and load grain, but only by special license. After 1551, the needs of Constantinople had swollen to such proportions, thanks to its increasing population, that no more such licenses were granted, with the result that one of the most important sources of grain for feeding Venice and other Italian cities was cut off.[5]

Political consolidation of western Europe also put fresh obstacles in the way of Venetian trade. French, Spanish, and English monarchs found taxing foreigners even more satisfactory than taxing their own subjects; and as large areas came effectively under a single administration, Venetians (and other Italians) found it harder to secure favorable treatment by threatening to take their business elsewhere to another jurisdiction. Moreover, western economic developments that had assumed large proportions toward the end of the fifteenth century—wine from Portugal, sugar from Madeira, alum from Rome—undercut older patterns of trade which had allowed Venice (and Genoa) to profit from the middleman's role by carrying commodities between the eastern Mediterranean and northwestern Europe. It is symptomatic of these changing commercial conditions that the Flanders galleys, which had played so prominent a role in Venetian affairs since the 1330s, ceased to be profitable. From 1492 the *muda* to Flanders became irregular; none were dispatched in the crisis years between 1508 and 1516; and efforts to revert to the old pattern resulted in only six additional voyages between 1516 and 1533, when Venetian oared merchantmen appeared in the English channel for the last time.[6]

Yet Venice did survive economically as well as politically. First of all, the ancient spice routes from India to Alexandria and Syria and thence to Venice soon recovered from the blows inflicted at the beginning of the century by Portuguese naval superiority in the Indian Ocean.[7] The Mediterranean route was shorter and navigationally safer than the voyage around Africa; and Portuguese officers in the Indian Ocean quickly found it worth their while to allow spices to travel along the old routes.[8] As a result, the price of spices delivered to Antwerp around Africa soon came to match quite exactly the price of spices delivered to Venice (and other Mediterranean ports) via Syria and Egypt. Competition may have lowered prices somewhat; at any rate, the European spice market approximately doubled its intake during the sixteenth century. By the 1560s purchases divided almost evenly between the two supply routes. Consequently for about fifty years, from the 1520s to the 1570s, Venetian merchants distributed as much or even slightly more in the way of spices than they had before 1500.[9]

Successful competition with the Portuguese probably required middlemen all along the line from India to Venice and beyond to lower their markups.[10] It certainly required the Venetians to lower their transport costs by shifting away from galleys to cheaper round ships. Merchant galleys of the type that had carried precious goods for Venice since the early part of the fourteenth century were costly and safe, because of their large crews. But with continued improvements in the design of ships and rigging, and especially as cannon came into use for the protection of round ships, merchant galleys ceased to be economical. In 1513 the Venetian government recognized this fact by permitting round ships to load spices and other goods previously reserved for the merchant galleys of the *muda*. As a result, transport costs (not charges, necessarily) sank to about one-third their former level;[11] and the economics of Venetian merchant shipping changed, since freights for precious commodities could now help to meet the costs of operating ordinary privately owned round ships, most of whose cargo, as before, had to come from coarser, cheaper goods: wine, cotton, wheat, salt, and the like. Old-fashioned merchant galleys were not abandoned at once; but when they lost their legal monopoly of the spice trade they lost their economic raison d'être and became unprofitable. The last *muda* sailed to Alexandria in 1535; thereafter Venice, like the rest of the world, depended solely on round ships, privately owned, for carrying trade goods.

The traditional concern of the Venetian government for navigation and shipbuilding did not disappear with the abandonment of the system of state-owned merchant galleys. On the contrary, regulations, subject to frequent adjustment in accordance with changing conditions, continued to envelop all aspects of Venetian shipbuilding and operation. Subsidies for construction of desired types of vessels were instituted and withdrawn according to need; freight rates were subject to regulation too; so were such matters as how deeply a ship could be laden, and where certain commodities—grain especially—could legally be discharged. Market conditions interacting with elaborate public supervision kept the Venetian merchant marine in comparatively prosperous condition until about 1570. Total tonnage at the disposal of the Venetians increased in the sixteenth century; the disappearance of the merchant galleys meant not decay (as was once believed) but modernization.[12]

The abandonment of merchant galleys at the beginning of the sixteenth century had one important implication; thenceforward the Venetian navy and the Venetian merchant marine were more sharply separated than before. Expenditures required for maintaining a suitable level of naval strength had to be met directly from taxes without the income formerly accruing from the operation of the merchant galleys. To be sure, in wartime, privately owned round ships could be conscripted for use as supply vessels for the navy; but they played only a marginal part. Ships of the line, designed for battle, remained oared, and adhered to the old boarding tactics, despite the development of naval gunnery which had allowed the Portuguese at Diu, for example, to destroy the Moslem fleet sent against them without ever coming to close quarters.

In view of what happened in the Mediterranean after 1580, it is clear that the failure of Venice and other Mediterranean naval powers to shift away from galleys to the new style of gunnery from round ships was a mistake, since it allowed the Atlantic navies to outstrip Mediterranean fleets technically. Various factors conduced to this result, among them the relative scarcity of metals and a mounting shortage of fuel in the Mediterranean lands. This made gun casting on a really big scale appallingly expensive, though this is what was needed to equip large numbers of vessels with an adequate number of heavy guns. It seemed easier to fall back on slavery as a means of manning the galleys—appallingly expensive, too, but mainly for foreigners and the lower classes[13]—than to pay the price the new technology required.

There were, of course, positive reasons for keeping galleys as ships of war. The Arsenal at Venice and similar institutions in other Mediterranean naval headquarters had refined the design and perfected the organization of skills for building and equipping galleys. This made their product dependable. Experienced managers could calculate precisely the costs and gains of building one to one hundred galleys. Shift to an entirely new technical basis for naval war involved high initial risks: new designs might not work (as the Venetians in fact discovered in the last decades of the century when they did experiment with new types of vessels). It was clear from the start that sailing ships could not be coordinated tactically with galleys; hence a decision to go over to a new kind of naval war implied scrapping something tried and true for something that was, to begin with, completely unknown. Common sense as well as bureaucratic caution rebelled against such a drastic step.

Experienced Mediterranean sea dogs could point out that galleys, after all, could operate amphibiously, and move about close inshore, where sailing vessels dared not go; were able to travel directly upwind, as no sailing ship could do; and in general could maneuver far more nimbly than any unoared vessel. Under ordinary circumstances no heavy-gunned fleet, dependent on wind for every movement, could expect to corner a fleet of galleys. And even for the strategic offensive, where the advantage of big guns was already apparent by the first decade of the sixteenth century, naval gunnery was stymied in attacking defended cities and harbors by the clear superiority of shore batteries, which were far more accurate than guns placed on board a tossing ship. The very rational result was that as long as the Ottoman navy remained on the offensive and retained the galley and the time-hallowed style of naval warfare suited to that kind of ship (i.e., until 1581) all other Mediterranean fleets did the same, and confined their experimentation with big guns to the scale of armament that could be accommodated on the prow of an oared vessel.[14]

As far as the Venetian economy was concerned, the sharp

dichotomy between naval vessels and merchant vessels that came to prevail after 1530 meant an increase of protection costs, because ships needed for war no longer were capable of earning income in times of peace, as the old merchant galleys had done. Venice, in short, came round to the Byzantine naval posture of some five centuries before, when Venetian superiority to the Greeks had rested largely upon the convertibility that then prevailed between the Venetian naval and mercantile marines.[15] Moreover, it is worth pointing out that precisely the same fate befell the Venetian maritime establishment after 1580 as had befallen the Byzantine establishment after 1081. For the northern ships that began to infest the Mediterranean in the last decades of the sixteenth century were merchant and warships combined. Heavily gunned, they were manned by rude and warlike crews whose lust for plunder and keen eye for a bargain, whether within or beyond the pale of law, exactly reproduced the attitudes and aptitudes of the Venetians and their Italian competitors when they took over Byzantine commerce in the eleventh century. Thus, in the seventeenth century, English, Dutch, and Algerine pirate-traders did to the Italians what the Italians had done to the Greeks half a millennium before: all but drove them from the seas.[16]

Up until the 1570s, however, Venetian responses to the economic crises of the first decades of the century were generally successful. It was not only the spice trade that recovered; other branches of Venetian commerce attained a flourishing condition, even if the markets Venice served tended to shrink back toward the city's more immediate hinterland in north Italy, south Germany, and the Adriatic-Aegean coastlands. More intensive development of local resources in these regions made up for the undoubted weakening of Venetian commercial importance in the more distant markets of the Black Sea, the North Sea, and the western Mediterranean.

The commercial importance of Venice was reinforced by a massive industrial expansion. Textile manufacture was, as always, preeminent. From the 1520s fine woolen cloth, formerly produced mainly in Florence, began to come from Venetian looms in growing quantities. The city's main advantage was political. Skilled artisans fleeing from the military disasters and social upheavals that afflicted Florence and other mainland cities during the prolonged wars on the Italian mainland found congenial refuge in the peace and internal order the Venetian government maintained so successfully. As a result, between 1521 and 1569 there was an average annual increase of no less than 9.6 percent in the number of cloths registered with Venetian authorities to be washed, finished, and tagged with an official seal. Thereafter the growth rate was much slower. War with Turkey, 1569–73, transferred Ottoman cloth markets to the French; and more generally, the return of peace to Italy after 1559 removed the unusual advantage Venice had enjoyed. But woolen cloth production crested in Venice as late as 1602.[17]

Comparably precise data for other industries is not available, but it is clear enough that old Venetian specialties like glass manufacture, fine metal and leather work, jewelry, silks, and other luxury production all flourished; and the brand new industry of printing concentrated in Venice partly because of lenient censorship and partly because of the superior availability of paper, which was another of the city's important manufactures.[18]

Population statistics, which became remarkably accurate in the sixteenth century thanks to official census taking, reflect Venetian economic success. From about 115,000 inhabitants in 1509, the crisis year, the population grew to a recorded 168,-000 in 1563 and may have increased somewhat more before 1575, when a severe plague struck the city, killing more than 45,000 persons in the course of less than two years. A census of 1581 showed only 134,000 inhabitants, and until 1951 the city's recorded population never again attained the peak of the 1560s and early 1570s. Actual totals were undoubtedly somewhat higher than census records showed, since some classes of the population were not counted, Jews and clerics for instance; and some must have been missed. The city's population probably crested in 1575 at slightly over 180,000.[19]

Concentration of so many mouths on barren mudbanks created a perennial problem: How could Venetians assure an adequate food supply year in and year out, no matter how harvests might vary, wars interfere, or prices fluctuate? Elaborate rules and regulations, supervised by a special board of magistrates whose duty it was to foresee and head off grain shortages by active intervention in the market whenever necessary, had been inherited from earlier centuries. The work of the *Officio Delle Biave* underwent no remarkable further development in the sixteenth century. Immemorial experience, reactivated at frequent intervals by sudden fluctuations in available food supplies, had long since attained rational and efficient administrative embodiment; all that could be done was to create more officials to enforce the rules more strictly.[20]

On the other hand, food production in the immediate hinterland of the city was capable of considerable increase. Maize, introduced in the 1550s, provided a more abundant crop than had been available before; it spread throughout the Veneto within three generations and eventually became the staple of peasants' diet. Rice also was introduced in the sixteenth century and added significantly to the food supply.[21] Drainage and diking of waterlogged land around the head of the Adriatic took on a new importance; a special government board was set up in 1501 to regulate river courses; another, established in 1556, supervised reclamation, settling conflicting legal rights in the interest of increasing the area under cultivation.[22] During the sixteenth century some forty-one square kilometers of very fertile land was brought under cultivation by these efforts—no small supplement to the city's granary. Less spectacular, but more important overall, were improvements in techniques of cultivation, permitting a decrease in the amount of fallow land. On the other hand, the parallel process of bringing waste land under the plow had ambiguous results, depriving the Veneto of pasture and woodlands which were vital to long-run human occupancy of the region.[23]

Intensification of cultivation on *terra firma* required capital, sometimes on a rather large scale. This was supplied by landowners, many of whom were wealthy Venetians who bought land partly for prestige and partly because it seemed a more secure and less onerous way of investing funds than any other. Successful trade or manufacture, after all, required practically constant attention to detail; whereas a bailiff could be trusted to manage a country estate and bother the owner with an accountancy only once a year. In proportion as the wealthy classes of Venice busied themselves in public affairs or in the pursuit of pleasure—including pleasures of the mind as well as of the flesh—the attraction of leisured landowning increased and the burdens of business management became correspondingly more repellent.

New groups—Jews, Greeks, Germans, and strangers from elsewhere in Italy—sprang up in the city, eager and ready to take over business roles vacated by native-born Venetians. The city's industrial growth could not have occurred without such in-migration; and some branches of trade, e.g., the book trade with the Balkans, rested in the hands of foreigners from the beginning. Nevertheless, the commercial and financial traditions of the Venetian nobility and citizen classes faded only slowly; until 1575, the year when plague struck with devastating effect, commercial investments continued to attract the city's ruling class. Only when commerce became less profitable than landowning, i.e., after the crippling commercial crisis that set in during the 1570s, did landowning and other forms of rentier investment definitely become the norm among the Venetian nobility.[24]

Adjustments and readjustments at home and on the Italian mainland that allowed Venice to survive and indeed to prosper through the middle years of the sixteenth century were matched by similarly successful moves overseas. The definitive loss of Negropont to the Turks in 1479 was more than compensated for by the annexation of Cyprus in 1489, when the widow of the last Lusignan king of that island (herself a Venetian by birth and a descendant of the sugar-planting Cornaro family) resigned her regalian rights into the hands of the Venetian Republic. For the following ninety years, Cyprus remained, with Crete and Corfu, an economically valuable imperial possession for the Venetians. To be sure, the sugar plantations of Cyprus and Crete suffered from the competition of newer lands: first the Madeiras (where sugar boomed in the 1480s) and then Brazil (which eclipsed Madeira sugar in the 1570s). Other crops, however, continued to command a brisk market, cotton and wine especially. Still others, e.g., dried currants from the Ionian islands, attained greater importance than in previous times. Venice also imported grain from her imperial possessions (including the mainland and Dalmatia). This trade was rigged in favor of the Venetians, since all grain exports had (in law, if not always in fact) to go to Venice and nowhere else.

Venice's chain of island possessions served as a valuable series of rest stations and ports of refuge for ships trading with Egypt and Syria or with Constantinople; and in war against the Turks, the Ionian islands, Crete and Cyprus, offered an all but indispensable chain of naval bases, since a galley could not operate for very long without putting into port for rest, food, and water.[25] Lastly, Venice extracted tax income from her possessions overseas, both in the form of hard cash and in the form of labor services for building fortifications, manning galleys, and in other ways contributing directly to the military-economic strength of the Republic.

Venetian policy overseas was purely defensive. Most of the time, the Turks were quite willing to concede trade privileges, though only for a price. More often than not the real community of interest between the Ottoman rulers and Venetian merchants in maintaining a flow of trade made itself felt. The Turkish government, by charging relatively high tribute fees for license to trade, in effect became a sharer in mercantile profits. In addition, the government and the men who headed it were important customers for some of the commodities Venetians and other Franks brought to Ottoman markets. The Turks, for instance, needed metals for armaments, and these came most cheaply and conveniently from western Europe, and could be best delivered by sea. Luxury items of western provenance, from fine cloth to mirrors, jewelry, and the like, also were welcomed by the Turkish upper classes. Competing luxury goods, manufactured at home or in other Moslem lands, made these supplies relatively unimportant for the rulers of the Ottoman Empire; by contrast, the supply of metals, for which alternative sources were, generally speaking, quantitatively insufficient to meet the government's needs, was always vital.[26]

Actual resort to force or the threat thereof played a big role in the trade between Ottoman and Christian lands. This was nothing new: the Italian cities of the eleventh to fifteenth centuries had capitalized on their military prowess vis à vis Byzantium, turning their superior force into profit. From 1479, superiority of organized force rested with the Turks: Venetian and other Christian merchants had to pay fat fees for the rights to trade; and on the open seas, as always, each ship had to attend to its own defense against acts of piracy. Christians as well as Moslems engaged in piracy, not least the crusading order, the Knights of Saint John, who made Rhodes their headquarters until 1522 (when Sultan Suleiman besieged and captured it); whereupon the knights transferred the seat of their piratical activity to the island of Malta (1530).

Every so often the Ottoman government decided to step up the normal level of maritime violence by taking the offensive. In 1499 it was the Venetians who bore the brunt of such a campaign, losing Coron and Modon before peace was restored in 1503. Yet, in this case, too, Venice made up for the loss of these ports of call by taking firm possession of the southern Ionian islands, Cephalonia and Zante. Though less conveniently located than Modon and Coron, these islands thenceforward served well enough as way stations for Venetian ships en route to Crete and further east.

After 1503, however, the Turks' main naval antagonist ceased to be Venice. The whole scale of Mediterranean war altered. The long-standing Ottoman-Venetian naval duel in the eastern Mediterranean merged with the French-Spanish struggle for control of Italy and the western Mediterranean. As a result, by the 1530s, all the naval forces of the inland seas were gathered up into one or the other of two rival coalitions: a Turkish-French alliance *vs.* a Spanish-Italian alliance. Second-rate powers, like Venice, survived through the equivocation of their participation in these coalitions—never fully dependable from the point of view of the great powers, yet indispensable for the increment of naval strength their ships could bring to an allied fleet.

This merger between the eastern and western Mediterranean spheres of naval action began in 1504 when two venturesome Moslem buccaneers, known to their Christian antagonists as Barbarossa because of the reddish color of their beards,[27] began to raid Christian shipping in the narrows between Sicily and Tunis. Soon they gained control of bases along the coast of North Africa, and in 1516 were able to take possession of Algiers. Simultaneously, the Hapsburg heir, Charles of Ghent, succeeded his grandfather, Ferdinand, on the Spanish throne and took up the quarrel against the French for predominance in Italy. In the very next year, 1517, the Ottoman sultan, Selim the Grim, occupied Egypt (thus eliminating the only other Moslem naval power of any importance in the Mediterranean) and took the Barbarossa brothers under his protection. Thus a few months before Martin Luther inadvertently kindled a very different kind of struggle in remote northern Germany, Ottoman power extended along the North African coast from Alexandria to Algiers, challenging Spanish and Christian naval predominance in the western Mediterranean as never before.

Genoa, long the plaything of rival factions and foreign dominion, regained a limited independence under the new naval circumstances that thus came to prevail in the western Mediterranean. Under the leadership of the famous admiral, Andrea Doria, Genoese ships served first with the French, then (from 1528) with the Hapsburgs. Doria was able to tip the naval balance between the two rivals as he shifted sides; and took advantage of that fact to free Genoa from foreign (i.e., French) control and reestablish an independent regime under his own semiautocratic control. Thereafter, Doria became the usual admiral of the array of Christian naval vessels that gathered under Hapsburg banners to fight a series of epic campaigns against their Moslem-French antagonists.[28] As for the Barbarossa brothers, the elder was killed in action in 1518; the younger, having earned the honorific appellation Khair ed-Din (Defender of the Faith), removed his headquarters to Istanbul in 1533 where he, an outsider like Doria, became commander of the Ottoman navy. He held the post until his death in 1546.

In 1536, the French concluded a formal treaty of alliance with the Turks; and in 1543–44 a Turkish fleet wintered in Toulon harbor rather than making the long journey back to Istanbul after a summer spent raiding in the western Mediterranean. This marked the apex of effective naval cooperation between the Turks and the French; in later campaigns, the Ottoman fleet acted pretty much alone, in spite of various efforts to concert naval strategy between the two mutually distrustful allies.[29]

The high point in the Ottoman naval offensive came in 1565, when a large Turkish expedition besieged Malta unsuccessfully. As that campaign demonstrated, improved fortress design could make a defended place proof against cannon fire, save after prolonged siege. This quickly created a military stalemate within the Mediterranean, since the effort needed to man and equip a fleet capable of capturing a worthwhile shore base got to be entirely out of proportion to any possible gain that could accrue, even from victory.

A similar stalemate simultaneously set in along the Ottoman land frontier with Austria, and for exactly the same reason. The great Suleiman died in 1566 in the field while his forces were vainly besieging the Hapsburg fortress of Szigeth in Hungary. The double failure of Malta and Szigeth, 1565–66, plainly indicated that the days of Ottoman expansion and easy victories had come to an end. The invasion and eventual capture of Cyprus (1570–73), matched as it was by the naval disaster of Lepanto in 1571, did not change the situation; and after 1574 neither Spain nor Turkey ever again had the will or the resources to invest in large-scale naval operations in the Mediterranean. This was confirmed by the fact that from the 1580s a new era of naval technology, based no longer on galleys but on heavy-gunned sailing vessels, dawned in the Mediterranean. All older naval installations and organizational structures became obsolete; but no Mediterranean power, except France, was able or willing to make the massive readjustment and heavy investment this technological transformation required. The Mediterranean, accordingly, became a naval backwater, a playground for pirates and for ships based on North Atlantic ports.[30]

Venice played a reluctant, marginal part in this vast struggle. The Venetian fleet remained a considerable force in the overall Mediterranean balance; and Venice in fact increased the number of its warships and the scale of its naval expenditure in the sixteenth century in a delibrate effort to keep up with the expanded scale of naval war.[31] From a Spanish and papal point of view, therefore, full and enthusiastic cooperation from Venice was much to be desired. A weighty propaganda (directed also against France) claimed that all Christian governments owed loyal adherence to Hapsburg-led coalitions against the Moslems as a matter of religious duty. This view of international politics merged with papal efforts to reform the church and revivify Christian commitment in all aspects of life.

Insofar as the Venetians refused to go along with this propaganda, they found themselves also resisting the transformative force of the Catholic reformation, with the result that they kept the Italian renaissance alive in their city, almost inadvertently, making Venice a locus of old-fashioned secularist, civic spirit for decades after that spirit had flagged and been driven underground elsewhere in Italy. This conservatism had great importance for the outreach of Venetian cultural influence toward the Orthodox Christian communities of eastern Europe, as we shall see in the next chapter. The lengthened afterglow of the renaissance in Venice also attracted Protestant Europe. As a result, between about 1530 and 1630 the University of Padua became the premier university of Europe, and a most significant meeting place of Europe's intellectual elites from east and west.

From a practical point of view, Venice had strong reasons to stand aloof from Spanish and papal efforts to recruit help against the Turks and French. Particularly after the Ottomans took control of Egypt and the Syrian coast (1517), the Venetian economy could only prosper if merchants had access to ports under Ottoman control. War did not bring solid economic returns, as it had in earlier days when Venetian ships had been the terror of the Aegean. On the contrary, it brought only physical hardship and financial difficulties. The principal gain from a victory at sea was an enhanced supply of galley slaves, who, however useful in war, were nonetheless an economic liability inasmuch as even they had to have food. Raiding coastal settlements seldom brought much return; too many pirates and slave raiders had already ravaged Mediterranean coastlands. Anything really worthwhile was secured behind formidable walls that would yield only to prolonged siege and after a very substantial expenditure of money for the upkeep of the besieging forces.

On the other hand, a heavily laden merchant vessel was a prize worth having. Those who made a living by this kind of robbery obviously maximized their income by attacking all comers, Christian or Moslem, regardless of nationality or prevailing diplomatic alignments. But regular governments and their specialized warfleets could not behave in such a manner without destroying the basis of their own existence, which depended on massive and predictable concentration of materials and manpower in their home ports by means of trade. In other words, if the warships of a numerous, well-equipped navy like that of Venice had preyed indiscriminately on Mediterranean merchantmen, the economic basis needed to support such a regular navy establishment would have quickly disappeared. The very scale and efficiency of the naval establishment thus condemned it to economic sterility—a fact which in turn limited the expansion of Venetian and all Mediterranean naval forces to what competing demands upon available tax income of the respective states permitted. Hence while piracy could and did pay, so long as it kept to a suitably modest scale, organized naval war most definitely did not. The Venetians were acutely aware of this fact, and therefore did all they could to minimize their involvement in the struggles that convulsed the Mediterranean great powers—Spain, Turkey, and France—during the sixteenth century.

Accordingly, the Venetians joined Spanish-papal coalitions against the Turks only when they found their own imperial territories and trade privileges under direct attack; and whenever the Turks showed willingness to renew peaceable relations, the Venetians were eager—treacherously eager from a crusading Christian point of view—to make peace and reopen trade with the Levant.

Successful maneuver between the Hapsburg and the Ottoman colossi was difficult. When a Turkish fleet set sail from Istanbul in the spring, it was hard to know just where it was headed. This recurrent uncertainty put a great premium on accurate information and appropriate diplomatic and military reaction to the latest intelligence from Istanbul and other ports and capitals of the Mediterranean. The Venetian diplomatic service served the city well in this circumstance, though it did not improve the Republic's reputation as a bulwark of Christendom.

Twice the resources of Venetian diplomacy were exhausted and the city found itself at war. In 1537 the Turks attacked the Venetian stronghold of Corfu but failed to take it; nevertheless, when peace was made three years later the Venetians had to surrender the fortress at Nauplion, on the east coast of the Morea, which had hitherto remained in their hands. Thirty years later, the Turks attacked the island of Cyprus and conquered it after a long siege of Famagusta. Relief proved impractical, since the Venetian fleet (allied with Spanish and papal contingents) was fully occupied by the main force of the Ottoman fleet in waters much closer to home.

In the first of these wars the Turks won a great naval battle off Prevesa (1538); in the second, the Christians wreaked havoc upon the Ottoman fleet at the battle of Lepanto (1571).[32] Yet neither the one victory nor the other had any lasting strategic value. Each side was capable of regenerating a formidable fleet within the space of a single year. The Turks very dramatically proved this in 1572 when they put to sea again in the spring with a fleet of almost undiminished size, despite the losses of the year before.[33] Since the Spaniards were unwilling to serve Venetian interests by fighting in Cyprus, and the Venetians were equally unready to expend effort on behalf of Spanish interests in North Africa, the Christian alliance fell apart after Lepanto. Being unable to relieve Famagusta on the strength of their own resources, and being equally unable to persuade the Spaniards to assist in the enterprise, the Venetians in 1573 made peace, surrendering Cyprus to the Turks. Thus the brilliant naval victory of Lepanto, in which Venetians ships, especially the new heavy-gunned galleasses, played a decisive and distinguished part, had no lasting importance, in spite of the enthusiasm that greeted the news in all of Catholic Europe, and the weight this Christian victory is still accorded in European history textbooks.

Yet the war in which the battle of Lepanto figured as a particularly dramatic episode did mark a major turning point

Four—Venice as a Marginal Polity

in Mediterranean history. In 1574, when the Turks recaptured Tunis, lost to the Spaniards just the year before, it was the last time that a large naval expeditionary force built around galleys[34] was able to accomplish anything of importance. Devastating plague struck the next year. By the time Venice and Istanbul and other Mediterranean ports had time to recover from that blow, creeping crises that had been long in the making began to afflict so much of the Mediterranean coastlands that full recovery proved impossible.

The first important setback to cripple the Venetian economy was the decay of the merchant marine. From 1590 English and Dutch ships began to appear in Mediterranean waters in large numbers, bringing grain from Danzig to hungry Mediterranean cities. These vessels were able to operate more cheaply than Mediterranean-built vessels, and speedily took over a large proportion of the carrying trade within the interior sea.[35] Venice responded to this new competition by allowing Venetian shipowners to buy the cheaper foreign-built ships. By tinkering with anchorage fees the government attempted to make it advantageous for ships of northern construction to register under the Venetian flag.[36] But these efforts backfired when foreign ships by-passed Venice in favor of competing ports. Accordingly, in 1607 the discriminatory rules were canceled,[37] though efforts to prevent foreign ships from dominating the city's carrying trade were not altogether abandoned. This both recognized and confirmed the fact that, between 1590 and 1610, Dutch and English ships had seized the lion's share of long-distance voyaging in the Mediterranean.[38]

English and Dutch ships were faster and more heavily gunned than the Italian ships they displaced; they were also cheaper to build because the supply of timber in northwestern Europe (from the Baltic in large part) was more abundant than in Italy. In addition, the social distance between crewmen and their officers was probably less among the newcomers; at any rate the Dutch and English speedily developed a well-deserved reputation for formidability that came as much from effective cooperation of all on board in battle as from superiority of armament.

The Barbary pirates, who initially were largely of Dutch

and English origin,[39] quickly learned that an attack on a Dutch or English ship was likely to produce hard knocks rather than a quick surrender. Accordingly, they tended to concentrate attention on Venetian and other less formidable vessels. This resulted in skyrocketing insurance rates, which still further handicapped the Venetian mercantile marine in trying to compete with the formidable newcomers. The Venetian navy was unable to check the new piracy, which, with tacit support from Hapsburg authorities of Croatia, became endemic even within the Adriatic.[40]

Despite decay of their merchant marine, foreign bottoms were abundantly available to Venetian trade, which continued at a high level through the first two decades of the seventeenth century. Receipts from the anchorage tax reached an all-time high in the years 1603–05, almost coinciding with the peak of woolen cloth production in the city, which came in 1602.[41] Thereafter the slope was downhill—with some precipitous drops (receipts from the anchorage tax in 1626 were only one-sixth of what they had been in 1603) and partial recoveries that always fell short of earlier peaks. Other manufactures, e.g., soap, also diminished; and by 1630 Venetian preeminence in printing was disappearing too. Only luxury craftsmanship survived, where skill and taste mattered more than cost of production.

During these same years Venice lost out to the Dutch in the spice trade. The Dutch East India Company (organized 1600) cut off the flow of spices at the source far more effectively than the Portuguese had ever been able to do. Dutch shipping was cheap, abundant, and seaworthy enough to be able to bring spices around Africa from the Moluccas and other points of origin more cheaply than they could be transported along the traditional routes via south India, Egypt, and Venice. As this pattern established itself during the first decade of the seventeenth century, the Venetian spice trade decayed finally and forever, and with it one of the sources of the city's prosperity faded into the past.[42]

Another of Venice's long-standing sources of commercial profit also slackened from about the middle of the sixteenth century and then faded away almost entirely with the outbreak

of the Thirty Years' War in 1618. For the yield from the gold
and silver mines of central Europe that had funneled a large
proportion of their product through Venice ever since the thirteenth century dwindled after about 1550. Exhaustion of some
lodes and the influx of precious metals from the New World
were responsible for this phenomenon.[43] Development of mining in Bosnia and other parts of the Balkans did little to fill
the gap as far as Venice was concerned, for this enterprise was
handled mainly by merchants operating from Ragusa, whose
surge of prosperity in the fifteenth century was assisted by the
freshet of precious metals (plus copper and lead) from the
western Balkans that debouched upon European markets
through their hands.[44]

The descending curve of Venetian prosperity reflected two
parallel and interrelated Mediterranean-wide crises that became crippling between 1575 and 1635. Food and fuel, fundamental to any society, both became critically short in
Mediterranean lands as the balance between cropland and
woodland shifted, in one region after another, beyond the
point at which forest growth could keep up with the rate of
tree destruction, whether by woodcutting, fire, or grazing
animals.

Fundamental to the entire phenomenon was a massive population growth that resulted in approximately doubling the
number of inhabitants of Mediterranean lands in the fifteenth
century.[45] Reasons for this are, to say the least, obscure. Perhaps the enhanced efficiency of local and long-distance market
relationships, which had been the *chef d'œuvre* of Italian city
state economy from the thirteenth to the fifteenth centuries,
meant both decrease in local violence destructive of life (as
a result of the concentration of organized force in fewer hands)
and a more frequent escape from famine (through rapid redistribution of available food supplies in cases of local crop failure). Still another factor which may have been of major
importance was the altered incidence of epidemic as a result
of speedier circulation of infectious diseases from port to port.[46]

Whatever its causes, the fact of massive population growth
both in Christian and in Moslem lands seems certain. The
result was that toward the end of the sixteenth century it be-

came increasingly difficult to find enough grain to feed Mediterranean cities in years of bad harvest. The spread of maize, which became a very important crop in the Balkans as well as in northern Italy, certainly increased the quantity of calories available per cultivated acre.[47] But this merely made the eventual collision between mounting population and available food supply more massive and more difficult to deal with effectively.

Shortage of wood was probably more pressing than shortage of food. Wood shortages meant that fuel as well as an indispensable raw material for construction and for innumerable manufactures became scarcer and scarcer, thereby raising costs to a point that gave north European producers (who, in England at least, had begun to shift to coal as their fundamental fuel)[48] a crushing advantage.

The importance of timber for shipbuilding is self-evident, and abundant records attest a critical shortage of suitable oak for Venetian shipbuilders from about the middle of the sixteenth century.[49] Other dimensions of the wood shortage do not seem to have attracted so much attention, either at the time or among scholars subsequently. Nonetheless, a moment's thought about the general importance of fuel in industrial and household routines is enough to convince anyone of how pervasive and important a reduction in the supply of wood must have been in places and times when fossil fuels were not available.

The question that cannot be answered with assurance is when and where, and how severely, wood shortages made themselves felt in Mediterranean lands; for it is one thing to lack oak timbers suitable for shipbuilding and a different matter to run out of scrub growth and other types of wood suitable for fuel. Mediterranean forests were, of course, particularly vulnerable to destruction. Once woodland had been cut over, the rays of the Mediterranean sun were so strong that young seedlings were liable to wither and die in the dry season. In a mature forest, the shade of established trees could prevent excessive desiccation; but in many Mediterranean landscapes, once big trees had disappeared, natural regeneration could become extremely slow, or even come completely to a halt.

Four—Venice as a Marginal Polity

Add the ravages of goats and sheep, erosion of exposed hillsides, and fire (sometimes set deliberately by shepherds to check the growth of scrub and increase the amount of grassland) and the factors working against Mediterranean forests become formidable indeed.

Without any definite data all one can safely say is that wherever natural regeneration of forests failed to keep up with the pace of destruction, a serious check to human occupancy swiftly followed. Only nomads (and Arctic hunters) were fully at home in an environment without a fairly copious supply of wood. In all probability, Mediterranean communities had often encountered this problem, even in ancient times.[50] The retreat of agriculture in Anatolia and the westward movement of nomads from the eleventh century may register not only the advance of Turkish and Moslem arms but also a crippling decay of accessible woodlands needed to sustain village and urban life. Similarly, the decay of the Sicilian economy under the late Norman kings offers another likely case in point. It is even possible that in better watered lands wood shortage sometimes limited industrial and urban development. The well-known industrial depression that hit the Low Countries in the latter part of the fourteenth century, for instance, might have been due to exhaustion of local wood supplies and the high cost of bringing fuel from afar, as much as to any of the other causes historians have adduced to explain what happened. For finishing woolen cloth, like most other manufactures, required fuel to heat the cauldrons of water used in fulling and dyeing.

It seems overwhelmingly probable that the economic depression that settled on Italy as a whole and upon Venice in particular after the 1630s was confirmed by persistent fuel shortages, though other factors—archaic techniques, high taxation, high wages, organizational rigidity supported by legal prescription, e.g., guild monopolies and work rules[51]—also played important parts.

Sociological changes of far-reaching import postponed the economic collapse of Venice, but this made decay particularly drastic when administrative and legal measures, designed to stave off disaster, no longer sufficed. The principal change in

146

Venetian society was this: by 1600, if not before, the Republic came to be governed by a small clique of rentiers, who drew their income mainly from land, and to a lesser degree from officeholding itself. Active management of industry and commerce passed into the hands of domiciled foreigners, who were tolerated cheerfully enough by Venetian authorities, but whose interests and opinions were not sensitively registered in the deliberations of official boards and governing bodies. As a result, the kind of commercial calculations that had governed Venetian state policy for centuries tended to lose persuasiveness. Simultaneously, considerations of social welfare and poor relief acquired greater scope, for the noble clique ruling the city recognized that its power could only remain secure if the mass of the populace continued to be more or less content.

Thus, for example, the increasing population of the city in the middle years of the sixteenth century called forth extensive efforts—part public, part private—to cope with hunger and poverty; and unusual crises, like the great plague of 1575–76, provoked correspondingly intense, though imperfectly effective, efforts to regulate public health, housing, and food distribution so as to reduce the effects of the disaster, especially upon the poor.[52] Insofar as such measures were successful in reducing human suffering, it seems obvious that they must also have cushioned the impact of changing economic conditions. This in turn presumably slowed adjustments in the allocation of resources, labor and capital alike.

Another way of describing the matter is to say that political and humanitarian considerations overrode economic and financial calculations. In view of the fact that the men who ruled Venice were no longer active in business, but devoted a large part of their official attention to regulating business behavior, this result is not surprising. In the short run, the measures taken by the Venetian government undoubtedly helped the city to survive acute crisis and gave the poor a definite stake in the maintenance of established administrative and political patterns. In the long run, official efforts at poor relief and public health regulation added to the overall costs of doing business in Venice, and made price competition with northern producers all the more impossible.

Four—Venice as a Marginal Polity

Idolization of the Venetian constitution as a supreme expression of political wisdom, uniquely capable of defending liberty and republican virtue, became explicit about the middle of the sixteenth century.[53] This no more than verbalized the principle upon which the ruling circle acted during and after the war of the League of Cambrai (1508–17), when they rejected any idea of expanding the number of persons allowed to participate in the government of the Republic.[54] Yet this hardening of political arteries did not prevent formal recognition of the ethnic pluralism that became a leading feature of Venetian society. Thus, for example, the Greeks were allowed to establish a community of their own in 1494, which drew up its own constitutional rules in direct imitation of the Venetian model. A more sensitive issue was the matter of allowing the Greeks to establish their own church. Yet this, too, was permitted as early as 1514, though actual construction of San Giorgio dei Greci began only in 1539 and the edifice was not complete until 1573.[55] The Greeks were authorized to use the Greek liturgy, while recognizing papal supremacy and dogmatic authority, as laid down by the Council of Florence. Nevertheless, Orthodox Christians felt quite at home in San Giorgio dei Greci, and the Venetian government resisted efforts to inquire too closely into just how the Greeks of San Giorgio straddled the issues separating the pope in Rome from the patriarch in Constantinople.[56]

Special "fondaci," i.e., buildings where goods could be safely stored and foreign merchants might reside, were established for Turks,[57] Tuscans, and Milanese on the model of the famous *Fondaco dei Tedeschi* where German traders had congregated since the fourteenth century. In addition, communities of Slavs (mainly from Dalmatia), Armenians, and Albanians clustered in particular districts of the city. Each developed a more or less organized and self-conscious corporate existence; but none of these foreign groups acquired a church of its own as the Greeks did, and none of them equaled the Greek community's importance, economically and culturally, either.

Jews, on the other hand, exercised important economic functions as bankers and moneylenders; and by the close of the sixteenth century also played a very important role in commerce with the Balkans and with the Ottoman lands generally.[58] In addition to overtly Jewish enterprises, various legal fronts disguised Jewish participation in legally forbidden manufacturing and retail selling. Conversely, Christians sometimes invested funds in Jewish banks, expecting to profit from the skill and shrewdness for which the Jews were famous.

The Jewish inhabitants of Venice divided into three quite distinct communities. The "Germans" were long established as moneylenders; after 1492 refugees from Spain and Portugal appeared, with quite different customs and language, and specialized more as merchants and, often, as doctors. A third group appeared only in the sixteenth century. Coming from the Levant, they enjoyed a superior legal status as subjects of the sultan, residing—at least in principle—in Venice only for short periods of time. Each of these groups organized separately to begin with, though all were consigned by Venetian authorities to the ghetto, designated for their occupancy in 1516. The first synagogue was built in 1529.[59]

The proliferation of ethnic corporate organizations in the sixteenth century did not signify that foreigners were only then beginning to live in Venice; nevertheless, the economic and cultural importance of these foreign communities certainly increased in proportion as various aspects of business and military enterprise were handed over to foreigners by tacit (or in the case of Jewish moneylending, explicit) consent of the Venetian government and population. Obviously, as wealthy Venetians transferred their capital to landholding, important economic roles were opened up for foreigners; hence the hardening of the caste lines that separated the Venetian nobility from the rest of society actually facilitated and went hand in hand with a deliberately widened tolerance for ethnic and religious pluralism within the city.

The Venetian ruling clique fully understood that their leisured privilege and political monopoly required others to take on business and commercial leadership roles; and by allowing these functions to cluster mainly in foreigners' hands, internal challenge to the political privileges of the noble caste was very effectually headed off. The wisdom and guile of the

Four—Venice as a Marginal Polity

Venetian nobility was never more evident than in the success this policy had in maintaining peace and order in the city, even in the face of economic crisis and eventual decay.

The tolerant, pluralist pattern of Venetian society became increasingly conspicuous in Italy as the Catholic reformation gathered momentum. Militant Catholics had much with which to reproach the Venetians, not least their unreadiness to fight the good fight against the Turks. Matters came to a head in 1606–07 when a bitter quarrel broke out between the papacy and the Venetian government. The great majority of the Venetian clergy chose to obey the magistrates of Venice rather than the pope in this encounter; and after a few months of vigorous propaganda battle, the French were able to arrange a face-saving compromise.

Behind this crisis loomed the shadow of Hapsburg policy. In 1596 the Spanish-educated, fanatically Catholic Ferdinand of Hapsburg took power in Styria, Carinthia, and Carniola, thus acquiring a common frontier with Venetian possessions on *terra firma*. Spanish governors of Naples and the Milanese naturally wished to secure their communications with this new bastion of the Catholic reformation by overcoming Venetian resistance. Indeed, the strategic advantages were so considerable that even after the papal interdict had been withdrawn, the Hapsburgs did not give up the attempt to overthrow their Venetian enemies. Accordingly, Ferdinand of Styria encouraged pirates to prey on Venetian shipping from bases within Hapsburg territories at the head of the Adriatic. This led to war (1613–17), when the Venetians attempted, with only modest success, to capture the pirate ports. In 1617, however, Ferdinand saw fresh problems looming ahead, as he was about to succeed to the throne of Bohemia. He therefore made peace with Venice, promising to remove the pirates from the coast and destroy their ships in return for retrocession of those coastal points the Venetians had captured. Then in the next year a "Spanish plot" agitated Venice. Rumors that Spanish agents planned to seize the seat of government by *coup de main*, with the help of bravos recently discharged from Venetian service in the war against the pirates, led to the arrest and execution of as many as three hundred persons.[60]

Thereafter, tensions diminished. Catholic zeal and Hapsburg resources were diverted northward to Bohemia and the Germanies with the outbreak of the Thirty Years' War in 1618; and when that struggle finally ended, Venice had come to terms with militant Catholicism at a time when the burning commitment of the missionary generations had begun to wear out. By the 1640s, with ideological frictions reduced almost to the disappearing point, the Hapsburg encirclement of Venetian territories therefore became tolerable to both parties. In truth, Venice had no choice. War with the Turks, 1645–69, compelled the Republic to come to terms with its other imperial neighbor, the Hapsburgs. So it remained until Napoleon upset the regime of Italy in 1797.

This upshot depended as much on the exhaustion of Venetian civic spirit as upon the decay of the Counter-Reformation vision of a purified and reunited Christendom. No doubt the economic disasters that pressed in upon the city after 1610 had a great deal to do with the manner in which Venetian civism ebbed in the following decades. In a sense, indeed, the ideal that inspired the defense of Venetian ecclesiastical practices against papal claims to plenary jurisidiction appealed to the city's leaders largely because they hoped by defending old practices and autonomies to restore the old-time commercial prosperity Venice once had known.[61] When, instead, shipping and manufactures both decayed, much of the force behind this belatedly old-fashioned Venetian version of the renaissance spirit evaporated. But what decisively broke the back of the tolerant, pluralist outlook was another severe bout of plague, which paralyzed the entire community in 1630–31. The disease killed no fewer than 46,490 persons in the city proper, and a total of more than 93,000 in Venice and the adjacent communities of Murano, Malamocco, and Chioggia.[62] This brought down the total population of the city to a mere 102,243, according to the official registers of 1633; thereafter the enumerated inhabitants of Venice never exceeded 140,000 during the seventeenth century.

The psychic impact of a two-year bout of plague, killing up to one-third of the population with small regard for social rank or station in life, is hard for us to grasp, living as we do in a society from which heavy epidemic death has disappeared. But in an age when all agreed that disease came from God, it was easy to believe that public policies displeasing to the pope might somehow be to blame for bringing down such a clear demonstration of God's displeasure upon the Republic of Saint Mark.

Moreover, the style of baroque Catholic piety that had developed in Italy and in the Hapsburg lands to the north was attractive in itself, capable of appealing vibrantly to sophisticate and peasant alike. Hence it is not surprising that in the face of acute epidemiological crisis on top of persistent economic difficulty, resistance to the papacy, to the Hapsburgs, and to the culture and outlook of Catholic reform all crumbled rapidly away. A far-reaching change in the tone of Venetian cultural life ensued as the new religious current flooded in. Correspondingly, the attraction Venice had formerly had for both Protestant and Orthodox antipapalists diminished as the life of the city and of the University of Padua were brought more and more into conformity with papal standards of Catholicity.

Yet this change of front did not save Venice from further disaster. The devastation of the Thirty Years' War, 1618–48, damaged Venetian markets and long-standing trade partnerships throughout southern Germany. This economic setback was swiftly succeeded by a Turkish invasion of Crete. The ensuing war of Candia dragged on from 1645 to 1669 and proved a crowning blow to Venetian power and prestige. The fact that hostilities could stagger on so long was in itself significant. In earlier times, when the Venetians had been the principal carriers between Ottoman ports and western Europe, neither side could afford prolonged warfare. But once English, Dutch, and then French ships took over the commercial role formerly played by Venetians, the Turks could afford indefinite suspension of peaceable relations with the one-time Queen of the Adriatic. Correspondingly, the damage to Venice was less acute when the city had already learned to live without large-scale Levantine trade.

This explains the long-drawn-out, sporadic character of the war of Candia. The Turkish expeditionary force quickly overran the whole of Crete except for the town of Candia. One of the longest sieges of European history then ensued, for the Venetians were able to supply the well-fortified Cretan capital by sea, but could not assemble a force strong enough to drive the Turks out of the island. Conversely, Turkish cannon were no longer capable of knocking down modernized fortifications designed to resist cannonade. A twenty-four-year stalemate resulted.

For the Venetians, decisive naval victory that would permanently isolate the Turks in Crete from their base of supplies was the obvious way to resolve the deadlock on land. But when the war began, the Venetian navy was in parlous condition, and for three years all that could be done was to supply the beleaguered garrison of Candia. Then in 1649 a small but formidable fleet[63] took the seas and attempted to blockade the straits. In 1654 the Venetians even penetrated the Dardanelles and defeated the Turkish fleet defending Istanbul; yet these successes were never enough to compel the Turks to withdraw from Crete, where in the absence of any sort of reliable supply from elsewhere, the Turkish soldiers simply lived off the land, wreaking very considerable destruction to the island's agriculture in the process.

In 1658 the Venetian fleet got caught in a storm and suffered serious damage. The effort required to fit out a fresh fleet capable of taking the offensive was more than the city could or was ready to afford.[64] Yet the war dragged on for eleven years; and sympathy for the Venetian struggle against the Moslem enemy even persuaded the premier military power of the age, France, to betray its Ottoman ally and come briefly, though ineffectually, to the aid of the Christian cause. When the French withdrew their expeditionary force, the Venetians decided that there was nothing to do but make peace. Accordingly in 1669 they ceded the island of Crete, the keystone of their empire since 1211, to the Turks.

By 1669, therefore, Venetian possessions overseas were confined to Dalmatia and the Ionian islands. The city's radius of action had shrunk back to merely local proportions; and even within the Adriatic, Venetian ships were no longer preeminent. Instead of acting as an interregional market and far-flung coordinator of economic and other kinds of human activity, as in its days of greatness, Venice had become a backwater, a city living on its past and on the (mainly agricultural) productivity of the immediate Italian hinterland. Of its erstwhile pan-European functions, only one remained: for even in the days of economic and military decay, Venice remained a favored playground for the rich, a pioneer of the tourist trade, and a place where the more corrupt pleasures and more licentious patterns of aristocratic behavior had freer scope and more perpetual exercise than anywhere else in Europe.

The city's role as pleasure capital and tourist trap was an afterglow of its earlier function as cultural center and beacon. The next chapter will examine this side of Venetian life in the period 1481–1669, when, though the political-military might of the city was in decay, Venetian cultural power attained its apogee.

FIVE

Venice as a Cultural Metropolis 1481-1669

FLORENTINE INNOVATIONS began to flood into Venice after the long Turkish war (1463–79) had ended. For a century and a half thereafter Venice became an extremely active center of renaissance culture, and a haven in war-troubled Italy for men and ideas that found it increasingly hard to flourish elsewhere in the peninsula. Foreign troops never occupied and plundered the Queen of the Adriatic, as happened to Naples, Genoa, Milan, and Rome; civil disturbances never broke the peace of the lagoons, as happened in Florence and Genoa. And just as the cloth trade migrated from the mainland to Venice to escape the wars and accompanying disorders, so also Venice assumed leadership or had it thrust upon her in the further development of renaissance art, music, theater, not to mention the art of printing. Moreover, the University of Padua, since 1405 the only institution of higher learning in the Venetian domain, became the seat of a distinguished school of philosophy and, in the sixteenth and early seventeenth centuries, led the entire world in the development of medical and related sciences.[1]

As usual, the history of art provides a sensitive indicator of cultural transformation and development. Gentili Bellini (ca. 1429–1507) and his brother Giovanni (ca. 1430–1516), with their brother-in-law, the Paduan painter Andrea Mantegna (1431–1506), made Venice and the Veneto the seat of an art

Five—Venice as a Cultural Metropolis

style distinct from yet comparable with the fine flowering of Tuscan art which reached an apogee with Leonardo da Vinci (1452–1519), Raphael (1483–1520), and Michelangelo (1475–1564). A distinct Venetian school took shape. Two of Giovanni Bellini's pupils, Giorgione (real name, Giorgio Barbarelli, ca. 1478–1511) and Titian (real name, Tiziano Vecelli, 1477–1576), made Venetian painting famous throughout Italy and much of western Europe.

Tuscan, Byzantine, and Gothic traditions flowed together to create the distinctive Venetian style of high renaissance painting. Developments in which the Florentines had pioneered—in particular the techniques of mathematically exact perspective and the general notion that a painted picture should emulate optical experience as exactly as possible—became constitutive assumptions for the Venetian painters, too. This, indeed, is what justifies classifying Venetian art of the late fifteenth and sixteenth centuries as "renaissance."

But the Byzantine and Gothic inheritances from former times were not lost. The coloristic virtuosity of Titian, for instance, seems clearly to descend from Byzantine mosaic art; and Byzantine echoes are also clearly perceptible in the composition of some of the best Venetian painting, whether it be a Bellini altarpiece or, much later, the work of Tintoretto (real name Jacopo Robusti, 1518–94).

Similarly, the trans-Alpine "Gothic" influence upon Venetian art of the sixteenth century was important, if only because the Venetians adopted the practice of using oil paints and applying them to canvas in imitation of techniques developed initially in Flanders. The textured surfaces and very complex palette permitted by this technique distinguished Venetian work from the tempera on plaster favored by most fifteenth-century Florentines. The technical challenge of exploring the illusionistic possibilities of the new medium gave Venetian painters ample scope for creativity, permitting them to draw freely upon all three of the art traditions available to them, Byzantine, "Gothic," and Tuscan. Without this possibility, the Florentine achievement of the fifteenth century might have stunted or even entirely inhibited fruitful innovation, condemning the Venetians, like painters elsewhere in Italy, to a strained "mannerist" search for escape from the heavy hand of the great Tuscan masters.

Giorgione and Titian departed from precedent in another and quite different way. A piece of painted canvas, framed and hung on a wall, is an easily transportable object, capable of being bought and sold, and subject to appreciation not only for its beauty but also as a piece of property. Religious and institutional uses for painting remained important in Venice; but from the time of Giorgione, great and famous artists of the city no longer had to depend entirely upon public commissions for their livelihood. An art market sprang up, and the use of paintings to decorate the walls of private houses became significant for the economic support of art and artists.[2]

Here, too, it seems likely that the Venetians were innovative with respect to Italian high art because they could draw on traditions from Byzantine (and, perhaps also from the Flemish-Burgundian?) world. Certainly, the purchase and sale of portable icons, destined for use in private homes, was a well-established custom among Orthodox Christians as early as the thirteenth century, if not before. Sale of icons for private use provided the economic basis for the guild of "madonneri" that existed in Venice from 1271, when it was organized, until the eighteenth century.[3]

It was not only painters who were in a position to profit from the confluence of divergent traditions that characterized Venetian culture in the sixteenth century. Venetian music achieved first rank, for instance, with the simultaneous arrival of a distinguished Flemish musician, Adrian Willaert (ca. 1480–1562), who became choir master at Saint Mark's in 1527, and of a cluster of refugees from the papal musical establishment who fled from Rome after the sack of that city by Emperor Charles V's troops in the same year.[4]

Printing also arrived in Venice from the Rhinelands, beginning in 1469, when John of Speyer began publication of such authors as Pliny, Livy, Cicero, and Augustine. Venice quickly became the most active center of printing in all Italy, and led in the process of cheapening books to reach a larger and larger market. Musical printing, map printing, medical printing with anatomical illustrations, and the publication of popular light literature in the vernacular[5] all either began at Venice or were there first developed on a substantial scale. One of the greatest achievements of the early Venetian printers was the publication of the Greek classics. The man principally responsible was Aldus Manutius (1450–1515) who set up his press in Venice in 1494 and with the help of a distinguished group of Greek scholars, come from Crete and elsewhere, began to edit and publish the principal pagan authors of Greek antiquity, most of them for the first time. By 1506, when the wars started to interfere with the enterprise, Aldus had made carefully edited Greek texts of Plato, Aristotle, Thucydides, Aristophanes, Euripides, Sophocles, Homer, Demosthenes, Aesop, Plutarch, and Pindar available to the learned world; and he did so in relatively cheap (and widely circulated) editions. The learning of western Europe was fundamentally and permanently enriched by the easy access to the Greek classics pioneered so vigorously by Aldus Manutius and his Greek assistants.[6]

The famous Aldine editions had been aimed principally at the learned and would-be learned of western Europe; other Greek presses established in Venice created a market for books in the Greek-speaking world itself. This branch of the book trade fell into the hands of Greek entrepreneurs from the start, and they made Venice the principal source for the entire Greek orthodox world of printed texts ranging all the way from the classics and Church Fathers to extremely cheap elementary schoolbooks and works of popular piety. Even when Venice ceased to be a particularly important center of publication for the western market—after 1570, roughly—the city continued until well into the eighteenth century to play the central role in printing and distributing books to speakers of Greek.[7] Thus in printing, as in art and music, it was the confluence of a trans-Alpine technique with Italian and/or Byzantine traditions that gave the Venetian achievement of the early sixteenth century its peculiar vibrancy and historical importance for Europe as a whole.

Intellectual developments in Venice and more particularly at the University of Padua also exhibited a fruitful mingling of trans-Alpine, Greek, and Italian learning. Andreas Vesalius (1514–1564), the most famous anatomist who ever taught at Padua, was a Fleming, and a numerous body of students from Germany and other trans-Alphine lands consistently attended the university,[8] which in the course of the sixteenth century became the most famous in all Europe. The Greek element was even more conspicuous. A professor of Greek was first appointed at Padua in 1463 and the new chair was continuously occupied through the fifteenth and sixteenth centuries by scholars of Greek origin.[9] Far more significant, however, was the introduction in 1497 of a course of lectures based upon the Greek text of Aristotle. This may not seem a world-shaking event at first glance; but it had immensely fertile and unsettling implications for the inherited scholastic tradition of philosophy and theology. These were based on texts of Aristotle as filtered through a double language barrier, first Arabic, then Latin. A heavy overburden of commentaries and commentaries upon commentaries altered profoundly the apparent meanings of many passages of the original texts. By going directly to the Greek, a new, naturalistic Aristotle could be discerned; and philosophers of Padua, who had been more closely allied to the medical faculty than to theology from the very beginnings of the university, responded vigorously and indeed recklessly to the vision of rational truth that emerged from closer inspection of Aristotle's own authentic words.

An influential early propagator of such views was Pietro Pomponazzi (1462–1524) who graduated from the medical faculty at Padua in 1487 and lectured as professor of philosophy there from 1495 to 1509 (when the university closed as a result of the war of the League of Cambrai). Pomponazzi withdrew first to Ferrara and then to Bologna, where he remained until his death. His first and most famous work, *On the Immortality of the Soul*, published in 1516, argued that soul and body were inextricably linked, being mutually related in men as form and matter are in ordinary objects. At the same time, however, Pomponazzi said that the soul may, through knowing, rise above the material realm to grasp eternal and immaterial truths, though without escaping its natural bodily integument. He advocated a naturalistic ethics, and declared that immortality could only be known through supernatural revelation and required a no-less-supernatural resurrection of the body. Such reviews aroused animated debate. Pomponazzi spent the rest of his life defending himself against charges of atheism and heresy, without losing influence among students or, for that matter, forfeiting the support of the city fathers of Bologna.[10]

The propagation of neo-Aristotelianism at Padua and Bologna was closely related to, and in some respects a mere by-product of, the development of medical studies, which took on the characteristics of modern science at Padua during the sixteenth century. In particular, discovery of new knowledge by empirical observation and dissection became normal. The authority of Galen was not rejected; but modification in detail, as his errors were discovered, altered the climate of opinion and made the study of medicine less bookish, more experimental, than before.

Dissection of human corpses had been started at Bologna before 1275; but the practice remained suspect on religious grounds until Pope Sixtus IV (reigned 1471–84), a former student at both Bologna and Padua, formally legitimated the practice.[11] The nasty task of cutting up the cadaver (usually an executed criminal) was left to an assistant, however, while the professor lectured aloofly from his chair. Then in 1537, the youthful Vesalius, fresh from his medical studies in Paris and Louvain, having been appointed professor of surgery and anatomy at the age of twenty-four, began to dissect human and animal bodies with his own hands. Under this regimen, discrepancies between Galen's text and observed details of human anatomy multiplied rapidly, for Galen had dissected only monkeys and pigs. Vesalius soon recognized this as the source of many of Galen's errors, and conceived the ambition of publishing a corrected treatise on human anatomy, illustrated with exact and precise drawings. This he succeeded in doing in 1543, thereby transforming Europe's anatomical knowledge.[12] Fresh discoveries in anatomy and physiology continued throughout the century, as a group of bold and empirically minded professors of medicine continued to exploit the possibilities offered by the freedom of inquiry and a regular supply of corpses which the Venetian magistrates, who directed the University of Padua, continued to permit and, indeed, encourage.

The fame of Padua's medical school drew students from all Europe. Greeks and Jews as well as Lutherans and other Protestants were not penalized for their religious views so long as they refrained from conspicuous, organized proselytism. The prevailing climate of university opinion discouraged religious fervor and positively encouraged the open expression of differing views. Two professors were appointed for most subjects, and they were even required to lecture at the same hour.[13] Such a system invited, indeed imposed, rivalry. Differences of opinion were underlined and elaborated, as it were automatically, since personal vanity impelled the *concurrens* (as they were termed) to compete for students. Knowledge assumed a pluralistic, open aspect under such conditions. No single unassailable doctrine could dominate the scene. Scope for individual judgment, discovery, elaboration widened. In addition, the Venetian state paid high salaries to attract and hold particularly famous professors; and from 1517, when the university resumed operation after the interruption incident to the war of the League of Cambrai, the magistrates appointed to supervise the affairs of the university kept ecclesiastical influence to a minimum. Practical success in the form of thousands of students, many come from afar, sustained these organizational peculiarities.[14]

Under such circumstances, it is not perhaps surprising that through most of the sixteenth century the University of Padua escaped the religious storms that embroiled Latin Christendom after 1517. Padua's insulation from religious controversy did not end until the 1580s, when the fierce conviction stirred in men's minds by a dogmatic and reformed Catholicism collided with the traditions of the university and provoked a series of notable debates and a political struggle to which we will return later in this chapter.

Venetian cultural creativity in the first decades of the sixteenth century had close analogues in the merchant republic of Ragusa, where a Slav patriciate presided over a vigorous commerce and a slender but significant cultural effloresence.

More important for the future was the similar development that took place in Crete, mainly at Candia, among the Greeks. In both cases, Italian and especially Venetian stimulus was central, and a literature that borrowed heavily from Italian prototypes, but employed, respectively, the local Slavic and Greek vernacular, sprang into existence.[15]

Crete also became the seat of a powerful art, carrying forward the Byzantine inheritance and, indeed, reexporting it to the Balkan mainland through new paintings, executed by Cretans, at Mount Athos and other major monastic centers. A key figure of this dispersal was the monk Theophanes, who was commissioned to paint murals at Meteora in Thessaly in 1527 and later did similar work at Mount Athos.[16] The Cretan style became normative for mural painting in the Greek world thereafter, though restrictions on church construction imposed by Ottoman authorities meant that mural painting did not remain a particularly vigorous or important art. Innovation concentrated instead on the creation of icons, where Cretan masters also played a major role, working sometimes in Venice, sometimes in Candia. As in the literary field, so also in art; the power of Italian renaissance models was acknowledged by varying degrees of appropriation and borrowing. But, generally speaking, the force of the Byzantine art tradition was such that Cretan and other Greek artists made only marginal and often evanescent borrowings from the west. The "Greek manner" remained an autonomous, recognized style in painting, whereas in literature the absence of any inherited vernacular tradition opened wide the gates for a far more complete assimilation of Italian models.[17]

There was a brief period at the beginning of the sixteenth century when it looked as though the Italo-Slavic cultural mix that developed in Ragusa might arouse significant resonance among the Serbs of the Balkan interior; but after 1526, when the kingdom of Hungary collapsed before the armies of Sultan Suleiman, the Serbs found symbiosis with the Ottoman regime more attractive; and from 1557, when Grand Vizier Mehmed Sokollu (né Sokolovic) restored autocephaly to the Serbian church and appointed his own brother as patriarch of Peć,[18] the Serbs turned their backs upon the siren song issuing from

Ragusa and the rest of the Dalmatian coast. For, despite its intrinsic charms, the Ragusan culture still carried an unmistakable Latin and papal taint. In Wallachia, however, where the Turks exercised only an indirect suzerainty in the sixteenth century, émigrés from the Ragusan and Dalmatian cultural world found ready welcome. One such, a monk named Makarius, printed (or at least distributed) two Church Slavonic books in Wallachia between 1508 and 1512.[19] Until 1711, when Greek princes replaced native hospodars, the Rumanian rulers remained undismayed by the whiff of Latinity emanating from the Adriatic, and in fact consciously cultivated slender but real cultural connections with Venice.[20]

Still further afield, in Muscovy, Italian participation in the construction of the Kremlin continued into the reign of Basil III (1505–33); but in proportion as native craftsmen acquired the skills required for gun casting, fortification, and monumental construction, the need for foreign experts diminished.[21] Consequently, when Ivan IV the Terrible (reigned 1533–84) wished to erect a magnificent church to commemorate his victories of 1552–56 over the Tatar khans of Kazan and Astrakhan, he entrusted the task to two Russian architects, who used old Russian wooden churches as prototypes for the strange and wonderful structure they created, the Church of Saint Basil on Red Square.[22]

But as the Russians' need for technological assistance diminished, other needs came to the fore. In particular, the Russian church, having severed its ties with Constantinople after 1453, was ill-equipped to resist new winds of doctrine that began to blow across the Russian lands in the 1490s. A group labeled "Judaizers" by its enemies came to light in Novgorod in the 1480s and soon attracted powerful supporters at Ivan III's court.[23] Among the Orthodox clergy themselves a sharp difference of opinion arose over the rightfulness of monastic ownership of property; and there were also problems in defending Russian church traditions against the propaganda of Latin clerics (based mainly in Novgorod) who forcefully propounded the papal claim to headship over the entire Christian church with arguments from Scripture and other holy authorities.

The great majority of the Russian clergy shrank in horror from "Judaizers" and Roman Catholics alike; but their only effective refutation was resort to force. Unlike his father, Basil III was prepared to use the secular arm against the Judaizers, and did so; but at the same time it seemed clear to everyone that burning heretics was not enough. Adequate refutation required learned argument based on authentic holy texts. But the Russian church lacked some important texts (the Church Fathers were only sketchily available in Church Slavonic) and suitably learned men for such a task did not exist. Hence in 1515 the Russian tsar sent a mission to Constantinople to ask the œcumenical patriarch for a qualified "translator of books" who might be able to meet the Judaizers and papalists on their own ground and demonstrate the superior truth of Orthodoxy.

This inquiry opened dazzling and supremely important prospects for the œcumenical patriarch. The embassy brought generous gifts, and if the Russian church could be persuaded to recognize once again the seniority and Orthodoxy of Constantinople, a flow of such gifts and other forms of support for the hierarchy of the hard-pressed Greek church could be expected.[24] As it happened, the œcumenical patriarch had at hand just the man for the job of reopening relations with the Russians by acting as a "translator of books." He was a monk of Mount Athos who had deliberately reaffirmed the traditions of his Orthodox ancestors after spending long years of his youth in Italy, where, as Michael Trivolis, he secured an excellent humanist education and briefly (1496–98) put his knowledge to work editing Greek texts for Aldus Manutius in Venice.[25] Trivolis also became thoroughly conversant with Latin theology after enrolling as a Dominican friar in Savonarola's convent at Florence (1502–04); but his fundamental intellectual experience came from association with the Platonic circle in Florence. Exploration of the mystical side of Platonism confirmed his distaste for official Latin theology. This eventually led him to leave the Dominican cloister in Florence and enroll in Mount Athos as a simple monk. There he took the name of Maxim by which he was subsequently known. His superiors recognized Maxim's unusual talents and sent him on missionary journeys to Wallachia to combat Latinism there. He also seems to have made other evangelical tours, aimed at carrying the faith to the common people in the manner of the Latin friars—an ideal he adhered to all his life.

This was the man, therefore, who accompanied the Russian mission on its return to Moscow and duly set up (1518) a center for translating Greek texts into Church Slavonic. Maxim got on well with the so-called Non-Possessors of the Russian church, i.e., with those who argued that monks should not possess lands and other income-producing property. But he soon fell out with their opponents, supporters of the ideal of a decorous, disciplined, and magnificent service of God within a church whose wealth would guarantee effective independence of secular control. Maxim's Platonism, his confidence in himself and his skills, and above all the belief he had that in altering Russian manuals and prayer books to accord with Greek texts he was personally inspired by the Holy Ghost, soon led to charges of heresy. In 1525 he was adjudged guilty. Six years later, after a second legal process, he was exiled to a remote northern monastery and remained there under surveillance for twenty years. After disarming even his foes by exemplary personal piety, Maxim was released in 1551, just five years before his death.

Throughout his years of exile, Maxim continued an active literary life, writing polemical and devotional tracts as well as continuing the task of translating the works of the Greek Fathers into Church Slavonic. Through his writings, Maxim introduced into Russia the philological and philosophical sophistication of contemporary Italy, inaugurated the study of grammar as applied to Russian and Slavonic languages, and brought the learning of the Russian church more closely into line with the corpus of Greek Orthodox theology.

Like his contemporary, the great Lutheran scholar and apologist Philip Melanchthon (1497–1560), Maxim the Greek used the skills and intellectual armament of Italian humanism to defend a dogmatic faith. He was a man in whom a convulsive reaction against the intellectual pluralism and open-endedness of Italian renaissance culture had provoked a crying need for certainty. He found what he needed in the hesychast pattern of Orthodox piety; whereupon he put the intellectual acuity, erudition, and literary skills he had acquired in the course of his secular education to new uses: exploring, defending, and expositing old truths with sophisticated new techniques.

Through Maxim's work in Russia, the fundamentally Greek orientation of Muscovite Christianity was confirmed, and by planting the humanist skills of Italian scholarship and learning in the chilly, inhospitable soil of Russia, Maxim did much to armor the Russians intellectually against the force of Catholic proselytism. His importance for the Russian church is illustrated by the fact that in the seventeenth century, when bitter quarrels divided the official hierarchy from the Old Believers, both factions claimed him as their own.[26]

Nonetheless, in the short run Maxim's mission must have been judged a failure in Constantinople. Formal reconciliation between the œcumenical patriarch and the metropolitan of Moscow did not ensue until 1589. The gap between Maxim's Platonizing, speculative mind and the xenophobic piety of Russian churchmen was too great to be bridged all at once, as his condemnation as a heretic made evident. Only toward the end of the sixteenth century, when a much intensified Roman Catholic propaganda began to make real inroads upon Orthodoxy, did the seeds Maxim had sown in Russian minds begin to bear fruit.

Maxim's own career and his collision with the intolerant, fearful hierarchs of the Russian church were symptomatic of a very widespread reaction against too much innovation and resultant psychological uncertainty that set in between 1480 and 1520 at many points around the periphery of the field of force that Italian renaissance culture had created for itself. Wherever Italian influence penetrated it carried with it a kind of professional expertise that grated upon local custom and offended indigenous amour propre. Hostility normally took religious form. Incandescent clerics mobilized wider groups to oppose the impious secularism characteristic of the rich and privileged foreigners. In doing so they verbalized and focused the otherwise inchoate resentment against the disturbances Italians brought to customary routines. The Italians' nascent professionalism—as bankers, merchants, engineers, architects, Latinists, musicians, actors, or arbiters of taste—was in fact not tied in any close or binding way to Christian or any other kind of faith. This exposed the intruders to religious attack; and rightly so, because the secular attitudes and values developed in the urban environments of the Italian renaissance were basically irreconcilable with sacred local custom.

This encounter coincided, of course, with other kinds of social dislocation. In particular, political relations altered drastically with the spread of artillery, enhancing the outreach of a few distant and, from a local point of view, often tyrannous courts. The whole mix simultaneously became more volatile thanks to the cheapening of communication that followed upon the invention of printing. Such conditions produced personal and psychological distress, at least among an elite of serious and sensitive persons. Most of them responded as Maxim the Greek did by demanding a clear, unambiguous definition of truth, to provide a firm basis for conduct. Many went further, demanding ruthless repression of all who propagated error and sowed confusion, i.e., all who disagreed with the truth upon which they pinned their personal faith.

Toward the center of western Christendom, where urban complexity was of long standing, experts and rulers had gotten used to putting up with a plurality of views, however uncomfortable the resulting conflicts of opinion might be. Really convulsive responses to the widening uncertainties of life developed mainly on the periphery of Europe. Here simpler societies collided, sometimes all at once, with the incoherent totality of skills and ideas that had developed so cancerously in northern Italy since the thirteenth century. Two options opened: either revolutionary challenge to constituted authority in the name of old-fashioned truth and righteousness, or, if preexisting governing institutions were not too deeply entangled in detestable pluralism and professionalism, an administrative purge aimed at extirpating error, however defined and wherever discoverable.

The lower classes of Italy and adjacent regions shared some of the characteristics of geographically peripheral regions, being in their own way also peripheral to the thought-world of the urban upper classes. Thus the fervent response to Savonarola in Florence, 1494–98, was a revolutionary thrust after holiness and certainty, very similar to the spirit that informed subsequent peripheral revolts triggered by Shah Isma'il (1499) and Martin Luther (1517). But in Italy there were powerful countervailing forces that soon mobilized themselves to crush Savonarola's movement, whereas, in remote Azerbaidzhan and Saxony, Isma'il (d. 1524) and Luther (d. 1546) both lived to see their revolutionary movements well on the way to lasting institutionalization.[27]

Spain, Muscovy, and the Ottoman Empire were the three great states that resorted to revolution from above, capturing and canalizing the emotional force of this sort of revulsion against pluralism by using constituted administrative channels to express it.[28] In the short run, each of these vast imperial structures probably gained strength and stability from the identification of state power with a fixed form of faith; in the long run, however, it seems clear that each of them suffered from the rigidity of the belief system which their early sixteenth-century success imposed on later generations.

The case of Spain is of only marginal concern here. Ferdinand and Isabella assigned the task of assuring uniformity of Catholic belief to the Inquisition. This was a special ecclesiastical and royal court established in the 1480s to unmask and punish Marranos and Moriscos, that is, persons who had ostensibly accepted Christian baptism while secretly retaining the Jewish or Moslem faith of their fathers. From relatively modest beginnings, the effort to purify Spain of unbelief went into high gear after 1492, when the last Moorish kingdom of the peninsula was conquered. First Jews (1492) and then Moslems (1502) were officially expelled from Castile, and the jurisdiction of the Inquisition was extended over all the kingdoms of Spain, despite some vigorous local resistance.

Simultaneously, under the leadership of Cardinal Ximenes (1437–1517), the learning and discipline of the Spanish clergy was strenuously upgraded. As a result, Spanish Catholicism took on a distinctive somber fanaticism (initially directed against Moslems and Jews) before colliding head-on with the twin challenges of Italian secularism and Lutheran heresy, which, between them, seemed to threaten the innermost citadel of Latin Christendom during the first half of the sixteenth century. Spanish faith and Spanish arms undertook the task of averting the danger, whatever the cost. Once committed thoroughly to the struggle, even the extraordinary adventure overseas in the Americas and beyond failed to divert Spaniards from their self-set task. Crises and uncertainty were met by more impassioned prayer and penitence. Intellectual reservations and doubts, if any, were rigorously repressed as much by private conscience as by public authority.[29]

Ottoman revulsion against secularism and unbelief is far less well known. Clearly, the death of Mehmed the Conqueror in 1481 triggered a reaction that put Sunni piety back into prominence at court.[30] Not long thereafter, in 1499, pursuit or religious conformity took on a new urgency and emotional intensity when Shah Isma'il Safavi challenged the legitimacy of Ottoman power by claiming to be the sole rightful heir of the Prophet. Many Moslems of Anatolia supported Shah Isma'il's revolutionary movement; thousands of them were slaughtered before Sultan Selim I (reigned 1512–20) felt himself secure. Moreover, in order to forestall any linkup between Shah Isma'il and the rulers of Egypt, and to keep the shah from fastening his power over Mecca and Medina and thus gaining a stronger basis for his claim to inherit the mantle of Muhammad, Sultan Selim seized Syria, Palestine, Egypt, and the Moslem holy cities of Arabia himself (1517), thus for the first time making the Ottoman state policeman to the heartlands of Islam. The Ottoman Empire thereby ceased to be a marginal polity within the Moslem world and instead took over heirship to the traditions of classical Islam. The shift meant stronger Arabic influence upon Ottoman life than before. Symbolic of the changed consciousness was the fact that beginning with Suleiman (reigned 1520–66), the older title, "Sultan of Rum [i.e., of Rome]," gave way to "Padishah of Islam" in the Ottoman rulers' official style.[31]

The task of securing a suitable level of religious uniformity throughout the vastly enlarged empire fell mainly to Selim's son and successor, Suleiman, known to Latins as "The Magnificent" and to Moslems as "The Lawgiver." As lawgiver, Suleiman gave the religious establishment of his empire a much firmer and more regular structure than earlier Islamic statesmen had ever dreamed of. He made experts in the Sacred Law of Islam into state officials, appointing them as *cadis* (judges) in each important town and city of the empire. Supervision of the establishment as a whole lodged in the capital, where an officer known as the *Sheik-ul-Islam* took on responsibilities for Moslems of the empire parallel to those borne by the œcumenical patriarch for Christians.[32] Like Ximenes in Spain, Suleiman also established new and reformed old schools and higher educational institutions (madrassas) where suitably pious persons could be trained for staffing the religious hierarchy he had brought, for the first time, under effective administrative discipline.[33]

The Ottomans did not, however, follow the Spanish example of trying to destroy religious dissenters. Selim toyed with the idea, then abandoned it; Suleiman never considered such a gross infraction of Moslem principles. Moreover, a wide spectrum of religious heterodoxy continued to exist just beneath the surface of Ottoman society, since diverse dervish communities remained in existence and taught mystical and latitudinarian doctrines to their initiates, without however daring to challenge official Sunni Islam and the Sacred Law as administered by the *cadis* of the empire, at least in public.

Suleiman could content himself with this residual (and traditional) diversity because it proved possible to discharge Moslem religious anxiety by warring successfully against Christendom, the hereditary enemy. A long series of victorious wars in the Mediterranean and on the Danube validated Ottoman legitimacy in the eyes of the Moslem community as a whole far more effectively than any sort of religious persecution at home could ever have done. As a result, after 1520 the crisis faded rapidly away, not least because the successors of Shah Isma'il (d. 1524) neither wished nor were able to sustain the white-hot enthusiasm of the initial sectarian outbreak.

Nevertheless, once bitten, twice shy: the Ottoman court never again treated Sunni Islam and outward manifestations of piety as lightly as Mehmed the Conqueror had done; and eventually the Sheik-ul-Islam became capable of legitimating and even of instigating the dethronement of a sultan who failed to measure up to expected standards of competence and piety. In harmony with the attitudes of the court and *ulema,* Moslems of the Ottoman Empire in general decided that it was unwise and unnecessary to be interested in novelties of any kind coming from beyond the pale of Islam. Hence such inventions as the printing press were deliberately rejected.[34] Members of the Moslem establishment of the Ottoman Empire, having been frightened by the Safavi religious challenge only to be reassured by the success of Suleiman's armies, simply closed off their minds from concern with, or interest in, anything that Christian Europe had to offer. A rigidity of mind and imperviousness to new experience resulted, far surpassing anything attained in Spain, despite the fact that Spanish official efforts at guaranteeing religious uniformity were far more strenuous.[35]

In Muscovy, Joseph of Volotsk, abbot of Volokolamsk (1440–1515), led the hue and cry against heretics. The so-called Judaizers were his immediate target; when Ivan III proved reluctant to persecute them vigorously (and even allowed some to find refuge at court), a church council of 1504 reproved his dereliction of duty, and the doughty saint persuaded the government to introduce the Spanish practice of burning condemned heretics at the stake.[36]

In the course of the next half century, men sharing the point of view championed so energetically by Joseph of Volotsk took control of the Russian church. They systematically repressed the anarchic striving after holiness which had been such a prominent feature of monastic life in the time of Saint Sergius of Radonezh, when the hesychast pattern of piety had first penetrated Russia.[37] As a result of disciplinary visits and heresy hunts, the Russian "trans-Volgan" monasteries, where the hesychast style of mysticism and holiness flourished, were reorganized along cenobitic lines; and within a few decades the sort of saints who had revivified Russian religiosity in the fourteenth and fifteenth centuries almost ceased to emerge.[38]

By 1551, when Ivan IV the Terrible (reigned 1533–84) summoned another council, Russian churchmen were prepared to defend their property even against the tsar, who wished to assign at least some monastic lands to the support of fighting men; they were also ready, no less vigorously (and frequently in ignorance of exact patristic precedent), to lay down Orthodox doctrine on points of dogma and ritual.[39] This implied complete disdain for the tradition of Greek Orthodoxy which held that only a general council of all the churches could define doctrine authoritatively, and that all essential doctrine had already been determined by the seven œcumenical councils of the early church.

Behind the Russian drive for regularity and discipline lay another, difficult ambivalence, affecting relations with the Latins. Latin influence had been felt in Novgorod from medieval times, thanks to the continual presence of German and other western merchants in that city. It had been the principal early center of the Judaizers, and a port of entry for uniate propaganda. In some respects, therefore, the tightening of discipline in the Russian church between 1480 and 1550 was part of an effort to expunge the traces of Latin religious and intellectual influence which had taken root in the merchant republic before its annexation (in 1478) by Moscow. Yet while administrative methods were capable of repressing and destroying such traces, a lingering sense of inferiority vis à vis western learning and other skills could not be exorcised entirely.

After the Stoglav council of 1551 had sealed the victory of the Josephists within the Russian church, however, this problem was temporarily relieved when Muscovy's neighbor to the west, the Polish-Lithuanian Commonwealth, began to witness a luxuriant growth of clashing religious opinions—Lutheran, Calvinist, and even Unitarian—together with large-scale confiscation of church lands. Such a spectacle gave Russian churchmen a more comfortable sense of the correctness of their chosen ecclesiastical path.[40]

The Russian Orthodox Church, therefore, could afford to remain smugly aloof from the controversies of the Reformation era in western Europe. The Spaniards, already engaged in Italy and tied dynastically to Germany, had no such option. But Spanish zeal did not falter even when faced with the task of reducing first Italy and then all of Christendom to Spanish ideals of piety, uniformity, and disciplined acceptance of Catholic truth. Such a program, even as very imperfectly realized through the Catholic reformation of the second half of the sixteenth century, reacted powerfully on eastern Europe and, as we shall see, provoked some striking and important realignments among the Greek and Slavic intellectual elites in the seventeenth century.

As a matter of fact, the Catholic reform as it impinged on eastern Europe, like the Protestantism it opposed, was the product of an extremely subtle and complex interaction between "Reformation" strivings after certainty and the "renaissance" thrust for professional autonomy and free elaboration of expertise, even when the latter involved potentially painful discrepancies of belief both within individual minds and amongst different professional groupings within society. This profound ambivalence was felt throughout Latin Christendom and, indeed, throughout Europe. Luther, like Ximenes and Maxim the Greek before him, relied upon humanist philology to guarantee the verbal accuracy of saving truths in biblical texts; and the rival theological camps regularly resorted to the tactic of "spoiling the Egyptians" whenever resources of secular culture and learning promised any advantage to their holy cause. Art, music, rhetoric, learning, history, and logic, disseminated as never before by busy printing presses, were freely appropriated for sacred purposes; and even while Spanish viceroys were doing all they could in the first half of the sixteenth century to bring unruly Italy to heel, skilled and ambitious Italians (mostly Genoese) were busy exporting to Spain for use in the Americas techniques of overseas empire and economic administration which had first been worked out in the Levant.[41] John Cabot (1450–98) and his son Sebastian (1476–1557), born respectively in Genoa and in Venice, performed a similar service for England, the latter being a founder and governor of the Merchant Adventures of London, the first successful London-based joint stock company which opened trade with Russia via Archangel in 1555.[42]

Spain's domination of Italy, sealed by the Peace of Cateau-Cambresis in 1559, involved the domestication of Spanish intolerant religiosity in Italy, though of course there was no simple and wholesale transference, and important elements within the papal court remained resentful and suspicious of Spanish preponderance long after the papacy had aligned itself unambiguously behind the effort, inspired initially from Spain, to enforce newly defined Catholic uniformity on all Christendom, wherever political conditions would permit.

Generally speaking, it was in the decade of the 1540s that the papacy began to take seriously efforts at religious reform; but not until after 1559 did the popes acquiesce in Spanish political preponderance in Italy and undertake a concerted effort to roll back Protestant heresy and other forms of religious error in trans-Alpine lands. Until the 1570s the Venetians went along with papal policy for the most part, fearing the Turks, who continued to advance ineluctably both by sea and land, even more than they disliked the encroachment of Spanish power within the Italian peninsula.

Thus Venetians played no very active role in the Council of Trent (1545–47, 1551–52, 1562–63) which did so much to consolidate the papal monarchy over the Roman church. The papal Inquisition was admitted to Venetian territory in 1542, the year of its establishment; but its activities were circumscribed by the fact that lay magistrates appointed to cope with heresy were required to participate in and approve the Inquisition's acts. As a result, trials for heresy were unimportant in Venice, and the city continued to allow foreigners of diverse religious faiths to come and go as they pleased. Similarly, the Jesuits were permitted to establish a lower school at Padua and to set up other establishments elsewhere on Venetian soil, but they were not permitted to teach at an advanced level in open rivalry with the secularly minded professors of the university.

Tolerance of religious diversity did not imply indifference. On the contrary, many Venetians cultivated a vigorous personal piety, and the state supported due and decorous observation of all traditional rituals and regulations. Consequently, among Venetians of the sixteenth century, Protestantism met with as little positive response as did Spanish-style Catholicism. Venetian society had already invented effective safety valves for the psychological strains inherent in their mode of life, and no particular crisis arose to require or provoke abandonment of the inherited patterns.[43] Instead, the rites of carnival continued to undergo elaboration, and aspects of carnival behavior broke the calendrical limitations by becoming more or less a year-round feature of the Venetian scene. Thus, for example, theater productions, open to the public on purchase of a ticket through most of the year, were established in Venice in 1565, when the world's first commerical theater, constructed specially for play-acting, opened. The method of finance and the character of the plays performed derived largely from practices initially confined to the carnival season.[44] Social satire, usually involving sexual entanglements, thus became a normal and very popular element in the public cultural life of Venice.

How this so-called *commedia dell'arte* began remains obscure, although the traditional attributes of Harlequin and his fellows clearly point to Venice, Padua, and Bologna as their locus of origin. From the 1550s, however, touring companies going from festival to festival and before long from court to court made the art pan-Italian; and after the organization of the "Gelosi" company, whose earliest surviving record dates from 1568, a level of professionalism was attained which soon attracted royal patronage as far away as Paris (1571). Thereafter the new Italian style of theatricals spread throughout Europe, penetrating Turkey in the sixteenth, Poland in the seventeenth, and Russia in the eighteenth centuries.

Thus within Italy what began as unrecorded popular and public entertainment entered surviving records as it began to attract princely patronage. Association with royal courts in turn made the art exportable beyond the Alps, where in varying ways and degrees it reversed the earlier pattern of social drift by again becoming popular. This involved, of course, alteration and blending with local traditions until the Italian element became only dimly recognizable.[45]

Closely related to the emergence of the *commedia dell'arte* and year-round commercial theatricals, open to the public, was the extraordinary elaboration of courtesan life in Venice. This developed a style and culture of its own. Witty conversation, elegant dress, music, poesy, play-going, gambling, and refinements of food and drink came to be intimately associated with prostitution as patronized by the upper classes. The attraction of such styles of life was attested by artists, many of whom, including Titian and Dürer, portrayed Venetian courtesans and used them as models for both pagan and sacred scenes. Even more significant was the fact that Venetian ladies of aristocratic family began to ape courtesan dress and behavior, not only in carnival season but throughout the year.[46]

The sensuality on display in Venice, as some of Titian's nudes may remind us, increased rather than diminished as the century wore on. This stood in growing contrast to the effort to repress all sinful lusts that constituted a major thrust of the Catholic reformation in other parts of Italy. Indeed, in proportion as sexual and other kinds of repression actually took root in Italy and in Europe generally under the goad of Protestant and Catholic forms in puritanism, it is plausible to believe that the flamboyant indulgence of the senses permitted by Venetian law and custom acquired a peculiar power over the imagination of Europe's upper classes—compounded of repugnance and fascination, admiration and fear, love and hate. As a result, by the end of the seventeenth century, Venetian styles of dissipation, if nothing else, had become normative for the aristocrats of the whole of Latin and Germanic Europe.[47]

Simultaneously, the intellectual venturesomeness of Paduan medicine and philosophy reached its apex. Anatomists carried on the tradition of Vesalius, correcting details he had missed. Gabriello Fallopio (1523–62), for instance, gave his name to the oviducts he discovered; and on his death the chair of anatomy at Padua passed to Fabricius ab Aquapendente (1537–1619), "the greatest of all teachers of anatomy,"[48] who raised embryology and comparative anatomy to a new level of accuracy and scope through close observation of how tissues differentiate in embryos and how the organs of one animal species match those of others. Such studies, obviously, narrowed the gap between men and animals, and made the traditional distinction between men, possessing immortal souls, and animals, without any such endowment, more and more implausible.

In philosophy, the Paduans confronted this problem head-on, following the path Pomponazzi had first traced out. Careful philosological study of Aristotle's texts, with special emphasis upon his biological and other scientific writings, abstracted the pagan philosopher's thought from its scholastic, Christian integument. Jacopo Zabarella (1532–1589) brought this development to full flower, treating the human soul as no more than a bodily function.[49]

The notion that knowledge was capable of advancement through new discoveries, deriving from observation and generalization from such observations, came to clear expression in Zabarella's writing. Such a point of view was profoundly unsettling to all who sought to close off uncertainty by affirming all-embracing truths, whether of theology or metaphysics. Yet in a university where medical discoveries were matters of course, and in an age when geographical and ethnographic discoveries stormed in upon Europe with the report of every new transoceanic voyage,[50] any view of knowledge as a closed system, discoverable in some authoritative text—biblical, philosophical, or mystical—could only be maintained by an act of faith. The leading professors at Padua declined to make this sacrifice of their intelligence, with the result that the university became the leading center of scientific discovery in Europe.

The intellectual tone of the university had a significant effect, too, upon the mental outlook of the Venetian ruling class. A good many young Venetian noblemen spent some time as students at the university,[51] but few of them ever learned to take abstract ideas seriously.[52] That ran counter to something very deep in the ethos of the Venetian noble class, whose concerns were practical and whose preferred avocations were sensual rather than cerebral. Nonetheless, in 1571 Venetian subjects were legally forbidden to attend any other institution of higher learning. It seems clear that this prohibition was intended to exclude the contagion of Counter-Reformation papalism, championed principally by the Jesuits, from Venetian soil. The men directing the Venetian state viewed doctrines making the pope superior to any and all temporal sovereigns as subversive. By virtue of their reaction against Jesuit teachings with respect to papal power more than from any deep sympathy or inward acceptance of the implications of Aristotelian scientific naturalism as taught at Padua, the clique of nobles ruling the state thus came to identify Venetian patriotism with the free-ranging traditions of Paduan science and philosophy.

Jesuit and other pious efforts to check heretical thoughts therefore met systematic resistance from Venetian magistrates, who saw behind all such initiatives the sinister hand of the pope seeking to extend his authority into Venetian territories at the expense of their own rightful jurisdiction. As long as cooperation with the pope in questions of Italian and Mediterranean politics seemed necessary, the Venetians compromised and fudged, rather than taking abstract issue with papal claims as defined by the Council of Trent and championed by impassioned Jesuit agents. After the breakup of the Holy League in 1573, however, latent conflicts burst into the open. At the same time, papal missionary activity turned to Orthodox Christendom with renewed energy, rudely awakening Greek and Russian churchmen from the dogmatic slumber that had dominated the hierarchy of both these branches of the Orthodox church since 1453. Sharing a common plight as targets of papal attack, Venice and Orthodox Christendom were thrown together in the period 1573–1630 as never before or after.

Even before this time of special Venetian-Orthodox collaboration, Venice's vigorous intellectual and artistic life stirred a slender but significant response among the Greeks. Crete, the capstone of Venetian empire overseas since 1211, played a key role as go-between. We have already noted the faint but perceptible Italian traces upon the style of the influential Cretan artist, Theophanes (d. 1559).[53] In intellectual matters, Crete also was able to act as an effective intermediary. A small learned class had existed in the island ever since 1453, when a number of highly educated Greeks arrived in Crete after the Turkish capture of Constantinople. Some remained there and established a considerable reputation in the world of Italian scholarship by copying Greek manuscripts. About the middle of the sixteenth century, a trickle of Cretan young men showed up in Padua. Two of them, Meletios Pigas (ca. 1535–

1601) and Maximos Margunios (ca. 1549–1602), became note-worthy scholars. Unlike earlier generations of learned Greeks, these men had the possibility of returning home to make a career in Greek-speaking lands. Margunios, for example, was twice invited to Constantinople to take charge of the patriarchal academy there. He did return to Crete on completing his studies at Padua and became a monk; visited Constantinople in 1584 but decided not to take responsibility for the academy; and spent most of the rest of his life in Venice, trying to reconcile Latin and Greek theology by writing learned treatises on the Trinity. Pigas, on the other hand, made his entire career in the east. On returning to Crete, he was probably responsible for organizing (or reorganizing) a school at Saint Catherine's monastery in Candia which, from about 1550, became an effective preparatory school for the University of Padua. Five years later, another Padua alumnus, Theodore Zygomales (d. 1580), took charge of the patriarchal academy in Constantinople, with the result that in the second half of the sixteenth century a flow of bright young men began to issue both from Candia and from Constantinople to attend the University of Padua. Medical training was particularly sought after; but such training was usually combined with liberal arts and always involved a considerable exposure to the kind of naturalistic Aristotelianism dominating Padua's philosophic instruction.

Some three-score Greeks had earned degrees from Padua and then returned to Greek-speaking lands by the 1570s, when relations between Catholic and Orthodox communities took on a new character, thanks to the papacy's effort to organize systematic missionary endeavor among the Orthodox. This meant that when Orthodox churchmen first felt the force of the new Catholic propaganda, a handful of strategically placed persons within the fold of Orthodoxy were ready and able to meet the Catholic challenge more or less on its own terms, thanks to their prior exposure to the full array of Latin learning at the University of Padua.[54]

This, then, was the situation as the clash of rival world views, generated by Europe's profound and painful sixteenth-century transmogrifications, moved toward a climax in the years 1573–1630. The Dutch revolt (1568–1609) and the wars of religion in France (1562–98), together with the beginning of the Puritan movement in England, were dramatic enough and pregnant for the future not merely of western Europe but of the whole world. The simultaneous perturbations in eastern Europe were no less dramatic, and as northwestern Europe's nineteenth-century dominance over the world diminishes perhaps the pattern of events that worked itself out in this other part of Europe can also claim world-wide significance, if only because Muscovy became Russia in passing through what traditionally, and very aptly, is called the "Time of Troubles" (1604–13).

From a political and sociological point of view, the upheavals through which eastern (and much of western) Europe passed after 1573 may be seen as a conflict between aristocratic and bureaucratic patterns of social management. In western Europe, with its more complex social stratification and more numerous towns, no single, unambiguous upshot of this struggle can be discerned; but in the relatively thinly occupied parts of eastern Europe, bureaucratic empire won out clearly and emphatically by 1650.[55] In the Ottoman Empire, however, where urban and ethnic complexity was far older and more fully developed than in Russia and the Danubian lands, bureaucratic elements in the state continued in dubious battle (and symbiosis) with various kinds of upstart landowners into the nineteenth century.[56]

In ideological terms, dogmatically defined religious groupings became the protagonists of a bitter struggle conducted on a continent-wide basis. By the last quarter of the sixteenth century, Calvinism and Catholicism were the rivals that everywhere disturbed and challenged conservative-minded Europeans. Each claimed full possession of saving Christian truth; each had clear and logically impressive evidences and authorities with which to buttress its own vision of the truth; and each was served by a body of educated, eloquent, and deeply committed true-believers who felt that nothing was more important than spreading their knowledge of God's truth to men everywhere for the salvation of souls.

Such missionaries made things uncomfortable for Venice,

and for Orthodox Christians, whether adherents of the Greek, Russian, or one of the lesser (Serbian, Rumanian, Ukrainian) churches. Despite great initial success in both Poland and Hungary, Calvinist reform had only fleeting significance for Orthodox Christendom. Calvin's rejection of most traditional ceremonies ran counter to an element that was central to Orthodox (as well as to Venetian) forms of Christianity. Perhaps for this reason, as well as because Calvinist preachers and reformers were less well organized and disciplined than their Roman Catholic counterparts, Calvinism never took hold seriously either in Venetian or in Orthodox territories. On the other hand, Roman Catholic missionary activity in eastern Europe achieved a new level of organized purposiveness under Pope Gregory XIII (r. 1572–85) and his successor Sixtus V (r. 1585–90), with the result that both Venice and all parts of the Orthodox world had to look to their defenses against the arguments and organizational energy of Jesuit and other agents of Catholic renovation.

From a Roman point of view, the period between 1573 and 1617 was immensely promising, yet also disturbing. After the breakup of the Holy League in 1573, alliance with and reliance upon Spanish power ceased to be a practicable policy. Entanglements with the Dutch and English attracted all the military strength the Spanish monarchy could spare from routine maintenance of its world-girdling empire. This meant that the papacy was freer to act on its own, even in Italy, than before 1559 when Spanish power had been aggressively advancing through the peninsula. It also meant that across the broad expanse of central and eastern Europe there was no single strong state upon which the popes could rely to advance the cause of Catholic reform. Not until Ferdinand II (r. 1617–37) succeeded to the Hapsburg possessions of Austria, Bohemia, and associated lands did such a champion emerge. Before his time the Austrian lands, like the rest of central and eastern Europe, were heavily infiltrated by varying forms of heresy: Lutheran, Calvinist, Hussite, not to mention more radical Unitarian and other sectarian movements.

Between 1573 and 1617, therefore, the Roman church had to rely on its own resources more completely than either before or after. This was, accordingly, the Jesuits' greatest age, when missions in Japan, China, and the Americas advanced with giant steps, matched by successes no less spectacular in south Germany, Poland, Constantinople, and the Ukraine. To be sure, in northwestern Europe—Holland and Britain above all Jesuit and Catholic efforts met with conspicuous failure in these years. Venice, too, stubbornly resisted papal power, and the Venetian example of how to oppose papalism naturally attracted sympathetic attention among Protestants and Orthodox alike.

This was of considerable importance for European history as a whole, for the Venetians found themselves, willy-nilly, defending on very old-fashioned grounds a cluster of ideas and practices that anticipated in important respects the liberal, pluralist outlook of subsequent generations. In the late sixteenth century when most sensitive and highly educated Europeans sought for a single, all-embracing truth as a necessary guide to conduct and hope for salvation, Venice continued to defend a different way of life. In doing so, the Venetians, quite unwittingly of course, played a conspicuous part in transmitting the idea and practice of pluralism from Italian to trans-Alpine parts of Europe. In similar fashion, important elements of Venetian thought and culture filtered into the Orthodox world, giving an intellectual cutting edge to Greek and Russian resistance to Roman Catholic propaganda on the one hand, and on the other, implanting a secular and scientific style of learning among the Greeks which eventually permitted them to take over the role of go-between for the Turks in dealings with the European powers.

Obviously, changing conditions within the Ottoman Empire had much to do with the remarkable receptivity a handful of strategically well-placed Greeks showed to stimuli emanating from Venice and Padua between 1573 and 1617. The fundamental fact was that by the 1570s Turkish territorial expansion had almost reached its limit. The spectacular Ottoman advances into Hungary of Suleiman's youth ended during the 1550s as a hedgehog of frontier fortresses sprang up, making it impossible for the Turks to advance securely more than a few miles beyond their recognized borders.[57] Further east, an unruly band of border states—Transylvania, Wallachia and Moldavia, Crim Tartary and the Cossack *sech*—admitted a hazy, shifty dependence upon one or more of the neighboring great powers—Turkey, the Hapsburg Empire, Poland, or Muscovy—though really successful local rulers were regularly tempted to aim at full and sovereign independence. Acute political instability resulted; but this, in turn, reflected the fact that each of the great powers, Turkey included, had to operate at its extreme effective range of action when seeking to bring any of these marginal polities under control.

The cessation of Ottoman expansion meant that Venice had more room for maneuver and could, in fact, court Turkish and French (not to mention Dutch and English) support against Hapsburg-papal pressures. The consequences for Ottoman society were far more serious. From its inception the Ottoman government had found income from booty and freshly conquered lands very helpful in maintaining the extraordinary centralization of power that Mehmed the Conqueror and his successors to the time of Suleiman the Lawgiver had wielded. Without booty windfalls, the government had to extract more money, goods, and services from the population within Ottoman borders. This, together with the rigid consolidation of a Moslem landlord class interested in market sale more than in a supply of goods in kind for mere subsistance (which was all simple-minded, hard-riding *timariots* in times past had expected), tended to harden class and religious-ethnic lines as never before.

The Ottoman Empire, of course, shared in the general Mediterranean crisis that set in toward the end of the sixteenth century, discussed in chapter 4. Matters were exacerbated for the Turks by a sharp change in the character of the reigning sultans, which resulted from a change in the succession law. Previously, the sons of a reigning sultan, as soon as they came of suitable age, were expected to serve an apprenticeship as provincial governors. Succession often depended on which of several rival sons was closest to the capital at the moment of his father's death. The grim custom of eliminating possible rivals by executing brothers (and half-brothers) on each new sultan's accession raised a possibility that the House of Osman might die out if a particular sultan failed to have children. Accordingly after the time of Ahmed I (reigned 1603–17) it became customary to confine the reigning sultan's close male relatives to "cages" within the palace,[58] where they lived under the watchful eye of the palace guards, insulated from war and politics, but available as a stud to produce heirs for the House of Osman, or in case of need to assume the throne themselves. This system meant that each succeeding sultan came to the throne untrained and unprepared for the tasks of running a great state. As a result, high officials had far freer range; deposition of a sultan could and did occur without much changing the realities of power; and the skills that brought men to the top came to be those of harem intrigue as much or more than the military virtues which had once mattered so much.

Conversions to Islam from among the sultan's Christian subjects continued, and their scale probably increased. On the other hand, forcible recruitment to the sultan's slave family by rounding up Christian boys from the western Balkan villages ceased to be important after Selim II (reigned 1566–74) permitted members of his household to insinuate their sons into the ranks of the janissary corps. This meant that social mobility decreased. Men like Grand Vizier Mehmed Sokolu, born a Christian who nonetheless became, as grand vizier, (1560–79) the most powerful man in the entire Ottoman state, almost ceased to exist. Social status, in other words, tended to become more nearly hereditary.

As a consequence, the counterpoise between peasant and townsman, Christian and Moslem, which had been maintained by means of the recruitment pattern to the imperial slave family, altered sharply. Townsmen and Moslems, having preferred access to nearly all positions of power, began to exploit the Christian peasantry more ruthlessly than before. Correspondingly, the Serb-Turk alignment, which had depended upon Serbian preponderance within the ranks of the sultan's slave family, wore itself out.[59]

On the other hand, Jews, especially those who had come to Ottoman lands as refugees from Spain, came to play an important role in the empire's economic life, and some of them were able to influence government policies. The most spectacular instance of this was the extraordinary career of Joseph Nasi (ca. 1520–1579), friend and confidant of Sultan Selim II, and from 1566 Duke of Naxos. Nasi was instrumental in arranging for the Turkish attack on Cyprus in 1571;[60] he also reorganized the Aegean wine trade by developing export markets in Poland and around the coasts of the Black Sea. Through his efforts and those of others, the medieval east-west axis of the Mediterranean wine trade which had brought malmsey to England in exchange for wool was superseded by a north-south flow, supplying Polish palates with the same wines. The Polish nobles paid mainly in cash, which they had at their disposal thanks to mounting grain exports to western Europe and, after 1590, to the grain-short Mediterranean itself.[61]

Nasi owed some of his success to the thorough familiarity with western Christendom which he brought with him from Flanders where he had spent his youth. Other Jews, especially medical men, shared this sort of expertise. Doctors who acquired such a reputation that sultan and grand vizier commanded their services found themselves automatically catapulted into positions of great strategic importance. It was easy for an Ottoman official, having entrusted his bodily welfare to a stranger, to learn also to rely on the same man's advice and information relating to political, military, and diplomatic matters. The career of Solomon Askenazi, born a Venetian subject and educated in Padua, exemplifies this avenue to power. He served as personal physician first to the king of Poland, then to the grand vizier, who, among other things, entrusted him with negotiation of the peace of 1573 with Venice.[62]

With the passage of time, however, the Jewish community of the Ottoman Empire tended to lose its connections with the Christian west. Access to professional training in Italy and elsewhere in Catholic Europe became much more difficult as papal anti-Jewish regulations took effect.[63] As a result, the age in which Jews were able to act as principal go-betweens for the Turks in their dealings with western Europe ended in the seventeenth century, when they were displaced by Greeks.

As might be expected, these far-reaching sociopolitical realignments within the Ottoman Empire also affected the Turks themselves. Among Moslems everywhere, the approach of the millennium of Islam[64] excited considerable speculation about the probable end of the world. The fact that after 1584 a galloping financial crisis beset the central government, resulting in sharp monetary devaluation and an upheaval of traditional price levels, lent special edge to such speculations. The artisan classes of the empire suffered some real damage from about this time, partly as a result of price instabilities, partly because of foreign competition. A more rigorous organization of guilds and official government sanction for various kinds of restrictive practices were intended to cushion (or at least insure an equal sharing of) such hardships. But such behavior was counterproductive in the long run, making effective competition with foreign imports increasingly difficult.[65]

More important politically was the fact that salaried officials and soldiers saw their income diminish drastically. As a result, state services suffered serious erosion, and the efforts of particular officials to recoup losses by demanding bribes for performance of routine duties did nothing to remedy the situation. Only a few bureaucrats and soldiers had contacts with the public that allowed them to increase their income by accepting bribes while continuing to perform prescribed and traditional functions with undiminished efficiency. Most officials worked within the administrative structure itself, assuring an appropriate flow of information, manpower, and material resources up and down the hierarchy of tax collectors and tax expenders. When such persons had to take on additional jobs to make ends meet—as happened among the janissaries *en masse,* so that they became at least as much artisans as soldiers by the middle of the seventeenth century—or when officials began to steal government supplies to sell or use for themselves, then the effectiveness of the Ottoman government as a device for mobilizing the resources of the society at large for public purposes underwent rapid and palpable decay. Among other things, such a development almost guaranteed continued failure in warfare against the Christian states of Europe whose capacities to mobilize their subjects' energies for war increased sporadically under the whiplash of recurrent intestinal struggles. The Thirty Years' War (1618–48) was particularly important in this

186

connection, provoking and permitting the Austrian Hapsburg power to begin to overtake Ottoman levels of mobilization. Yet while the Ottoman polity as a whole undoubtedly suffered, some high officials profited handsomely from bribes, and landowners benefited directly from price inflation. By organizing the production of marketable crops, including such new, labor-intensive commodities as tobacco, an estate owner had everything to gain from rising prices since he did not have to pay wages in cash. Enterprising landlords relied instead on force or threat of force to conscript peasant labor for the tasks of cultivating domain land—the so-called *chiflik*. Alternatively, landlords could commandeer an increasing proportion of the peasants' own crop by direct seizure. Such acts were illegal, but those enforcing the law were inclined to wink at acts of oppression against the peasantry, since they were themselves often doing exactly the same thing.

Thus a small but conspicuous Moslem upper class was able to flourish while Ottoman government and society at large suffered. Indeed, the government's financial crisis, exactly like that which had paralyzed the Byzantine government in its last days, arose fundamentally from the fact that landowners succeeded in intercepting more of the yield of the land than before, while permitting less to reach the central offices of government. Correspondingly (and again recapitulating the Byzantine experience), landowners were no longer compelled to rally regularly to the sultan's colors and accept the hardships of a campaign. Instead they stayed home and concentrated on finding ways to increase their income at the expense both of the peasants who tilled the soil and of the central government.[66]

Economic difficulties at home and the cessation of victory abroad had serious implications for Moslem thought and self-confidence. As long as success had continued to crown Ottoman standards, the Moslems of the empire could and did argue that the favor which Allah continued to shower upon Ottoman arms attested the correctness of their faith. When successes ceased, the inference was obvious. Clearly, Allah was displeased; and reasons were not far to seek. From almost the beginning of Islam, pious and fanatical puritans had taught that all innovation that went beyond the practices attested in the

Koran was displeasing to God. This was a doctrine that demanded reformation of existing Ottoman religious practices every bit as radical as anything dreamed of by the Calvinist reform program for Christianity. The two movements coincided closely in time, for in the final decades of the sixteenth century and throughout the first half of the seventeenth, so-called *faki* preachers inflamed popular discontents, already acute for economic reasons, by demanding uncompromising adherence to Koranic models of piety. The *faki* attacked the official hierarchy of Ottoman Islam for criminal laxity in condoning innovations of all sorts. They attacked the dervish orders no less vigorously for the heterodoxy of their opinions and ritual practices.[67]

Despite their passion and popular following, the *faki* did not prevail and were never able to seize political power. Their cultural influence was negative, inhibiting all but the rich and privileged from exploring novelties, whether intellectual or otherwise, for which Koranic sanction was lacking. Even long-established rational sciences—imported into Moslem learning in Abbasid times—withered away as subjects of instruction in public institutions of higher learning. Symbolic of this transformation was the fact that in 1580 the Sheik-ul-Islam ordered the destruction of the sultan's private observatory. This institution had been as well equipped as any in Europe; but when popular preachers interpreted an outbreak of plague in Istanbul as a sign of Allah's displeasure at the sultan's impious efforts to penetrate God's secrets by astrological science, the observatory (which was, in fact, inspired by astrological curiosity) had to go.[68]

When well-established Moslem cultural traditions came under such attack, innovations from the Christian world obviously invited double damnation. When even the rich and powerful had to be careful in pursuing traditional but religiously dubious diversions, serious efforts to come to terms with the swarm of new things arising in the Christian west was out of the question. On the other hand, the development of a leisured landlord class in the provinces, freed from the burden of regular military service, enlarged the public for fundamentally Persian, but long since Islamicized, styles of genteel living.

Yet the fact that this tradition flirted with religious heresy made it safer to pursue the delights of love poetry, for instance, within the privacy of the harem than in more public places.[69]

Hence it is not really surprising that the private and personal sides of Ottoman high culture (as distinct from such public arts as architecture, which attained its apogee with the work of Sinan [1491–1588][70] but decayed after 1617 when financial difficulties began to paralyze the state) continued to flourish during the seventeenth century. Literature and art remained strictly within lines laid down earlier, mainly in the sixteenth century, when Ottoman poetry, miniature-painting, and other arts attained their classical definition. By that time, the Turks had had time to digest the Persian and Arabic inheritances that they had imported wholesale in the fifteenth century. Accordingly, during the empire's greatest days, a cluster of poets and artists succeeded in creating their own distinctively Ottoman modulation of the wider Islamic tradition. Creativity continued in the seventeenth century, with some loss of vigor perhaps but with no decay of virtuosity.[71]

Natural science was especially vulnerable to *faki* attack. There was no social class or secure institutional refuge within which such studies could continue in spite of *faki* assaults. The Moslems of the empire therefore abandoned even such traditional pursuits as medicine and mathematical astronomy-astrology. Doctors and fortune-tellers could be found among Jews and Christians, after all. Such religiously suspect professions were accordingly handed over to unbelievers, leaving the field of Moslem higher education to narrowly traditional religious studies and skills. Geography alone survived, for the Turks could not afford to neglect entirely the new information and new concepts (longitude and latitude, magnetic variation, etc.) available in the west. Thus in 1583 a Spanish work on the discovery of America was translated into Turkish. More significant was the translation of Mercator's *Atlas*. This was carried through by Haji Halfa (1608–1657), a polymath and the first Turk who seriously attempted to come to grips with some of the scientific advances which came so rapidly to western Europe in the seventeenth century.[72]

Nevertheless, attention devoted to novelties from the alien

world of Christendom was minimal. The weight of a thoroughly conservative educational system inherited from the time of Suleiman the Lawgiver entirely overbalanced concern about new things. Novelty in matters of religion and law were by definition wrong, indeed dangerous and deserving punishment. Memorization of sacred texts and of commentaries upon them was the substance of higher education; divagation from well-worn and accustomed verbal formulae was the way to perdition. With such training, it is small wonder that Moslems paid almost no attention to the religious and intellectual upheavals that beset Christendom in the sixteenth-seventeenth centuries. No Moslem even bothered to inquire into the dogmatic quarrels and innovations that kept Christendom in such an uproar.

The Orthodox clergy of Constantinople were, for the most part, inclined to do exactly the same as their Moslem counterparts. Concentrating on the art of getting ahead by ruthless fiscality and intrigue, church leaders had little time even for legal training;[73] and were normally content to argue that whatever was, was right because it had been handed down in that way from their Orthodox forerunners.

When challenged to react to the Lutheran definition of the Christian faith in 1559, the œcumenical patriarch chose not to reply; when in 1574 Lutheran divines of Tübingen again solicited Greek doctrinal support against the papacy, Patriarch Jeremias II called on Paduan-trained Theodore Zygomales to formulate a reply. The Greek scholar took up each article of the Augsburg Confession, and expressed agreement and disagreement courteously but firmly. The Germans responded by trying to minimize differences. This provoked a series of increasingly tart responses from the Greek side, until the correspondence was broken off in 1581 at the request of Patriarch Jeremias.[74]

On the whole, the Greeks emerged from this initial brush with western theologians very creditably, thanks to the availability of Theodore Zygomales, whose education in the west allowed him to move intellectually on the same plane as the Lutheran divines. Yet the fundamental weakness of the œcumenical patriarchate was plain enough. What forced the reluctant patriarch to embark upon theological debate with the

Germans in the first place was pressure from the Hapsburg ambassador to Turkey (who was a Lutheran). Catholic-minded ambassadors soon followed suit, bringing pressure to bear upon Greek prelates to accede to Catholic interests. The Greek church therefore found itself riven with intrigue as ambitious prelates began to seek patronage and promotion through association with one or another foreign embassy. And since westerners, whether Protestant or Catholic, insisted on credal definitions and precise catechetical commitment, the old custom of defining Orthodoxy simply as the way things were no longer sufficed. If Orthodoxy were not to be engulfed entirely, new formulations somehow had to be found that would define the faith in forms equivalent to those brandished so vigorously by the rival Protestant and Roman Catholic propagandists.

Before considering subsequent orthodox efforts to cope with western missionary zeal, it seems best to summarize the manner in which the Venetian government and their intellectual champions clashed with the papacy, and then return to a survey of how the echoes of this and the other controversies of the age affected Orthodox Christendom.

To many at the papal court, the peace which Venice concluded with the Turks in 1573 seemed unforgivable. Just when at long last the infidels were on the run, Venice chose to withdraw, thereby playing traitor to the cause of Christendom! A generation before, Venice had also made peace with the Turks under somewhat similar circumstances; but on that occasion hard feelings were papered over again because both Venetians and Hapsburgs soon found it necessary to renew cooperation against Turkish aggressiveness. No such compulsion modulated the resentments generated in 1573; on the contrary, a kind of stiff-necked civic pride took hold among the leaders of the Venetian state which induced them to oppose papal policy more and more openly.

Venetians, first of all, felt it was their contribution to the allied fleet—the new galeasses above all—that had won at Lepanto. Perhaps the old hegemony of the sea was not lost forever, if Venetian resources could only be redirected from land defenses toward more strenuous naval modernization! Unfortunately, however, this policy collided with a crippling shortage of timber for ship-building; and, as we saw in the preceding chapter, a no less crippling commercial collapse swiftly followed in the first decade of the seventeenth century.

Nevertheless, when an energetic and ambitious clique took over the principal magistracies of the Venetian Republic, 1582–83, these failures lay hidden in the future. The *giovani*, as the new men were called, boldly set out to revive the marriage with the sea that had made Venice great, developing commerce with the Levant in every way possible, while remaining, as before, passively defensive on land. The leading spirits among the *giovani* had been shaped at the University of Padua and took a lively interest in scientific and secular ideas. Galileo, for instance, appointed professor at Padua in 1592, became a member of a circle that met in the Morosini house, where other distinguished professors—including the anatomist Fabricius—rubbed shoulders with an inner circle of Venetian nobles and learned men, of whom the friar Paolo Sarpi (1552–1623) was destined to become the most famous. In religious matters, they were thoroughly conservative, proud of their city's claim to derive its faith from Saint Mark, and entirely unwilling to concede to the pope the kind of administrative supervision over religious institutions which reformed Catholicism, emerging from the Council of Trent, legitimated.[75]

Efforts on the part of the Venetian government to limit the growth of church properties and unwillingness to submit to papal visitations and other encroachments on the autonomy of the Venetian church reflected fundamentally divergent ideals: papal universal monarchy *vs.* the sovereignty of the secular state. At Padua a Jesuit school chartered by the pope (1550) aroused the enmity of the students and professors of the university by offering competing instruction; in 1591 a famous professor of philosophy, Cesare Cremonini, heir to the Aristotelianism of Pomponazzi and Zabarella, persuaded the senate to prohibit the Jesuits from awarding degrees on Venetian soil. Obedience to religious authority in matters intellectual as against the free-ranging professionalism of the Padua tradition thus became another source of disagreement between Venice and the papacy. The issue remained a very lively one, for the Jesuits did not submit tamely to their defeat of 1591, but repeatedly renewed their efforts to set up an effective intellectual counterweight to the stronghold of secularism which was the university. Political machinations behind the scenes, student riots, and virtriolic debate continued until 1606, when, at the height of the papal-Venetian clash, the Jesuits were expelled from the whole Veneto.[76]

A third dimension of the quarrel was the flagrant disregard of the crusading principle involved in the treaty Venice concluded with the Turks in 1595, reaffirming and extending good relations between the two states, at a time when the Hapsburgs had commenced a long and difficult war against the Ottoman Empire, 1593–1606.[77] Hapsburg agents and all the fiercely dedicated spirits who believed the salvation of mankind depended on the magnification of papal power agreed, therefore, that Venice was a varitable cancer in the fair body of Catholic Christendom. Strong measures against such a caitiff community seemed fully justified.

In 1606 Pope Paul V brought matters to a head by putting Venice under formal interdict. He demanded that the Venetians repeal certain laws affecting ecclesiastical property and give up the practice of trying clerics before secular courts. But the propaganda that swiftly sprang up on both sides extended the issue much further, bringing into the open a long list of petty grievances as well as fundamental issues as to how human society and government should be structured. Papal champions claimed the right to override local government of whatever kind in the interests of the church and religion; Paolo Sarpi, who became the principal pamphleteer on the Venetian side, argued for separation of spiritual from temporal authority, claiming that civil government derived its powers directly from God as legitimately as the pope derived his spiritual dominion from Christ.

The controversy excited wide attention in western Europe. Protestants, especially in England, allowed themselves to think that Venice might soon join their ranks; but the religious opinions of the Venetian rulers remained thoroughly conservative. They criticized the pope and his minions for innovation in exalting and exaggerating the monarchical authority of the papacy; it was no more than logical for them to resist change as stoutly in matters theological as in matters jurisdictional. Catholic monarchs, even the Spanish, tended to sympathize with Venetian principles as broadcast to the world through Sarpi's pamphlets; and when the Venetian clergy and people failed to obey the pope's interdict, continuation of the propaganda debate clearly tended to harm rather than help the papal cause. Hence, after a year's deadlock, in spring 1607, the French arranged a compromise, whereby two clerics, who had been condemned by a Venetian court, were handed first to French and then to papal jurisdiction for final disposition. In this way the papacy could pretend that Venice had yielded on at least one of the points at issue. But in fact the Venetians had won, for the same men and ideas remained in control of the city, and the tone of Venetian culture remained unaltered.

Nevertheless, conditions were not propitious for the long-term survival of Venetian civism. One economic disaster after another damaged the city's prosperity, as it turned out, irretrievably. Personal hardship and disappointments multiplied. In view of the fact that their policies had produced such disasters, it was hard to believe that those who had directed the state in its collision with the papacy were either wise or good. Hence, by 1612, when Doge Leonardo Donà, one of the most energetic of the *giovani*, died, the city's mood had altered. Sarpi and his friends were relegated to the margins of public life, and a readier acquiescence to papal claims gained ground within the Republic.[78]

This meant that the intellectual liberty and innovativeness of the University of Padua and the ethnic and cultural pluralism of the city of Venice were thrown on the defensive—never entirely repudiated, but no longer vigorously sustained either. Other centers arose—in Holland especially—where rising wealth sustained pluralism and toleration; and when Galileo left Padua (1610), the greatest days of Paduan science began slowly but surely to fade into the past. The medical school remained famous and influential throughout the seventeenth century; but despite Galileo's eighteen fertile years as professor of mathematics there, the new kind of European science—

mathematical, quantitative, and concerned rather with physics than with medicine—failed to establish permanent roots at the University of Padua.

One reason, surely, was that Galileo Galilei left Padua within a few months of attaining a pan-European reputation through the publication of his telescopic discoveries—the moons of Jupiter, mountains on the moon, and so on. The professors who remained behind were predisposed to reject Galilean discoveries; the qualitative, hierarchical universe of Aristotle was fundamentally irreconcilable with Galilean mechanics. The Aristotelians particularly resisted erasure of the difference between terrestrial and celestial regions which Copernican heliocentric doctrines implied. Indeed, Galileo announced his Copernicanism publicly only after leaving Padua. When this brought the wrath of the Inquisition upon him, no one in Padua was interested in defending such doubly subversive doctrines—offensive to the church and offensive as well to Aristotelian natural philosophy.[79]

Hence, by leaving the University of Padua when he did, to take a position at the Medici court in his native Florence, Galileo severed institutional connections that might have allowed his teachings to perpetuate themselves among students and pupils in Italy. When the costs of espousing such ideas in Italy became plain to everyone through Galileo's condemnation and detention by the Inquisition (1616, 1633),[80] few cared or dared to run such risks. At Padua and other Italian universities, the vested interest in Aristotelian science was so overwhelming that what had been fruitful and propitious for the development of anatomy and related medical studies became inimical and deadly for the free, organized pursuit of the newer mathematical physics.

All such tendencies to intellectual rigidity were directly and powerfully reinforced by the organized authority of the papacy, and confirmed by the economic crisis that pervaded, not just Venice, but the whole of Mediterranean Europe during the first half of the seventeenth century. Hence it is not really surprising that in the 1620s and 1630s intellectual leadership of Europe departed Italian soil, where it had so long been domiciled. Padua and Venice, where the latter phases of Italian renaissance intellectual development had been principally at home, acquiesced in the loss through the same conservatism which had, until then, sustained the preservation of local, civic and pluralist attitudes of mind so jealously.

In such a climate of opinion, the plague of 1630–31, which brought death to nearly one-third of the city's inhabitants, came as a crowning, crushing blow. God's will seemed clear: humility before the divine displeasure and submissiveness before God's Vicar on earth, the pope, recommended itself as never before to high and low.[81] A similar plague, almost as severe, 1575–77, had provoked a proliferation of theories about contagion as well as far-reaching practical measures for the control of public health.[82] Fifty-five years later, when plague struck again, no similar response was possible; and with the declining curve of economic prosperity, which ran its ineluctable course throughout the seventeenth century, Venetian political initiative and intellectual leadership also decayed. Nevertheless, institutional conservatism, and the continued accessibility of the Paduan medical school to Greeks and Jews, endowed that institution with a prolonged afterglow in the east at a time when, in northwestern Europe, more active centers of intellectual innovation, located in Holland, France, and England, had already begun to eclipse the achievements of the Italian renaissance.

Decay was not uniform. Some aspects of Venetian culture retained their vivacity after the University of Padua faded from the forefront of European intellectual development. Musically, for instance, Venice entered upon its most influentian period only in the first half of the seventeenth century. Professionalized performance of secular music, addressed to a general audience who paid for admission to the performance, had its genesis in Venice, where the first public opera house was opened in 1637. Composers and performers pioneered new dimensions of music. The most famous, Giovanni Gabrieli (1557–1612) and Claudio Monteverdi (1567–1643), were musical directors of Saint Mark's, though they are most remembered for secular musical compositions: concertos, madrigals, operas.[83]

The practice of renting opera boxes to noble families[84] created a very experienced audience in short order, for it became customary for boxholders to attend the opera house almost every evening, where in the back they might play cards, dine, and amuse themselves in other ways between bouts of serious listening and watching the performance. When attending to one another, singers and boxholders were, in fact, both on display; and both had an area for recuperation and private retreat— behind scenes on stage and in the rear compartment of the boxes. Under these circumstances, taste evolved rapidly; performers and impresarios alike were stimulated to high achievement through intimate interaction with the Venetian audience. Commoners, occupying the open seats, learned to rival the aristocrats in the professionalism of their taste; opera became a focus of delight, education, and distraction from the difficulties of everyday. Like professional sport in twentieth-century America, the most recent operatic performance became a topic of conversation for the entire city, and a political safety valve and sounding board of very considerable importance.[85]

Similarly, Venice's reputation as a city of pleasure, where gambling and sex could be pursued with fewer inhibitions and greater elegance than anywhere else in Europe, did not decay, for by the time papal clericalism broke through the last barriers of Venetian civism, reformed Catholicism had come to terms with human sinfulness on such a scale as to take Venetian sensuousness in stride.

Sensuousness certainly had its appeal for Turks and Orthodox Christians of eastern Europe, though Ottoman culture had a ripe tradition of its own in these matters. Ottoman sensuous expression (at least in its heterosexual manifestations) was strenuously private, however; an affair of the harem. Hence Venetian plays and operas titillated and shocked the Turks, who accepted some embellishments into their shadow theater, but on the whole rejected such public exhibitions as indecent.[86]

More significant for the course of public events were the intellectual affinities that converted a small but important company of Greeks into apostles of Paduan versions of philosophical and scientific truth. A talented group of Orthodox young men studied at Padua during the decades when the quarrel between Jesuit and Paduan forms of Aristotelianism kept the university in an uproar.[87] The sympathetic interest that Sarpi and his fellows showed in Orthodox and patristic patterns of church-state relationship was reciprocated by the sympathy and support for Venetian resistance to papal and Hapsburg pressures that were manifest both in learned Orthodox and in official Ottoman circles. A common enemy, particularly a strong and threatening one, is the best cement for any alliance; and the fact that Venice was so stoutly antipapal in matters of politics and religion made it seem safer for Orthodox Christians to come to Padua for study. However novel or subversive the ideas they might imbibe at the university, the simple fact that the pope and his storm troopers, the Jesuits, abominated Paduan principles made them seem less dangerous. The further fact that the philosophic basis and inspiration for the Paduan intellectual tradition was the Greek text of Aristotle also appealed to Greek pride and made it easier to feel that even clearly heretical ideas such as the mortality of the soul and the eternality of the material world—ideas very widely accepted at Padua—were somehow less repugnant to an Orthodox Christian because they descended from the pagan Greek past. On top of this was the further fact that the island of Crete continued to provide a staging ground and transmission point for interchange between Venice and the Orthodox world. As a result, even abstract and recondite aspects of culture began to move back and forth beween Venice and the Greek world more freely than ever before.[88]

The careers of two Cretan artists nicely illustrate the mingling and mutual enrichment of Greek and Latin high cultural traditions that became possible through the rapprochement that occurred toward the end of the sixteenth century within the framework of the Venetian empire. The first of them, Michael Damaskinos (ca. 1535–1591), became famous as an icon painter in Crete. In 1574 he came to Venice, where he had been commissioned to help decorate the new, nearly completed church, San Giorgio dei Greci. He remained in Venice until 1582, and during these years deliberately attempted to blend Venetian technique with Cretan and age-old Orthodox traditions of icon painting. In his old age, however, Damaskinos returned to Crete and reverted to a more strictly traditional

"Paleologue" style. Nevertheless, others paralleled, preceded, and carried on the effort to blend the two art styles, introducing clouds of figures, for instance, into a single icon and sketching in background to suggest three-dimensionality. As a result, a vigorous and technically very skilled school of icon painters arose, working both in Venice and in Crete, and supplying a market for part-Italian, part-Greek religious art that arose among citizens of Candia and among the Orthodox communities of Venice, the Ionian islands, and parts of the Balkans as well.[89]

This hybrid art tradition provided a springboard for another Cretan painter, Domenicos Theotocopoulos (ca. 1540–1614), known to the Spaniards among whom he settled in 1576 as El Greco. His blending of Byzantine, Venetian, and a more purely personal vision of reality was, of course, far more successful than anything attained by Damaskinos and his fellow icon painters. El Greco, after all, arrived in Venice while still a young man,[90] when his skills as a painter (and perhaps also his religious views) were still malleable to a degree that was not true of Damaskinos, who arrived a decade later as a mature man with an established reputation. Individual genius and prolonged isolation from the religious and artistic environment of his youth, which residence in Spain involved, were no less important to El Greco's career, though he never entirely turned his back upon the Byzantine heritage he had brought with him from Crete.[91]

As usual, these episodes of art history are sensitive indicators of the larger cultural scene. In the Roman Catholic west, El Greco founded no school and remained a great though isolated figure; whereas the Italianizing icon painters of the sixteenth-seventeenth centuries, though lesser artists than El Greco, nonetheless had a pervasive importance in the Orthodox east. Newfangled Italianizing and far older "Greek" styles persisted side by side into the eighteenth century; often the same painter could produce an icon to meet either taste, depending on what a prospective purchaser preferred. Such skill mirrored widespread social circumstance. Hability in playing one role or the other in response to the wishes of those with whom they had to deal became a prominent characteristic of all members of the Greek elite, whose precarious position as subjects of the Turks and objects of Catholic missionary propaganda encouraged, if it did not require, such chameleonlike behavior.

A Cretan literary renaissance paralleled the sixteenth-century development in art. Writers, like painters, found western and specifically Venetian models worthy of imitation. This interest was institutionalized sometime after 1571 through the foundation of an *Academia de Extravaganti*. This society was consciously modeled on the famous Florentine Academy, founded by Cosimo de Medici in the aftermath of the Council of Florence when an interest in Greek learning had attained peculiar intensity among a few intellectually inclined Florentines. The new Cretan Academy deliberately set out to repay the compliment, for it was organized by Greeks who were inspired by an intense and unprecedented interest in Italian and specifically Venetian literature and life style. As such, it provided a stimulus for the development of formal literary composition in a colloquial Cretan form of Greek. The academy likewise maintained a theater, where new-minted tragedies and comedies could be presented before a select company of fellow spirits.[92]

A few texts survive, and show that these plays were closely modeled on Italian prototypes. One of the authors, Giorgios Chortatsis, seems to have studied at Padua, though exact dates of his life are unknown. But Cretan drama was never more than a hothouse plant, important mainly as a proving ground for the development of literary language close enough to popular speech to give Greek *belles lettres* a fresh start. The man who capitalized on the possibilities this opened was Vincent Cornaros—his name suggests a Venetian ancestry—who wrote a heroic poem, *Erotokritos*, some time in the seventeenth century. This poem became extremely popular not only in Crete but throughout rural Greece. It spread by recitation, becoming so well known that a full three hundred years later familiar quotations from *Erotokritos* remained common coin among speakers of Greek, regardless of the level of their formal education. This poem, far more pervasively than the Italianizing icons of the age, entered into the life of the common people of Greece, reaffirming and recasting in modern form a much older heroic tradition dating back to Homer and *Digenes Akritas*.[93]

It was, however, in the field of theology and the practice of piety that the interpenetration of Greek and Italian traditions was most active and emotion-fraught, for both parties treated matters of doctrine and religious observances with the greatest seriousness. As early as the 1520s and '30s the Venetian printing press began to issue popular books of piety in a demotic, unstandardized form of Greek. Authors translated and adapted their texts from similar books published in Italian.[94] In 1570 a more learned theologian, Damaskinos Studites, metropolitan of Naupactos, published a *Thesauros* of popular piety which corrected some Latinizing dogmatic errors of the earlier collections and therefore became standard among Orthodox Greeks for centuries thereafter.[95] Even such a dignified and learned scholar as Maximos Margunios published a collection of saints' lives in demotic Greek in 1603, arranged to fit the calendar of the church year.

Publications such as these, peddled throughout the Balkans by the Greek book publishers of Venice, must have very much affected the substance of Orthodox piety, especially as manifested in lay circles. Until the 1570s, remarkably little trace of Orthodox-papal conflict showed in such works. Published in Venice, where public policy required cooperation with the papacy, no open contradiction of Catholic doctrine would have been allowed, even if the Greek entrepreneurs, who engaged in the business of book publishing and distribution in a thoroughly commercial spirit, knew or cared about details of the tangled theological issues separating pope from patriarch.

After the failure of the Holy War against the Turks (1573), however, the situation changed. Force having failed, Pope Gregory XIII felt impelled to resort to more strenuously spiritual methods for the propagation of Catholic truth. Dramatic successes came first in Poland-Lithuania, where a handful of Jesuit missionaries, beginning in 1565, were able in less than twenty years to bring the majority of the Polish and Lithuanian nobility back to the papal obedience. Learned argument, education, rather dubiously effective royal support, and their own disciplined, pious example proved quite enough to rout the quarreling Protesant factions. Encouraged by such results, the pope refounded the college of Saint Athanasius (1577), in hope of attracting bright young Greeks to Rome and training them to become missionaries to their fellow Christians. The shape of things to come became clearer in 1583 when the first Jesuit mission arrived in Constantinople itself[96] and met with considerable initial success, before its members succumbed to plague in 1586. Two years later the new pope, Sixtus V, approved a crusade against Moscow initiated by the Polish king, Stephen Bathory (reigned 1576–86).[97] But Polish arms met with only modest success, and in 1582 a Jesuit father, Antonio Possevino, negotiated a ten-year truce ending the long and difficult Livonian war between Muscovy and its western neighbors. Possevino at first even hoped that tsar Ivan IV the Terrible might be converted to Catholicism.[98] Simultaneously, other energetic Catholic missionaries pushed into the Balkan interior from Ragusa and Croatia, though without achieving any very dramatic results.[99]

As Roman Catholic missionary enterprise made itself felt along the entire Orthodox-Catholic borderland in this fashion, the œcumenical patriarch, Jeremias II the Magnificent (reigned 1572–95 with two brief periods of dethronement), reacted by trying to put the Orthodox church into better order. His first and most significant move was to effect a reconciliation with the Muscovite church. In 1588–89 he broke precedent by making a trip to the Russian lands; and while in Moscow he assisted in a ceremony which formally raised the metropolitan of all the Russias to the rank of patriarch.

Thereby the doctrinal estrangement between Greek and Muscovite branches of the Orthodox church formally ended, although the Russians did not, of course, surrender the administrative autonomy they had enjoyed since 1448. In order to make room for Moscow among the five patriarchates of the church,[100] Rome was officially stricken from the roster. Such an act tended to pit confederated Orthodoxy against the monarchy of papal Rome. Yet there were many Greek churchmen who resisted such a polarization, and efforts to find a basis of reconciliation with the pope remained vigorously alive within Orthodox ranks.[101]

After his return to Constantinople, the patriarch called a synod which met in 1593. Through this synod Jeremias attempted to reinvigorate the hierarchy immediately under his control. Improvement of the quality and accessibility of education was a special concern, for one of the main means by which the Jesuits had won their successes in Poland and elsewhere was through schools that attracted bright and ambitious young men by the excellence (and cheapness) of the instruction they offered.

The Synod of Constantinople in 1593 was significant in another way. It served as a showcase where the handful of Greek ecclesiastics who had been trained at Padua were able to show how well the sort of education they had acquired in the west fitted them to cope with the troublesome range of issues that Roman Catholic propaganda had raised. Meletius Pigas, by now patriarch of Alexandria, was particularly prominent, and on the death of Patriarch Jeremias in 1595 he became *locum tenens* when agreement on a successor to the office of œcumenical patriarch could not be achieved immediately. He it was, therefore, who met the crisis that arose when almost all of the Orthodox bishops of Poland-Lithuania decided to subscribe to the Union of Florence, as updated and spelled out in detail by a pair of synods that met at Brest, 1594–95.

Meletius Pigas responded by sending a special Orthodox mission to Poland, and made his cousin and fellow Cretan, Cyril Lukaris (ca. 1572–1638), then still fresh from six years of study at Padua, second in command. An effort to form a common front between the Orthodox and Protestants proved fruitless and was broken off in 1599; but the experience posed for the young Cyril, and for Greek churchmen everywhere, the dilemma of how best to react to the sort of missionary propaganda that had produced such a spectacular victory for the papal cause.[102]

The dilemma came far closer to the seats of Orthodoxy in 1609. In that year, a Polish force invaded Muscovy and for a while was able to occupy Moscow itself. In the same year, a new Jesuit mission arrived in Constantinople under the special protection of the French embassy.[103] Both the political and religious situation in Russia remained in utmost confusion during the Time of Troubles, but by 1612 Orthodox feeling and Russian xenophobic sentiment clearly began to converge in opposition to the Catholic Polish invaders. A new tsar, Michael Romanov, was elected in 1613; his father, Filaret, patriarch of Moscow, acted as his coadjutor in the exercise of power. The combination successfully drove back the foreigners, and Holy Russia emerged from its tribulation fiercely suspicious of Roman Catholic aggression as exemplified by the conduct of its Polish and Lithuanian neighbors.

In the south, where Moslem Turks held the reins of power, the struggle had to be fought out differently. The Jesuits started off very successfully. They set up a school that soon attracted an elite student body. Greeks and Jews mingled there with the sons of western residents of the city, and imbibed Roman Catholic theology along with secular subjects. The Jesuit missionaries, with the help of the Catholic ambassadors in Constantinople, were also able to create a party of sympathizers within the Orthodox hierarchy who committed themselves with varying degrees of openness to a uniate policy. In their approach to Orthodox clerics, Jesuit missionaries went very far to accommodate Greek[104] sensibilities, making the most of the principle accepted at Florence, that local church rituals and customs might differ from those of Rome so long as a minimal doctrinal statement and recognition of the pope's primacy were agreed to. The Jesuits often chose to instruct their converts to remain ostensibly Orthodox, dissembling their acceptance of papal claims to rule the church. The hope was in this way to win over the entire Orthodox hierarchy little by little, without the scandal of an open schism.[105]

Roman Catholic successes, however, soon created an opposing party within the Greek Orthodox hierarchy. The whole matter became entangled with international rivalries, as Dutch and English ambassadors strove to counteract the support French and Hapsburg representatives gave to the Catholic cause. And when the quarrels of Christendom flared into the Thirty Years' War (1618–48), maneuver and counter-maneuver in Constantinople took on an especially fevered quality. The Turks watched it all with a certain amused detachment, favoring now one and now another of the rivals in Constantinople in response to the fluctuations of the diplomatic situation. When important interests of state were not engaged, Turkish authorities were quite willing to respond to bribery; and reacted with predictable annoyance to local acts of violence and public disorders, inspired from time to time by the zeal of the conflicting parties.[106]

In 1622 the struggle assumed a new intensity. In that year Catholic missionary activities were brought under central command through the organization of the *Congregatio de Propaganda Fide.* Thenceforward, important moves were concerted in Rome and implemented by means of a genuinely international, indeed world-wide, command structure. In the same year, Cyril Lukaris became œcumenical patriarch for the first time. Until 1638, when Jesuit intrigue succeeded in persuading the Turks to seize and execute him as a traitor to the Ottoman regime, Cyril Lukaris remained the central figure in the impassioned struggle that went on in Constantinople and in other centers of Greek population between supporters and opponents of the Catholic cause.[107]

Since the time of his youthful efforts to counter Catholic propaganda in Poland, Lukaris had become the most conspicuous foe of papal pretensions among Orthodox prelates. His Paduan education no doubt predisposed him in this direction, for he had listened to the philosopher Cremonini and lived through the most acute phase of student agitation against the Jesuits in his university days. But the situation in Constantinople practically guaranteed that someone would arise as leader of the antipapal element among the Orthodox clergy. It was the Jesuit's ill luck that a man as well trained and as competent as Lukaris was available for the role; no less critical was the fact that he could call upon a cluster of fellow alumni of Padua for help in his efforts to meet papal arguments and formulate an effective Orthodox rebuttal.

Details of the struggle are not important here. Lukaris' own effort to define a confession of faith met with disaster. He came strongly under the influence of Antoine Léger, a Calvinist chaplain attached to the Dutch embassy, who, on his arrival in Constantinople (1628), set out to prepare a translation of the New Testament into the popular tongue and proposed, likewise, to prepare a suitably concise Confession of Faith for Orthodox use that would underline and make unmistakably clear the abominable errors of papal Christianity. Lukaris cooperated in both these enterprises, and was almost certainly the author of a Confession of Faith, attributed to him and pubished in Latin at Geneva in 1629. The Jesuits had long accused Lukaris of Calvinism; now the charge began to have the color of truth in the eyes of many Orthodox Greeks. At least one of the items in the Genevan Confession—that dealing with the use and value of icons—was clearly incompatible with traditional Orthodox belief; and the whole document leaned in a Protestant and Calvinist direction. Even more disturbing to Greek Orthodox sensibility was the effort to bring the Bible to the people in colloquial Greek, rather than holding fast to the sacred words of the New Testament in their original form. The argument that New Testament Greek had become incomprehensible to the laity in no way diminished the sense of outrage generated by Lukaris' readiness to tamper with God's sacred and authentic word.[108]

It is therefore not surprising that after Lukaris' death in 1638 a strong reaction against his policy of consorting with Protestants and Protestantism manifested itself in Constantinople. A synod condemned the Genevan Confession and repudiated the translation of the Bible into demotic, though the Greek prelates saved appearances by denying that the confession was authentically from the dead patriarch's hand. Yet repudiation of the Protestant path did not of itself solve the problem of how to define Orthodoxy in some handy fashion that could be referred to and relied upon in controversy with Roman Catholic missionaries, whose catechisms and abundant supply of handbooks of piety constituted very powerful weapons in the struggle for souls.

This defect was repaired in the 1640s when a Confession of Faith, drafted originally by the metropolitan of Kiev, Peter Moghila (reigned 1632–47), met with general acceptance. The success that thus came to Moghila's credal formulation gave recognition to the remarkable recovery of Orthodox morale, and the revivification of Orthodox learning, that had been achieved in the Ukraine in the half-century following the Union of Brest. The Orthodox cause actually benefited from Polish disdain. For as Polish attitudes became ever clearer, Ukrainian national self-consciousness and popular distaste for aristocratic domination of society found indirect but heartfelt expression through stubborn adherence to Orthodoxy. When the Polish government and Polish nobles refused to accept the uniate bishops as completely equal to their Roman Catholic counterparts, the attractiveness of the uniate church to socially ambitious Ukrainians was drastically undermined; and when the government authorities in Warsaw decided that they needed military help from the Orthodox Cossack community, the support of the secular arm for the uniate church all but disappeared. Thus the Jesuit program for converting Orthodox Christians to the uniate rite was already in serious difficulty when in 1621 the patriarch of Jerusalem secretly ordained a number of Orthodox bishops for the Ukraine. The restored hierarchy soon found it safe to come out in the open, sheltered by the mounting military importance of the Orthodox Cossack hordes.

This was the situation when the high-born, Paris-educated, Peter Moghila[109] decided to become an Orthodox monk and set up a school at Kiev (1631) for the instruction of prospective priests. Elevated to the rank of metropolitan in 1633, he used the resources of that office to expand his school into an academy, which speedily became a very influential center of higher education. The language of instruction was Latin, and the theology of Aquinas ranked with the thought of the Greek Fathers of the church in the curriculum.

Moghila, like his contemporary Lukaris, recognized the practical need for a concise Orthodox Confession of Faith. Accordingly, he drew one up on his own authority about 1640. Simultaneously, the hospodar of Moldavia, Basil Lupu (reigned 1634–54), decided to intervene in the troubled affairs of the œcumenical patriarchate, trying to pacify the quarrels that had boiled to the surface following Lukaris' death. He accordingly paid off some of the debts that had been burdening the patriarchal office, and thereby secured an effective, if informal, protectorate over the Greek church. A preliminary move was to summon a synod at Jassy, his capital, where in

1642 a slightly modified form of Moghila's confession was accepted as an authoritative definition of Orthodox belief. Subsequently, a series of other local synods endorsed the Jassy confession so that by the end of the decade Greek Orthodoxy, too, had been effectively armored with a credal formula, short enough to be memorized and definite enough to separate the faithful from both Protestant and papal forms of error.[110]

The upgrading of education among Orthodox Slavs, resulting from the establishment of the Kiev academy, was paralleled by a thoroughgoing transformation of the patriarchal academy in Constantinople. Major investment in higher education had been initiated by Patriarch Jeremias at the Synod of 1593, which had instructed Greek bishops to establish a school in every diocese; but a decisive new turn came under Cyril Lukaris, who felt it vital to establish on Greek soil an institution of higher learning that would be as nearly as possible equivalent to the University of Padua where he had himself been trained. He therefore entrusted direction of the patriarchal academy to Theophilos Korydaleos (ca. 1570–1646), like himself a Paduan alumnus and a passionately intellectual man.[111]

Korydaleos had absorbed the vision of a rationally comprehensible natural world from Cremonini and his other professors at Padua. He was seized by an enormous enthusiasm for scientific knowledge as exemplified by Paduan neo-Aristotelianism; and the fact that the basis of the entire doctrine was by origin Greek did nothing to diminish his emotional commitment to the new outlook. By explaining nature rationally, theology retreated to its proper domain—the suprasensible and suprarational. This struck Korydaleos and many of his students as a marvelous liberation from obfuscation and folly. Mystical faith and rational science each had its sphere; clear separation of one from the other was the precondition of achieving a healthy condition for religion as much as for natural knowledge.

Between 1613 and 1620, accordingly, Korydaleos composed a series of works, systematically laying down the truths of Aristotelian science for the benefit of his students. He wrote in classical Greek, as befitted an educated man, explaining all the latest knowledge and defending the complete autonomy of reason in the realm of natural science with a passionate conviction that he had picked up during his student days at Padua. On taking charge of the patriarchal academy, Korydaleos proceeded to make his philosophic and scientific texts the core of the curriculum. Even after Lukaris had been overthrown, the new curriculum remained, and indeed continued to dominate Greek Orthodox higher education until the last decades of the eighteenth century.[112]

The Paduan influence did not remain confined to Constantinople. In 1646 an academy modeled on the institution in Constantinople was set up at Jassy as part of Basil Lupu's program for the defense of Orthodoxy; another arose in Bucharest about 1678. A third important institution of higher education appeared in Jannina in 1677; and in 1687 the Russians set up a Greek academy in Moscow that brought the Paduan style of Aristotelianism to that part of the world for the first time. It is not clear that all these institutions enjoyed a continuous existence; and in Russia and the Rumanian provinces a struggle between the Greek and a Latin curricular model—the latter deriving largely from Kiev—distracted and complicated the scene. After 1711 the Greek Orthodox Constantinopolitan pattern for higher education won out in Rumania, imposing the stamp of Paduan Aristotelianism just as it was becoming obsolete; in Russia, the Greek curriculum did not survive Peter the Great's turn toward the west in the 1690s. Nevertheless, it is safe to say that the upgrading of Orthodox philosophical and scientific knowledge that followed in the wake of the educational reforms associated with Korydaleos on the one hand and with Peter Moghila on the other meant that the old indifference to, and ignorance of, new currents of thought sweeping in from western Europe was gone for good. A small but sophisticated intellectual elite took shape among the Orthodox, laity and clerics alike.[113]

As a result, by the 1640s Orthodox champions no longer had any difficulty in opposing the arguments of Roman Catholic missionaries effectively. Simultaneously, the Hapsburg-Catholic program for the suppression of Protestantism in Germany faded as the French intervened in the Thirty Years' War to save the Protestants from defeat. Little by little, therefore, the hope of winning all branches of the Christian church back to papal obedience lost its vibrancy, even among the missionary fathers of the Society of Jesus, who, more than anyone else, had embodied that ideal and done all they could to realize it—not solely in eastern Europe, but literally all round the earth.[114]

The relaxation of the Counter-Reformation thrust coincided, as we have seen, with the relaxation of resistance to papal intervention in church administration within Venetian territories, and with the weakening of the tension between a debilitated Venetian civism, on the one hand, and Baroque Catholic forms of high culture on the other. By the time the war of Candia (1645–69) had dragged its weary length along, exposing the helplessness of Venetian arms even when aided by Hapsburg and (briefly) French forces in war against the Turks, Venice was ready and willing to assimilate local styles of thought and culture to patterns prevailing within the territories of both her old rivals: the papacy to the south and the Hapsburgs to west and north. Culturally as much as economically and politically, Venice had ceased to be a Great Power.

In the east, however, the relaxation of Roman Catholic missionary pressure did not bring a halt to important cultural realignments and socioeconomic shifts. From the 1640s if not earlier, a conscious competition existed between the Latinate learning of Kiev and the Greek learning of Constantinople for dominance among Orthodox Slavs. This tipped, at least temorarily, in favor of the Greek definition of intellectual culture as a result of the reform associated with Patriarch Nikon of Russia (reigned 1652–66).

Nikon was of peasant origin, and associated himself with a reforming party of Zealots who earnestly and energetically sought to improve the moral and religious life of Russia. His vision of what the church should be achieved clear definition in 1649 when Paisios, patriarch of Jerusalem, visited Moscow seeking alms. Being an educated and sophisticated Greek, who knew how to flatter as well as cajole, Paisios opened Nikon's eyes to a magnificent vision of Russia's rightful role in Christendom: nothing less would do than the creation of a New Jerusalem, modeled accurately and authentically on the church established by Christ himself at the see over which Paisios presided.[115] This meant, in practice, remodeling the Russian church on prevailing Greek patterns, since the Orthodoxy of the patriarch of Jerusalem was identical with the Orthodoxy of Constantinople and of the other Greek-administered branches of the Christian church.

Being a man of commanding presence and demanding piety, who walked familiarly with God and believed firmly that his own opinions were the immediate reflex of God's clear and unambiguous will, Nikon had a lot to do when he became patriarch of Moscow in 1652. He had extracted a special oath of obedience from Tsar Alexis (reigned 1645–76) and the Russian court before agreeing to accept the office, and therefore felt his way clear to carry through the massive reform needed to bring Russian practices into line with Christ's authentic establishment as preserved and passed down among the Greeks. What mattered most to Nikon and other Russians were details of ritual, not doctrinal formulae of the kind Protestants and Roman Catholics had quarreled over in the west. Hence the number of fingers extended when making the sign of the cross and the number of hallelujahs used in the liturgy were the issues upon which the Russian church divided; not the proper definition of the eucharistic Real Presence.

Nikon had a printing press at his disposal, already established by his predecessors in the patriarchal office; and when he set out to correct Russian church books, he relied upon a Greek scholar (and graduate of Padua), the monk Arsenios,[116] as guide. Despite the oath he had exacted, Nikon's effort to exalt the patriarchate above the tsar soon brought him into conflict with Alexis. His imperious methods of bringing Russian church practices into line with those of Jerusalem simultaneously antagonized the Zealots from whose ranks he had emerged. Having created such a constellation of enemies, Nikon found it impossible to continue to function as patriarch. He therefore withdrew to his New Jerusalem monastery, just outside Moscow, refusing to abdicate or permit a successor to take the patriarchal office. After a long stalemate, Nikon was finally deposed against his will by a council that met 1666–

67; and, ironically, the courtiers who contrived the legal process required for his deposition relied upon another clever and thoroughly unscrupulous Greek prelate, Paisios Ligarides, metropolitan of Gaza,[117] to construct a legal case in canon law and muster support from the sister Orthodox churches for Nikon's dethronement.

The council that deposed Nikon did not reject his Hellenizing policy. On the contrary, the council also denounced those Zealots who refused to accept the innovations Nikon had decreed. Thus began the "Raskol," a split in the Russian church as profound and disruptive as the Protestant-Catholic split that had distracted Latin Christendom in the previous century. The "Old Believers" preserved more fully than their enemies the traditions of hesychasm that had so deeply transformed Russian piety in the fourteenth and fifteenth centuries. Thus both the innovators and the opposition represented successive waves of Greek cultural impress upon the Russian church. By way of reciprocity, in the latter part of the seventeenth century, Greek Orthodox prelates more and more openly began to look to the north, not merely for alms but for political support against the Turks, finding little to hope for and less and less to admire in Italy and western Europe.

The ecclesiastical linkup between the Greek and Russian churches was forwarded by a number of simultaneous changes in political and socioeconomic relations within the Ottoman Empire and in the steppelands adjacent to the Black Sea. The collapse of Ukrainian political-military independence after 1654 obviously diminished any chance for an autonomous Kievan style of culture to attain fuller development. The parallel Hellenization of the high culture of the Rumanian provinces —a process consciously and very successfully advanced by Basil Lupu and continued by most of his successors as hospodar[118] interdicted any possibility of effective collaboration between the South Slavs of the Balkans (who remained intellectually torpid) and the Ukrainians to create a distinctively Slavic style of high culture that might have been capable of resisting the advancing Greek tide.[119]

These massive Greek cultural successes depended fundamentally upon the extraordinary position the Greeks secured for themselves in the Ottoman Empire itself, thanks to commercial skills they had inherited from time immemorial,[120] and to the advantages their improved educational pattern conferred upon especially talented young men. Even in the sixteenth century, a Greek magnate from Chios, Michael Cantacuzene (d. 1578), monopolized the Russian fur trade and lived like a prince, rivaling Joseph Nasi. Others, less spectacular, followed in his path and made the trade of the Black Sea increasingly their own. Greek merchants and tax collectors, for instance, opened up the Rumanian provinces to commercial agriculture. This was, in turn, the essential underpinning for the Hellenization of the hospodars' court culture that occurred in the course of the seventeenth century. In other parts of the Ottoman Empire the economic role of Greek traders was less apparent, but their activity probably also extended into fresh regions of Asia Minor, rivaling a similar Armenian diaspora.[121] In the western Balkans, semi-Hellenized Vlachs and Albanians seem to have been the most active commercial element;[122] Basil Lupu, for instance, was of Albanian background and a successful merchant before he became hospodar.

The heights to which a clever Greek could rise with the further advantage of a first-rate education was illustrated by the career of Panagioti Nicoussias, who took a medical degree from Padua about 1650 and set up a practice in Constantinople. He achieved such a reputation that the grand vizier, Mehmed Köprülü, made him his personal physician soon after coming to power in 1656. The grand vizier gradually learned to rely on Nicoussias for political advice about western states and rulers; and there is a kind of symbolic significance in the fact that when the Venetians finally determined to give up the long struggle over Crete and make peace with the Ottomans (1669), the man who was entrusted with the responsibility of conducting negotiations for the Turks was none other than the ex-medical student of Padua, the Greek Nicoussias.

Knowledge and skills he had perfected through his education at Padua had served him well indeed. On his return from negotiating a victorious peace, the Turkish authorities were so pleased with his accomplishments that they invented a new title, Grand Dragoman of the Porte, to dignify functions which became approximately equivalent to the duties of a foreign minister in European cabinets. After his death in 1673 the office passed to another brilliant medical alumnus of Padua and Bologna, Alexander Mavrocordato (1642–1709), who started his career with a treatise on the circulation of the blood and climaxed it by negotiating the Treaty of Carlowitz in 1699.[123]

The rise of the Greeks within Ottoman society went hand in hand with a similar enhancement of the role of Moslem Albanians. These rough and ready mountaineers achieved a strategic place in Ottoman society through their military formidability, on the one hand, and through the much more remarkable fact that they could be trusted to remain loyal to a master whose service they entered voluntarily.[124] Mehmed Köprülü, who became grand vizier in 1656 at a time of intense crisis in Istanbul,[125] founded a veritable dynasty of Albanian grand viziers that lasted until almost the end of the century. It was the Köprülüs, men of limited formal education themselves, who sealed alliance with the Greek educated class through their reliance on Nicoussias and his ilk.

The people who suffered most from this realignment were the Jews, who lost the professional advantages they had formerly enjoyed, largely, perhaps, because they lacked any secular system of education to match that which the Greeks, from the time of Korydaleos, had created for themselves.[126] The remarkable career of Sabbatai Zevi (1626–1676) was both a symptom and a cause of the further undermining of the Jews' position in the Ottoman Empire. For Sabbatai Zevi announced in 1666 that he was the long-awaited Messiah. Jews all over Europe paid respectful attention, and many Ottoman (and Polish) communities experienced intense emotional upheavals in anticipation of the end of the world's injustices. A man commanding such reverence and claiming to be King of the Jews obviously excited attention also among Turks and Christians; but when the Ottoman authorities arrested Sabbatai and offered him the choice of death or acceptance of Islam, the would-be Messiah chose the latter course, to the intense disgust of most of his coreligionists. Others excused his apostasy on the ground that good could only overcome evil by entering into it totally. A few even followed him into the Moslem fold, where they survived as a distinct community until the twentieth century.[127]

The upshot, therefore, by 1669 was extraordinarily favorable to the Greeks. Having undermined the Jews, decapitated the Balkan Slavs, seduced the Rumanians, and persuaded the Russians of the superior value of Hellenic high culture over alternative models, the Greeks had also made themselves indispensable to the Turks! An Orthodox Hellenic style of culture had emerged from the shadows of the first Ottoman centuries, enriched by a strong infusion of skills from the Latin (mainly Italian, largely Venetian) west. Politically this reinvigorated Hellenism divided itself awkwardly between Ottoman and Russian allegiance; a corollary was that the Ottoman style of civilization tended to split apart. In the time of Mehmed the Conqueror and Suleiman the Lawgiver, the Turkish culture of court and city had been supremely confident, seemingly capable of keeping Orthodox Christians, with their distinct but impoverished style of civilization, in a safely subordinate place as a humble part of the overall symphony of peoples and customs that together and traditionally made up Moslem civilization. Jews, willy-nilly, conformed to such a role; but with the upsurge of Greek Orthodox wealth, skills, and knowledge that resulted from the reception of and reaction to Italian renaissance and Counter-Reformation culture, the older pattern of Ottoman society and civilization began to develop two heads, one Moslem, one Christian. Neither was capable of existing without the other, yet the two were fundamentally and, as it turned out, in the long run fatally, at odds.

Northwestern Europe was more fortunate. Receiving and reacting to Italian renaissance and Counter-Reformation impulses successively rather than simultaneously, the western peoples had more time to meld old with new, thus achieving more solid results than Greeks and other Orthodox peoples were ever able to do. This, in turn, was largely due to the fact that in western Europe a larger proportion of the entire population took active part in the upheavals of renaissance and Reformation than was true of eastern Europe, where only a rather narrow elite of the Greek and Slavic worlds (and even fewer Moslems) shared actively in the cultural transformations we have been following. Finally, the political structure of western Europe permitted various nations to go different ways, compounding the common elements of their culture in varying proportions to suit local circumstances, without constricting pressure from such vast imperial structures as weighed upon Ottoman, Russian (and, erelong, Hapsburg) subjects in eastern Europe.

Nonetheless, we must admire the achievements of eastern Europeans in mastering the challenges to their accustomed ways inherent in the extraordinary attainments of the north Italian city states in the long period from 1281 to 1631, when Italian skills dominated most of Europe. It remains, in a final chapter, to consider briefly how it was that the Italian model of culture lost its hold upon east European minds in the final years of Venetian political independence, between 1669 and 1797.

· SIX ·

Venice becomes Archaic and Loses Influence Abroad 1669-1797

BY THE middle of the seventeenth century, if not before, the most active centers of creativity in Europe had moved north of the Alps. Italy and the entire Mediterranean region became, generally speaking, laggard in matters technical, intellectual, organizational. Northern Italy no longer acted as metropolitan center against which the achievements and skills of other peoples and regions of Europe could be measured and found wanting; instead, the cities and countryside of Italy began to fall short of Dutch, English, and French achievements in one field of endeavor after another.

It did not take the peoples of eastern Europe long to notice what had happened. Peter the Great went to Holland (1697) to see how ships were built and never thought of visiting the Venetian Arsenal, once so famous; and leading Greek intellectuals soon discovered that there were more interesting new ideas to be gleaned in Amsterdam, Paris, and London than in Padua,[1] even though most Greeks who studied abroad continued to come to Padua where they could work amidst a circle of other Orthodox Christians, who were busily seeking valuable professional training in medicine without really having the time to come to grips with such disturbing intellectual

217

novelties as the Cartesian world machine or the mathematical elegance and emptiness of the Newtonian universe.

Undoubtedly the ecological and demographic crises that struck Mediterranean lands so sharply, 1580–1630, were fundamental in the sense that creeping poverty set harsh limits upon Mediterranean societies in general and upon those of Italy and of Venice in particular.[2] But dogmatic rigidity that had been so energetically imposed on Italian minds by the true believers of the Catholic Reformation also hampered creativity, especially in intellectual and literary fields. This, in turn, was sustained by organizational rigidities that shored up things as they were at the cost of making adjustment to changing circumstances more and more difficult as time went on.

In politics, for example, the division of Italy into a patch-work of small states condemned the peninsula to remain a sphere of influence and sporadic battleground for greater powers until the nineteenth century. In economics, restrictive practices among craftsmen protected them in local markets at the price of increasing technical backwardness and perpetual vulnerability to cheaper foreign imports. Most of all, perhaps, the enormous resources assigned to the support of religious institutions of all kinds sustained and reinforced routine and repetition as the surest way to heaven. Catholicism, tempered and elaborated by the pious practices of the reform era, had become nearly perfect in all its parts, armed with handy truths and ready practical prescriptions for almost every human circumstance. Short of the drastic and painful step of rejection in toto, Catholic dogma and morals left almost no room for improvement or new departures. Cultural creativity concentrated therefore on the side of sin: for secular music, theatrical performances, gambling, and other forms of stylish depravity —the fields in which Italy in general and Venice in particular continued to excel the rest of Europe until almost the end of the eighteenth century—all carried with them at least a whiff of brimstone, curable, of course, by a timely resort to the confessional.

Such generalizations overlook isolated individual efforts at intellectual invention—bypassing such figures as the Neapolitan, Giovanni Battista Vico (1668–1744), for instance, whose new science of human history attracted little attention in his own lifetime but has been much admired since. Moreover, men of the age itself, who accepted one or another of the dogmatic definitions of religious truth that divided Europe so emphatically in the sixteenth and seventeenth centuries, could not be expected to believe that the new mathematical physics was a noticeable improvement upon traditional faith in the governance of Divine Providence; and even the improvements in technology that carried Holland, France, and England to the forefront of European economic development seemed to most of those affected by the changes to be more detestable than admirable.

Thus there were strong psychological forces supporting the conservatism of thought and action which dominated Venice from the middle years of the seventeenth century until the final extinction of the Republic in 1797. Yet the most rigorous conservatism still offered alternative models for political action. Even after 1669, and the defeat of Candia, Venice could aspire to a glorious resumption of its imperial role in the east. Such an aspiration gained plausibility in proportion as ills within the Ottoman Empire came into the open and made that once formidable foe increasingly vulnerable to Christian attack. Alternatively, the Republic of Saint Mark could fall back upon a more passive policy of neutrality as between the Great Powers, and remain satisfied with the more modest policy of merely retaining the territories and upholding the usages passed down from former times.

The first of these lines of action came to be identified with the person of Francesco Morosini (1618–1694), who established a European reputation for courage while commanding the garrison of Candia during its last, tenacious stand against the Turks, 1667–69. When Turkish arms, tempered by a decade of difficult war in the Ukraine, turned again westward and in 1683 penetrated to the heart of Austria and laid siege to Vienna, as had happened only once before (1526) in the days of Sultan Suleiman, the Venetians rallied to the Holy League which the pope and the Hapsburgs cooperated in creating. To be sure, the Venetians did not abandon their accustomed caution. They began hostilities only in 1684, after the siege of Vienna had failed and the destruction of the Ottoman field army made attack in Dalmatia and on the slimly defended Morea look temptingly easy. Morosini was placed in charge of an expeditionary force of about 9,500 men (including a large detachment of Hanoverians). He quickly won a series of brilliant victories, and, with the help of local Greek irregulars, drove the Turks entirely out of Morea in 1687.[3] The next year an effort to invade Negropont failed as malaria and other diseases cut down the strength of the invading forces. In the same year, Morosini returned to Venice and was elected doge. Despite his years, he then went off to the east once again as commander-in-chief of Venetian forces.[4] He died there in 1694, almost as full of years and far more elaborately honored than his predecessor, Enrico Dandolo, leader of the Fourth Crusade.

Efforts to revive the Venetian navy met with modest success, too: a fleet of gunships of northern design supplemented the galleys which the Venetians still sent to sea. Turkish warships proved inferior, but Venice found the cost of keeping a fleet at sea very heavy to bear for any length of time. Sea and land fighting alike fell off after a futile attack on Crete (1692) was followed by an equally futile expedition that briefly occupied the island of Chios (1694). The final phases of the war depended on events in Hungary, Moscow, and along the Rhine: once the Russian tsar joined the war against Turkey and Louis XIV had made peace with the Austrians at Ryswick (1697), thus allowing the Hapsburgs to concentrate all their resources against the Ottoman armies in Hungary, the scales tipped decisively against the Turks. Reluctantly, therefore, they made peace at Carlowitz in 1699, ceding most of Hungary to the Hapsburgs and all of the Morea to Venice.[5]

However glorious Morosini's conquest had been, it soon became obvious that there were costs of empire that the Venetians were unable or unwilling to bear. Defense of the Morea required modern fortifications and professional soldiers to man the fortresses. The Venetians naturally enough, decided that the local inhabitants should pay for these necessities, and began to install a rational administration to make sure they did so. But despite some statistically and visually impressive achievements,[6] the effort to conscript labor to work on fortifications and to collect taxes to pay for a meddlesome administration and garrisons of foreign troops quickly alienated popular sentiment. Venetian religious policy, which in the enthusiasm of the Holy War had become aggressively Roman Catholic,[7] provided all such discontents with an effective ideological rallying cry. The establishment of Roman Catholic bishoprics in the Morea roused deep misgivings among almost all Greeks who soon rallied behind the local Orthodox clergy in more and more open opposition to the Venetian overlords. The result was that when the Turks, having humbled Peter the Great of Russia at the Pruth (1711), gathered their forces for an attack on the Venetians (1714), the Greeks of the Morea welcomed them back. Without local support Venetian resources were entirely inadequate to resist the Turkish armies; and despite all the handsome new fortifications of Corinth and Nauplion, the garrison forces—short of men, guns, and supplies as they often were—put up no very determined resistance. As a result, the Turks won back all they had lost within a few months, and projected the capture of Corfu and Dalmatia to roll back Venetian power from the Balkan peninsula entirely. Intervention of Austrian armies in the north prevented this dénouement; but when peace was again concluded at Passarowitz on the basis of *uti possidetis* (1718), Austrian gains along the Danube were counterbalanced by Venetian losses in the Morea and the Aegean.[8] Venetian possessions overseas were thereafter confined to the island of Cerigo off the southernmost tip of the Morea, together with the Adriatic coastlands and the Ionian islands. Morosini's great adventure utterly collapsed, and Venetians ceased to dream of resurrecting their past imperial greatness. They did so with what amounted to a sigh of relief. The manpower and much of the money for this final military fling had come from sources outside of Venice itself. Foreign, mainly German, troops, hired with funds provided by the pope from gifts of the pious all over Europe, had provided the backbone of Morosini's forces;

and when papal subsidies ceased to flow as the excitement of the initial victories subsided, the Venetians had been left with their own and the Morea's inadequate resources.[9]

What remained, therefore, was to revert to a less ambitious policy of neutrality in the wars which subsequently blew up, whether fought in Italy (War of the Polish Succession, 1733–35) or in the Balkans (1736–39) when Austria lost Serbian territories won at Passarowitz, and 1768–74, and 1787–92 when Catherine II's armies advanced Russian borders to the Dniester.

The Venetians played no part in these upheavals. Their alliance with the Hapsburgs had been proclaimed eternal at Passarowitz; and since the Hapsburgs were the only European rulers in a position to threaten Venetian mainland territories, the Republic could relax its landward guard safely enough, at the price of perpetuating the city's relation of clientage to Vienna. The only significant military problem therefore was safeguarding the Adriatic from the raids of Barbary pirates, who developed a taste for attacking Venetian ships because the Venetian navy was seldom in a position to retaliate effectively. The practical solution was to pay protection money to the bey of Tunis and other potentates of the North African coast; but since these rulers could not always control piratical entrepreneurs operating from their ports, this solution was only partially efficacious.

Plans to make Venetian vessels capable of self-defense by equipping them with more cannon were initiated in 1736. This met with modest success for a few years until nullified by parallel improvements in the armament and sailing abilities of the Barbary pirate ships. Naval bombardment of Tunis, though tried on more than one occasion, was expensive and unproductive. As the century wore on, however, the control exercised by Moslem authorities in North Africa over the corsairs increased so that after 1763–65, when the Venetians negotiated a new set of agreements to pay protection money to the rulers of Tripoli, Tunis, Algiers, and Morocco, the problem of piracy was effectively solved at last. As a result, the Venetian merchant marine almost doubled its tonnage in the final thirty years of the city's independence.[10]

In spite of some elaborate efforts to restore Venetian long-distance trade,[11] high-cost shipping, low-quality crews, and discriminatory tariffs[12] combined to thwart even the best-laid plans. The war of 1684–99 interrupted Venetian commerce with Ottoman lands; it never recovered. Thereafter, except for a few articles of luxury[13] like the mirrors with which Venetian glassmakers continued to decorate the boudoirs and drawing rooms of much of Europe, Venetian manufactures shrank to the level suited to supply local consumption in the Veneto and along the Adriatic coast. Even book publishing for the Greek market ceased to be important from the time when well-organized Greek printing presses were set up in the Rumanian provinces (1670).[14]

Within the Adriatic, however, and on the canals and rivers of the Veneto, shipping continued to play its traditional role, bringing food into the city from the countryside, and distributing various commodities—salt, iron, and other manufactures—to the local markets in exchange. Venice, of course, continued to be the hub of this kind of intraregional exchange;[15] but inasmuch as the city was thrown back upon local resources for its support, urban elements in the population could not bulk as large proportionately as had been true in the days of Venetian greatness, when the city had been able to draw sustenance from as far away as the shores of the Black Sea.[16]

Rural population rose from an average density of 51 per km.[2] in 1548 to 75 per km.[2] in 1790. By the end of the period there were clear signs of an agricultural crisis. Overcropping, and shortages of manure resulting from plowing up pastures, lowered productivity as population continued to grow. Harsh collision between population and food supply had been postponed—but became all the more massive when it came—by the spread of maize. This high-yield crop became the main source of food for the peasantry during the seventeenth century and accounted for half the Veneto's cereal acreage by 1750.[17] Techniques of cultivation were not noticeably improved after the sixteenth century. Landlords usually remained passive rent collectors, or received a share of the crop without taking active charge of farm management or finding it worthwhile to invest capital in newfangled forms of tillage.[18] Absenteeism was the rule, and an increasing proportion of the land came into the hands of nobles and other citizens of Venice who resided in town, at least most of the year.[19]

The decay of trade and manufactures and the increased importance of landholding obviously transformed the economic character of the Venetian ruling classes, bringing the business behavior of the nobility of the city much closer to the aristocratic norms of the rest of Europe. The critical shift probably occurred between 1570 and 1630; but events thereafter confirmed what had happened. Venice's urban economy came to depend very largely upon the city's role as a pleasure ground for rentiers, where they could enjoy the amenities of life more fully than by living in isolation on their estates. Of course the city continued to provide goods and services for lower ranks of society; but this aspect of Venetian life remained humble and inconspicuous, all the more so because a substantial tourist trade developed, especially at the carnival season,[20] reinforcing local rentiers with aristocrats and adventurers from all over Europe, come to enjoy the pleasures, licit and illicit, for which Venice had become renowned throughout Europe.

Venetian society exhibited some remarkable characteristics in the latter seventeenth and eighteenth centuries. The nobility maintained a complete monopoly on political office, as had been the case since the thirteenth century, and generally kept aloof from the swarms of pleasure-seekers who infested the city's public places. Fortunes invested in land and government bonds were fundamentally inelastic, unlike trading capital. It therefore became customary for noble families to arrange *mariages de convenance* for only one son—often the youngest—and that late in life when it seemed necessary to beget a legitimate heir to carry on the family name. Such schemes sometimes miscarried: and many noble families died out.[21] Still others lost their wealth through improvident or spendthrift behavior, so that real power in the state devolved upon no more than thirty to forty families. The decision to admit new families by selling patents of nobility, although it replenished the ranks of the Venetian nobility in significant proportion, did not change the concentration of political control, for the newcomers were systematically excluded from all important offices of state.[22]

There were those among the nobility who resented the concentration of political and economic power in the hands of so few. But efforts to mobilize the voting power of the poor and excluded noble families against the dominant oligarchs regularly broke down. The group at the top could always rally enough votes to keep themselves in command by offering crumbs of office and other advantages to individuals among the poor nobles who often needed such income in order to live at all. Hence there was no effective challenge from within to the small clique at the top of Venice's government.

What made the regime stable was the activity of professional bureaucrats who staffed the numerous government offices, boards, councils, and commissions. These men were *cittadini*, a privileged rank in itself. They studied law and public administration at the University of Padua and then qualified for office by passing an examination. Not infrequently it was they rather than the noble magistrates who really made decisions and executed them. These bureaucrats created remarkably full statistical records, to the delight of social historians and demographers; and their high professional morale (reinforced no doubt by careful bookkeeping techniques) prevented any widespread peculation. Oddly enough, where almost everything else was for sale, the public administration, by and large, was not. Venice therefore continued to enjoy the services of an efficient and on the whole benevolent bureaucracy, which made the façade of noble government tolerable to the majority of the city's inhabitants.[23]

It should, however, be understood that what was good for the city and its inhabitants was often hurtful to the peasants of the Veneto whose economic plight became increasingly dismal as the eighteenth century advanced. Within the city, in effect, administrative actions redistributed resources as between social classes on a fairly large scale: this was, fundamentally, what maintained social stability within Venice. Rich and poor of the city combined to profit from the rents and taxes a punctilious administration managed to collect from the populations of *terra firma*. Ecclesiastical properties contributed a good deal to the process also, for hospitals, foundling homes, and the like were commonly staffed and managed by clergy and supported by endowments which more often than not were put into land. Small wonder, therefore, that the constitution remained inviolate and an object of almost superstitious reverence! Those who benefited from its operation were close to the seat of power and conscious of their stake in its continued operation, whereas the peasants who carried the burden of the city on their backs were scattered, ignorant, and often so ill-fed as to lack the energy to revolt.[24]

Another way to describe the transition from a commercial-manufacturing economy to a rentier economy which the Venetian government and people executed with such skill by about 1675 (when the city's economic retrogression reached bottom) is this: In the days of Venetian greatness, the city's commerce concentrated resources drawn from all parts of the Mediterranean and Black Sea coastlands, and even beyond. This trade dealt predominantly in luxuries; it prospered by sales to local landlords who were able to buy such goods because they found ways to exact unrequited goods and services from peasants around them. With the breakdown of long-distance Venetian trade after 1630, a more intensive, local exploitation of the peasantry in the immediate hinterland of the city achieved similar results, permitting the fragile fabric of the Queen of the Adriatic to remain externally intact.

Similar alternation between distant and close-in urban parasitism upon rural populations had occurred before in Mediterranean history—notably in Attica after 404 B.C. and in Liguria after about A.D. 1400; but nowhere had it been achieved without violent political strife until the Venetian administrators of the seventeenth century managed to perform that feat. The constant and more or less rational readjustment of ends to means, which had been built into the consultative structures of the Venetian government from the thirteenth century (if not before), never met a severer test than this. Equally, the deficiencies of rationality applied for the benefit of a limited segment of humankind—in this case the inhabitants of the city of Venice—can seldom be more plainly observed than in the way Venetian political institutions worked in the eighteenth century to preserve the urban fabric at the peasantry's expense.

From one point of view it may not seem to make much difference whether a city battens on the economically unrequited labor of cultivators far removed or close by. Yet this is not really the case. A managerial elite that lives by trade and manufacture must maintain an active, inquisitive, energetic mode of life. Merchants deal, mostly, with equals, buying from and selling to men of power in their own communities. To prosper in such encounters a man must perpetually respond to new situations, be ready to defend himself or flee, calculate margins, take risks. Men so engaged constantly experience new things, whether at home or abroad. In other words, the renaissance spirit of Venice and other Italian cities was a natural and necessary response to the economic relationships which Italian townsmen established with the rest of Europe between the thirteenth and sixteenth centuries.

Landlords and tax collectors who squeeze goods and services from a sullen and resentful peasantry have a far less stimulating experience of life, particularly when custom has made it unnecessary to resort openly to force. Men's minds quite naturally close up when new experiences cease to be a normal part of life; this, as much as the plague of 1630–31 and the missionary persuasiveness of Catholic reform, accounts for the narrowing of Venetian outlook (and of that of Italy at large) which followed upon the change of Venetian socioeconomic structure in the second half of the seventeenth century.

Yet, within its own terms and range of sensibilities, the refinement and elegance of Venetian high culture remained very great. Venetian music and theater were among the most admired in Europe, as the names of Antonio Vivaldi (1676–1741) and Carlo Goldoni (1707–1793), both of them Venetian born and bred, may remind us. Yet soon after Vivaldi's death, musical leadership of Europe moved north of the Alps, with Bach (d. 1750), Haydn (d. 1809), and Mozart (d. 1791); and when Goldoni left Venice in 1761 to take up a position at Paris, the Venetian stage soon sank to merely parochial significance.[25] Yet wherever the improvisational *commedia dell'arte* had taken root, Goldoni's plays and the way he built upon that older tradition had great influence into the eighteenth and indeed until the twentieth century. Like light from a dead star, the power of the Venetian theater continued to be felt in trans-Alpine

Europe long after the creative energy that gave it birth had been dissipated.[26]

Venetian art, too, maintained a high European reputation throughout the eighteenth century, yet signs of the city's decay are evident. Giovanni Battista Tiepolo (1696–1770), for instance, the last of the Venetian masters in the grand style, did his most famous work in Germany and Spain, where princely patronage was more lavish than anything the Venetians themselves could possibly afford. His contemporary, Antonio Canale (or Canaletto, 1697–1768), made a living by painting Venetian cityscapes for the tourist trade; his pupil, Francesco Guardi (1712–93), did the same. The way in which Canaletto and Guardi made the city of Venice itself the subject of their art seems symptomatic of a self-conscious turning to the past, which seemed grander and more admirable than anything the present could show. It is as though the aging Queen of the Adriatic, raddled with age and feeling the pinch of poverty, still found pleasure in contemplating herself in the mirror of art, coquettishly prepared to flaunt her surviving charms in the hope of being noticed and remembered for conquests and seductions of the past, if for nothing else.

In matters intellectual, the University of Padua and Venice generally ceased to be an important center of innovation after 1620. The competency of medical training obtainable at Padua remained very high, and students from the Balkans continued to come in substantial numbers. Special endowments were set up by wealthy Greeks to facilitate the education of their countrymen, the most famous of them being the Collegio Cotunios at Padua, established in 1653, and the Collegio Flanginis at Venice, established in 1664.[27] The practical usefulness of a Paduan medical degree was what sustained this flow of students from the east. The value of an M.D. degree in real life allowed the intellectual leaders of the university to hold fast to the Aristotelian scientific-philosophical pattern of thought long after the cutting edge of European science had gravitated toward a mathematical-mechanical model, for which the doctors and philosophers of Padua had no use whatever.[28]

In the second half of the eighteenth century, a few Venetians began to react to the ideas of Voltaire and other exemplars of the French Enlightenment, but they were never more than passive receivers of new things from France; and their openness to such ideas aroused opposition, not only from the Paduan faculty, but also among the magistrates of Venice who found Voltairean ideas dangerous to society and religion alike.[29] When a sense of falling behind intellectually became inescapable and oppressive, Venetian administrators reacted by investing directly in technology, founding new chairs at Padua in agriculture, chemistry, and water engineering. Some worthwhile work resulted, but the more ambitious hydraulic projects developed by the new professors of engineering were never implemented, owing to lack of sufficient capital for realizing their plans. Official suspicion, meanwhile, drove free thought in matters metaphysical and social more or less underground, mainly into Masonic channels.[30]

In spite—indeed, because—of the care and intelligence with which the Venetian officials supervised the affairs of the University of Padua, the scientific and intellectual leadership of Europe which that institution had enjoyed for a few decades in the sixteenth and early seventeenth centuries was never restored. Venice and *terra firma* became a struggling province of Italy, overshadowed by Hapsburg power, facing intractable socioeconomic problems with an administration so skilled in maintaining things as they were that the kinds of new growth which a more disorderly society might have allowed were regularly nipped in the bud. It required the ruthlessness of a Corsican upstart, supported by the military as well as by the intellectual forces of the French Revolution, to shatter forever what so many generations of Venetian rulers had sustained, for in 1797, after his first great victories over the Austrians in northern Italy, the young Napoleon advanced toward Venice and in the name of popular liberty rudely demanded abrogation of the age-old constitution of the Republic.

The doge and great council abdicated without attempting armed resistance. The might of the conqueror was too great, and the conviction with which even its most privileged beneficiaries supported the existing regime was too weak to permit any other course of action. As a result, the Republic of Saint Mark exited from the stage of history with scarcely a whimper

—too old and weak to fight any more, even for life. The final lines of Wordsworth's sonnet "On the Extinction of the Venetian Republic" express not only the poet's feelings at the time but also strike a note of elegaic acquiescence that has since prevailed, among Venetians and outsiders alike:

> Once did she hold the gorgeous east in fee;
> And was the safeguard of the west: the worth
> Of Venice did not fall below her birth,
> Venice, the eldest Child of Liberty.
>
> . . .
>
> And what if she had seen those glories fade,
> Those titles vanish, and that strength decay;
> Yet shall some tribute of regret be paid
> When her long life has reach'd its final day:
> Men are we, and must grieve when even the Shade
> Of that which once was great is pass'd away.

Yet the departing Shade, to the moment of its extinction (and beyond, for that matter) continued to exert influence in Orthodox Europe—more through the momentum of cultural relationships antedating 1669 than through new impulses, to be sure, yet tangibly enough for all that. Until 1797, after all, Venice retained imperial control of the Greek-speaking Ionian islands, where an uninterrupted process of acculturation to the Venetian model produced an almost perfectly Italianized upper-class style of life by the end of the eighteenth century. As so often, the history of art sensitively reflects the larger cultural scene, for on the island of Zante a second-rate painter, Panagiotis Doxaras (d. 1729), founded a school of painting by consciously repudiating Byzantine rules and no less consciously striving to imitate nature in the spirit of Leonardo da Vinci and the other great artists of the high renaissance. Interestingly, when the kingdom of Greece sought to establish cultural institutions worthy of a modern state, it was to this school the authorities turned by inviting artists from the Ionian islands to set up shop in Athens in 1835.[31]

The Ionian islands, however, were a backwater of little importance for the general interaction of cultural styles between eastern and western Europe. During some three decades after

1669, the tide of Padua's influence upon Orthodox Christendom continued in full flood. Alexander Mavrocordato's career as Grand Dragoman of the Porte, 1673–1709 (with a brief period of disgrace, 1703), was, after all, the best possible advertisement for the merits of a Paduan education; and his very real intellectual interests—he wrote voluminous if unoriginal histories and philosophical-scientific works with the aim of spreading knowledge among his fellow countrymen—set a fashion among wealthy and ambitious Greeks for cultivating at least the appearance of learning.[32]

The most fertile ground for the new style of Orthodox high culture was in the Rumanian provinces. Rapid agricultural development of Wallachia and Moldavia provided an expanding economic base, and the administrative structures erected by the hospodars with the help of Greeks from Constantinople proved extremely effective in concentrating surpluses in the hands of a small landowning and mercantile class, commonly called "Phanariots" because so many of them lived or had originated in the Phanar district of Constantinople, where the Orthodox patriarchate had its headquarters. A few members of reigning families as well as lesser members of the Rumanian aristocracy went to study at Padua.[33] A rising level of taste and learning among the rulers supported a rapid development of schools and scholarly publication; in addition, some very impressive churches and monasteries were constructed in a style interestingly intermediate between Russian and Byzantine, with admixture of Armenian and western elements as well, e.g., in decorative motifs. The overall result was striking and original, though art historians conventionally prefer earlier, less ornate, Moldavian structures. For secular uses, a strongly Italianate palace architecture, replete with loggias and façades imitative of those of Venetian palazzos, presumably reflected the personal taste of the hospodars and their court circle.[34]

The central figure in the flowering of Greek learning on Rumanian soil was Patriarch Dositheos of Jerusalem (1641–1707).[35] Dositheos saw himself as responsible for the defense of Greek Orthodoxy everywhere. He it was who organized the establishment of a Greek academy in Moscow for example; and he devoted considerable attention to forwarding Greek theology among Georgian- and Arab-speaking Christians. He was a busy polemicist and founded a press at Jassy in 1670 to propagate Orthodox truth by publishing not only in Greek but in Arabic, Georgian, and Rumanian as well. A similar press was started at Bucharest soon afterward; its proudest achievement was the publication of an impressively learned translation of the Bible into Rumanian in 1688.[36]

This flurry of scholarly propaganda was certainly stimulated by the fact that the Rumanian provinces were a borderland between Greek, Slavic, and Latin linguistic provinces, so that the Greek learning and ecclesiastical tradition, so redoubtably defended by Dositheos, found itself confronting the heavily Latinized Church Slavonic learned tradition ensconced at Kiev since the time of Peter Moghila; and both confronted Protestant and Roman Catholic propaganda couched in Rumanian peasant speech! This contest was won decisively by the Greeks after 1711, when native Rumanian hospodars were displaced by Greek rulers come from Constantinople, who used the power of their office to support and confirm the Greek character of the provinces' ecclesiastical and secular culture.

Two products of Dositheos' busy pen contributed conspicuously to this result. The first of these was a new Confession of Faith, sharply anti-Protestant in tone, but more authentically Greek in theological nuance than Moghila's earlier Confession had been. Dositheos' Confession was approved by a synod at Jerusalem in 1672, and thereafter tended to displace Moghila's text as the preferred summation of Orthodox doctrine. No subsequent effort to define Orthodoxy has ever been made. Dositheos' Confession therefore ended a process of dogmatic definition begun a century earlier when Lutherans first tried to get Orthodox clerics to support them in their dogmatic debates with the pope.[37]

Dositheos' second great achievement was to give the Orthodox tradition a historical definition. He did this by writing a *History of the Patriarchs of Jerusalem*, published in 1715, eight years after his death. This is a vast work, incorporating many documents culled from all ages of church history down to and including Dositheos' own lifetime. The tone is polemical: he marshaled the record of the past to expose the errors of the west, whether Catholic or Protestant; but, of course, the scholarly technique Dositheos used was itself a child of western humanistic scholarship.[38]

Dositheos probably received his higher education at the patriarchal academy in Constantinople, where John Karyophylles, the pupil and loyal intellectual heir of Korydaleos, remained in charge until 1664. Yet in 1691 Dositheos felt impelled to bring an accusation of heresy against Karyophylles, and after a formal trial (at which Alexander Mavrocordato presided) Dositheos prevailed. Karyophylles was compelled to abjure his errors, and his offending manuscripts were burned.[39] Such an affair is reminiscent of Patriarch Gennadios' destruction of the works of Gemistus Pletho after 1453; and the circumstances that provoked such an obscurantist action were also similar. In Gennadios' age, Latin rational theology pressed the mystical tradition of Orthodoxy very hard. After a youthful, ardent flirtation with human reason as elaborated among the Latins, Gennadios reacted violently against what he came to feel was religiously irresponsible and dogmatically dangerous presumption. By burning Pletho's manuscript, he aimed to preserve Greek Orthodoxy from such speculative contamination. Almost exactly the same situation recurred toward the end of the seventeenth century, when defenders of Orthodoxy, like Dositheos, began to feel that the Orthodox faith was again threatened by too much reasoning about man and nature—reasoning, moreover, inspired from abroad and therefore liable to carry the taint of heresy as well as indulging the sin of pride.

The fact is that the precarious balance that had been struck early in the seventeenth century at Constantinople and other Orthodox centers between the Paduan style of Aristotelian rational science and religious truth threatened to topple over by the end of the century. New and more radical forms of rationalism, like that of Descartes (d. 1650), seeped into the Orthodox world, mainly via Jesuit schools, where the mathematical and physical doctrines of Cartesianism were regularly taught in the latter seventeenth century.[40] Moreover, the rise of a cultured upper class of layman (as in Pletho's time, too) created a small but sophisticated public for any and every intellectual novelty coming from the west. Under such circumstances, high ecclesiastics easily became alarmed. Their accustomed monopoly of abstract thought was being challenged by laymen who promulgated new doctrines recklessly, and with small regard for the fact that their new ideas could only be reconciled with Orthodoxy by redefinition of the boundaries between sacred and secular truth.

The career of Demetrius Cantemir (1673–1723), a younger contemporary of Dositheos, illustrates the problem Orthodox churchmen confronted. Born the son of the reigning hospodar of Moldavia, the young prince was introduced to intellectual concerns by a Greek who had studied at Leipzig and Vienna. A Rumanian nobleman named Miron Costin, who had been trained by Jesuits in Poland, also had strong influence over the young man. On his father's death, he went to Constantinople where he spent many years in semidetention, until in 1710 he managed to persuade the Turks to appoint him hospodar. The very next year, having compromised himself by dealings with Peter the Great, he lost his throne and spent the rest of his life in Russia.

His importance for us rests upon the books he wrote. They were very numerous: histories, theological works, and scientific-philosophical treatises all flowed freely from his pen. His central purpose was to reconcile the latest in western science with the traditions of Orthodoxy as Cantemir understood and was prepared to defend those traditions.[41]

Under ordinary circumstances the leaders of the Greek church might have been able to put up with the adventurous and eager search after truth that inspired laymen like Cantemir, even if it involved continued revision of doctrine in matters of natural science. This was what Orthodox churchmen had done in the 1620s, when Korydaleos' reform of education had proved tolerable, despite some sharp initial frictions. But by 1700 two events had put Greek prelates on guard, with the result that a narrow-minded, defensive mood surged in upon all those in strategic, responsible positions and led the hierarchy of the Greek Orthodox church for a second time to turn its back emphatically on everything new from the west.

The first shock to Orthodox sensibilities resulted from the renewal of Holy War under papal auspices, 1683–99. This drove a deep wedge between Latin and Greek Orthodox Christians, compelling the Greeks in effect to choose between Turkish and Latin subjection. Venetian and Hapsburg religious policy was such that the various halfway houses in matters of faith and ritual which had proliferated in the seventeenth century through the work of Roman Catholic missionaries in the Levant became uninhabitable. To be sure, many Orthodox Serbs did find a new halfway house by emigrating. In 1690 a large number of families followed the patriarch of Peć, Arsenios III, onto newly won Hapsburg territory north of the Sava River. There the Serbs set up an autonomous community; but the Hapsburg presence nevertheless meant an increasing permeation of thir cultural life with western ideas in the course of the eighteenth century.[42]

Greeks, on the other hand, scarcly wavered in their loyalty to the Ottoman regime. They had a lot to lose, having worked their way into so many positions of power and influence within the Ottoman fabric; and it soon became evident that Venetian or Hapsburg rule would involve religious oppression far greater than anything the Turks were accustomed to exert. To be sure, there were manifestations of welcome for the Venetians when first they appeared in the Morea in 1695; but, as we saw, the fiscal and religious policy of the Venetian administration quickly alienated their new Greek subjects. This made it easy for the Orthodox hierarchy and Phanariot laymen in Constantinople to demonstrate a genuine as well as a politic preference for Turkish as against western rule. One way to show such loyalty, of course, was to reject intellectual and other cultural influences coming from abroad. This the Orthodox clergy were already inclined to do because the tumultuous flow of new and radical thought was so difficult to deal with anyway. The proceeding against John Karyophylles in 1691 was therefore a political as well as a philosophical demonstration of where the loyalties of the Greek church lay.

A second, reinforcing experience was the way in which Tsar Peter the Great of Russia (ruled 1689–1725) destroyed Greek influence over the Russian church. This influence had never been unchallenged; both Roman Catholic and Protestant ideas had continued to flood into Russia during the entire seventeenth century. Nikon's thrust after certainty by basing himself upon the tradition of Jerusalem and Greek Orthodoxy, although it continued to attract a powerful party within the church after the great patriarch's overthrow, was never able to dam the flow of contrary thoughts and opinions coming from the west.[43] From early youth, Peter had been attracted to western things, and when he took over Russia's government he launched a general and ruthless westernization. Nearly all of the Russian prelates opposed Peter's policies. The consequence was that in 1700, when the reigning patriarch died, Peter refused to replace him and instead put the governance of the Russian church under a synod like that familiar among Lutherans.

The leading spirits of Peter's new ecclesiastical regime, Stephen Javorsky and Theofan Prokopovich,[44] were both Ukrainians, heirs of the learned tradition established by Peter Moghila. They followed a consciously anti-Greek, pro-western policy. Peter's action therefore undid the Greek successes of 1589–1685; even the Greek Academy, so recently established in Moscow, was overhauled and a Latin curriculum modeled on Kiev's put in place of the Greek studies that had been imported from Constantinople!

In art as in thought, Peter directed his attention westward, building upon Ukrainian precedents. Baroque church edifices had first come to the Ukraine in the early part of the seventeenth century;[45] this style, firmly associated with reformed, proselytizing Roman Catholicism, was imported to Moscow for the first time in 1693; and when Peter set out to construct his new capital, he employed western architects (including several Italians) to make Saint Petersburg a thoroughly contemporary artistic monument, with no telltale traces of either the Greek or Russian Orthodox past.[46]

The Greek hierarchy, with Patriarch Dositheos leading the pack, protested vigorously against what Peter was doing to the Russian church, but could do nothing but deplore the tsar's disdain for true religion and the loss of their influence in the tsar's territories. Yet this quarrel made it easier in 1711, when Peter attacked the Ottoman Empire and penetrated as far as the Pruth River in Moldavia, for Greek prelates and secular magnates to refrain from any gesture of sympathy for the Russians, despite efforts Peter made to sound the tocsin for a general Christian revolt against the Turks.[47]

The effect, therefore, of these events was to bring the Greek Orthodox hierarchy and the Turkish government into a tacit alliance very similar to that which Patriarch Gennadios and Sultan Mehmed the Conqueror had formed after 1453. The Greek church had come full circle: both in the fifteenth and in the eighteenth century, the leaders of Greek Orthodoxy became deeply suspicious of the west and fearful of new ideas coming from that direction, even though in both ages the intellectual tradition which the Orthodox clergy cherished incorporated important elements—scar tissue mayhap—deriving from earlier encounters with that same ever-restless west.[48]

The Greeks soon reaped practical rewards for their demonstrated loyalty to the Ottoman regime. Beginning in 1701, Phanariots established a stranglehold on the high office of Dragoman of the Fleet, which carried with it effective jurisdiction over most of the islands and some coastal areas of the Aegean. After 1711, too, the rich Rumanian provinces were governed by Phanariot Greeks appointed from Constantinople. Both regimes lasted until 1821, when Greeks in their turn proved ready to betray the Turks. In the ecclesiastical field, the Turks permitted the œcumenical patriarch to complete the administrative consolidation of the Orthodox churches within Ottoman borders by abolishing the Serbian patriarchate of Peć and the Bulgarian patriarchate of Ochrid in 1766–67. These were not great events in themselves, for both patriarchates had fallen on evil days and were already administered by Greeks at the time of their formal suppression.[49] It was, nevertheless, symptomatic of a general tightening up of legal and administrative procedures within the Greek Orthodox church,[50] a development which, like the way in which Greek Orthodoxy had been pressed into the narrow confines of a precise Confession of Faith, made the œcumenical patriarch more like an Orthodox pope than before. The patriarchate even began to organize schools and missions in Albania, in an effort to check conversion to Islam which early in the eighteenth century had been proceeding at a fairly rapid rate.[51] This, too, was a direct imitation of papal policy. Thus even in rejecting the west, the prelates who ruled over the Greek Orthodox church found themselves constrained, almost in spite of themselves, to imitate their Roman rivals.

After 1700, with the hardening of Greek Orthodox sentiment against further truck with the west, the weight and influence of Venice and of Italy generally ceased to count for much in eastern Europe. The Catholic missionary presence, which continued to exacerbate relations with the Greek church throughout the eighteenth century,[52] had become entirely French; and after 1700 it was French culture and French ideas along with French trade and French techniques that infiltrated Ottoman society, Christian and Moslem alike. France, in other words, took over the role of metropolitan center which had previously been filled by northern Italy, ever since the end of the thirteenth century. With that shift, the pattern of cultural relationship which this book has tried to explore broke up and disappeared; yet even in its declining days there were still occasions on which the old, familiar link between Venice and the east asserted a spasmodic existence.

The mainstream, however, set in emphatically for France. In the course of the eighteenth century a few Greek clerics were attracted to French Enlightenment ideas.[53] The top hierarchy, of course, always resisted. It was mainly laymen, especially the prospering merchants who took over more and more of the Ottoman Empire's carrying trade, who propagated new tastes and new ideas among the Orthodox communities of eastern Europe, including, after 1774, the entire region of the Black Sea and especially south Russia.[54]

Among the Turks, too, a circle of high officials and courtiers became mildly interested in French culture along with French military technique after the Treaty of Passarowitz in 1718.[55] By that time, two successive defeats, 1683–99 and 1714–18, at Austrian hands convinced many Turks in high positions that something drastic would have to be done to improve Ottoman artillery. This meant teaching artillery officers elementary mathematics and engineering, for which purpose a school with instructional materials translated from French manuals was opened at Scutari in 1734. A handful of men realized that a far broader upgrading of Turkish skills and knowledge was required to keep pace with the west. The most interesting of these, Ibrahim Müteferrika (ca. 1670–1745), was a Unitarian from Hungary who turned Turk without, however, changing his religious views or surrendering the high intellectual culture he had acquired in his youth. Ibrahim was probably instrumental in getting the artillery school set up; he was certainly the man who persuaded the Ottoman *ulema* to authorize the establishment of a Turkish printing press at Constantinople in 1727, on the understanding that he would print only books on science, mathematics, geography, and such indifferent subjects, leaving religious texts strictly to the guild of calligraphers.[56]

Turkish art reflected the new interest in French models of civilization, especially during the so-called Tulip era, 1718–30;[57] and French merchants who dominated east-west Mediterranean trade after 1713[58] imported various articles of luxury made in France for sale to the Ottoman upper classes—Christian and Moslem alike.

Yet the number of Turks who took any serious interest in French or any other form of Christian civilization in the eighteenth century was very small; and when in 1736–39 Ottoman armies confronted a combined Austro-Russian attack, yet managed to defeat the Austrians and conclude an advantageous peace at Belgrade into the bargain,[59] the leaders of the empire concluded that it was quite unnecessary to continue the fundamentally distasteful efforts at reform that had been launched after 1718. Printing virtually stopped, for instance, after Ibrahim's death in 1745. It was not resumed until 1783, when fresh defeat at the hands of the Russians in 1774 had reopened the whole question of how to cope with superior foreign military forces. In architecture, however, Ottoman baroque, using motifs borrowed from Italian prototypes, started about 1755 and continued to dominate the taste of Istanbul thereafter until almost the end of the eighteenth century.[60]

Russia's course was fundamentally different. From the time of Peter the Great (d. 1725) there was no turning back for the clique of adventurers who ran the Russian government, many of whom were themselves of foreign, mainly German, extraction. The only question was whether the French or the German cultural model was the more persuasive. The payoff came in 1768–74 when Russian armies proved themselves far superior to their Turkish enemy and succeeded in opening up the Black Sea to Christian shipping for the first time since 1453.

Yet the Russian example reminds us that other cultural traditions lay buried, like archeological strata, among the lower classes of Orthodox society. Of these the most active and powerful was undoubtedly the hesychast pattern of piety which had been preserved within monasteries of Mount Athos ever since the fourteenth century. It welled up afresh in the later eighteenth century through the writing and personal example of a number of holy monks, chief among them Saint Nicodemus, the Hagiorite (1748–1809). His monumental work of piety, entitled *Philokalia*, was published in Venice in 1782. It drew freely on Roman Catholic as well as Orthodox mystical writings, and the regimen Saint Nicodemus prescribed (e.g., frequent communion) owed something to Jesuit rules of piety which he had encountered as a schoolboy in his native island of Naxos. Nevertheless the essence of Saint Nicodemus' teaching was consciously Orthodox and Greek. The *Philokalia* became extremely influential in forwarding a revival and spread of hesychast styles of piety—especially the practice of ecstasy-inducing prayer—not only among Greeks but in the Russian lands as well.[61]

There is something suitably valedictory in the fact that this last important contribution to Orthodox Christendom's development in which Venice had a hand was rather a reaffirmation of eastern elements in the Orthodox inheritance than renewal of western aggression against the east. The Venetian establishment as much as the Orthodox establishment had become fixedly backward-looking by 1782; each felt challenged by ill-understood and insistent revolutionary innovations; and insofar as either deigned to speak to the other, it was, appropriately, with accents and ideas drawn from a distant past. The shared Aristotelianism of their respective educational establishments attested earlier intercourse; but for both Orthodox and Venetian minds that common inheritance had become a burden and a barrier to rigorous, original thought by the last decades of the eighteenth century.

Not surprisingly, both establishments crumbled before the same antagonist: revolutionary France. Venice fell in 1797; the Orthodox establishment of the Ottoman Empire collapsed in 1821, when the revolutionary ideals of freedom and equality, invoked by leaders of the Greek revolution, shattered beyond repair the Phanariot-Ottoman symbiosis within which the Greek upper classes had nestled—albeit uncomfortably—ever since 1700.

As for Russia, the last notable contribution Venice made to that country's history was fittingly enough of an entirely opposite intellectual character. For John Capodistrias (1776–1831), Tsar Alexander I's friend and foreign minister during his doctrinaire and liberal years, 1815–22, started life in the Venetian island of Corfu and, like so many Greeks before him, took an M.D. at the University of Padua before entering politics and joining the Russian service in 1809. Dying as first president of independent Greece, Capodistrias in his person bridged the gap, or at least tried to do so, between the old and new regimes of Europe as experienced among the Greeks; and the guidelines he chose were none other than the cluster of enlightened and revolutionary ideas which the rulers of Venice and the Greek Orthodox hierarchy had so systematically rejected until force overthrew them both.

Yet while the words he used and the ideals he voiced were certainly new, the pattern of his career, shifting from medicine to politics and acting as go-between and *homme de confiance* for the mighty, was completely conformable to the tradition established by Capodistrias' illustrious predecessors, Panagiotis Nicoussias and Alexander Mavrocordato. Thus as late as 1821, a generation after the end of Venetian political independence, old patterns of interaction between the Latin and Orthodox portions of Europe continued to manifest themselves, even in the final revolutionary act itself.

Notes

One—*The Frankish Thrust into the Levant, 1081–1282*
1. The three-century time lapse between the initial invention of the techniques of knighthood and their manifestation on Mediterranean battlefields was due to difficulties northern Europeans had in supporting any significant number of such expensively equipped fighters. This was solved by about 950 through far-reaching agricultural and sociopolitical changes in the region between the Loire and Rhine. See Marc Bloch, *Les caractères originaux de l'histoire rurale française* (Oslo, 1931). Thereafter properly equipped and trained knights multiplied rapidly, so that by 1050 considerable numbers of younger sons became available for ventures far afield. The thrust toward the Levant was only one of several similar expansive moves—into Iberia, England and Ireland, trans-Elbia, and down the Danube. On knighthood see Lynn White, Jr., *Medieval Technology and Social Change* (Oxford 1962), pp. 1–38.
2. Even in their heyday, knights needed infantry support on the battlefield, as tanks did in World War II. See R. E. Smail, *Crusading Warfare 1097–1193* (Cambridge 1956), pp. 192–203 and passim.
3. The earliest known chrysobull defining the conditions of Venetian trade in Constantinople, which dates from 922, refers to "old custom" as normative for that trade. See H. F. Brown, "The Venetians and the Venetian Quarter in Constantinople to the close of the Twelfth Century," *Journal of Hellenic Studies* 40 (1920): 68–70.
4. The chrysobull enumerated a total of 32 towns where Venetian traders would not have to pay excise. See Silvano Borsari, "Il commercio veneziano nell' Impero Bizantino nel XII secolo," *Rivista Storia Italiana* 76 (1964): 985–86, for the full enumeration. The Black Sea remained closed, however; so did Cyprus and the islands of the Aegean, except Chios and Negropont. In addition, Alexius

assigned space along the waterfront of the Golden Horn to the Venetians for quays, warehouses, and other amenities needed for trade in the Byzantine capital.

5. See Hélène Antoniades-Bibicou, *Recherches sur les Douanes à Byzance* (Paris, 1963), pp. 222–24.

6. In matters of religion as in other respects, Venice long remained marginal between Latin and Orthodox Christendom. The patriarch of Grado enjoyed Venetian protection. His lofty ecclesiastical titulature descended from the days when the headquarters of the western half of the Roman empire had been situated at the head of the Adriatic. By the eleventh century the patriarchal title had become a convenient vestige, implying association with rather than subordination to the œcumenical patriarch of Constantinople.

Local ecclesiastical autonomy was further reinforced in 828 when a party of Venetians surreptitiously brought back the relics of Saint Mark from Alexandria. This provided Venetian piety with apostolic patronage independent of, even if junior to, that enjoyed by Saint Peter's successor in Rome. Such powerful sanctions for ecclesiastical independence of both pope and patriarch existed nowhere else in Latin Christendom.

7. This word is a contraction of "rivo alto," i.e., high bank or shore.

8. By 1188, less than a century after its establishment, the Arsenal was capable of readying between 40 and 100 galleys within six months. See Heinrich Kretschmayr, *Geschichte von Venedig* (Gotha, 1905), 1: 185.

9. This feat was performed for King Henry III of France during his visit to Venice in 1574. See W. Carew Hazlitt, *The Venetian Republic: its Rise, its Growth, and its Fall* (London, 1915), 2: 549; Frederic C. Lane, *Venetian Ships and Shipbuilders of the Renaissance* (Baltimore, 1934), p. 144.

10. Pisans paid a 4 percent excise tax; Venetians paid none; the standard rate was 10 percent. See Freddy Thiriet, *La Romanie vénitienne au moyen âge* (Paris, 1959), p. 40.

11. Cf. Kretschmayr, *Venedig*, 1: 224–25.

12. It proved to be the longest lived of all European overseas empires, since it endured, with many ups and downs, for six and three-quarter centuries, until 1797.

13. For details see Hélène Ahrweiler, *Byzance et la mer* (Paris, 1966), pp. 175–267.

14. Ibid.; pp. 230–32, 288 ff.

15. George I. Bratianu, *La Mer Noire: des Origines à la conquête*

Ottomane [Societas Academica Dacoromana, Acta Historica IX] (Munich, 1969), pp. 165–66.

16. See Maurice Lombard, "Arsenaux et Bois de Marine dans la Méditerranée Musulmane, VII-XIe siècles," in Michel Mollat, ed., *Le Navire et l'économie maritime du moyen âge au XVIIIe siècle principalement en Méditerranée* [Travaux du Deuxième Colloque International d'Histoire Maritime, 1957] (Paris, 1958), pp. 53–99.

17. Ahrweiler, *Byzance et la mer*, p. 438.

18. Cf. Lionel Casson, *Ships and Seamanship in the Ancient World* (Princeton, N. J., 1971), pp. 202–8 and passim. This is a fundamental and admirable book, but unfortunately breaks off just at the time when the eleventh-century "revolution," if such there were, was about to occur. I owe the hypothesis of a drastic change in shipbuilding in the eleventh century to a private communication from Professor Lynn White, Jr.

19. Ibid., pp. 338–39; George F. Bass, ed., *A History of Seafaring Based on Underwater Archeology* (London, 1972), pp. 143–46, describes a Byzantine ship dating from about A.D. 625 in which mortice and tenon construction was used for only part of the hull. By the twelfth century, another Byzantine wreck is known which exhibits rib and plank construction throughout, giving a *terminus ad quem* for the change. But as of 1972 gaps in available evidence remain enormous.

20. Gino Luzzatto, *Storia economica di Venezia dall'XI al XVI secolo* (Venice, 1961), pp. 25–28, gives details of personal investments made by Sebastiani Ziani (doge, 1172–78) and his son Pietro (doge, 1205–29). The Ziani family was the richest in Venice and sustained that status by investing in a large number of different trading ventures.

21. See Wilhelm Heyd, *Geschichte des Levanthandels im Mittelalter* (Stuttgart, 1879), 1: 110–21, 207–8).

22. This seems to have been the fate of the Byzantine empire after 1082, and of the Norman kingdom of Sicily after the end of the twelfth century. On Byzantium see below, pp. 29, 78; on Sicily see Denis Mack Smith, *A History of Sicily: Medieval Sicily, 800–1713* (New York, 1968), pp. 43, 55–56, 59.

23. Frederic C. Lane, "Economic Consequences of Organized Violence," *Journal of Economic History* 18 (1958): 401–17, reprinted in *Venice and History: The Collected Papers of Frederic C. Lane* (Baltimore, 1966), pp. 412–28.

24. The technical conditions of moldboard tillage are made admirably clear in C. S. and C. S. Orwin, *The Open Fields* (Oxford,

1938). The importance of the moldboard plow in medieval agriculture was first emphasized by Marc Bloch, *Les caractères originaux de l'histoire rurale française;* Lynn White, Jr., *Medieval Technology and Social Change,* pp. 41–57, convincingly elaborates on Bloch's ideas.

25. Intuitive judgments of "national character" suggest that there is a close coincidence between a special capacity to cooperate for peaceful purposes and the boundaries of moldboard cultivation. Mediterranean Europe, where vines and olives grew, never knew the moldboard plow; these are the regions of Greek "philotimo," Spanish pride, and Sicilian "omertà." Ireland also escaped the discipline of the moldboard plow for the most part; so did Slavic Europe, except for Bohemia, Slovenia, and part of Croatia. On geographical range of the moldboard plow cf. the distribution of "long acre" fields as described in the monumental work of August Metzen, *Siedlung und Agrarwesen der Westgermanen, Ostgermanen, Kelten, Römer, Finnen und Slawen* (3 vols. and Atlas; Berlin, 1895). Meitzen did not relate long acre fields with moldboard plows but attributed differences in field layouts to race. Nevertheless, his data remain the most complete ever assembled.

There are, of course, other bases for transfamilial cooperation than the plow team. Military and hunting bands are the most important of these, being all but universal in human societies. But the attitudinal biases appropriate to cooperation in the application of violence are not easily compatible with dull, persistent, routinized, and purposive activity. The contrary was true of the work teams created to drive the moldboard plow through the soil of west Europe.

26. The quarters and eighths of modern stock exchange prices descend directly from this practice.

27. There is an extensive literature on the *colleganza,* which came later to be used for loans to artisans and others who remained in situ. Cf. G. Padovan, "Capitale e lavoro nel commercio veneziano dei secoli XI e XII," *Rivista di Storia Economica* 6 (1941): 1–24; Gino Luzzatto, *Studi di storia economica veneziana* (Padua, 1954), pp. 59–81; Robert S. Lopez and Irving W. Raymond, *Medieval Trade in the Mediterranean World* (New York and London, 1955), pp. 174–84; Frederic C. Lane, "Investment and Usury," *Explorations in Entrepreneurial History* 2, ser. 2 (1964): 3–15, reprinted in Lane, *Venice and History,* pp. 56–68.

28. Notably Florence and Genoa.

29. Luzzatto, *Storia,* pp. 28–34, 108–9.

30. Artificial brotherhoods, sealed by some ritual act, were important in Moslem artisan life, and this did something to transcend the limits on wider scale cooperations imposed by pervasive and well-grounded attitudes of extrafamilial distrust. The so-called "akhi" that developed between the eleventh and thirteenth centuries among Moslems were part artificial brotherhood, part craft guild, part mystical encounter group. Cf. Bernard Lewis, "The Islamic Guilds," *Economic History Review* 8 (1937): 20–37. The identity of Venetian legal forms with those of Egypt for interregional trade comes clear in S. D. Goiten's *A Mediterranean Society: The Jewish Communities of the Arab World as portrayed in the documents of the Cairo Geniza* 1: *The Economic Foundations* (Berkeley and Los Angeles, 1967): 169 ff. Abraham L. Udovich, *Partnership and Profit in Medieval Islam* (Princeton, 1970), p. 173, derives the *commenda* form of contract from pre-Islamic Arabian commercial practices.

31. Cf. Luzzatto, *Studi,* p. 62, for details of one instance: a man who at the time of his death had twenty-five separate *colleganze.* Such diversification was usual because it reduced the risk of losing too much trading capital in any single shipwreck or other disaster.

32. Cf. Armando Sapori, *Le Marchand Italien au Moyen Age* (Paris, 1952), pp. xi-xiii.

33. I have been unable to find any discussion of the arms industry in Byzantium under the Comneni; but the well-attested use of Latin knights in large numbers as mercenaries implies the need for a supply of arms *à la Frank,* a need that Milanese arms manufacturers were in a position to meet better than anyone else. For Latins in Byzantine armies see Speros Vryonis, Jr., *The Decline of Medieval Hellenism in Asia Minor and the Process of Islamization from the Eleventh through the Fifteenth Century* (Berkeley, Los Angeles, and London, 1971), pp. 75–76, 106–8.

34. Kretschmayr, *Venedig,* 1: 237–40. Such treaties were, of course, variants of the sort of trade treaties Venice maintained with more distant, much greater powers.

35. The crisis began when Venice refused (1166) to supply naval forces to the Byzantine emperor Manuel for operations against the Normans. This was an infraction of the obligations Venice owed the emperor as *quid pro quo* for their trade privilege. See H. F. Brown, "Venetians and the Venetian Quarter in Constantinople to the close of the Twelfth Century," *Journal of Hellenic Studies* 40 (1920): 84.

36. According to a Greek chronicler, as many as 10,000 Venetians were arrested on this occasion. See Luzzatto, *Storia,* p. 22. This

number is no doubt exaggerated, but at least suggests an order of magnitude for the Venetian presence in the Levant—thousands rather than hundreds.

37. Manuel in fact never did pay the promised sum, and Venetian commerce had not resumed full scale when, three years after his death, in 1183, trade relations between Latins and Greeks broke down afresh.

38. Cf. Vryonis, *The Decline of Medieval Hellenism*, pp. 184–94 and passim. Seljuk policy and the disturbed conditions of the interior of Anatolia combined to divert trade goods originating in the east to the south coast of the peninsula where Christian merchants operating from Cyprus took over.

39. See the judicious summary in Kenneth Setton, ed., *A History of the Crusades* (Madison, 1969), 2: 167–73, and Joseph Gill, "Franks, Venetians and Pope Innocent III," *Studi Veneziani* 12 (1970): 85–105.

40. The force that invaded and conquered the Peloponnese numbered only a few hundred, yet overcame Greek forces ten times the size without difficulty. On the other hand, sieges of strongly fortified places lasted until hunger reduced the garrison. See Donald M. Nicol, *The Despotate of Epiros* (Oxford, 1957), pp. 14–25.

41. Boniface of Montferrat claimed Crete in the initial distribution of the spoils; he sold his rights in the island to Venice in 1204. See Thiriet, *La Romanie vénitienne*, pp. 75–76.

42. Roberto Cessi, *Storia della Repubblica di Venezia* (Milan, 1944), 1: 195–210; Silvano Borsari, *Studi sulle colonie Veneziane in Romania nel XIII secolo* (Naples, 1966), pp. 89 ff.

43. A sixteenth-century chronicler says that soon after this reconciliation it was proposed to transfer the seat of Venetian government to Constantinople. Modern scholars are not agreed as to the accuracy of this report. See Thiriet, *La Romanie vénitienne*, pp. 92–93; Cessi, *Storia*, 1: 210.

44. A garrison of only 132 knights (each responsible for putting himself and two mounted squires into the field as needed) was judged sufficient to control the entire island of Crete. Silvano Borsari, *Il Dominio veneziano in Creta nel XIII secolo* (Naples, 1963), pp. 23–31. Total Venetian population resident in Crete in the thirteenth century has been estimated at 3,500. Thiriet, *La Romanie vénitienne*, p. 131.

45. The years immediately after 1204 were important in Venetian constitutional history. Under a successful buccaneer like Henry Dandolo, the office of doge threatened to become a personal mon-

archy. As leader of the crusade he took key decisions without consulting home authorities, and presented them with a series of *faits accomplis*. Under his successors, however, this development was reversed; the dogeship became definitely a magistracy and not a monarchy. The model offered by the dogeship of Candia may in fact have helped to define the dogeship of Venice. Giacomo Tiepolo, for instance, had a long career in the colonies, acting as doge of Candia, 1208–16, and as *podestà* in Constantinople, 1218–20 and 1224–27, before becoming doge of Venice, 1229–49. For such a man, having served the Venetian state as doge of Candia must have made it seem more natural to do the same as doge of Venice. On Tiepolo's career see Thiriet, *La Romanie vénitienne*, pp. 93, 125; Kretschmayr, *Venedig*, 1: 340–42.

46. See Silvano Borsari, *Il Dominio veneziano in Creta nel XIII secolo*, pp. 23–31.

47. The principality of Achaia, although it gave Venetian merchants free access to its ports and even accepted nominal subordination to Venice in 1209, was practically in a position to play Venetians off against other merchants coming from the Norman kingdom or from the west coast of Italy. Further east, in the Aegean, this was not really the case, so that Venetian influence over the lords of Negropont, for example, was always preponderant. See Thiriet, *La Romanie vénitienne*, pp. 80–88; Borsari, *Studi sulle colonie veneziane*, p. 43 ff.

48. George I. Bratianu, "Etudes sur l'approvisionnement de Constantinople et le monopole du blé a l'époque byzantine et ottomane," *Etudes Byzantines d'histoire économique et sociale* (Paris, 1938), pp. 129–81.

49. Among the peoples of the steppes, the role of honored guest could stretch to accommodate foreign merchants. This required appropriate behavior on the part of the merchants, of course; i.e., readiness to make a gift to the host in expectation of suitable return, and other forms of politeness. At least sometimes, bargaining took an inverse form—the partner coming off best who gave the gift of greatest value. Haggling was counterproductive; the dramatic gesture counted for a great deal. Marco Polo's *Travels* illustrate the advantages of handling so rare and portable a commodity as gems in appropriately "reckless" ways among steppe peoples.

It is possible that the fusion between noble and merchant that had taken place in north Italian towns from the twelfth century or before made it easier for Italian traders to conform to steppe ideals of calculatedly reckless generosity, whereas merchants accustomed only to grovel before the mighty found the steppes extremely inhospitable for their kind of shrewdness.

50. See George Bratianu, *La Mer Noire,* pp. 220–35; Roberto Lopez, *Storia delle colonie Genovesi nel Mediterraneo* (Bologna, 1938), pp. 250 ff.

51. The earliest example of open warfare between homeland and colony came in 1318, when Pera and Genoa, controlled by different factions, one Ghibelline, one Guelf, resorted to sea fights to settle their differences. Ibid., p. 292.

52. The last Norman king, William II (reigned 1166–89), married off his great aunt (and heir) to Barbarossa's son, Henry VI (reigned 1190–97). Henry had to fight for his wife's inheritance in southern Italy; his son and heir, Emperor Frederick II (reigned 1212–50), resided by preference in his southern dominions, quarreling bitterly with the popes who feared that any consolidation of the Hohenstaufens' imperial power in Italy would spell the end of their own long-standing sovereignty over Rome and central Italy.

53. When Charles formulated his ambitions, the imperial title in the west was in limbo, and from a Latin point of view the same was true in Constantinople. He dreamed therefore of assuming an undisputed imperial title after driving the Greeks from the Bosporos once more and then, perhaps, leading a united Christendom against the Moslems, as his brother King Louis twice vainly attempted (1249–50, 1270).

54. Cf. Deno Geanakoplos, *Emperor Michael Paleologus and the West, 1258–1282: a Study in Byzantine-Latin Relations* (Cambridge, Mass., 1959); Steven Runciman, *The Sicilian Vespers* (Cambridge, 1958).

55. Only the opportune intervention of a corps of crossbowmen saved the day for King Louis in Egypt in 1249. Setton, *Crusades,* 1: 501.

56. Cf. Ramon Muntaner, *Chronicle,* trans. by Lady Goodenough, Hakluyt Society, ser. 2, 47 (1920): 148, 192, 254, 279–80, 330.

57. Kenneth M. Setton, *Catalan Domination of Athens, 1311–1388* (Cambridge, Mass., 1948), seems unaware of the Catalans' armament but provides full details of a very tangled political story.

58. Romans had crossbows and their use never disappeared entirely thereafter in Mediterranean fighting. Charles Singer et al., eds., *A History of Technology* (Oxford, 1956), 2: 707–9. The crossbow was, in fact, a miniaturized version of one form of catapult, related to the larger weapons exactly as hand guns of the sixteenth

century were to siege cannon of the fifteenth. The problem in making crossbows effective was to find bow materials strong and flexible enough to develop sufficient power to penetrate armor without becoming awkwardly large and too heavy for a single man to lift and aim. There were equally important problems of finding ways to cock such a bow and release it by a suitable trigger mechanism. Cf. John F. Guilmartin, *Gunpowder and Galleys: Changing Technology and Mediterranean Warfare at Sea in the Sixteenth Century* (Cambridge, forthcoming), chap. 4; Ralph W. F. Payne-Gallwey, *The Crossbow, medieval and modern, military and sporting: Its Construction, History and Management* (London, 1958). Captain Guilmartin very kindly allowed me to read his ms.

I have been unable to discover of what the Catalan bows were made. Ramon Muntaner says: ". . . all Catalan crossbowmen are people who can renovate a crossbow and every one of them knows how to put it together and how to make light darts and bolts and how to twist and tie the string, and he understands all that pertains to a crossbow. And so he carries all his tools in a box, and it is as if he had a workshop. And no other people do this. . . . Wherefore the Catalans are the most superior crossbowmen of the world" (*Chronicle,* p. 330). These skills, plus the hitherto unexampled number of weapons the Catalans employed, appear to be the secret of their success.

59. Frederic C. Lane, "The Crossbow in the Nautical Revolution of the Middle Ages," *Economy, Society and Government in Medieval Italy: Essays in honor of Robert L. Reynolds* (Kent, Ohio, 1969), pp. 161–71.

60. Muntaner's description, quoted above, may indicate that the Catalan crossbows derived their strength from being made of more than one material. If so, it is probable that they were constructed on the well-known principle of the Turkish compound bow, which used sinews to reinforce wood and sometimes horn or bone. For details and excellent photographs see W. F. Paterson, "The Archers of Islam," *Journal of the Economic and Social History of the Orient* 9 (1966): 69–87. Construction and maintenance of such bows would be unfamiliar to most western Europeans in the thirteenth century; but without better information it seems fruitless to speculate on how the Catalans achieved their remarkable—though evanescent—dominance in missile weaponry. Payne-Gallwey, *The Crossbow,* pp. 62–63, and Charles Singer, ed., *A History of Technology,* 2: 723, say that steel crossbows came in ca. 1370, extending effective range of fire to about 400 yards. According to the same authorities, ear-

lier bows were of wood, bone, and sinew; but they say nothing of either Turkish or Catalan roles in developing the weapon.

61. Ferdinand Lot, *L'art militaire et les armées au moyen âge en Europe et dans la Proche Orient* (Paris, 1946), 1: 340 ff. Charles W. C. Oman, *The Art of War in the Middle Ages* (Boston and New York, 1924), 1: 378–79; 2: 111 ff.

62. Nicol, *The Despotate of Epiros*, pp. 32, 180 ff.; Ferdinand Chalandon, *Les Comnènes* (Paris, 1912), 2: 620.

63. Kenneth M. Setton, "The Byzantine Background to the Italian Renaissance," American Philosophical Society, *Proceedings* 100 (1956): 38–40; Bruno Lavagnini, *La letteratura neoellenica* (3d ed.; Florence, 1969), pp. 18–26; C. Th. Dimaras, *Histoire de la littérature neo-héllenique* (Athens, 1965), pp. 27 ff.

64. Geanakoplos, *Emperor Michael Paleologus*, pp. 65, 266–76.

65. Oman, *History of the Art of War in the Middle Ages*, 2: 24–52.

66. R. Janin, "Les Francs au service des Byzantins," *Echos d'Orient* 29 (1930): 61–72; William Miller, *The Latins in the Levant: A History of Frankish Greece, 1204–1566* (London, 1908), pp. 148–49.

67. Constantin Jireček, *Geschichte der Serben* (Gotha, 1911), 1: 288–302; 2: 16–17; Dimitri Obolensky, *The Byzantine Commonwealth: Eastern Europe, 500–1453* (London, 1971), pp. 237–43, 349–51.

68. Cf. Denis Mack Smith, *Medieval Sicily*, pp. 24–64. For details about Sicilian translations into Latin from Greek cf. Charles H. Haskins and Dean Putnam Lockwood, "The Sicilian translators of the twelfth century and the first Latin version of Ptolemy's Almagest," *Harvard Studies in Classical Philology* 21 (1910): 75–102; Charles H. Haskins, "Further notes on Sicilian translations of the twelfth century," Ibid. 23 (1912): 155–66.

69. Michael Huxley, ed., *The Root of Europe: Studies in the Diffusion of Greek Culture* (London, 1952), pp. 53–54.

70. I rely mainly on the elegant and judicious learning of Otto Demus, *Byzantine Art and the West* (New York, 1970), for what follows.

71. Otto Demus, *The Church of San Marco in Venice: History, Architecture, Sculpture* [Dumbarton Oaks Studies 6] (Washington, D.C., 1960); Sergio Bettini, *L'Architettura di San Marco* (Padua, 1946).

72. It is interesting to note that Kiev served a similar function in the northward diffusion of Byzantine art. Prince Yaroslav (ruled

1019–54), like the Norman rulers of Sicily, strove to express his royalty through mosaic decoration of the Cathedral of Saint Sophia in Kiev. Cf. G. K. Loukomski, *L'Architecture religieuse Russe du XIe au XVIIe siècle* (Paris, 1929), appendix, pp. 98–102; Arthur Voyce, *Art and Architecture of Medieval Russia* (Norman, 1967), p. 91.

73. Cf. Demus, *Byzantine Art and the West*, pp. 29–30. Kurt Weitzmann has ingeniously suggested that ateliers in the crusading states, especially at Acre, may have played a part in spreading Byzantine styles westward. Cf. Kurt Weitzmann, "Various Aspects of Byzantine Influence on the Latin Countries from the 6th to the 12th century," *Dumbarton Oaks Papers* 20 (1966): 3–24; Kurt Weitzmann, "Icon Painting in the Crusader Kingdom," Ibid., pp. 51–83.

Two—Venice as a Great Power, 1282–1481

1. Carlo M. Cipolla, *Moneta e civiltà mediterranea* (Venice, 1957), p. 70, calculates the ratio of land:sea transport costs ca. 1282 as 20:1. This at least suggests an order of magnitude for the change involved when ships began to ply regularly between Europe's northern and southern shores.

2. For details of the amazing career of Benedetto Zaccaria see Robert Lopez, *Genova Marinara nel Duecento: Benedetto Zaccaria, ammiraglio e mercanti* [Biblioteca Storica Principato XVII] (Messina-Milan, 1933).

3. Steering oars could be multiplied in number and enlarged, affixed permanently to the ship's frame by a pivot, and counterweighted so that human strength did not have to lift the entire weight of the oar. Such steering rigs competed with sternpost rudders until the latter part of the fifteenth century. See Jacques Heers, *Gênes au XVe siècle: Activité économique et problèmes sociaux* (Paris, 1961), p. 277. They were, however, inherently clumsier and more fragile than the single rudder, tucked close in under the stern and aligned with the keel. Cf. the nineteenth-century contrast between paddle wheelers and screw-driven ships.

4. Measured by an hourglass.

5. Comte Richard Le Febvre des Noëttes, *De la marine antique et la marine moderne: la Révolution du gouvernail: Contribution a l'étude d' esclavage* (Paris, 1935), was the first to emphasize the importance of the sternpost rudder; but his views were promptly contradicted on technical grounds by G. de la Roërie, "Les Transformations du Gouvernail," *Annales, Economics, Sociétés, Civilisa-*

tions 7 (1935): 564–83. A truly perspicacious account of the late medieval revolution in maritime affairs has yet to be written. Pierre Chaunu, *L'Expansion européene du XIIIe au XVe siècle* (Paris, 1969), pp. 273–307, is the best wide-ranging treatment of the matter that I have encountered. For more technical matters Romola and Roger C. Anderson, *The Sailing Ship: Six Thousand Years of History* (London, 1926), pp. 85–115, give some data; so do Frederic C. Lane, *Venetian Ships and Shipbuilders of the Renaissance* (Baltimore, 1934), pp. pp. 34–53; Jules Sottas, *Les Messageries maritimes de Venise au XIVe et XVe siècles* (Paris, 1938), p. 58 ff.; and Heers, *Gênes au XVe siècle*, pp. 267 ff. Significant aspects of nautical developments on either side of 1300 come clearer in a cluster of brilliant articles by Lane, all published in 1963 and reprinted in *Venice and History* (Baltimore, 1966): "The Economic Meaning of the Invention of the Compass," *American Historical Review* 68 (1963): 605–17; "From Biremes to Triremes," *The Mariner's Mirror* 49 (1963): 48–50; "Merchant Galleys, 1300–34: Private and Communal Operation," *Speculum* 38 (1963): 179–205.

The development of windlasses, block and tackle, and other means of exerting mechanical advantage for moving heavy objects (including rudders) is an aspect of the development that seems unexplored. Nor has anyone tried to connect the development of crossbows with the changes in ship design, though it seems clear that the big new cogs, relatively slow and cumbersome because of their size, had to depend on missiles for protection. There is reason to suspect, in other words, that the military revolution emphasized in the preceding chapter was connected intimately with the nautical developments that inaugurated the new "renaissance" age of Italian shipping; but exact information is hard to find. Paintings and drawings, though more reliable than words, are often puzzling; and scholars have not yet combed available sources with appropriate questions in mind.

6. Cf. Lane's remarks on the differentiation between bowmen and rowers in "The Crossbow in the Nautical Revolution of the Middle Ages," *Economy, Society and Government in Medieval Italy: Essays in honor of Robert L. Reynolds* (Kent, Ohio, 1969), pp. 161–69.

7. Italian shippers owed part of their success to the administrative rationality with which they developed differential freight rates for different commodities and different hauls calculated to keep their holds full as much of the time as possible. This had the effect of greatly reducing freight charges on some hauls, since it was

always better for the shipowner to have some cargo on board rather than have to return empty. See Frederigo Melis, "Il fattore economico nello sviluppo della navigazione alla fine del Trecento," in Manlio Cortelazzo, ed., *Mediterraneo e Oceano Indiano* [Atti del Sesto Colloquio Internationale di Storia Marittima, 1962] (Florence, 1970), pp. 99–105.

8. The term was applied to all costly goods (except gems) imported to Europe from the east, and extended to items no longer commonly called "spices": dyes, drugs, aphrodisiacs, sugar, etc.

9. George I. Bratianu, *La Mer Noire: des Origines à la conquête Ottomane* (Munich, 1969), p. 254; Julian Chrysostomides, "Venetian Commercial Privileges under the Paleologi," *Studi Veneziani* 12 (1970): 316, dates major grain imports to Venice from the Black Sea region to the year 1268.

10. See Michel Mollat, "Aux origines de la précocité économique et sociale de Venise: l'exploitation du sel," Centro di Cultura e Civiltà della Fondazione Giorgio Cini, *La Venezia del Mille* (Florence, 1965), pp. 185–202.

11. A corruption of Monemvasia, a port in the southeast Morea from which much of it was shipped.

12. See Gino Luzzatto, *Storia economica di venezia* (Venice, 1961), pp. 124–27.

13. For an interesting discussion of how distant regions of Europe and North Africa meshed together economically see Robert Sabatino Lopez, "The Origin of Merino Sheep," *Joshua Starr Memorial Volume: Studies in History and Philology* (New York, 1953), pp. 161–68.

14. See Lopez, *Genova Marinara nel Duecento*, pp. 23–39.

15. For details see Heers, *Gênes au XVe siècle*, pp. 273–79, 316–20. These specialized alum carriers of the fifteenth century resembled the giant oil tankers of our own time. They were uneconomic for other uses, since big ships (over 1,000 tons capacity) could not ordinarily pick up enough cargo to utilize their capacity. Wooden ships of later centuries were therefore smaller.

16. Charles Verlinden, "Le Commerce en Mer Noire des débuts de l'époque Byzantine au lendemain de la conquête de l'Egypt par les Ottomans (1517)," *XIIIe Congrès International des Sciences Historiques* (Moscow, 1970), p. 11. Cf. the same author's "La colonie vénitienne de Tana, centre de la traite des esclaves au XIVe et au début du XVe siècle," A. Giuffrè, ed., *Studi in onore di Gino Luzzatto* (Milan, 1950), 2: 1–25.

17. On Ottoman marriage patterns see A. D. Alderson, *The Structure of the Ottoman Dynasty* (Oxford, 1956), pp. 85–100.

18. Iris Origo, "The Domestic Enemy: Eastern Slaves in Tuscany in the 14th and 15th Centuries," *Speculum* 30 (1955): 321–66.

19. See Fernand Braudel, "Monnaies et Civilisations: De l'or du Soudan à l'argent d'Amérique," *Annales: économies, sociétés, civilisations* 1 (1946): 9–22.

20. See Berthold Spuler, *Die goldene Horde: die Mongolen in Russland, 1223–1502* (2d ed.; Wiesbaden, 1965), pp. 400–404.

21. An adventitious but by no means unimportant additional advantage accrued to Italian businessmen from their association with the papacy. Agents, almost always of Italian origin, who were stationed in distant regions of Latin Christendom to look after papal revenues were often also in a good position to develop other kinds of business. M. D. O'Sullivan, *Italian Merchant Bankers in Ireland in the Thirteenth Century* (Dublin, 1962), shows how this process operated in one of Europe's remoter corners; Marian Malowist, "Les routes de commerce et les marchandises du Levant dans la vie de la Pologne au bas Moyen Age et au début de l'époque moderne," in Manlio Cortelazzo, ed., *Mediterraneo e Oceano Indiano*, pp. 157–75, points out something similar for Poland.

22. In 1462 alum mines were discovered at Tolfa, near Ostia, in the papal states. In the sixteenth century the papacy organized a new monopoly on the basis of these mines, but in the latter seventeenth century several other deposits of the mineral were discovered, and long-range haulage of alum in large quantities ceased to make sense. See Jean Delumeau, *L'Alun de Rome XVe–XIXe siècles* (Paris, 1962).

23. For the geographic migration of the strong, sweet "malmsey" type of wine see Roger Dion, *Histoire de la Vigne et du Vin en France* (Paris, 1959), pp. 317–23.

24. The earliest mention of sugar growing in Crete dates from 1428, according to Raymond Matton, *La Crète au cours de siècles* (Athens, 1957), p. 116.

25. See Charles Verlinden, *Les Origines de la civilisation Atlantique* (Paris, 1966), pp. 157–78.

26. Wilhelm Heyd, *Geschichte des Levanthandels im Mittelalter* (Stuttgart, 1879), 2: 698–99.

27. Luzzatto, *Storia economica*, pp. 55, 68; Lane, *Venice and History*, pp. 113–16; Heyd, *Levanthandels* 2: 572–75.

28. See, for instance, David Herlihy, "Population, Plague and Social Change in Rural Pistoia, 1201–1430," *Economic History Re-*

view 18 (1965): 225–44. On the other hand, recovery from the Black Death in Venice came quickly, as in other leading Italian business centers. See Luzzatto, *Storia economica*, pp. 135–45.

29. The debate provoked by Robert S. Lopez, "Hard Times and Investment in Culture," in Metropolitan Museum of Art, *The Renaissance: a Symposium* (New York, 1953), pp. 19–33, seems inconclusive. Cf. Armando Sapori, "Economia e Cultura nell'Eta del Rinascimento," reprinted in Armando Sapori, *Studi di Storia economica* (3d ed.; Florence, 1955), 1: 649–52; Wallace K. Ferguson, "Recent Trends in the Economic Historiography of the Renaissance," *Studies in the Renaissance* 7 (1960): 7–26; Robert S. Lopez and H. A. Miskimin, "The Economic Depression of the Renaissance," *Economic History Review* 14 (1962): 408–26; Carlo M. Cipolla, "Economic Depression of the Renaissance?" *Economic History Review* 16 (1964): 519–24, with rejoinders by Lopez and Miskimin, pp. 525–29.

30. Not surprisingly, a diaspora of Italian experts and adventurers had much to do with the initial development of more efficient administrative and financial methods in territorially large states. See Armando Sapori, *Le Marchand Italien au Moyen Age* (Paris, 1952), pp. liii–lix. Sapori dates the peak of the Italian diaspora to 1400; thereafter, local rivals, having themselves acquired sufficient skills from association and competition with the strangers, slowly squeezed out the Italians.

31. See Heers, *Gênes aux XVe siècle*, pp. 385–406; Philip Argenti, *The Occupation of Chios by the Genoese, 1346–1566* (3 vols.; Cambridge, 1958).

32. See Charles Verlinden, *Précédents mediévaux de la colonie en Amérique* (Mexico, 1954).

33. Heers, *Gênes aux XVe siècle*, pp. 564–89, 97–190; Emilio Marengo, Camillo Manfroni, and Giuseppe Pessagno *Il Banco di San Giorgio* (Genoa, 1911).

34. Alexis Kallergis, leader of the rising, was in touch with Constantinople, but got little help from Emperor Michael VIII. Freddy Thiriet, *La Romanie vénitienne au moyen âge* (Paris, 1959), p. 153.

35. Lane, "Medieval Political Ideas and the Venetian Constitution," *Venice and History*, pp. 286, 306–7, suggests that from twenty to forty men controlled the Venetian state in the late twelfth century. By contrast, the Great Council, as defined at the end of the thirteenth century, included between one thousand and two thousand members, not all of whom took part in meetings, of course, but who all had the right to do so, and transmitted the right to their

sons automatically, even if they themselves remained politically inactive.

36. See the admirably instructive chart prepared by Alberto Tenenti and Corrado Vivanti, "Le film d'un grand système de navigation: Les galères marchandes vénitiennes, XIV-XVI siècles," *Annales: Economies, sociétés, civilisations* 16 (1961): pocket insert. It shows only five years between 1332 and 1534 in which *muda* were not auctioned off. Three of these years were when Venice was herself besieged during the war of Chioggia, 1379–81.

37. For details of dimensions, etc., see Alberto Sacerdoti "Note sulle galere da mercato venezianne nel XVe secolo," *Bolletino del istituto di Storia della Società e dello Stato Veneziano* 4 (1962: 80–105.

38. Under special conditions oars were used even in open sea. A detailed record of the use of sails and oars has been reported for a voyage in the sixteenth century by Elena Fasano-Guarini, "Aux XVIe siècle: Comment naviguent les galères?" *Annales: Economies, Sociétés, Civilisations* 16 (1961): 279–96.

39. Early merchant galleys were smaller than those built later. Their capacity rose from about 150 tons burden early in the fourteenth century to about 250 tons burden by the end of the fifteenth century. This was the upper limit practical with lateen-rigged sails, because the heavy spar that holds a lateen sail in place quickly becomes unmanageable with increased size. See Paul Gille, "Les navires des deux routes des Indes: (Venise et Portugal): Evolution des Types, Résultats économiques," in Cortelazzo, ed., *Mediterraneo e Oceano Indiano*, pp. 193–201; Sottas, *Les Messageries maritimes de Venise*, p. 68.

40. Lane, "Merchant Galleys, 1300–34: Private and Communal Operation," *Speculum* 38 (1963): 179–205, reprinted in *Venice and History*, pp. 193–226.

41. In 1423 the Doge Tomasso Mocenigo calculated Venetian maritime resources as follows:

3,000 small vessels, employing 17,000 crewmen
  300 large sailing vessels, employing 8,000 crewmen
    45 galleys, employing 11,000 crewmen, of which
      25 were merchant galleys
      15 were war galleys
       5 were specialized for carrying passengers
        —— pilgrim galleys to the Holy Land
        —— special vehicles for ambassadors and
        message-carrying.

Sottas, *Les Messageries maritimes,* p. 37. In time of war, of course, the number of galleys could be approximately doubled (maximum was about one hundred) by commissioning reserve ships from the Arsenal.

42. Genoa and other cities also built merchant galleys from time to time. See, for example, Michael E. Mallett, *The Florentine Galleys in the Fifteenth Century* (Oxford, 1967) pp. 24–39. Most Mediterranean galleys, however, remained ships of war. It was the special character of trade goods, i.e., the prominence of spices and other precious commodities, that made the galley a worthwhile carrier. In return, the development of merchant galleys and of the *muda* organization perpetuated Venetian emphasis on mixed trading in luxury goods in an age when others were pioneering the bulk transport of cheap commodities.

43. Sottas, *Les Messageries maritimes,* p. 50.

44. Only nobles were eligible to bid.

45. See the list of prices bid for galleys going to the Black Sea between 1332 and 1396 in Thiriet, *La Romanie vénitienne,* pp. 344–45.

46. Lane, "Rhythm and Rapidity of Turnover in Venetian Trade of the Fifteenth Century," *Venice in History,* pp. 109–27, translated from *Studi in onore di Gino Luzzatto,* 1: 254–73.

47. Lane, "Fleets and Fairs: the Functions of the Venetian Muda," *Studi in onore di Armando Sapori* (Milan, 1957), 1: 651–63, reprinted in *Venice and History,* pp. 128–41.

48. Until the 1340s, the Flanders voyage remained in private hands. A century and a half later, the famous diarist and chronicler, Marino Sanudo (1466–1536), explained why this was changed, as follows: "In 1349, there were built in the yards of Terranuova three great galleys for private persons, . . . with which they went to Flanders and returned in eight months and seven days and gained greatly. Thereupon it was passed that no more great galleys were to be built for private persons and that they should be made for the government. And three having been built and having been sent on the voyage to Flanders . . . , they made the voyage in ten months and twenty-six days." Quoted in Lane, *Andrea Barbarigo, Merchant of Venice, 1419–1449* (Baltimore, 1944), pp. 80–81. Sanudo's facts appear to be somewhat mixed up, but his words may be taken as an authoritative mirror of public attitudes, at least in his own time, when the galleys were already becoming obsolete.

49. See Lane's penetrating case study of Andrea Barbarigo, cited above, n. 48.

50. Citizens could, of course, become fronts for foreigners whether Jews, Greeks, Florentines, or other varieties of Latin Christian. But this was uncommon. Venetians continued to finance their own trade until the end of the *muda* system; and the foreign communities that established themselves in the city never became economically dominant.

51. Cf. the hymn to Venetian commercial-mindedness in Luzzatto, *Storia economica*, pp. 72–80; and the more quizzical analysis of Giorgio Cracco, *Società e stato nel medioevo veneziano, secoli XII-XIV* (Florence, 1967).

52. A young noble often began his career as a "bowman of the quarterdeck" aboard a merchant galley; this was an honorific and expeditious way to become acquainted with the world with which Venice had to deal. Not infrequently, such a man would then devote himself to trade, often living abroad for a decade or more before returning to Venice to marry and enter upon a political career. See Gino Luzzatto, "Les activités économiques du Patriciat vénitien," *Annales d'histoire économique et sociale* 9 (1937): 25–57. This meant, among other things, that wild oats were mostly sown abroad, while at home Venice remained very much a gerontocracy. Cf. an episode in 1373, when members of the Great Council under thirty years of age who were excluded from deliberations anent war with Padua protested in an unseemly manner and were disciplined for such behavior. W. Carew Hazlitt, *The Venetian Republic* (London, 1915), 1: 684–85. On the significance of age groupings in Venetian politics see D. S. Chambers, *The Imperial Age of Venice 1380–1580* (London, 1970), p. 82.

53. The size of the noble class made it literally possible for every Venetian noblemen of active years to know every other man of the same class. Luzzatto calculated the total as about 1,180 in the mid-fourteenth century. "Les activités économiques du Patriciat vénitien," *Annales d'histoire économique et sociale* 9 (1937): 55.

54. George I. Bratianu, "Les Vénitiens dans la mer Noire au XIVe siècle après la deuxième guerre des Détroits," *Echos d'Orient* 33 (1934): 148–62; Elena C. Skržinskaya, "Storia della Tana," *Studi Veneziani* 10 (1968): 3–46.

55. Thiriet, *La Romanie vénitienne*, p. 327, calculates that in 1342 Venice drew seven-tenths of its grain from regions not under Venetian political control, of which a large proportion came from the Black Sea. Cf. Marie Nystazapoulou-Pelekidis, "Venise et la mer noire du XIe au XVe siècles," *Thesaurismata: Bolletino dell'Istituto*

Ellenico di Studi Bizantini e Post-Bizantini, Venezia 7 (1970): 14–51.
56. Thiriet, *La Romanie vénitienne,* pp. 173–74, 251–56.
57. Cf. Heyd, *Levanthandels,* 2: 1–24, 406–26; George Hill, *A History of Cyprus* 2: *The Frankish Period, 1192–1432* (Cambridge, 1948): 369 and passim. From 1373, when the Genoese seized Famagusta and held the island government to ransom, the profits of trade concentrated largely in Genoese (and to a lesser extent also in Venetian) hands. The Genoese set up a *maona* for Cyprus like that which from 1346 had exploited Chios so successfully. The Cyprus *maona* never conquered the whole of the island, but very effectively weakened and impoverished the Lusignan rulers.
58. Heers, *Gênes aux XVe siècle,* pp. 366–68.
59. Bratianu, *La Mer Noire,* pp. 281–303; Marian Malowist, "Les routes de commerce et les marchandises du Levant dans la vie de Pologne au bas moyen âge et au début de l'époque moderne," in Manlio Cortelazzo, ed., *Mediterraneo e Oceano Indiano,* pp. 157–75; Skržinskaya, "Storia della Tana," *Studi Veneziani* 10 (1968): 3–46.
60. Kretschmayr, *Venedig,* 2: 229–40.
61. Ibid., p. 580. The ambassadorial function grew slowly, and the custom of maintaining permanent embassies, charged with sending back regular reports for the information of home authorities, did not achieve firm definition until the 1450s. Cf. Garrett Mattingly, *Renaissance Diplomacy* (Boston, 1955), chap. 7.
62. For the story of Carmagnola's trial see Kretschmayr, *Venedig,* 2: 341–42.
63. Marc Antonio Bragadin, *Repubbliche Italiane sul Mare* (Milan, 1951), p. 146.
64. Thiriet, *La Romanie vénitienne,* p. 402–3.
65. Navies have always been less liable than armies to organize *coups d'état,* presumably because in going ashore ties of discipline customarily—and almost necessarily—dissolve. Sailors fresh from long weeks at sea have other things in mind than seizing power on behalf of their commanders; an army, already in being, need only march to the seat of power.
In this connection, Venice's location offshore was surely a contributory factor to the city's immunity from military *coups d'état.* No army could march to the Square of Saint Mark's; swift surprise was therefore impossible.
66. Gino Luzzatto, *Studi di storia economica veneziana* (Padua, 1954), pp. 217–18.
67. Thiriet, *La Romanie vénitienne,* pp. 219–35.

68. In 1423, Doge Tomasso Mocenigo publicly estimated the annual income of the Venetian Republic as follows:

From Venice itself	774,000 ducats
From *terra firma*	464,000 ducats
From overseas	376,000 ducats
	1,614,000 ducats

Luzzatto, *Storia economica*, p. 165. This may have been boastful; another estimate puts Venetian income in the 1470s at only a million ducats per annum; but this was a good 40 percent larger than the annual income available to Milan and Naples, the next wealthiest of the Italian governments. See Denys Hay, *Europe in the Fourteenth and Fifteenth Centuries* (London, 1966), p. 186.

69. This idea derives from Robert Lopez, *The Birth of Europe* (New York, 1966), p. 266.

70. In particular, the interests of the state and interests of particular traders within the state did not always coincide. For interesting examples and discussion of this problem see Philippe Braunstein, "Le commerce du fer à Venise au XVe siècle," *Studi Veneziani* 8 (1966): 267–92.

71. A fundamental requirement for such management was a supply of well-trained clerks and professionalized administrators. This was secured through the establishment in 1402 of a Chancellery School which admitted boys at age twelve and put them through a rigorous training in Latin, law, administrative routines, etc. See Freddy Thiriet, *Histoire de Venise* (Paris, 1952), p. 92.

72. The despotate of Mistra had been established in the Morea between 1278 and 1308, as an appanage of the Byzantine Empire. See D. A. Zakythinos, *Le Despotat grec de Morée* (2 vols.; Paris and Athens, 1932–35). In the latter fourteenth and early fifteenth centuries, the part of the Morea under Greek rule shared in the commercial development that came to Crete in the same period, exporting wine northward to Constantinople and the Black Sea as well as westward to Venice and beyond.

73. Thiriet, *La Romanie vénitienne*, pp. 399–406. The Venetian government imposed the same condition on Latin clergy, for the pope was always a foreign power as far as the Venetian state was concerned. Pervasive antipapalism, which characterized the ecclesiastical life of Venice, made rapprochement with Orthodox Christians easier insofar as Latin Christianity impinged upon Orthodox consciousness in a papal guise. Rapprochement between the Venetian and Orthodox communities therefore assumed real importance only

with the emergence of the papacy as the director of Catholic reform in the sixteenth century. See below, chap. 5.

74. Freddy Thiriet, "La condition paysanne et les problèmes de l'exploitation rurale en Romanie Gréco-vénitienne," *Studi Veneziani* 9 (1967): 35–69, finds evidences of a small class of fairly prosperous peasants in Crete by the close of the fourteenth century.

75. Vera Hrochova, "Le Commerce vénitien et les changements dans l'importance des centres de commerce en Grèce du 13e au 15e siècle," *Studi Veneziani* 9 (1967): 3–34, traces the rise of new export centers trading with Venice in precise geographic detail. The grain trade used many ports, each supplying only small quantities for export, yet in sum amounting to substantial quantities for feeding a city the size of Venice.

76. On Fredrico Cornaro see Luzzatto," *Studi di Storia economica,* pp. 117–23. Sugar plantations appeared in Crete between 1400 and 1410 according to Thiriet, "Quelques Réflexions sur les enterprises vénitiennes dans les pays du sud-est européen," *Revue des Etudes Sud-Est Européenne* 6 (1969): 395–405.

77. Luzzatto, *Storia economica,* pp. 190–203; Philippe Braunstein "Le commerce du fer à Venise au XVe siècle," *Studi Veneziani* 8 (1966): 267–92.

78. Pera's trade in 1423 was only one-seventh what it had been in 1323; a similarly precipitous decay of business occurred in Genoa, according to Roberto Lopez, *Storia delle Colonie genovesi nel Mediterraneo* (Bologne, 1938), pp. 378, 404. Venice herself lost out to Ragusa (Dubrovnik) in some respects after about 1358. First the Hungarians and later the Turks on the whole preferred to open the interior of the western Balkans to traders from Ragusa rather than to the politically more troublesome Venetians. Hence the mining developments of Bosnia and adjacent regions that assumed some importance in the fifteenth century were financed by Slavic traders from Ragusa. See B. Krekić, *Dubrovnik (Raguse) et le Levant au Moyen Age* (Paris, 1961). On Balkan mining see Desanka Kovačević, "Dans la Serbie et la Bosnie mediévales: Les Mines d'Or et d'Argent," *Annales: Economies, Sociétés, Civilisations* 15 (1960): 248–58.

79. On Venetian public ceremonials see Pompeo G. Molmenti, *La storia Venezia nella vita privata dalla origini alla caduta della repubblica* (5th ed.; Bergamo, 1910), 1: 231–64; Bianca Tamassia Mazzarotto, *Le Feste veneziane; i Giochi populari, le Ceremonie religiose e di Governo* (Florence, 1961).

80. See Leon-Pierre Raybaud, *Le Gouvernement et l'administration centrale de l'empire Byzantin sous les premiers Paléologues, 1258–1354* (Paris, 1968).

81. Bratianu, *Etudes byzantines d'histoire économique et sociale,* p. 153. Price differentials for grain were substantial, even within the Mediterranean, offering shipowners an (often evanescent) chance for making substantial gains. In the 1480s, for example, grain prices in Salonika oscillated at a figure about one-fifth of those in Venice. Cf. Freddy Thiriet, "Les lettres commerciales des Bembo et le commerce vénitien dans l'empire Ottoman à la fin du XVe siècle," *Studi in onore di Armando Sapori,* 2: 913–33. This almost equaled the 1:7 price differential calculated as normal between Lvov and Valencia in the fifteenth century according to Pierre Chaunu, *L'Expansion européenne,* p. 343. These cities were respectively the cheapest and the dearest grain markets of the time in Europe for which price series are available.

This did not mean, of course, that a merchant might not lose his shirt by loading grain at inflated prices in time of dearth and carrying it to some distant market where, in the meantime, the price had dropped drastically due to the arrival of other ships. The leading feature of the grain market, in fact, was the rapidity of price fluctuation from year to year, season to season and region to region —depending on local harvest conditions.

Overall, of course, the development of the grain trade blunted the edge of local famine, and allowed more people to survive crop failure; but it was the urban segment that mainly profited. In time of local crop failure, peasants normally could not buy, having nothing of value to offer in exchange. Their only choice lay between flight and starvation.

82. The population of Byzantine cities decreased sharply in the fourteenth and early fifteenth centuries. See Peter Charanis, "A note on the Population and Cities of the Byzantine Empire in the 13th century," *The Joshua Starr Memorial Volume: Studies in History and Philology* (New York, 1953), pp. 135–48.

83. Under Andronicus II (reigned 1282–1328) strenuous efforts to increase tax income achieved a figure of one million depreciated gold coins per annum; a figure less than an eighth of the imperial income three centuries before according to George Ostrogorsky, *History of the Byzantine State* (2d ed.; Oxford, 1969), pp. 484–85. This sum soon shrank; by mid-century Genoese customs receipts at Galata were nearly eight times the customs receipts the imperial government collected in Constantinople itself (Ibid., p. 526). For

illuminating details of how Venetian traders escaped Byzantine taxation see Juliàn Chrysostomides, "Venetian Commerical Privileges under the Paleologi," *Studi Veneziani* 12 (1970): 267–329.

84. On the fraying out of the Frankish model of knighthood, see Raybaud, *Le Gouvernement et l'administration centrale de l'Empire Byzantin*, pp. 250–51, and above, pp. 38–40.

85. Cf. Peter Charanis, "Internal Strife in Byzantium during the 14th Century," *Byzantion* 15 (1940–41): 208–30. Had hesychasm and the Zealot social program joined forces, Byzantine society might have armed itself with an emotionally powerful popular ideal for which men would have been willing to fight. There was no inherent antipathy between mysticism and warlike prowess, as the Ottoman polity proved. On the other hand, the long-established symbiosis of the Mount Athos monasteries (where hesychasm had its primary seat) with Byzantine imperial circles made it easy for a champion of the aristocracy like John Cantacuzenus to take on the role of protector of the hesychast movement. Thus just as Byzantine feudalism came too late to protect Orthodoxy, so also hesychasm missed fire as a potential focus for popular mobilization in defense of Orthodoxy by allowing aristocratic patrons to capture it. The best treatment of hesychasm known to me is Jean Meyendorff, *St. Grégoire Palamas et la mystique orthodoxe* (Paris, 1959). On hesychasm see chap. three, below.

86. Cf. Dimitri Obolensky, *The Byzantine Commonwealth* (London, 1971), pp. 243–60.

87. Claude Cahen, *Pre-Ottoman Turkey: A General survey of the material and spiritual culture and history, c. 1071–1330* (London, 1968), pp. 314–18; Speros Vryonis, Jr., *The Decline of Medieval Hellenism in Asia Minor* (Berkeley, Los Angeles, and London, 1971), pp. 184–94.

88. The highly professionalized music of Turkish dervish rituals probably drew some of its technique from ancestral shamanism. In particular, the prominence of drums and the insistence of their beat seems likely to derive from shaman ritual practices.

To dance to such music magnifies the direct effect of rhythmic sound and stirs atavistic roots of human sociality. Our hunting ancestors in all probability danced rhythmically around their campfires —perhaps before speech had been articulated. The emotional effect of such an experience is duplicated in some degree by recent Anglo-American "rock" music. It seems clear that conversion to a doctrine and to a distinctive life style was facilitated and proclaimed by such music—both in our age and in Anatolia of the thirteenth-fifteenth centuries. I have been unable to find a history of dervish music in any language I can read; but having heard such music on the Turkish radio during Ramadan in 1971, some faint idea of its emotional force came home to me.

89. For details see Cahen, *Pre-Ottoman Turkey*, pp. 336–39.

90. Slaves were secured both by purchase and by capture in war; when these channels failed to supply enough manpower to make good the losses suffered by the sultan's household through heavy campaigning, the Ottomans resorted to the device of rounding up Christian boys from remote villages, where collection of money taxes was difficult or impossible. This so-called *devshirme* became customary in the fifteenth century, but never entirely supplanted other channels of recruitment. The *devshirme* became a dreaded blood tax for the mountain villages of the western Balkans, though the boys who survived and rose to high positions in the Ottoman government clearly did not regret their enslavement. The *devshirme* had precedents in other Turkish states, but only the Ottoman sultans set up a systematic training program to make the raw enslaved manpower maximally serviceable. See Speros Vryonis, Jr., "Seljuk Gulans and Ottoman Devshirmes," *Der Islam* 41 (1965): 224–52.

91. The above remarks derive mainly from Paul Wittek, *The Rise of the Ottoman Empire* (London, 1957), and Halil Inalcik, "The Emergence of the Ottomans," *Cambridge History of Islam* (Cambridge, 1970), 1: 263–91.

92. The spread of timars through the Balkans substituted small estates for large ones. In addition, estates held in return for strictly enforced service obligations replaced estates previously enjoying immunities from central jurisdiction or taxation. The overall effect was to destroy an old aristocracy that had been deeply engaged in export-import trade, replacing it with a far more numerous military class, who consumed more of the available agricultural surplus on the spot and marketed far less. Resources, in other words, were deflected toward military and away from civilian uses and brought under effective central control. The "feudalism" thus implanted in the Balkans differed greatly from other feudalisms, and there is little to be gained by belaboring the term, as does Ernst Werner, *Die Geburt einer Grossmacht—die Osmanen (1300–1481): Ein Beitrag zur Genesis des türkischen Feudalismus* (Berlin, 1966), pp. 219–304. Despite occasional exhibitions of doctrinal rigidity, this book is very instructive. For a contrary emphasis on the bureaucratic element in the Ottoman polity see Paul Wittek, "De la Défaite

d'Ankara à la prise de Constantinople," *Revue des Etudes Islamiques* 12 (1938): 1–34.

93. See Athanase Gegaj, *L'Albanie et l'invasion turque au XVe siècle* (Louvain-Paris, 1937).

94. The standard authority on Mehmed II is Franz Babinger, *Mehmed der Eroberer und seine Zeit* (Munich, 1953). Cf. also Inalcik, "The Rise of the Ottoman Empire," *Cambridge History of Islam*, 1: 295–308.

95. Ibid., pp. 305–6.

96. Mallett, *The Florentine Galleys*, pp. 68–69. After 1460, Mehmed's subjects paid only 4 percent tariff on goods coming in and out of Ottoman ports. This was 1 percent less than foreigners had to pay, thus reversing the tax advantage that had favored foreigners ever since 1081. The result was, as might be expected, to transfer the empire's internal trade and some of its export trade from Italian hands. Turks, Armenians, Greeks, and Jews were the principal beneficiaries. Cf. Halil Inalcik, "Bursa and the Commerce of the Levant," *Journal of the Economic and Social History of the Orient* 3 (1960): 131–47.

97. Roberto Lopez, "Il principio della guerra veneto-turca nel 1463," *Archivio Veneto*, series 5, 15 (1934): 45–131, gives full narrative details.

98. Ship for ship, Venetian traditions of seamanship continued to give them superiority; it was only strategically—the really important aspect of sea power—that the Ottoman fleet attained superiority.

99. Bratianu, *La Mer Noire*, pp. 322 ff.

100. The history of gold coinage accurately symbolized these basic shifts of power, for gold both followed and supported political strength. In 1284 the Venetians began coining the gold ducat, and maintained it with only very minute changes at a standard weight and purity until 1545. The Ottoman government first put out a gold coinage of its own in 1476, modeled on the ducat as to weight and purity; Spain followed suit in 1497. The importance of the ducat in international trade suffered from these new competitors, almost as much as the Venetian state itself suffered from the same two competitors on the political-military level. See Philip Grierson, "La Moneta veneziana nell'economia mediterranea del Trecento e Quattrocento," in Fondazione Giorgio Cini, Centro di Cultura e Civiltà, *La civiltà veneziana del Quattrocento* (Florence, 1957), pp. 77–97.

101. Galley warfare required access to land bases, preferably

fortified. Large-scale naval campaigns therefore turned upon sieges of strategically located, fortified ports. For a clear and convincing account of the differences between this style of naval warfare and that developed by men-of-war under sail in the seventeenth-eighteenth centuries cf. John F. Guilmartin, *Gunpowder and Galleys* (Cambridge, forthcoming), chaps. 1–3.

102. For details of Venetian troubles in Italy during and immediately after the Turkish war see Kretschmayr, *Venedig*, 2: 371–88.

103. The war of 1463–79 had strained Ottoman resources near the limit. Mehmed's death provided the occasion for a strong reaction on the part of Moslems who had lost *waqf* lands (confiscated wholesale in 1475) and been pinched by currency revaluations—and who distrusted the religiously tolerant atmosphere of Mehmed's court into the bargain. On Mehmed's policy toward Moslem landholders see Bistra Cvetkova, "Sur certaines réformes du régime foncier au temps de Mahomet II," *Journal of the Economic and Social History of the Orient* 6 (1963): 104–20. On Mehmed's death see Babinger, *Mehmed der Eroberer*, pp. 443–45.

104. Rhodes, too, remained Christian until 1522.

105. On guns in Ottoman society see V. J. Parry, "Warfare," *Cambridge History of Islam*, 2: 834 ff. On role of cannon in fifteenth-century Muscovy see Richard Hellie, *Enserfment and Military Change in Muscovy* (Chicago, 1971), pp. 154–55. A Bolognese architect, engineer, and cannon founder arrived in Moscow about 1475 and taught the Russians to make bronze guns. As military expert he took part in Ivan III's campaigns against Novgorod (1478), Kazan (1482), and Tver (1485). Both Novgorod and Tver were added to Muscovite dominions through these campaigns—a clear demonstration of the connection between the new weapons and the erection of hitherto unattainably large agricultural empires.

Three—Cultural Interactions, 1282–1481

1. Cf. Hans Baron, *The Crisis of the Early Italian Renaissance: Civic Humanism and Republican Liberty in an Age of Classicism and Tyranny* (Princeton, 1966), pp. 387–400.

2. Verona lost its independence initially to Milan in 1387.

3. The Dominican church, SS Giovanni e Paolo, was built between 1246 and 1430; the Franciscans' Santa Gloriosa dei Frari was started only in 1338.

4. See Rodolfo Pallucchini, *La Pittura Veneziana del Trecento* (Venice-Rome, 1964), *La Pittura a Veneta del Quattrocento* (Bologna, n.d.).

5. In 1451 the patriarch of Grado removed to Venice; the city thus became the seat of a prelate who claimed a rank almost equivalent to that of the pope himself. Significantly, the premier church of Venice, Saint Mark's, did not become the patriarch's seat, but remained the (ostensibly private) chapel of the doge.

6. A law of 1339 prohibited improper dress in carnival time, and mentioned specifically the custom of visiting churches and nunneries wearing masks. See Pompeo G. Molmenti, *La Storia di Venezia nella vita privata* (Bergamo, 1910), 1: 255. The Council of Ten—the principal wielder of police authority in Venice—had become permanent only four years before this law was passed.

7. I have been unable to find any history of carnival customs or of their spread through Europe and beyond. The contents of Julio Caro Baroja, *El Carnaval (Analisis Historico-Cultural)* (Madrid, 1965), belie the title; Adolf Spamer, *Deutsche Fastnachtsbräuchen* (Jena, 1936), and Higinio Vazquez-Santana y J. Ignacio Davila-Garibi, *El Carnaval* (Mexico City, 1931), are both narrowly local. It seems clear nonetheless that Venice played a special role in what took place. The use of masks, crucial to the psychology of carnival, is said to have come to Venice from the Levant, and is first mentioned in Venetian records in 1268. Molmenti, *La Storia di Venezia,* 1: 255. If this is so, Venice's pivotal role can scarcely be doubted.

Comparison of Venetian carnival with Ottoman dervish ritual is worth thinking about. Music, dance, and sex played a prominent part in both traditions. The Venetians compartmentalized their year between two sharply contrasting modes of behavior; the Turks compartmentalized their society. Both institutionalized an emotionally vibrant counterculture, thereby stabilizing an officially prescribed rigor.

8. See Paul O. Kristeller, "Die italienischen Universitäten der Renaissance," *Schriften und Vorträge des Petrarcha Instituts* (Cologne, n.d.), 1: 23; P. Heinrich Denifle, *Die Entsehung der Universitäten des Mittelalters bis* 1400 (Berlin, 1885), p. 289.

9. In 1354 Demetrios Cydones translated Aquinas' *Summa Contra Gentiles* into Greek, making the richness of Latin intellectual accomplishments available to Byzantine intellectuals for the first time. He went on to translate the *Summa Theologica* (1358) with the help of his brother Prochoros Cydones; and about 1360 became a Roman Catholic. See Kenneth M. Setton, "The Byzantine Background to the Italian Renaissance," American Philosophical Society, *Proceedings* 100 (1956): 52–57.

10. See the photographs in M. Berza, ed., *Cultura Mol-*

doveneasca in Timpul lui Stefan cel Mare (Bucharest, 1964), pp. 259–362; Wladimir Sas-Zaloziecky, *Die byzantinische Baukunst in den Balkanländer und ihre Differenzierung unter abendländischen und islamischen Einwirkungen* (Munich, 1955), pp. 109–10.

11. Barlaam subsequently taught Petrarch Greek at Avignon and ended up a bishop in southern Italy, having recognized the authority of the pope. For his biography and attainments see Setton, "The Byzantine Background to the Italian Renaissance," pp. 40–45.

12. Jean Meyendorff, *St. Grégoire Palamas et la Mystique Orthodoxe* (Paris, 1959), offers a penetrating and sympathetic treatment of hesychasm. Cf. also Jean Meyendorff, "Spiritual Trends in Byzantium in the late 13th and early 14th centuries," *Art et Société à Byzance sous les Paléologues* [Bibliothèque de l'Institut Hellénique d'Etudes Byzantines et post-byzantines de Venise, No. 4] (Venice, 1971), pp. 55–71; Basil Krivoshein, "The Ascetic and Theological Teaching of Gregory Palamas," *Eastern Churches Quarterly* 3 (1938–39): 26–33, 71–84, 138–56, and 193–214; and Timothy Ware, *The Orthodox Church* (Harmondsworth, 1963), pp. 70–79.

13. See the excellent little book of Emile Turdeanu, *La littérature bulgare de XIVe siècle et sa diffusion dans les pays roumaines* (Paris, 1947); Ivan Dujčev, "Les Slaves et Byzance," *Etudes Historiques* (Sofia, 1960), 1: 64–71; Petar Dinekov, "L'école littéraire de Tarnavo," *Etudes Balkaniques* 8 (1972): 5–14. After 1393, Tirnovo ceased to be the seat of a patriarchate, rivaling Constantinople; and the Bulgarian church lost its most active intellectual and organizational center. The metropolitan of Ochrid took over headship of the Bulgarian church, but his relations with the Greek hierarchy were far more amicable than Tirnovo's had been.

14. Cf. the detailed story of how the monasteries of Meteora in Thessaly were created in the 1340s by a pair of graduates from the Mount Athos school of mysticism, as recounted by Donald M. Nicol, *Meteora: The Rock Monasteries of Thessaly* (London, 1963), pp. 88–113.

15. Constantin Jireček, "Staat und Gesellschaft im mittelalterlichen Serbien: Studien zur Kulturgeschichte des 13–15. Jahrhunderts," Kaiserlichen Akademie der Wissenschaft in Wien, *Denkschriften* [Philosophisch-historische Klasse] 56 (1912): 53–54; Vojislav Djurić, "L'Art des Paléologues et l'Etat Serbe," in *L'Art et Société à Byzance sous les Paléologues* [Bibliothèque de l'Institut Héllenique d'Etudes Byzantines et post-Byzantines de Venise, No. 4], pp. 180 ff.; Sas-Zalaziecky, *Die byzantinische Baukunst*, pp. 108 ff.; A. Schmaus, "Zur Frage der Kulturorientierung der Serben im

Mittelalter," *Sudostforschungen* 15 (1956): 179–201. Court etiquette and manners retained a Latin imprint (part Hungarian, part Burgundian) until the Turkish conquest, however.

16. G. P. Fedotov, *The Russian Religious Mind* (Cambridge, Mass., 1966), 2: 195–229.

17. The most popular and influential of these, *Life in Jesus Christ*, was written by a layman, Nicholas Cabasilas (d. ca. 1371). This work had an importance for Orthodox Christianity similar to that of Thomas à Kempis' *Imitation of Christ* in Latin Christendom. On Cabasilas see Myrrha Lot-Borodine, *Un Maître de la spiritualité byzantine au XIVe siècle, Nicholas Cabasilas* (Paris, 1958).

18. See Viktor Lazarev, *Old Russian Murals and Mosaics from the XI to the XVI Century* (London, 1966), pp. 144–54, 181; Viktor N. Lazarev, *Andrej Rublev* (Milan, 1966).

19. See Svetozar Radojčič, *Geschichte der serbischen Kunst, von dem Anfängen bis zum Ende des Mittalalters* (Berlin, 1959); Vojislav J. Djurić, *Icônes de Yougaslavie* (Belgrade, 1961); Djurić, "L'Art des Paléologues et l'Etat Serbe," pp. 179–91.

20. Cf. Manolis Chatzidakis, "Contribution à l'Etude de la Peinture Post-Byzantine," in *1453–1953: Le Cinq-centième anniversaire de la Prise de Constantinople [L'Hellénisme Contemporaine, 2e série, fascicule hors de série]* (Athens, 1953), pp. 193–216; and, generally, David Talbot Rice, *The Art of Byzantium* (London, 1959), together with Kurt Weitzmann et al., *Icons from South Eastern Europe and Sinai* (London, 1968). These two handsome volumes, magnificently illustrated with color plates, will dispel any lingering idea that Byzantine art was static, unchanging, or rigidly hieratic.

21. Cf. Sergio Bettini, *La Pittura di Icone Cretese-Veneziana e i Madonneri* (Padua, 1933), pp. 4–16; Sergio Bettini, *Padova e l'arte christiana d'Oriente* (Venice, 1937). According to this authority, most Venetian families possessed icons painted in the Greek manner for private devotions, thus creating a substantial local demand for this kind of art. *Madonneri* continued to flourish in Venice until the eighteenth century.

22. Manoussas Manussacas, "Un Poeta cretese ambasciatore de Venezia a Tunisi e presso i Turchi: Leonardo Dellaporta e i suoi componimenti poetica," in Agostino Pertusi, ed., *Venezia e l'Oriente fra tardo Medioevo e Rinascimento* (Florence, 1966), pp. 283–307. Dellaporta wrote his poetry in jail, where he had been consigned for adultery; his principal work, *Dialogue with Truth*, is largely autobiographical.

23. Dellaporta's poetry survives in a single MS discovered by

Professor Manussacas in a monastic library at Mount Athos. It had no known successors—or predecessors. This may be misleading, for extensive plundering of Crete, incident to the war of Candia (1645–69), may have destroyed traces of a more nearly continuous literary culture than surviving texts allow one to assume. Cf. Franz Babinger, "Veneto-Kretische Geistesbestrebungen um die Mitte des XV. Jahrhundert," *Byzantinische Zeitschrift* 57 (1964): 62–77.

24. Manuel was a very cultivated man, a prolific author, interested in the pagan classics as well as in trying to attract Latin help against the Turks. See John W. Barker, *Manuel II Palaeologus, 1391–1425: A Study in Late Byzantine Statesmanship* (New Brunswick, N. J., 1969). For a convenient summary of the "Greek renaissance" see Steven Runciman, *The Last Byzantine Renaissance* (Cambridge, 1970).

25. See Setton, "The Byzantine Background for the Italian Renaissance," p. 58.

26. Pletho was a systematic thinker who took Plato seriously and seems to have hoped to be able to reform decadent Byzantine society by rational reorganization along lines derived from Plato's *Laws*, the example of ancient Sparta, and, perhaps, by borrowing something from contemporary Ottoman practices. Whether or not he was a Christian was hotly debated immediately after his death, and in modern times. The Patriarch Gennadios II destroyed Pletho's principal work after his death as being impious, so certainty as to his doctrines can no longer be expected. See François Masai, *Pléthon et le Platonisme de Mistra* (Paris, 1956); D. A. Zakythinos, *Le Despotat grec de Morée* (Paris and Athens, 1932–35) 2: 322–28, 372–74; F. Taeschner, "Georgios Gemistos Plethon, Ein Beitrag zur Frage der Ubertragung von islamischen Geistesgut nach dem Abendlände," *Der Islam* 18 (1929): 236–43.

27. The task of reconciling Greek and Latin theology seemed to some of the learned men assembled at the Council of Florence to be only a part of the larger task of reconciling Christian truth with rational metaphysics. Plato—understood always in a Neo-Platonic guise—was, of course, the prime guide to rational metaphysics; and the idea that such doctrines were fundamentally compatible with Christian truth—so long as both were properly understood—seems to have been generated initially in Byzantine intellectual circles. How else could the fullness and beauty of the pagan Greek literary inheritance be accommodated in a Christian age? See Paul Oskar Kristeller, "Umanesimo italiano e Bisanzio," *Lettre Italiane* 16 (1964): 1–15. The ambition of penetrating outward dissimilarities to

the intelligible essence of metaphysical reality through the exercise of reason was what Pletho and his ilk transferred to Italian soil during the Council of Florence. It is easy to see how such ideas constituted a kind of liberation from the brittle rationality of Latin theology as perfected by Aquinas.

28. Bessarion was a great bibliophile, and collected several hundred Greek codices which he willed to the city of Venice. His library thus became the nucleus of the Marciana library, where some of his volumes still survive. Bessarion's most famous literary work, written 1458–65, was entitled *Against the Calumniators of Plato.* It undertook to reconcile Platonism with Christianity and to minimize differences between Plato and Aristotle, "The Philosopher" of Latin theology. This work, and the debate over Aristotelianism *vs.* Platonism to which it contributed, played a very prominent role in renaissance intellectual development. Cf. L. Mohler, *Kardinal Bessarion als Theologe, Humanist und Steaatsmann* (3 vols.: Paderborn, 1923–42), and the still useful volume, Henri Vast, *Le Cardinal Bessarion* (Paris, 1878).

29. See Ihor Ševčenko, "Intellectual Repercussions of the Council of Florence," *Church History* 24 (1955): 291–323. The Council of Florence was also of great importance for the Latin church, since it ended the conciliar challenge to papal monarchy. The Greeks helped to assure this upshot by spurning the rival Council of Basel, whose terminal sessions overlapped in time the meetings of the Council of Ferrara-Florence, to which the Greeks came. The Greek choice was made on practical grounds. Military help seemed likelier from the pope than from any of the princes and prelates assembled at Basel.

30. Destruction in the western steppelands was countered by notable cultural efflorescence further east. Tamurlane and his heirs created an elegant and flourishing court culture in the central Asian borderlands of Transoxiana and Khorassan, where Iranian and Turkish populations intermingled. Moreover, in Anatolia and other more securely and anciently urbanized parts of the Moslem world, Tamurlane's meteoric career did not have lastingly destructive consequences. On the contrary, the exemplary force of Timurid court culture was felt for centuries, setting a new standard of refinement for other Moslem rulers to aspire after. See Halil Inalcik, *The Ottoman Empire: The Classical Age* (London, 1973), p. 176.

31. Jean Richard, "La Conversion de Berke et les Débuts de l'Islamisation de la Horde d'Or," *Revue des Etudes Islamiques* 35 (1967): 173–84.

32. The album in question remained in the private collection of the Ottoman sultans until 1923, and may or may not have belonged to Sultan Mehmed II, the Conqueror. Richard Ettinghausen, *Turkish Miniatures from the 13th to the 18th century* (London, 1965), p. 14, inclines to the opinion that these paintings derive from the Kipchak court of Astrakhan and date from the second half of the fifteenth century. He suggests that Selim the Grim (reigned 1512–20) was probably the sultan who acquired them for the Ottoman house.

The pages from this album on display in Topkapi Museum in November 1971 took me utterly by surprise, as they will most who look at the sample of reproductions that are available through the handsome UNESCO publication, *Turkey: Ancient Miniatures* [published by New York Graphic Society by arrangement with UNESCO], (n. p., 1961), pl. vii–xii.

33. In 1504 the khan of the Crim Tatars intercepted a Venetian architect and bronze founder on his way to Moscow and let him go only after he had demonstrated his skill by making a pair of metal doors for the khan's palace. See Sergio Bettini, "L'architetto Alevis Novi in Russia," in Agostino Pertusi, ed., *Venezia e l'Oriente fra tardo Medioevo e Rinascimento* (Florence, 1966), pp. 573–94. On Tatar culture generally see Boris Grekov and A. Iakoubovski, *La Horde d'Or* (Paris, 1939), pp. 148–62; Boris Ischboldin, *Essays on Tatar History* (New Delhi, 1963), pp. 36–57; Berthold Spuler, *Die Goldene Horde, Die Mongolen in Russland, 1223–1502* (2d ed.; Wiesbaden, 1965), pp. 424–38.

34. Edward G. Browne, *A Literary History of Persia* (4 vols., new impression; Cambridge, 1969), and Arthur Upham Pope ed., *A Survey of Persian Art* (3 vols.; London, 1938), offer monumental introductions to the two aspects of Iranian culture which westerners have long known and admired.

35. Cf. the fine photographs in Aptullah Kuran, *The Mosque in Early Ottoman Architecture* (Chicago, 1968).

36. Hanna Sohrweide, "Dichter und Gelehrte aus dem Osten im osmanischen Reich (1453–1600). Ein Beitrag zur türkisch-persischen Kulturgeschichte," *Der Islam* 46 (1970): 263–302.

37. See Alessio Bombaci, *La letteratura Turca* (Florence, 1969), pp. 302–4. The poem is available in English translation as Suleyman Çelebi, *The Mevlidi Sherif* [F. L. MacCallum, trans.], (London, 1957). In 1589, the sultan instituted a special celebration for the Prophet's birthday in Istanbul at which this poem was antiphonally recited.

38. Cf. Ernst Werner, "Häresie, Klassenkampf und religiöse Toleranz in einer islamisch-christlichen Kontaktzone: Bedr ed-Din und Bürklüce Mustafa," *Zeitschrift fur Geschichtswissenschaft* 12 (1964): 255–76; Franz Babinger, "Schejch Bedr ed-Din, der Sohn des Richters von Simâw. Ein Beitrag zur Geschichte des Sket-wesens in Altosmanischen Reiche," *Der Islam* 11 (1921): 1–106; Paul Wittek, "De la défaite d'Ankara à la prise de Constantinople," *Revue des Etudes Islamiques* 12 (1938): 1–34; Bernard Lewis, *Istanbul and the Civilization of the Ottoman Empire* (Norman, Oklahoma, 1963), pp. 19–22.

39. It is symbolic of the tensions within the Russian church that Saint Sergius, the key figure in establishing the new hesychast style of piety in Muscovy refused to accept appointment as metropolitan of all the Russians, and yet allowed himself to be used as a tool for fastening the power of the grand prince of Muscovy on neighboring princes' lands. See Fedotov, *Russian Religious Mind*, 2: 212, 223–29.

40. Cf. Ernst Werner, *Die Geburt einer Grossmacht* (Berlin, 1966), pp. 298–304.

41. Nevertheless, like his predecessors, Mehmed II relied on Sunni *ulema* to administer the law and founded eight *madrassas* for training the necessary experts in his new capital on the Bosporus. See Lewis, *Istanbul and the Civilization of the Ottoman Empire*, p. 104.

42. Kritovoulos, *History of Mehmed the Conqueror* [Charles T. Riggs, trans.] (Princeton, 1954), pp. 209–10; cf. Abdulhak Adnan, *La science chez les Turcs ottomans* (Paris, 1939), pp. 20–41.

43. Franz Babinger, "Maometto II, il Conquistatore e l'Italia," *Rivista Storica Italiana* 63 (1951): 469–505. Babinger says that one of Mehmed's most famous military moves, dragging ships overland to penetrate the Golden Horn as preliminary to the final assault on Constantinople in 1453, was suggested to him by an Italian who in turn had heard or knew how the Venetians in 1439 had dragged boats from the Adige to Lake Garda in an effort to relieve the siege of Brescia.

44. Cf. the remarkable letter addressed to Pope Pius II as quoted in Reschid Saffet Atabinen, *Les Turcs occidentaux et la Méditerranée* (Istanbul 1956), p. 97. Also Franz Babinger, *Mehmed der Eroberer* (Munich, 1953), p. 225.

45. Ibid., p. 511.

46. Ibid., pp 416–18. Bellini was by no means the first Italian artist to visit Mehmed's court. For details see Josef von Karabacek,

"Abendländische Künstler zu Konstantinopel im 15. und 16. Jahrhundert," Akademie der Wissenschaften in Wien [Phil-Hist Klasse], *Denkschriften* 52 (1918): 1–64.

47. Papal diplomacy followed up the success at Florence by concluding uniate agreements with the Armenian (1439), Coptic (1442), Syriac (1444), Chaldean (1445), and Maronite (1445) churches along lines similar to those agreed to with the Orthodox at Florence. See Aristide Brunello, *Le Chiese Orientali e l'Unione: Prospetto, Storico, Statistico* (Milan, 1966), p. 28. The papacy's readiness to allow local variations in rite, like those agreed upon at Florence with respect to the use of leavened bread in the Eucharist, made these negotiations far more successful—at least on paper—than earlier Latin efforts at subduing and correcting the errors of their fellow Christians had been.

48. By agreement between the œcumenical patriarch and Russian authorities, this office had been filled alternately, more or less, by men of Greek and men of Russian background. See Dimitri Obolensky, "Byzantium, Kiev and Moscow: a Study in Ecclesiastical Relations," *Dumbarton Oaks Papers* 11 (1957): 23–78.

49. For details see Albert M. Ammann, *Abriss der ostslawischen Kirchengeschichte* (Vienna, 1950), pp. 90–140.

50. In 1390 a monk from Tirnovo became metropolitan of Moscow. This was symptomatic of how powerfully the South Slav emigration affected the development of the Muscovite church in the late fourteenth and early fifteenth century. Chiliastic speculation, fed by the collapse of the Serbian and Bulgarian states before the advancing Turks, was highly developed among these *émigrés*. See James H. Billington, *The Icon and the Axe: An Interpretive History of Russian Culture* (New York, 1967), p. 56.

51. Michael Cherniavsky, "The Reception of the Council of Florence in Moscow," *Church History* 24 (1955): 347–59; Hildegard Schaeder, *Moskau das Dritte Rom: Studien zur Geschichte der politischen Theorien in der Slawischen Welt* (Darmstadt, 1929), pp. 21–37; Ammann, *Abriss der ostslawischen Kirchengeschichte*, pp. 138–62; William K. Medlin, *Moscow and East Rome: A Political Study of the Relation of Church and State in Muscovite Russia* (Geneva, 1952), pp. 60–74.

52. It is ironical, perhaps, that Gennadios was one of the most Latinate of Byzantine theologians, being a great admirer of Thomas Aquinas and thoroughly familiar with Aquinas' method of resolving seeming contradictions among authorities by drawing appropriate logical distinctions. Cf. the rather unfriendly sketch of Scholarios'

life in Joseph Gill, *Personalities of the Council of Florence and Other Essays* (Oxford, 1964), pp. 79–84.

53. Two hundred archers from Crete did arrive with Cardinal Isidore in 1452. This was a mere token of the military help the Byzantines had been promised.

54. Joseph Gill, *The Council of Florence* (Cambridge, 1959), offers by far the best overall treatment of the council and its results, though his Roman sympathies are evident. Cf. also Jean Décarreaux, *Les Grecs au Concile de l'Union Ferrare-Florence (1438–1439)* (Paris, 1970); and Deno J. Geanakoplos, "The Council of Florence (1438–39) and the Problem of Union between the Greek and Latin Churches," *Church History* 24 (1955): 324–46.

55. Latin Christendom's reactions are described by Rogert Schwoebel, *The Shadow of the Crescent: the Renaissance Image of the Turk, 1453–1517* (Nieukkoop, 1967).

56. To be precise, the command to tolerate People of the Book applied only to those who recognized Moslem superiority voluntarily; resistance justified forcible conversion or slaughter. The question therefore in Moslem law became whether or not the Balkan Christian had voluntarily surrendered to the Turks; if so, then toleration was mandatory; if not, then forcible conversion was permissible. Mehmed chose to act on the former assumption, less perhaps from respect for principles of the Sacred Law than from practical considerations of how best to govern his empire. See Gunnar Hering, "Das islamische Recht und die Investitur des Gennadios Scholarios, 1454," *Balkan Studies* 2 (1961): 231–56; Hilal Inalcik, "The Policy of Mehmed II towards the Greek Population of Istanbul and the Byzantine Buildings of the City," *Dumbarton Oaks Papers* 23–24 (1969–70): 231–49.

57. Gennadios is said to have helped to draw up the terms of his installation as patriarch, and at the sultan's request he wrote a summary of Christian doctrine which was translated into Turkish. The two men discussed points of theology face to face on several different occasions. See Louis Petit, X. A. Siderides and Martin Jugie, eds., *Œuvres Complètes de Scholarios* (8 vols.; Paris, 1928–36), 3: xxiv; G. Georgiades Arnakis, "The Greek Church of Constantinople and the Ottoman Empire," *Journal of Modern History* 24 (1952): 235–50.

58. Cf. the instructive organizational chart prepared by Theodore H. Papadopoullos, *Studies and Documents Relating to the History of the Greek Church and People under Turkish Domination* (Brussels, 1952), p. 94.

59. The patriarchal dignity was first purchased in this way in 1466. Steven Runciman, *The Great Church in Captivity: A Study of the Patriarchate of Constantinople from the Eve of the Turkish Conquest to the Greek War of Independence* (Cambridge, 1968), pp. 193–94.

60. Attributed to a Greek notable, Luke Notaras, by the historian Ducas, *Historia Turco-Byzantine*, ed. V. Grecu (Bucharest, 1958).

61. Calculation from biblical narratives produced a consensus among Orthodox experts that Creation had occurred on or about 1 September 5509 B.C. Since a thousand years are as a day in God's sight (Psalm 90.4), and since the destruction of the world seemed appropriate only after the same length of time it had taken God to create it, the experts figured that seven days equaled seven thousand years; and seven thousand years from 1 September 5509 B.C. came out A.D. 1491–92. Cf. Schaeder, *Moskau das Dritte Rom*, pp. 49–50.

62. *Œuvres Complètes de Scholarios*, 4: xxix.

63. I have been unable to find any adequate scholarly biography of Gennadios, but compare the biographical sketches in *Œuvres Complètes de Scholarios*, 1: ix–xiv; 8: appendix 5, pp. 20–47; Gill, *Personalities of the Council of Florence*, pp. 79–84; Vast, *Le Cardinal Bessarion*, pp. 117–37; Papadopoullos, *Studies and Documents Relating to the History of the Greek Church and People under Turkish Domination*, pp. 16–20.

64. The œcumenical patriarchate did not get around to formal repudiation of the acts of the Council of Florence until 1484; but from the time of Gennadios' enthronement there was no question of further dealings with the pope.

65. The house of Osman was itself extensively infiltrated by Christian influences. Intermarriage with Christian princesses dated back to the time of the second sultan, Orhan I (reigned 1324–60), and most of the slaves of the harem were also of Christian birth. Mehmed II maintained very close ties with one of his father's wives, the Lady Mara, who remained a Christian. Throughout his reign she played an important role as patron of the Orthodox church. Almost certainly, the Lady Mara was not Mehmed's mother, though this has sometimes been asserted. Cf. A. D. Alderson, *The Structure of the Ottoman Dynasty* (Oxford, 1956), table xxvi.

66. On Cretan developments cf. below, chap. five.

67. For details see Deno J. Geanakoplos, *Greek Scholars in Venice: Studies in the Dissemination of Greek Learning from Byzantium to Western Europe* (Cambridge, Mass., 1962), pp. 28–58; Geanakoplos, *Byzantine East and Latin West: Two Worlds of Christendom*

in Middle Ages and Renaissance (Oxford, 1966), pp. 114–18, 139–44.

68. See Speros Vryonis, Jr., "The Byzantine Legacy and Ottoman Forms," *Dumbarton Oaks Papers* 23–24 (1969–70): 253–308.

69. See N. J. Pantazopoulos, *Church and Law in the Balkan Peninsula during the Ottoman Rule* [Institute for Balkan Studies publication No. 92], (Thessalonica, 1967), pp. 39–45.

70. The failure of the Second Coming to manifest itself as expected in 1492 must have disconcerted those who had looked upon their subjection to the Turks as a short-term disaster. I have found no discussions of fluctuations of morale among Orthodox monks; though it is clear that by the seventeenth century many monasteries had lost the intense, burning conviction that had sustained hesychasm when it was still a new and revolutionary form of the faith. Cf. Virgil Candea, "Les intellectuels du sud-est européen au XVIIe siècle," *Revue des Etudes Sud-Est Européennes* 8 (1970): 211 and n. 80, 632–35.

71. Casual use of this title started as early as 1473. When it came regularly into use, Ivan III based the claim not on his own marriage to the imperial heiress, Zoë (Sophia) Paleologus, but on the marriage of Vladimir I (Saint Vladimir, 980–1015, the ruler who Christianized Russia) to the sister of the then reigning Byzantine emperor. Medlin, *Moscow and East Rome*, pp. 76–77.

72. The phrase is first recorded from 1492. Ibid, p. 78.

73. The resemblance to Moslem "akhi" of an earlier age is striking, though no one seems to have explored possible relations. Cf. George Vernadsky, *Russia at the Dawn of the Modern Age* (New Haven, 1959), pp. 33–34, 269–73, on Orthodoxy in Lithuania.

74. See Ettore Lo Gatto, *Gli Artisti Italiani in Russia* (Rome, 1934), 1: 23 ff.; Arthur Voyce, *Art and Architecture of Medieval Russia* (Norman, Oklahoma, 1967), p. 91. Fioravanti had been preceded by an Italian mint master, who had been instrumental in arranging the marriage with Zoë. Vernadsky, *Russia at the Dawn of the Modern Age*, p. 18. Long-standing trade patterns running southward to the Crimea had brought the Russians into contact with Italians beginning in the thirteenth century. A small Italian colony existed in Moscow, for instance, in the mid-fourteenth century. Such items as vodka and paper, along with astrology and alchemy, appear to have been introduced into Russia by this route. Moreover, the close alignment between Genoese and Tatars in matters of trade tended to make the Russians favor the Venetians, whose establishment at Tana, at the mouth of the Don, was more accessible to cen-

tral Russia than was the Genoese headquarters at Caffa, on the south coast of the Crimea. On these earliest contacts between Muscovy and the Italian trading cities see Billington, *Icon and Axe,* pp. 84–88.

75. See V. N. Lazarev, "L'art de la Russie Médiévale et l'Occident, XI-XV siècles," *XIII Congrès International des Sciences Historiques* (Moscow, 1970), pp. 41–52.

76. For details see Arthur Voyce, *The Moscow Kremlin: Its History, Architecture and Art Treasures* (Berkeley & Los Angeles, 1954), pp. 18–47.

77. On Muscovite military developments cf. Richard Hellie, *Enserfment and Military Change in Muscovy* (Chicago, 1971), and Thomas Esper, "Military Self-Sufficiency and Weapons Technology in Muscovite Russia," *Slavic Review* 28 (1969): 186–90. On Muscovite music cf. Gerald R. Seaman, *History of Russian Music* (Oxford, 1967), 1: 40–44.

Four—Venice as a Marginal Polity, 1481–1669

1. The Flemish frontier between France and the Hapsburg lands was almost as rich and considerably closer to Paris and the other main centers of French power, yet wars in that region remained small scale until the age of Louis XIV. The Pyrenees frontier, too, remained quiet. This has puzzled some modern historians, e.g., Charles Oman, *History of the Art of War in the 16th Century* (New York, 1937), pp. 14–27. The primacy of Italian battlefields, 1494–1559, may have owed something to accident: battle once having been joined, the contestants kept on coming back in hope of recovering losses or consolidating gains. Rivalries among the Italian states themselves repeatedly invited the reentry of foreign powers; but from a French or Spanish monarch's point of view, there was a rational enough motive for intervention in Italy. Success meant control of one or more of the prexisting Italian states. And taking over the administrative structure of Naples or Milan as a going concern meant cash in hand on a scale unattainable elsewhere in Europe of that day. And money paid for armies. For an estimate of the annual cash value of the five major Italian powers in the late fifteenth century see Denys Hay, *Europe in the Fourteenth and Fifteenth Centuries* (London, 1966), p. 186.

2. Heinrich Kretschmayr, *Geschichte von Venedig* (Gotha, 1905), 2: 423–48.

3. In 1508–09, the noble patriciates of Padua, Verona, and Brescia

welcomed liberation from the Venetian yoke, aspiring to take control of their own affairs once again. From the start, the poorer classes preferred Venetian magistrates and proconsuls to home-grown tyrants; and the facts of foreign military occupation, with all the plundering and violence this brought with it, soon discredited the patricians' aspiration for local independence they could not defend from foreign intruders. See Angelo Ventura, *Nobilità e popolo nella società veneta del '400 e '500* (Bari, 1964), pp. 167–86.

4. In 1511 Antonio Contarini proposed adlecting the nobility of Zara to the Venetian Senate as a means of pacifying that ever-restless city and expanding the political base of the Venetian state. His suggestion, supported by only a handful of senators, was rejected. By declining to remodel the constitutional base of the Venetian state along such lines, the city in effect surrendered its best chance of reenacting ancient Rome's career of the third century B.C. and uniting Italy. The Venetian elite, frightened at the ring of enemies created by their earlier policy of expansion, opted for security within the tight little world defined by hereditary registration in the famous Golden Book of the Venetian nobility. Ibid., pp. 170–72.

5. Maurice Aymard, *Venise, Raguse et le Commerce du Blé pendant la seconde moitié du XVIe siècle* (Paris, 1966), p. 46; Halil Inalcik, "Bursa and the Commerce of the Levant," *Journal of the Economic and Social History of the Orient* 3 (1960): 131–47; Halil Inalick, "Captial Formation in the Ottoman Empire," *Journal of Economic History* 29 (1969): 97–140.

6. Alberto Tenenti and Corrado Vivanti, "Le film d'un grand système de navigation: Les galères vénitiennes au XIV-XVI siècles," *Annales: Economies, Sociétés, Civilisations* 16 (1961): pocket insert.

7. Until 1513 Venetian imports of pepper and other spices remained only about a quarter of pre-1500 quantities. Nevertheless, by the 1530s the Venetian spice trade again achieved its former volume. Frederic C. Lane, "Venetian Shipping during the Commercial Revolution," *American Historical Review* 38 (1933): 219–39; Ruggiero Romano, Alberto Tenenti, and Ugo Tucci. "Venise et la Route du Cap, 1499–1517," in Manlio Cortelazzo, ed., *Mediterraneo e Oceano Indiano* (Florence, 1970), pp. 109–39.

8. Portuguese agents in the Indian Ocean attempted to choke off the Red Sea route and build up the Persian Gulf route for spices. Tolls collected at Ormuz could then pay for the Portuguese garrison and fort. From the Venetian point of view it made little difference

whether spices arrived at Alexandria or Beirut. I owe insight into Portuguese policy in the Indian Ocean to a forthcoming book by Bentley Duncan which he kindly showed me in MS.

9. Frederic C. Lane, "The Mediterranean Spice Trade: Further Evidence of its Revival in the Sixteenth Century," *American Historical Review* 45 (1940): 581–90, reprinted in Lane, *Venice and History* (Baltimore, 1966), pp. 25–34.

10. In 1505 the Venetians quarreled with the sultan of Egypt over the price of spices, and until 1509 trade was actually broken off between the two partners. Obviously, customary patterns of pricing were being brought under unaccustomed pressure; and it is significant that it was only after the battle of Diu that Egyptian-Venetian trade relations were resumed. The Moslem defeat of 1509 must have convinced the rulers of Egypt that price competition was more practicable than naval competition with the Portuguese; though after the Ottoman conquest of Egypt in 1517, the Turks made three additional efforts to recover naval supremacy, in the Indian Ocean for Moslem shipping. See Fernand Braudel, *La Méditeranée et le monde méditerranean à l'époque de Philippe II* (2d ed.; Paris, 1966), 2: 458–60.

11. Paul Gille, "Les navires des deux routes des Indes: (Venise et Portugal) Evolution des types. Résultats économiques," in Cortelazzo, ed., *Mediterraneo e Oceano Indiano*, pp. 193–201.

12. Lane, "Venetian Shipping during the Commercial Revolution," pp. 219–39; Ruggiero Romano, "La Marine marchande vénitienne au XVIe siècle," in M. Mollat, ed., *Les Sources de l'histoire maritime en Europe du Moyen Age au XVIIIe siècle* [Actes du Quatrième Colloque de'Histoire Maritime], (Paris, 1962), pp. 33–68. Romano points out that the success in keeping the Venetian merchant marine afloat in the sixteenth century was attained by massive and skillful state intervention. State revenues supported ship construction, and shippers were allowed to charge high rates for such monopolized articles as salt. Rising costs were thus distributed to the whole population of Venice and/or customers who bought from Venetian suppliers. Such methods staved off but could not ultimately escape the problem of rising costs. Collapse, when it came after 1580, was correspondingly sudden—and irremediable.

13. Prisoners were first used as rowers on Venetian war galleys in the 1540s; by 1600, since free men held back, prisoners predominated, and systematic recuitment of condemned men from other states became a recognized way to man the oars. Until the 1720s, however, some free men were conscripted to serve as rowers in the

Venetian fleet—usually peasants from the country (especially Dalmatia), not residents of the city itself. See Mario Nani Mocenigo, *Storia della Marina Veneziana da Lepanto alla Caduta della Repubblica* (Rome, 1935), p. 42. Other Mediterranean war fleets were similarily manned, though proportions between slave and free rowers varied. At Lepanto (1571), for instance, only twenty-five of the Turkish ships were rowed by slaves; of the remaining two hundred most were manned by Moslem conscripts, according to Fernand Braudel (lecture at Fondazione Cini, Venice, in October 1971). Spain led the way toward slave rowers, having come to rely on such crews by about 1550. Cf. John Guilmartin, *Gunpowder and Galleys* (Cambridge, forthcoming), chap. 3. Capture meant transfer to slave status; and some individuals passed back and forth between Moslem and Christian fleets several times. Such a system created a brutalized international pool of galley slaves, part criminal, part war captive, part Christian, part Moslem; but generally godless and driven only by hunger and fear.

Overall loss of efficiency was very great when a part of the fighting force on every galley had to guard against the danger of revolt among the galley slaves! See Ruggiero Romano, "Economic Aspects of the Construction of Warships in Venice in the Sixteenth Century," in Brian Pullan, ed., *Crisis and Change in the Venetian Economy in the 16th and 17th Centuries* (London, 1968), pp. 65–67. This is a translation of an article, "Aspetti economica degli armamenti navali veneziani nel secolo XVI," *Rivista storica Italiana* 66 (1954): 39–67.

14. Experimentation and adjustment to the changing capacities of guns was incessant among Mediterranean fleets during the entire sixteenth century. See, for instance, Frederic C. Lane, "Naval actions and fleet organization, 1499–1502" in John R. Hale, ed., *Renaissance Venice* (London, 1973) pp. 146–73. In many ways the most significant changes came in fortress design, checkmating by about 1530 the initial overwhelming advantage big siege guns gave the attacker against medieval "curtain" walls. As sieges again became difficult, the long-standing symbiosis between galley fleets and defended shore bases set in once more. For an admirably perspicacious analysis see Guilmartin *Gunpowder and Galleys,* chap. 6 and passim. Climax of the adjustment to shipboard artillery came with the introduction of the galleass, introduced to Mediterranean warfare by Venice shortly before the Battle of Lepanto (1571). It was an oared gun platform, stoutly built to withstand the recoil of heavy cannon. This made it clumsy to maneuver and incapable of keeping up with

the rest of the fleet, despite a change to larger oars, rowed by as many as five men in place of the single man per oar of earlier designs. When galleasses were able to reach the scene of battle, as at Lepanto, their heavy guns were indeed effective; but to hold the light galleys to the maneuver speed of the galleasses surrendered the main advantage galleys had over sailing vessels. Cf. R. C. Anderson, *Oared Fighting Ships* (London, 1962), pp. 74–83.

15. See above, chap. one.

16. Cf. Alberto Tenenti, *Piracy and the Decline of Venice, 1580–1615* (London, 1967).

17. Domenico Sella, "The Rise and Fall of the Venetian Woollen Industry," in Brian Pullman, ed., *Crisis and Change in the Venetian Economy*, pp. 108–10.

18. For the importance of Venetian paper in the Levant see Franz Babinger, "Papierhandel und Papierbereitung in der Levant," reprinted in Babinger, *Aufsätze und Abhandlungen zur Geschichte Südosteuropas* (2 vols.; Munich, 1962, 1966), 2: 127–31. On sixteenth-century Venetian industry generally see Gino Luzzatto, *Storia economica di Venezia* (Venice, 1961), pp. 257–60.

19. Danieli Beltrami, *Storia della popolazione di Venezia dalla fine del secolo XVI alla caduta della Repubblica* (Padua, 1954), pp. 57, 59; Karl Julius Beloch, *Bevölkerungsgeschichte Italiens* (Berlin, 1961), 3: 1–23; Aymard, *Venise, Raguse et le Commerce du Blé pendant la seconde moitié du XVIe siècle*, p. 16.

20. Details, ibid., pp. 72–73.

21. According to Pierre Chaunu, *L'Expansion Européenne* (Paris, 1969), p. 338, rice yields 7.35 million calories per hectare as against 1.51 million calories for wheat. These are obviously inexact figures, but the 5:1 ratio gives an idea of how important rice was in increasing food supply in places where suitable flooding during the growing season was possible. The calorie yield from maize is intermediate between rice and wheat—but in practice, of course, local conditions of soil and rainfall make all the difference. Rice required flooding; this limited its spread to flat, irrigable lands. Maize needed more rainfall than wheat, but these two crops were mutually substitutable almost everywhere in the Veneto.

22. Extensive canalization of *terra firma*, using locks (invented in the mid-fifteenth century in Lombardy) to overcome changing heights of land, allowed far cheaper delivery of grain and other agricultural commodities to urban consumers by reducing expensive overland haulage. See Frédéric Mauro, *Le XVIe Siècle Européen: Aspects économiques* (Paris, 1970), p. 144.

23. Daniele Beltrami, *Saggio di storia dell'agricoltura nella Repubblica di Venezia durante l'erà moderna* (Rome-Venice, 1955), pp. 21–36.

24. Luzzatto, *Storia economica,* p. 252, emphasizes the continued importance of commerce for Venice; Beltrami, *Saggio di storia dell' agricoltura,* and the same author's *La Penetrazione economica dei veneziani in terrafirma: Forze di lavoro e proprietà fondaria nelle campagne venete dei secoli XVII e XVIII* (Venice-Rome, 1961) emphasizes the shift from commerce to land.

25. Guilmartin, *Gunpowder and Galleys,* chaps. 3 and 6, offers a careful discussion of factors affecting galley fleet radius of action. A distance of 1,000 miles from home base was extreme; and as the sixteenth century advanced, the effective range for Mediterranean fleets shrank owing to use of heavier guns and connected adjustments of galley design.

26. How conscious the Ottoman rulers were of their need for metals is illustrated by the fate of the island of Chios. This island remained under Christian sovereignty until 1566, even though the Turks could easily have seized it at any time after the 1430s, if not before. They refrained from doing so, however, because the Genoese *maona,* that ruled Chios, supplied the Ottoman government with tin, brought from England; and the Turks feared that if they drove the Genoese out, their supply of tin, essential for bronze gun casting, would dwindle, or at best become unreliable. When an alternative supply arriving direct from Cornwall in English bottoms became available, the Turks at once picked a quarrel with the Maona and occupied the island. I owe this information to conversation with Halil Inalcik. The status of Hong Kong, 1949–69, offers a modern parallel.

Philip Argenti, *Chius Vincta, or the Occupation of Chios by the Turks (1566) and their administration of the Island, 1566–1912* (Cambridge, 1941), does not mention the tin trade; the same is true of his three-volume work, *The Occupation of Chios by the Genoese, 1346–1566* (Cambridge, 1958). On the relation between English shipping in the Mediterranean and the tin trade cf. Braudel, *La Méditeranée,* 1: 554 ff., 567.

27. The two "Barbarossas" were sons of a janissary of Mytilene. Their mother was a Greek. Cf. Ernle Bradford, *The Sultan's Admiral: The Life of Barbarossa* (New York, 1968), pp. 16–18. In spite of its popular tone this is a well-informed book.

28. As a good Genoese, Doria disliked and distrusted the Vene-

tians; a sentiment fully reciprocated. This did nothing to consolidate the anti-Turkish naval coalition.

29. For details see R. C. Anderson, *Naval Wars in the Levant,
1559–1853* (Princeton, 1952), pp. 5–59.

30. See Braudel, *La Méditerranée,* 2: 451–68. The whole tenor
of my remarks about Venice and the Mediterranean at large in the
second half of the sixteenth century is fundamentally shaped by this
masterwork.

31. Romano, "Economic Aspects of the Construction of Warships in Venice in the Sixteenth Century," in Pullan, ed. *Crisis &
Change,* pp. 39–67.

32. For the political signficance of Lepanto see Andrew C. Hess,
"The Battle of Lepanto and its Place in Mediterranean History," *Past
and Present* 57 (1972): 53–73. For military details see William
Ledyard Rodgers, *Naval Warfare under Oars, 4th-16th Centuries:
A Study of Strategy, Tactics and Ship Design* (Annapolis, 1939),
pp. 143–239. Guilmartin, *Gunpowder and Galley,* is technically
more informed and informative.

33. Even more impressive: the galeass, which had been a new
type of ship at Lepanto and proved its value in that battle, was
immediately adopted by the Turks too. In the Turkish fleet that
took the seas in 1572, according to Robert Mantran (lecture at
Giorgio Cini Fondazione, October 1971), there were several heavily
gunned galeasses, comparable to those the Venetians had used with
such effect the preceding year.

34. Of a design not fundamentally different from that with
which Phoenicians had explored Mediterranean waters some 2,300
years previously.

35. On the arrival of northern shipping in the Mediterranean
see Fernand Braudel and Ruggiero Romano, *Navires et Marchandises à l'entrée du Port de Livourne, 1547–1611* (Paris, 1951), pp.
51–53; Braudel, *La Méditeranée,* 1: 543–78; Alberto Tenenti,
Naufrages, corsaires et assurances maritimes à Venise, 1592–1609
(Paris, 1959), pp. 13–27.

36. Romano, "La Marine marchande vénitienne au XVIe siècle,"
M. Mollat, ed., *Les Sources de l'histoire maritime en Europe,* pp.
47–50.

37. English ships were permitted to pay the same taxes as Venetian ships in this year. See Frederic C. Lane, "The Merchant Marine
of the Venetian Republic," *Venice and History,* p. 157.

38. The northerners reversed medieval relationships with Venice by establishing a small but active commercial colony in the city.

See Wilfred Brulez, *Marchands Flamands à Venise, 1568–1605* (Brussels, 1965).

39. Privateering ended in Atlantic waters with the signing of the Anglo-Spanish treaty in 1604 and with the truce between Spain and Holland in 1609. Ex-privateers based themselves on North Africa and taught the local seafaring populations how to use specialized, speedy, and heavy-gunned ships. Cf. Ralph Davis, "England and the Mediterranean 1570–1640," in F. J. Fisher, ed., *Essays in the Economic and Social History of Tudor and Stuart England in Honour of R. H. Tawney* (Cambridge, 1961), pp. 127–29.

40. See Tenenti, *Naufrages, corsaires et assurances maritimes à Venise, 1592–1609.* On the political connections of the Adriatic pirates see Gunther Rothenberg, "Venice and the Uskoks of Senj, 1537–1618," *Journal of Modern History* 33 (1961): 148–56.

41. Lane, "The Merchant Marine of the Venetian Republic," in *Venice and History*, p. 153; Sella, "The Rise and Fall of the Venetian Woollen Industry," in Pullan, ed., *Crisis and Change*, pp. 108–9. English cloth exports moved into the gap created by the decay of Venetian manufacture. See the statistics of English woolens export to the Ottoman empire presented in Ralph Davis, *Aleppo and Devonshire Square: English Traders in the Levant in the 18th century* (London, 1967), p. 97.

42. Braudel, *La Méditerranée*, 1: 568–73. In 1626, Venetian merchants found it cheaper to import pepper from Holland than from Egypt! See Ralph Davis, "Influences de l'Angleterre sur le déclin de Venise au XVIIe siècle," in Fondazione Giorgio Cini [Civiltà veneziana studi, No. 9], *Aspetti e Cause della decadenza economica veneziana nel secolo XVII* (Venice-Rome, 1961), pp. 185–235.

43. See Vitorino Magalhaes-Godinho, "Crises et changements géographiques et structuraux au XVIe Siècle," *Studi in Onore di Armando Sapori* (Milan, 1957), pp. 981–98.

44. On spread of hard rock mining into the Balkans in the fifteenth-sixteenth centuries see Desanka Kovačević, "Dans la Serbie et la Bosnie médiévales: Les Mines d'or et d'argent," *Annales: économies, sociétés, civilisations* 15 (1960): 248–58.

45. Braudel, *La Méditerranée*, 1: 368.

46. In an age when devastating plague struck cities like Venice repeatedly, it may seem perverse to suggest that disease may have been less destructive to human populations than in other ages. Nevertheless, the only epidemic diseases of importance in the fifteenth-seventeenth centuries in the Mediterranean were typhus, bubonic plague, and syphilis; in other ages, when the childhood

diseases of modern society were less homogeneously distributed, it is probable that the roster of killing epidemic diseases was far greater. In early modern times, more or less accurate demographic data for the first time begin to make the impact of epidemic diseases on human populations measurable; but this should not lead us to suppose that diseases played a more murderous role in that age than in earlier times about which we are less well informed. For a most instructive overview of pestilence in early modern times see Roger Mols, *Introduction à la démographie historique des villes d'Europe du XIVe au XVIIIe siècle*, 2 vols. (Louvain, 1955).

47. On spread of maize in Ottoman lands see Traian Stoianovich and George C. Haupt, "Le maïs arrive dans les Balkans," *Annales: Economies, Sociétés, Civilisations* 18 (1962): 84–93.

48. Cf. the classic work of John U. Nef, *The Rise of the British Coal Industry* (London, 1932).

49. Lane, *Venetian Ships and Shipbuilders of the Renaissance*, pp. 217–33.

50. Cf. Plato's account of how Attica was denuded of its trees and soil in *Critias* III: ". . . for although some of the mountains now only afford sustenance to bees, not so very long ago there were still to be seen roofs of timber cut from trees growing there, which were of a size sufficient to cover the largest houses. . ." (Jowett, trans.).

51. Cf. Aldo Stella, "La Crisa economica veneziana della seconda metà del secolo XVI," *Archivio Veneto* (5th series) 58–59 (1956): 17–69; Carlo M. Cipolla, "The Economic Decline of Italy," in Pullan, ed., *Crisis and Change*, pp. 127–45. This is a translation of "Il declino economico dell'Italia," *Storia dell'economica italiana* (Turin, 1959), which was in turn an expanded and corrected version of an earlier essay appearing in *Economic History Review* 5 (1952): 178–87.

52. Brian Pullan, *Rich and Poor in Renaissance Venice: The Social Institutions of a Catholic State to 1620* (Cambridge, Mass., 1971), pp. 287–371 and passim.

53. In the fifteenth century Venice had enjoyed a reputation as a tyrant and threat to liberty, thanks to its successful territorial expansion; after 1509 Italian patriots began to view the Republic in a more friendly light as all of the other important Italian states lost their liberty in course of the wars, 1494–1559, either to foreign viceroys, as in Naples and Milan, or to home-grown, absolute sovereigns, as in Florence and Rome. Outside Italy, Jean Bodin (1530–1596) was the principal popularizer of the view that Vene-

tian constitutional arrangements were peculiarly admirable; various Protestant publicists picked up the idea, 1606–07, during the last and most spectacular collision between Venice and the papacy. See Fredrico Chabod, "Venezia nella politica Italiana ed Europea del Cinquecento," in Centro di Cultura e Civiltà della Fondazione Giorgio Cini, *La Civiltà veneziana del Rinascimento* (Florence, 1958), pp. 29–55; Lane, "At the Roots of Republicanism," in *Venice and History*, p. 533, reprinted from *American Historical Review* 71 (1966): 403–20.

54. It is a striking fact that after the previous supreme crisis of the war of Chioggia, a few families had been enrolled among the nobility in recognition of their services to the city during the war, whereas the opposite happened in the sixteenth century. On the very eve of the war of the League of Cambrai, in 1506, the government set up a birth and marriage register for the nobility as a way of definitively excluding everyone who did not have an attested, legitimate claim to the rank. See James Cushman Davis, *The Decline of the Venetian Nobility as a Ruling Class* (Baltimore, 1962), p. 19.

55. Deno Geanakoplos, *Greek Scholars in Venice* (Cambridge, Mass., 1962), pp. 63–65.

56. For details see Giorgio Fedalto, *Ricerche storiche sulla posizione giuridica ed ecclesiastica dei Greci a Venezia nei secoli XV e XVI* (Florence, 1967).

57. A treaty of 1595 required Venetians to allow Turkish subjects free movement within their territories in return for similar rights accorded Venetians in Ottoman lands. See M. A. Belin, "Relations diplomatiques de la République de Venise avec la Turquie," *Journal Asiatique* 8 (1876): 419. A *Fondaco dei Turchi* actually opened in 1621, according to Halil Inalcik, "Capital Formation in the Ottoman Empire," *Journal of Economic History* 29 (1969): 113.

58. Brian Pullan, *Rich and Poor in Renaissance Venice*, pp. 511–13, 568–73. Jewish influence in Istanbul was sufficient to make the Ottoman government an effective protector of Jews in Venice. In 1573, for instance, when the Venetians made peace after Lepanto, a preliminary to successful negotiations was the relaxation of anti-Jewish measures that had been undertaken in the heat of crusading enthusiasm. The Turkish agent in these negotiations was a Venetian-born Jew, Solomon Askenazi, who in all probability insisted on the abrogation of the new anti-Jewish regulations before he would start serious negotiation. Cf. ibid., pp. 538–39; M. Franco, *Essai sur l'histoire des Israélites de l'Empire Ottoman* (Paris, 1897), pp. 62–73.

59. Jews had previously been permitted to live at Mestri on the

289

mainland whence they could visit Venice for business purposes during the day. This system broke down during the war of the League of Cambrai, when Jewish refugees swarmed into Venice. Until 1516 they scattered throughout the city. Concentrating them into the ghetto (literally "foundry") was conceived as a compromise between expulsion and allowing them the enjoyment of ordinary civic rights. The ghetto was an abandoned cannon foundry when the Jews moved in, walled completely around.

60. See Kretschmayr, *Venedig*, 3: 112–25, 281–89.

61. See William J. Bouwsma, *Venice and the Defense of Republican Liberty: Renaissance Values in the Age of the Counter Reformation* (Berkeley and Los Angeles, 1968), pp. 105 ff.

62. Beltrami, *Storia della Popolazione di Venezia*, pp. 58–59. These are the figures officially recorded.

63. The Venetian Arsenal experimented with new types and designs of warships, aiming always at heavier broadsides; yet the shipbuilders were not willing to give up oars until 1660 and completed construction of the first Atlantic-type warship, dependent entirely on sails, only in 1667, too late to play any decisive part in the war. See Mario Nani Mocenigo, *Storia della marina veneziana da Lepanto alla caduta della repubblica* (Rome, 1935).

64. It was only after this disaster that the decision to go over to sailing vessels of Atlantic design, carrying unprecedented quantity of cannon, was finally made. But it took the Arsenal seven years to construct a copy of an English warship—a measure of the heavy cost the changeover from galleys involved. By then the confidence of the Venetian government in the capacity of the fleet to win decisive strategic success had vanished; offensive naval strategy was not even attempted. For details of the shift (only partial; in 1718 the Venetian navy comprised sixteen galleys and twenty sailed vessels) to warships of Atlantic design see ibid.

Five—Venice as a Cultural Metropolis, 1481–1669

1. Cf. the graceful and penetrating essay by H. G. Koenigsberger, "Decadence or Shift? Changes in the Civilization of Italy and Europe in the 16th and 17th centuries," *Transactions of the Royal Historical Society* (series 5), 10 (1960): 1–18.

2. See Galienne Francastel, "De Giorgione au Titien: l'artiste, le public et la commercialisation de l'oeuvre d'art," *Annales: Economies, Sociétés, Civilisations* 15 (1960): 1061–75; Oliver Logan, *Culture and Society in Venice, 1470–1790* (London, 1972), pp. 129–219.

3. I have not found any history of the economics of art; Francastel's article, cited above, suffers from myopia, comparing Venetian practice only with that of earlier Italian painters whose names happen to have been enshrined in art histories.
4. Guglielmo Barblan, "Il Cinquecento musicale veneziana," *La Civiltà veneziana del Rinascimento* (Florence, 1958), pp. 59–79. According to Charles Van den Borren, *Les Débuts de la Musique à Venise* (Brussels, 1914), pp. 9–11, the beginnings of a distinctive Venetian musical style date from the 1490s when the installation of a second organ in Saint Mark's allowed the invention of "double choir" arrangements, which caught on and spread rapidly to other parts of western Europe. It was, however, a Flemish choirmaster who first exploited the technical possibilities of two organs. He it was who first brought Flemish music to Venice in 1491, so that Willaert had a tradition to build upon when he arrived a generation later.
5. A literary circle formed around the famous scholar and churchman, Pietro Bembo (1470–1547), during the decade of 1529–39 when he resided in his native Venice as official historiographer to the Republic. Bembo and his friends consciously set out to make the, by then archaic, Florentine dialect of Dante and Petrarch standard for literary Italian; and with the help of Venetian printers, who circulated the works of the great Florentines widely in Italy, Bembo and his circle were remarkably successful. One result was thereafter to condemn the language of Venice to merely comical and topical uses in formal literature. This may have contributed to the relative barrenness of Venice in the realm of *belles lettres,* for the differences between Florentine and Venetian speech were in fact substantial. Cf. W. Theodore Elwert, "Pietro Bembo e la vita letteraria del suo tempo," *Civiltà veneziana del Rinascimento,* pp. 126–76, and "Venedigs literarische Bedeutung: Ein bibliographischen Versuch," *Archiv fur Kulturgeschichte* 36 (1954): 261–300; P. O. Kristeller, "The Origin and Development of the Language of Italian Prose," *Renaissance Thought II: Papers on Humanism and the Arts* (New York, 1965), pp. 119–41.
6. For early printing in Venice, Horatio F. Brown, *The Venetian Printing Press: an Historical Study* (London, 1891), is an excellent guide.
7. Details may be found in Emile Legrand, *Bibliographie Hellénique ou description raisonnée des ouvrages publiés en grec par des grecs au XVe et XVIe siècles* (4 vols.; Paris, 1885–1906). Turkish prejudice against printing inhibited the development of Christian

presses in Ottoman territories until the late seventeenth century. This had the effect of prolonging Venetian predominance in the field of printing for Greeks.

8. A total of 6,060 German students graduated from Padua in the second half of the sixteenth century; 5,083 in law, 977 in arts. Pompeo G. Molmenti, *Storia di Venezia nella Vita Privata* (Bergamo, 1910), 2: 265.

9. Deno J. Geanakoplos, *Greek Scholars in Venice* (Cambridge, Mass., 1962), p. 38.

10. An English translation of Pomponazzi's treatise is available in Ernst Cassirer et al., eds., *The Renaissance Philosophy of Man* (Chicago, 1948), pp. 255–381. Pomponazzi did not know Greek himself; only later, among his successors, of whom Jacopo Zabarella (1532–1589) was the most distinguished, did a full command of Greek philological learning and abstract philosophical interest in expounding the authentic Aristotle come together in one man. Pomponazzi was, nevertheless, deeply influenced by the work his contemporaries undertook to uncover the authentic Aristotelian text. See Paul O. Kristeller, *Renaissance Thought: the Classic, Scholastic and Humanist Strains* (New York, 1961), pp. 40–42; John Herman Randall, Jr., *The School of Padua and the Emergence of Modern Science* (Padua, 1961), pp. 69–114.

11. Charles Singer, *A Short History of Anatomy and Physiology from the Greeks to Harvey* (New York, 1957), pp. 72, 86.

12. Vesalius' book was published in Basel, but the woodcuts that gave his words a clear meaning had been made in Venice, probably on the basis of drawings produced by artists working for Titian. See C. D. O'Malley, *Andreas Vesalius of Brussels, 1514–1564* (Berkeley and Los Angeles, 1964), pp. 124–28. The intersection of extremely skilled draftsmanship and an intellectual posture that allowed Vesalius and his students to overcome the normal emotional reactions to the sight (and smell) of a dead and mangled human body was what made the sudden scientific advance at Padua possible.

13. Randall, *The School of Padua and the Emergence of Modern Science*, p. 90.

14. I have not found a modern history of the University of Padua, but compare Biagio Brugi, *Gli scholari dello studio di Padova nel Cinquecento* [Discorso Inaugurale, 6 November 1902], (Padua, 1903); Antonio Favaro, *Galileo Galilei e lo Studio di Padova* (Florence, 1883; reprinted Padua, 1966), 1: 51–77; Giovanni Fabris, "Professori e scolari greci all'università di Padova," *Archivio Veneto* 30 (1942): 120–65. According to Charles Yriarte, *La Vie d'un*

patricien de Venise au XVIe siècle (Paris, 1874), p. 256, in 1571 there were eighteen thousand students at Padua and one hundred professors!

15. For Ragusa see Barisa Krekić, *Dubrovnik in the 14th and 15th centuries: A City between East and West* (Norman, Oklahoma, 1972), pp. 112–44; Josef Matl, *Europa und die Slawen* (Wiesbaden, 1964), pp. 120–31; Luigi Villari, *The Republic of Ragusa* (London, 1904), pp. 339–81. For Crete see Alexandre Embiricos, *La Renaissance crétoise, XVIe et XVIIe siècles: I. La Littérature* [Collection de l'Institut Néo-Héllenique], (Paris, 1961); M. Valsa, *Le Théâtre grec moderne de 1453 à 1900* (Berlin, 1960), pp. 22–161.

16. See Manolis Chatzidakis, "Recherches sur la peinture de Théophane le Crétois," *Dumbarton Oaks Papers* 23–24 (1969–70): 309–43.

17. For Cretan art see Manolis Chatzidakis, "Contribution à l'étude de la peinture post-Byzantine," *1453–1933: Le Cinqcentième anniversaire de la prise de Constantinople* (Athens, 1953), pp. 193–216, and his *Icônes de St. Georges des Grecs et de la collection de l'Institut Hellénique de Venise* (Venice, 1962); Alexandre Embiricos, *L'Ecole crétoise, dernière phase de la Peinture Byzantine* [Collection de l'Institut d'Etudes Byzantines et néo-Helléniques de l'Université de Paris, Fascicule XX], (Paris, 1967). These Greek scholars emphasize continuity with Byzantium; Sergio Bettini, *La Pittura di Icone Cretese-Veneziana e i Madonneri* (Padua, 1933), perhaps predictably, emphasizes the Italian element in Cretan art.

18. Sokollu was, of course, a Serb by birth and was eighteen years old before becoming a member of the sultan's slave household. He obviously remembered his origins. Serbs in fact predominated among the sultan's slaves in the sixteenth century and used their native language as a kind of private patois at the court. Suleiman is said to have spoken it too. See Ladislas Hadrovics, *Le Peuple Serbe et Son Eglise sous la Domination Turque* [Bibliothèque de la Revue d'Histoire Comparée, VI], (Paris, 1947), pp. 44–52; W. E. D. Allen, *Problems of Turkish Power in the 16th Century* (London, 1963), p. 13.

19. Emile Turdeanu, *Le Livre roumain à travers les siècles* (Paris, 1959), p. 8. According to Virgil Molin, "Venise, Berceau de l'imprimerie glagolitique et cyrillique," *Studi Veneziani* 8 (1966): 347–445, these books were actually printed in Venice, not, as previously believed, in Rumania.

20. Hospodars financed publication of several books in Venice

in the seventeenth century; and, in 1708, Constantin Brancoveanu invested thirty thousand ducats in the Venetian public debt as a means of assuring income for a school he established in Bucharest in that year. A. D. Xenopol, *Histoire des Roumains* (Paris, 1896), 2: 174–76. For sidelights on Venetian-Rumanian ties see Nicholae Iorga, *Ospiti Romeni in Venezia (1570–1610): Una Storia ch'è un romanzo ed un romanzo ch'è una storia* (Bucharest, 1932). A consciousness of Latin origin and affinities on the part of educated Rumanians dated from the sixteenth century, when Lutheran and Calvinist proselytism in Transylvania led to the first printing in the Rumanian language. Ten such books were published between 1558 and 1582. Turdeanu, *Le Livre roumain*, p. 10.

21. The last important Italian architect and technician active in Russia was known as Alevis Novi, i.e., the new Alevis. He arrived in 1504 and had built no fewer than eleven churches in Moscow by the time of his death in 1551. See Sergio Bettini, 'L'architetto Alevis Novi in Russia," in Agostino Pertusi, ed., *Venezia e l'Oriente* (Florence, 1966), pp. 573–94.

22. Arthur Voyce, *The Moscow Kremlin* (Berkeley, 1954), pp. 95–101.

23. Astronomical and cabalistic lore lay near the heart of this movement. Its reception was facilitated by the fact that Orthodox astronomical and calendrical ideas suffered an awkward shock when the world failed to come to an end in 1492, as many Russian as well as Greek Orthodox clerics had thought would happen. (The Easter calendars prepared centuries before expired in that year; and this had confirmed speculation to the effect that the year 7000 from Creation would see the Last Day). Jews, with trade connections southward to the Crimea and Constantinople, may have been instrumental in bringing the new lore into Muscovy. Similiar ideas, after all, were in high repute at Mehmed II's court. Cf. George Vernadsky, 'The Heresy of the Judaizers and the Policies of Ivan III of Moscow," *Speculum* 8 (1933): 436–54.

24. The Russian embassy arrived at an especially critical time in the history of Moslem-Christian relations within the Ottoman Empire. Sultan Selim the Grim had, in 1514, defeated the armies of his Moslem rival, Shah Isma'il Safavi, drowning the sectarian uprisings of Asia Minor in blood. Having treated heterodox Moslems so roughly, the sultan bethought himself of treating his Christian subjects in the same way, with the aim of producing (as Ferdinand and Isabella were then doing in Spain) complete religious uniformity within his domains. He was dissuaded by Sunni experts

in the Sacred Law of Islam, who pointed out that the orthodoxy he proposed to impose required toleration for Christians and Jews! But at the time when the tsar's emissaries arrived, this upshot was not yet clear, and the Orthodox patriarch had reason to fear the worst. Having no liking for the Latins, Russia was the patriarch's only possible outside source of help. See Elie Denissoff, *Maxime le Grec et l'occident: Contribution à l'histoire de la pensée religieuse et philosophique de Michel Trivolis* (Paris-Louvain, 1943), pp. 347–56.

25. Denissoff (see above) proved for the first time the identity of Michael Trivolis and Maxim the Greek, as he came to be known in Russia. This book is a triumph of scholarly detective work, though it suffers a bit from hero worship.

26. My remarks on Maxim derive from Denissoff, pp. 3–19, 387–90, and passim. See also Alexander Vucinich, *Science in Russian Culture; A History to 1860* (Stanford, 1963), pp. 5–10; George Vernadsky, *Russia at the Dawn of the Modern Age* (New Haven, 1959), pp. 159–61; R. Klosterman, "Legende und Wirklichkeit im Lebenswerk von Maxim Grek," *Orientalia Christiana Periodica* 24 (1958): 353–70.

27. In the first half of the twentieth century totaliatarian forms of Marxism won wide success in former peasant lands marginal to industrial Europe for psychological and sociological reasons closely parallel to what happened some four hundred years earlier in lands similarly marginal to renaissance Italy.

28. Cf. James H. Billington, *The Icon and the Axe* (New York, 1957), pp. 67–72, for interesting remarks about the resemblances between Spain and Muscovy. He does not, however, consider the Ottoman Empire as a member of this family of states, as I think it was.

29. Cf. the judicious summary of J. H. Elliott, *Imperial Spain 1469–1716* (London, 1963).

30. In 1494 a distinguished mathematician and professor at a madrassa of Istanbul was executed for irreligion, after attaining fame and fortune under Mehmed the Conqueror and enjoying the patronage, also, of Beyazid II (reigned 1481–1512). Abdulhak Adnan, *La Science chez les Turcs ottomans* (Paris, 1939), pp. 43–46. This was a *cause célèbre* at the time, demonstrating the high price of impiety under the new regime.

31. Bernard Lewis, *Istanbul and the Civilization of the Ottoman Empire* (Norman, Oklahoma, 1963), p. 45.

32. A Grand Rabbi and an Armenian Catholikos completed the

system by exercising comparable responsibilities and jurisdiction over Jews and Armenian Christians. In addition, Roman Catholics came under the protection of the French ambassador in 1604, thanks to a new clause in the "capitulations" treaty negotiated in that year. This proved fateful for eighteenth-nineteenth century Ottoman history but was merely a minor administrative convenience in the seventeenth century, making an appropriate authority responsible for managing the affairs of a small and otherwise unorganized religious community.

33. The *étatisation* of the *ulema* in the Ottoman Empire had begun earlier, notably under Mehmed II the Conqueror. Suleiman, however, perfected, stabilized, and regulated the system. Cf. Lewis, *Istanbul and the Civilization of the Ottoman Empire*, pp. 104 ff.

34. *Ulema* opposed the printing press as an innovation but rejected it primarily on the ground that it would permit improper replication of God's word, the Koran. The prohibition was enforced until 1727.

35. On Ottoman religious and administrative policy under Selim I and Suleiman cf. Marshall Hodgson, *The Venture of Islam* (Chicago, 1974); *Cambridge History of Islam* (Cambridge, 1970), 2: 313–42. Barnette Miller, *The Palace School of Muhammed the Conqueror* (Cambridge, Mass., 1941), deals in detail with one of the key institutions of the state, not only under Mehmed but throughout its history. Albert H. Lybyer, *The Government of the Ottoman Empire in the Time of Suleiman the Magnificent* (Cambridge, Mass., 1913), despite schematic oversimplification, is also useful.

36. Joseph had been informed of Spanish methods by an ambassador from the German emperor who passed through Novgorod when the first Russian prosecutions for heresy had begun. Cf. W. K. Medlin, *Moscow and East Rome* (Geneva, 1952), p. 85.

37. Maxim the Greek, of course, belonged within this hesychast tradition. His insistence on personal autonomy in the search for religious salvation and truth was fundamentally incompatible with the Josephist effort to organize and defend a truth already known.

38. G. P. Fedotov, *The Russian Religious Mind* (Cambridge, Mass., 1966), 2: 377–92.

39. E. Duchesne, *Le Stoglav ou les Cent Chapitres: Recueil des décisions de l'assemblée ecclésiastique de Moscou, 1551* (Paris, 1920), contains an instructive introduction and commentary. Cf. also Medlin, *Moscow and East Rome*, pp. 107–13.

40. In 1568, however, Ivan IV the Terrible executed the metro-

politan of Moscow, an act that weakened the alliance of throne and altar for half a century.

41. Charles Verlinden has devoted much attention to this continuity. His views are summed up in three partially overlapping books: *Précédents médiévaux de la colonie en Amérique* (Mexico City, 1954); *Les Origines de la Civilisation atlantique: de la Renaissance à l'Age des Lumières* (Paris, 1966); *The Beginnings of Modern Colonization* (Ithaca, New York, 1970).

42. Cf. Merrill Jensen and Robert L. Reynolds, "European Colonial Experience: A Plea for Comparative Studies," *Studi in Onore di Gino Luzzatto*, 4: 75–90; Charles Verlinden, "L'héritage de Venise en Occident," in Cortelazzo, ed., *Mediterraneo e Oceano Indiano*, pp. 357–72.

43. A small circle of aristocratic adherents of the "devotio moderna" imported from the Netherlands came into existence in Venice during the crisis of the war of the League of Cambrai; and between the 1540s and 1560s both Calvinism and Anabaptism excited some attention. But all such heretical groups remained trifling in size and their practical importance was nil. Cf. Edouard Pommier, "La Société vénitienne et la réforme protestante au XVIe siècle," *Bolletino dell'Istituto di Storia della Società e dello Stato Veneziana* 1 (1959): 3–26. The vigor and variety of Catholic piety in Venice is learnedly displayed in Alberto Vecchi, *Correnti religiose nel sei-settecento veneto* (Venice-Rome, 1962). Cf. also Hubert Jedin, "Gaspero Contarini e il contributo veneziano alla riforma cattolica" *La Civiltà veneziana del Rinascimento* (Florence, 1958), pp. 105–24.

44. Molmenti, *La Storia di Venezia nella vita privata*, 2: 309–11; Allardyce Nicholl, *The World of Harlequin: A Critical Study of the Commedia dell'Arte* (Cambridge, 1963), pp. 159–69 and passim.

45. On Venice and *commedia dell'arte* see Diego Valeri, "Caratteri e valori del teatro comico," in *Civiltà veneziana del Rinascimento*, pp. 3–25; for diffusion through trans-Alpine Europe cf. Nicholl, *World of Harlequin*, pp. 167–202; for Turkish theater see Metin And, *A History of Theatre and Popular Entertainment in Turkey* (Ankara, 1963–64), pp. 31–42; Otto Spies, *Türkischen Puppentheater* (Emsdetten, 1959), pp. 65–70. Turkish popular theatricals shared some stock characters with the *commedia dell'arte*. Whether Turks borrowed from Italians or vice versa is an open (and unexplored) question; their interaction is beyond doubt. The Turkish puppet theater may derive from ancient shamanistic rituals. But

Italian stimulus may lie behind the elaboration that ensued when imperial patronage became available to puppet masters and to a parallel and related tradition of entertainment by live actors. The first record of an imperial command performance dates from 1582.

46. Molmenti, *La Storia di Venezia* 2: 572–90; Yriarte, *La vie d'un patricien de Venise au XVIe siècle*, pp. 43–61, offers a vivid description of the seclusion Venetian ladies rebelled against; Ernest Rodenwalt, "Untersuchungen über die Biologie des venezianischen Adels," *Homo* 8 (1957): 1–26, presents some remarkable figures on marriage rates among the Venetian nobility, as follows:

> Sixteenth century: 51 percent males remained unmarried
> Seventeenth century: 60 percent males remained unmarried
> Eighteenth century: 66 percent males remained unmarried

Unmarried noblemen consorted with courtesans as a matter of course; marriage was a matter of property and family. To forestall dispersal of wealth it became common for only one son to marry and beget legitimate heirs.

47. In 1638, a gambling house, the Ridotto, was set up under private management, but licensed by the state. This became the prototype of the European casino, where ladies and gentlemen, even if perfect strangers, could gamble elegantly with one another, or against the house, all according to clearly defined and punctiliously enforced rules. Cf. Pompeo Molmenti, *La Storia de Venezia* 3: 227–28.

48. Singer, *A Short History of Anatomy*, p. 153.

49. Randall, *The School of Padua and the Emergence of Modern Science*, pp. 106–7 and passim.

50. Venetian printers played an active role in diffusing data about the great European voyages of discovery. The most important such work was the collection made by Giambattista Ramusio, *Delle Navigazioni e Viaggia* (3 vols.; Venice, 1550–59). This became a fundamental reference work, making otherwise rare and fugitive reports available to learned men in all of Europe.

51. In 1554 more than one hundred noble Venetians were registered as students, according to Brugi, *Gli scolari dello studio di Padova nel Cinquecento*, p. 16.

52. The fate of the Venetian Academy, established in 1557 on the initiative of a prominent nobleman, Frederigo Badoer, is symptomatic. Modeling his enterprise on the famous Aldine Academy of the beginning of the century, Badoer projected an ambitious publishing program for his new academy, got state support and approval,

but mixed his personal business affairs with those of the academy in such a fashion as to bring both to bankruptcy and discredit in 1571. See Paul Lawrence Rose, "The Accademia Venetiana: Science and Culture in Renaissance Venice," *Studi Veneziana* 11 (1969): 191–215.

53. See above, p. 162.

54. G. Chassiotis, *L'Instruction publique chez les grecs depuis la prise de Constantinople jusqu'aux nos jours* (Paris, 1881), pp. 25–26; Cléobule Tsourkas, *Les débuts de l'enseignement philosophique et de la libre pensée dans les Balkans; La vie et l'oeuvre de Théophile Corydalée (1570–1646)* (2d ed.; Thessalonika, 1967), pp. 16–18; Cléobule Tsourkas, *Gli scolari greci di Padova nel rinnovamento culturale dell'Oriente ortodosso* (Padua, 1958), p. 4; Giovanni Fabris, "Professori e scolari greci all'università di Padova," *Archivio Veneto* 30 (1942): 130–34; Deno J. Geanakoplos, *Byzantine East and Latin West* (Oxford, 1966), pp. 141–43, 166–69; Geanakoplos,*Greek Scholars in Venice* (Cambridge, Mass., 1962), pp. 46–52.

55. Cf. William H. McNeill, *Europe's Steppe Frontier, 1500–1800* (Chicago, 1964), pp. 54–123.

56. Profits to be made from exporting grain and other agricultural products strengthened the landowning, local element in Ottoman society at the expense of central authorities. Cf. Maurice Aymard, *Venise, Raguse et le commerce du blé*, pp. 46–53. There are statistical measures of this change. O. L. Barkan, on the basis of Ottoman tax records, estimates that when Suleiman the Lawgiver ascended the throne in 1520, 51 percent of all tax income reached the sultan's treasury. A century later the percentage had shrunk to 25 percent. A harder figure still: in 1527 the sultan's income totaled about four million gold pieces; in 1667 his income had risen only to 4.9 million gold pieces, despite a price rise of more than 200 percent in the interim! (Lecture, Giorgio Cini Institute, Venice, October 1971.)

57. An operational alliance of Turkish with Serbian (and Bosniak) manpower was what permitted Suleiman to conquer and administer Hungary, 1526–43; a similar sociomilitary alliance between Croats and Germans under the Hapsburg aegis, which was sealed in these same decades, checked further Ottoman advance by mustering an equivalently formidable manpower on the Christian side. For details of how the Hapsburgs organized their marches against the Turks see Gunther Rothenberg, *The Austrian Military Border in Croatia, 1522–1747* (Urbana, 1960).

58. Syphilis may have had something to do with the decay of the house of Osman; but conditions in the cages guaranteed physical as well as mental debility for anyone who spent much time immured therein. Kept like a zoo animal, confined in luxury with absolutely nothing to do all day, sensual indulgence and overindulgence was all that remained to make life bearable. On Ottoman dynastic patterns cf. A. D. Alderson, *The Structure of the Ottoman Dynasty* (Oxford, 1956).

59. Symbolic of the change was the fact that in 1594 the Grand Vizier Sinan pasha ordered the body of Saint Sava disinterred and publicly burned in Belgrade. Saint Sava, it will be remembered, was the patron saint and organizer of the Serbian church. On the changing Serbian role in the Ottoman Empire, George V. Tomasevich, "Continuity and Change in Serbian Civilization in the Wake of Ottoman Conquest" (Chicago, 1957, unpublished Ph.D. dissertation) is of some value.

60. Cf. Cecil Roth, *The House of Nasi; The Duke of Naxos* (Philadelphia, 1948); P. Grunebaum-Ballin, *Joseph Nasi, Duc de Naxos* (Paris, 1968).

61. Marian Malowist, "Les routes de commerce et les marchandises du Levant dans la vie de Pologne au bas Moyen Age et au début de l'époque moderne," in Cortelazzo, ed., *Mediterraneo e Oceano Indiano*, pp. 157–75; Halil Inalcik, "Capital Formation in the Ottoman Empire," *Journal of Economic History* 29 (1969): 123.

In the last decade of the sixteenth century, vines transplanted from the Aegean to Hungary provided the basis for the rise of the famous "Tokay" vintage. Being much nearer to Poland, Hungarian vintners were able to take over the Polish wine market in the early decades of the seventeenth century. This exactly recapitulated the western Mediterranean's reception of "vinoble" in the fourteenth and fifteenth centuries. See above, p. 56.

Incidentally, a similar cycle asserted itself in the time of the Roman Empire, when the spread of ordinary grapes from Italian to Spanish, Gallic, and even German soil created a severe marketing crisis in Italy under the Emperor Domitian (reigned A.D. 81–96). The loss of first the western and then the northern market had similarly depressing consequences for the Aegean regions in early modern times, compounded and obscured, however, by the destruction wrought upon the export vineyards of Crete during the long war of Candia, 1645–69.

On Polish-Ottoman wine trade my colleague, Professor Arcadius Kahan, has kindly provided me with a summary of two Polish authorities: Roman Rybarski, *Handel i Polityka Handlowa Polski v XVI stuleciu* (Warsaw, 1958), 1: 121; Ignacy Schiper, *Dzieje Handlu Zydowskiego na Ziemiach Polskich* (Warsaw, 1937), pp. 32–33, 86–91.

62. Roth, *The House of Nasi,* pp. 156–60; Grunebaum-Bellin, *Joseph Nasi,* pp. 147–53. Western-trained Jewish doctors doubling as diplomats were not new in the Ottoman Empire in the sixteenth century. Mehmed the Conqueror relied upon such a man, despite Venetian efforts to bribe him to poison his patient. See Franz Babinger, "Ja-qub Pasha, ein Leibartz Mehmeds II: Leben und Schicksal des Maestro Iacopo aus Gaeta," *Revista degli Studi Orientali* 26 (1951): 87–113.

63. A decisive turn of papal policy against Jews took place in 1555 when Pope Paul IV organized persecutions in Ancona and confined the Jews of Rome to a ghetto for the first time. See Leon Poliakov, "La Communauté Juive à Rome aux XVIe et XVIIe siècles," *Annales: économies, sociétés civilisations* 12 (1957): 119–22. Then in 1564 the papacy laid down the rule that the award of every advanced degree should be accompanied by a formal and public profession of Catholic faith on the part of the candidate; and in 1581 Pope Gregory XIII forbade Christians to resort to Jewish doctors. Presumably such rules were effective in most of Catholic Europe, though at Padua, after the Venetian government quarreled openly with the pope, a special ceremony was arranged in 1616 to permit Protestants, Orthodox Christians, and Jews to secure degrees without forswearing their religion. See Cecil Roth, *Venice,* (Philadelphia, 1930), pp. 186, 288–91; Giovanni Fabris, "Professari e scolari greci all'università di Padova," *Archivio Veneto* 30 (1942): 139.

64. Since the Moslem year was lunar and about two weeks shorter than the solar year, the thousandth anniversary of the Hegira (A.D. 632) as reckoned by Moslems fell in the year 1590 as reckoned by Christians.

65. Gabriel Baer, "Monopolies and Restrictive Practices of the Turkish Guilds," *Journal of Economic and Social History of the Orient* 13 (1970): 145–65. Guilds and dervish orders entered into a close symbiosis in Ottoman towns; but exact information is lacking. Cf. Hans Joachim Kissling, "The Sociological and Educational Role of the Dervish Orders in the Ottoman Empire," *American Anthropologist Memoirs,* no. 76 (1954): 23–35.

66. Cf. Traian Stoianovich, "Land Tenure and Related Sectors of the Balkan Economy," *Journal of Economic History* 13 (1953):

298–411; Deena R. Sadat, "Rumeli Ayanlari: The Eighteenth Century," *Journal of Modern History* 44 (1972): 346–63. The price of revolution in Turkey was, of course, related to the influx of American silver and the general world-wide changes of monetary values that resulted.

67. Halil Inalcik, *The Ottoman Empire: The Classical Age* (London, 1973), pp. 183–85.

68. Ibid., p. 179. By way of contrast, the plague of 1575–77 in Venice provoked a series of remarkably rational administrative and theoretical efforts to cope with the phenomena of contagion. See Ernst Rodenwalt, *Pest in Venedig, 1575–77; Ein Beitrag zur Frage der Infektkette bei den Pestepidemien West Europas* (Heidelberg, 1953).

69. Coffee drinking and tobacco smoking dated from 1555 and 1601 respectively in Istanbul. These novelties aroused much opposition among pious and puritanical Moslems, but were not in the end confined to merely private consumption. As a compromise, the keeping of public coffee houses was consigned to Christians, even though Moslems might patronize them. See Lewis, *Istanbul and the Civilization of the Ottoman Empire*, pp. 132–33.

70. By universal consent, the greatest Ottoman architect was Sinan (1491–1588), a member of the sultan's slave family, janissary officer and only subsequently architect. He began with military construction, bridges, etc., before becoming chief architect to Suleiman the Lawgiver. In that capacity, he was responsible for all public construction in the empire, and kept this office all the rest of his life. His two masterpieces are the mosque in Istanbul named after Suleiman, and the even more magnificent mosque named after Selim II in Edirne. The dome of the Selimiye mosque, completed in 1575, was slightly larger than the dome of Hagia Sofia, a fact symbolic of Sinan's conscious rivalry with his Byzantine predecessors. His buildings are of a truly classical beauty, and to my eyes, at least, easily surpass the clumsier bulk of Hagia Sofia. On Sinan cf. Ernst Egli, *Sinan: Der Baumeister osmanischer Glanzzeit* (Zurich, 1954); Godfrey Goodwin, *A History of Ottoman Architecture* (Baltimore, 1971), pp. 192–333.

71. It remains exceedingly difficult to arrive at anything like a just appreciation of Ottoman cultural achievements, for beyond the still imperfectly studied arts of poetry and miniature painting, other important elements of Ottoman high culture remain unknown and perhaps unknowable. Calligraphy, for example, was accounted an art and underwent extraordinary elaboration. Music, too, was

highly professionalized, but skills were passed on by apprenticeship patterns, and there was no effort to develop a notation to record virtuosity. With the breakup of the various musical organizations that took place in the nineteenth and twentieth centuries, traditional high skills were therefore permanently lost. In 1638 Sultan Murad IV conquered Baghdad and brought back to Istanbul a famous musician named Shah Culi who is said to have given a new direction to Ottoman court music; and in 1691 Demetrius Cantemir wrote a treatise on Turkish music and tried to reduce it to a form of European notation, but the effort was not taken up by the performers themselves. Barnette Miller, *The Palace School of Muhammed the Conqueror* (Cambridge, Mass., 1941), p. 118 ff., has something to say of the importance of music in Ottoman education and public life.

72. On Turkish art cf. Celel Esad Arseven, *L'Art turc* (Istanbul, 1939), pp. 171–74; Oktay Aslanapa, *Turkish Arts; Seljuk and Ottoman Carpets, Tiles and Miniature Paintings* (Istanbul, n.d.) and Ekren Akurgal, Cyril Mango and Richard Ettinghausen, *Treasures of Turkey: The Earliest Civilizations of Anatolia, Byzantium and the Islamic Period* (Geneva, 1966). The last two are not really histories but reproduce some impressive photographs. No really satisfactory history of Turkish art appears to exist.

On Turkish literature, Alessio Bombaci, *La Letteratura Turca* is the best available handbook. Cf. also E. J. W. Gibb, *A History of Ottoman Poetry* (3 vols.; London, 1902–4); and the more summary evaluations of Bernard Lewis, "Some Reflections on the Decline of the Ottoman Empire," *Studia Islamica* 9 (1958): 111–27; Virgil Candea, "Les Intellectuels du Sud-Est Européen au XVIIe siècle," *Revue des Etudes Sud-Est Européennes* 8 (1970): 627–28. On Turkish science, Abdulhak Adnan, *La Science chez les Turcs Ottomans* (Paris, 1939), pp. 91–124. Copernican astronomy did not assail Turkish minds before the eighteenth century.

73. In 1561 a *Nomocanon* was compiled, codifying the law to be enforced by church courts. This brought Greek Orthodoxy into line with Islam, where the body of Sacred Law had been codified since the ninth century of the Christian era. On the *Nomocanon* see N. J. Pantazopoulos, *Church and Law in the Balkan Peninsula during the Ottoman Rule* (Thessalonika, 1967), p. 45.

74. Cf. George Elias Zachariades, *Tübingen und Konstantinopel: Martin Crusius und seine Verhandlungen mit der griechisch-orthodoxen Kirche* (Göttingen, 1941); Steven Runciman, *The Great Church in Captivity* (Cambridge, 1968), pp. 238–58; Ernst Benz,

Wittenberg und Byzanz: Zur Begegnung und Auseinandersetzung der Reformation und der ostlich-orthodoxen Kirche (Marburg, 1949), pp. 94–128. The great literary monument to Lutheran interest in the Greeks is Martin Crusius' *Turco-Graeciae* (Basel, 1584). This stout volume records all a professor of Greek at Tübingen was able to discover about contemporary Hellenism. Part of Crusius' data is reprinted in Otto Kresten, *Das Patriarchat von Konstantinopel im ausgehenden 16. Jahrhundert* (Vienna-Cologne-Graz, 1970).

75. William J. Bouwsma, *Venice and the Defense of Republican Liberty: Renaissance Values in the Age of the Counter Reformation* (Berkeley, 1968), pp. 236, 250–69.

76. Antonio Favaro, *Galileo Galilei e lo Studio di Padova* (2 vols.; Padua, 1968), 1: 60–75.

77. One of the provisions of this treaty assured Moslems the right to reside and trade in Venetian territories. See above, p.289, n.57.

78. Bouwsma, *Venice and the Defense of Republican Liberty*, pp. 339–416 and passim; Gaetano Cozzi, *Il Doge Nicolò Contarini, Ricerche sul patriziato veneziano agli inizi del Seicento* (Venice, 1958); Frederico Seneca, *Il Doge Leonardo Dona* (Padua, 1959).

79. The split between Galileo and the Aristotelian establishment at the University of Padua dated back to 1604 when a *nova* appeared in the skies and provoked much debate among astronomers all over Europe. Cremonini, who had made his reputation by opposing the Jesuits in 1581, and continued to be the university's most honored professor until his death in 1631, knew that the heavens were incorruptible; therefore, the *nova*, whatever appearances might say, had to be sublunar. When Galileo discovered defects on the surface of the moon, Cremonini refused to look through the telescope himself on the ground that it would make him dizzy. He believed that whatever Galileo saw through the new instrument was no more than an optical illusion of some kind, a trick with which a promising young man had gulled first himself and then the public. Cf. Antonio Favaro, *Galileo Galilei et lo Studio di Padova*, 2: 28–32.

80. Cf. Giorgio di Santillana, *The Crime of Galileo* (Chicago, 1955).

81. Cf. Alberto Vecchi, "La Vita Spirituale," in Centro di Cultura e Civiltà della Fondazione Giorgio Cini, *La Civiltà veneziana del Settecento* (Florence, 1959), pp. 133 ff.

82. Rodenwalt, *Pest in Venedig 1575–77*; Pullan, *Rich and Poor in Renaissance Venice*, pp. 314–26.

83. Manfred F. Bukofzer, *Music in the Baroque Era: from*

Monteverdi to Bach (New York, 1947), pp. 20–25, 33–38, 55–68.

84. Boxes became hereditary; and assignment of an empty one turned into a matter of state, entrusted to the doge himself. See Simon Towneley Worsthorne, *Venetian Opera in the Seventeenth Century* (Oxford, 1954), pp. 2–17.

85. Opera as produced at Venice quickly established an international reputation. In 1675 the grand vizier of Turkey commanded an operatic performance in Constantinople; and when the Venetian *bailo* demurred for want of time, the Turks were miffed. See John Covel's Diary, reproduced in J. Theodore Bent, ed., *Early Voyages and Travels in the Levant* [Hakluyt Society, First series, 87], (London, 1893), p. 202.

86. Ottoman dancing boys who performed in public were just as shocking to Latin sensibility, for they apparently manifested homosexuality much as the Italian stage manifested heterosexuality.

87. Among those who later became famous were Cyril Lukaris, œcumenical patriarch, 1621–38; Theophilos Korydaleos, who transformed the curriculum of the patriarchal academy in Constantinople beginning in 1624; Michael Bassarab, hospodar of Wallachia, 1632–54.

88. Such interaction was forwarded by the fact that from about 1550 Venetian authorities permitted Greeks to establish schools freely within the territories under Venetian imperial administration. Such schools were staffed by graduates of the University of Padua and created a slender but real group of well-educated Greek schoolboys, some of whom in their turn came to Padua for higher education. See Philip Sherrard, *The Greek East and the Latin West: A Study in Christian Tradition* (London, 1959), p. 175–76.

89. In 1551 the Stoglav Council in Russia prohibited icons that departed from traditional style; this did not permanently prevent importation of icons with western contamination into Russia, however, for the Patriarch Nikon found it necessary in 1655 to stage a public destruction of westernizing icons, which he had confiscated from private homes. See George Vernadsky, *The Tsardom of Moscow, 1547–1682* (New Haven, 1969), pp. 567–68.

90. Probably about 1566. He stayed there until about 1570, when he went to Rome, and thence to Toledo.

91. On Damaskinos and the Italianizing Cretan School of icon painting see Manolis Chatzidakis, *Icônes de Saint Georges des Grecs et de la Collection de l'Institut hellénique de Venise* (Venice 1962); Sergio Bettini, *Il pittore Michel Damasceno e l'inizio del secondo periodo dell'arte Cretese-Veneziana* [Atti del Reale Istituto

Veneto di Scienze, Lettere ed Arti, XCIV, part 2, 1934–35], (Venice, 1935); Alexandre Embiricos, *L'école Crétoise, dernière Phase de la Peinture Byzantine*, pp. 131–243; on El Greco cf. Embiricos, pp. 244–88; Pal Kelemen, *El Greco Revisited: Candia, Venice, Toledo* (New York, 1961); J. F. Willumsen, *La Jeunesse du peintre El Greco, essai sur la transformation de l'artiste byzantin en peintre Européen* (2 vols.; Paris, 1927).

92. See N. M. Papagiotakis and A. L. Vincent, "Nea stoicheia gia tin Akademia ton Stravaganti," *Thesaurismata* 7 (1970): 52–81, and Papagiotakis' earlier article, "Ereunai en Venetia," *Thesaurismata* 5 (1968): 45–118. Three major monuments of the Cretan theatrical tradition are available in English translation. See F. H. Marshall, trans., *Three Cretan Plays: The Sacrifice of Abraham, Erophile and Gyparis* (London, 1929). Cf. also Linos Politis, "Il teatro a Creta nei suoi rapporti con il teatro Italiano del Rinaschimento e in particolare con la commedia Veneziana," in Agostino Pertusi, ed., *Venezia e l'Oriente* (Florence, 1966), pp. 225–40.

93. The poem was published in Venice in 1713 but must have been written before 1669, though perhaps only after 1645 when the war of Candia began. For a long time even the name of the author was unclear; almost nothing is known of his life.

The plot was lifted from an obscure Provençal romance dating back to the fourteenth century. *Erotokritos* was, in fact, a belated example of the chivalric romance of the sort Cervantes satirized; but this archaic character, combined with a distinctly anti-Turkish tone, fitted it for the vast success it had among Greek villagers and simple folk. A portion of the poem is available in translation in John Mavrogordato, *The Erotokritos of Vicenzo Kornaros: A Greek Romantic Epic* (London, 1929). Cf. Embiricos, *La Renaissance Crétoise I: La Littérature*, pp. 205 ff; C. Th. Dimaras, *Histoire de la littérature néo-hellénique* (Athens, 1965), pp. 78–96; Bruno Lavagnini, *La letteratura neoellenica* (Florence, 1969), pp. 76–111.

94. The first published work of popular piety in demotic Greek appeared at Venice in 1524; the two really influential collections were those of Joannikos Kartanos, *Flowers of All the Bible*, published in 1536, and an anonymous work, *Flowers of Charity*, published in 1546. These books remained in print until the nineteenth century. (Last edition of *Flowers of Charity*, Venice, 1866). They were used as schoolbooks in Greek-speaking lands everywhere. See the excellent little monograph by Philipp Meyer, *Die theologische Litteratur der griechischen Kirche im 16. Jahrhundert* (Leipzig, 1899), pp. 105–137.

95. Twelfth edition, Venice, 1899.

96. Similar missions arrived in the Lebanon in 1580 and in India in 1585, aiming at reconciliation with Maronite and Saint Thomas Christians respectively. See Joseph Hajjar, *Les Chrétiens uniates du Proche-Orient* (Paris, 1962), pp. 205–7. In 1590 a Jesuit mission was set up also in Chios. Emile Legrand, *Relation de l'établissement des PP. de la Compagnie de Jésus en Levant* (Paris, 1899), p. 6.

97. The plan was first to conquer Moscow, then use Russian resources for a final attack on the Turks.

98. See Paul Pierling, *La Saint-Siège, la Pologne et Moscou, 1582–1587* (Paris, 1885); Oscar Halecki, *From Florence to Brest, 1439–1596* (2d ed.; New York, 1968), pp. 210–11.

99. In 1586 the archbishop of Ochrid, head of the Bulgarian church, entered into complex and in the end fruitless negotiations with the papacy, offering recognition of papal primacy in return for a suitable subvention. Since the metropolitan's power lacked clear legitimacy, it all came to nothing. See Oscar Halecki, "Rome, Constantinople et Moscou au Temps de l'Union de Brest," in *1054–1954: L'Eglise et les Eglises,* (Chevetogne, 1954), 1: 453–54. Rather better success was achieved in Sofia among Bulgars, mainly converted Paulicians. See Ivan Dujčev, *Il Cattolicesimo in Bulgaria nel secolo XVII* [Orientalia Christiana Analecta, III], (Rome, 1937), pp. 12–22; M. Murko, *Die Bedeutung der Reformation und Gegenreformation für das geistige Leben der Südslawen* (Prague and Heidelberg, 1927), pp. 27 ff.

100. Defined since patristic times as Jerusalem, Antioch, Alexandria, Constantinople, and Rome. Even before the reconciliation with Moscow, obscure changes in personnel and administrative procedures had brought the patriarchates of Jerusalem and Alexandria securely under the influence of the œcumenical patriarch in Constantinople. By Jeremias' time, these sees were occupied by Greeks, and the incumbents characteristically spent as much time in Constantinople and adjacent areas as in their supposed seats. Ottoman conquest of Syria, Palestine, and Egypt, 1515–17, was of course fundamental; thereafter all relations with Turkish authorities tended to be channeled through the œcumenical patriarch. But Hellenization was not inevitable: the patriarchate of Antioch remained in the hands of Arabic-speaking Christians, and its relation with Constantinople was much more distant.

Generally, the rise of a sharper pan-Orthodox consciousness seems attributable both to an improved level of education among Greek prelates, dating from about the middle of the sixteenth century (see above, pp. 178–79) and to a general reaction against Roman Catholic missionary efforts, which, for instance, drove the patriarchs of both Jerusalem and Alexandria to seek support in Constantinople. Cf. Runciman, *The Great Church in Captivity*, pp. 176–77; Hajjar, *Les Chrétiens uniates du Proche-Orient*, pp. 201–17, 240.

101. Early in his career as patriarch,Patriarch Jeremias, for instance, managed to create the impression in Rome that he was a good Catholic; and his behavior in Lithuania en route back to Constantinople in 1589, where he reorganized the Orthodox hierarchy, deposing specially scandalous prelates and blessing others nominated by the Catholic king, may reflect some disposition on his part to conciliate the Roman Catholics after his sharp defiance of papal prerogative in Moscow. See Halecki, *From Florence to Brest, 1439–1596*, p. 233.

102. For details see Halecki, *From Florence to Brest, 1439–1596*.

103. A clause in the Treaty of Zitva-Török (1606), ending the long and inconclusive war between the Turks and the Hapsburgs that had started in 1593, guaranteed Roman Catholic missionaries access to Ottoman territory. Thus the new Jesuit mission had Hapsburg as well as French support.

104. And Armenian. The Jesuits in fact won over a large segment of the Armenian hierarchy to the uniate position, though not without provoking an eventual schism (1735) that kept a part of the Armenian church outside the papal fold. In general, Jesuit missionary efforts concentrated on winning the Armenians after their efforts to infiltrate the Greek church had clearly failed, i.e., after the 1680s. See Friedrich Heiler, *Urkirche und Ostkirche* (Munich, 1937), pp. 514–15; M. A. Belin, *Histoire de la Latinité de Constantinople*, (2d ed.; Paris, 1894), p. 266.

105. Communist "boring from within" tactics of the 1920s and 1930s paralleled Jesuit methods both in intention and result, creating costly backlash in the form of revulsion on the part of their intended victims whenever the tactic was unmasked.

106. Some acts of violence were deliberately contrived, as when Catholic agents employed a body of janissaries to attack a printing press that had been set up adjacent to the English embassy in response to a request from the Orthodox patriarch for printing facilities. For details see Georg Hofmann, "Griechische Patriarchen und römische Päpste: II. Patriarch Kyrillos Lukaris und die römische Kirche," *Orientalia Christiana* 15 (1929): 778 ff.

107. Lukaris held the patriarchate most of this time, but his tenure was always precarious, and he often experienced temporary

exile and dismissal from office. In actual fact he mounted the patriarchal throne no less than five separate times; but those who held the office in rivalry to him were minor figures, and their tenure short.

The Jesuits, too, were expelled from Constantinople several times and then allowed to return, depending on which of the rival ambassadors from the west the Turks chose to listen to, or whose bribes the grand vizier deigned to accept.

108. The storms of controversy that surrounded Lukaris in life continue to disfigure the only recent book-length treatment of his career, George A. Hadjiantoniou, *Protestant Patriarch: The Life of Cyril Lukaris (1572–1638), Patriarch of Constantinople* (Richmond, 1961). Runciman, *The Great Church in Captivity*, pp. 259–88, offers a brief though excellent summary; so does Germanos, metropolitan of Thyateira, *Kyrillos Lukaris, 1572–1638* (London, 1951). For the envenomed exchanges of an earlier generation, cf. Hofmann, "Griechische Patriarchen und römische Päpste," Paul Trivier, *Cyrille Lucar, sa vie et son influence* (Paris, 1877), a rebuttal to the still older Aloysius Pickler, *Geschichte des Protestantismus in der orientalischen Kirche im 17. Jahrhundert, oder der Patriarch Cyrillos Lucaris und seine Zeit* (Munich, 1862).

Three great Orthodox patriarchs richly deserve scholarly and detached biographies: Gennadios, Cyril Lukaris, and Nikon.

109. He was the son of a hospodar of Moldavia; his mother was of a noble Ukrainian family. His education at the Sorbonne made him thoroughly conversant with western high culture. See Eduard Winter, *Byzanz und Rom im Kampf um die Ukraine, 955–1939* (Leipzig, 1942), pp. 83–88. In spite of the time and place of its publication, this is a careful, scholarly work.

110. This procedure had the advantage of not committing the church in legal form to any innovation. Only a general council, by Orthodox law, had the power to define doctrine officially: and it was traditional to argue that all Orthodox doctrines had already been defined by the general councils of the early church. The central charge against the papacy, in fact, was innovation that went beyond the teachings of these councils. Hence it was important to Orthodoxy to secure the substance of a new definition of faith without officially altering anything. This was what Basil Lupu's policy achieved.

111. Korydaleos attended Saint Athanasius College in Rome, 1602–07, before moving north to Padua, where he studied 1607–13, emerging with both an M.D. and Ph.D. He then taught at Athens,

perhaps privately, 1613–19, and was in Zante when Lukaris called him to take charge of the patriarchal academy in 1624. See Tsourkas, *Les débuts de l'enseignement philosophique et de la libre pensée dans les Balkans*, pp. 34–46.

112. Raphael Demos, "The Neo Hellenic Enlightenment," *Journal of the History of Ideas* 19 (1958): 530–31; Tsourkos, p. 11 and passim. Tsourkos gives a precise and detailed account of Korydaleos' ideas as well as of his life. The author is clearly partisan and may exaggerate the "libre pensée" element in Korydaleos' thought; but there can be no doubt that Korydaleos freed and stimulated Orthodox minds to come to grips with contemporary Italian science and secular culture as had not been attempted by Greeks since the Paleologue age. I owe a great deal to this book for whatever understanding I have of seventeenth-century Orthodox intellectual developments.

113. A warm debate has developed between Tsourkas and Rumanian scholars about the beginnings of higher education in Jassy and Bucharest, with Tsourkas claiming almost exclusive importance for Korydaleos' thought and the Rumanians insisting on a more complicated (and later) development. Victor Papacostea, "Les Origines de l'Enseignement supérieur en Valachie," *Revue des Etudes Sud-Est Européennes* 1 (1963): 8–39; 4 (1966): 115–47; and Virgil Candea, "Les intellectuels du sud-est européen au XVIIe siècle," *Revue des Etudes Sud-Est Européennes*, 8 (1970): 202, are rebutted by Cléobule Tsourkos, *Germanos Locros, Archevêque de Nysse et son temps, 1645–1700* (Thessalonike, 1970). Eduard Winter, *Frühaufklärung: Der Kampf gegen den Konfessionalismus in Mittel- und Osteuropa und die deutschslawische Begegnung* (Berlin, 1966), pp. 272–73, is less detailed but has the virtue of being uninvolved in this controversy, which bears telltale traces of rival Greek and Rumanian nationalisms.

114. Another element that may have weakened the Catholic missionary drive was the questionable—not to say repulsive—moral character of some of their converts. For instructive details on how doctrinally indifferent and crassly mercenary a Catholic "convert" from Orthodoxy could be see V. Laurent, "Le patriarche d'Ochrida, Athanase II et l'Eglise Romaine," *Balcania* 3 (1945): 3–65.

115. Nikon's effort to create a New Jerusalem was very literal. He sent an envoy to Jerusalem to make a model of the Church of the Holy Sepulchre so as to be able to duplicate its form in the "New Jerusalem" monastery which he founded outside Moscow. He also reenacted the role of Christ on Palm Sunday, riding on a

donkey, led by the tsar; and in many ritual ways undertook to assert the primacy of the Church over lay society. See Billington, *Icon and Axe*, pp. 131–37.

116. Arsenios had a checkered career. Educated at Rome and Padua (where he earned an M.D.), he arrived in Russia in 1649 in the train of the patriarch of Jerusalem, Paisios. He stayed behind, only to be denounced by Paisios, who had learned in the meanwhile that Arsenios had accepted Catholicism while in Italy, reverted to Orthodoxy on returning east, only to profess Islam when arrested by the Turks as a Venetian spy! When called to account in Moscow, telltale circumcision compelled him to confess to these charges. Accordingly, he was sent off to a monastery, where his piety and authentic learning somehow convinced Nikon that he was the right man to entrust with the task of revising Russian manuals of worship to bring them into line with Greek practices! See Vernadsky, *The Tsardom of Moscow, 1547–1682*, pp. 568–69.

117. Educated in Rome, Ligarides was despatched to Constantinople as an agent of the *Congregatio de Propaganda Fide* in 1641, with instructions to bore from within. Accordingly, in 1651 he took Orthodox monastic vows and was ordained metropolitan of Gaza, while remaining in correspondence with the *Congregatio* and dunning Rome for money to forward the work of conversion. Nikon extended an invitation to this dubious character in 1657 to come to Russia and help in the scholarly tasks of revising the sacred books; he arrived in 1662 in time to take charge of the legal maneuverings incident to Nikon's deposition. *The Tsardom of Moscow*, pp. 589–90.

118. See Nicolae Jorga, *Geschichte des Rumanischen Volkes in Rahmen seiner Staatsbildungen* (Gotha, 1905), 2: 45–74, 115–16.

119. The lethargy of Serbian and Bulgarian ecclesiastics and laymen arose principally from the fact that as soon as a Balkan Slav acquired more than the rudiments of education or advanced very far in urban occupations, he became Greek—as it were, without knowing it. This process continued in the Balkan interior until the nineteenth century, and guaranteed that South Slav culture (except among those Serbs who had emigrated to Hapsburg lands in 1690) would remain at a simple peasant level, incapable of resisting the intellectual and organizational sophistication of Hellenism. Conversely, part of the élan of the Greek community in the seventeenth and eighteenth centuries derived from the fact that the most talented individuals from any Balkan Christian community were regularly recruited into Greek ranks; while the leakage

from Greek (and Serbian) communities into the Turkish Moslem class, which had been of great importance in the sixteenth century and earlier, came almost to a halt.

Statistics are of course lacking; so is serious scholarly investigation, since the crossing-over from one nationality to another that was a normal accompaniment of social mobility in seventeenth and eighteenth-century Ottoman society became profoundly repugnant to nineteenth and twentieth-century nationalistic historians, who do all they can to close their eyes to the phenomenon.

120. An uninterrupted urban and commercial tradition among speakers of Greek reached back to the sixth century B.C. Equally significant for the nurture of the Greek commercial spirit was the fact that Greek rural communities, by and large, and prior to the remarkable expansion of Greek urban culture that occurred in the seventeenth and succeeding centuries, had been confined to regions of the Balkans and Asia Minor where vines and olives could be raised. These are commercial crops par excellence; they were—I think always—cultivated by nuclear peasant households. In medieval centuries Greek peasants probably never knew the complicated joint tenancies and shared workloads which prevailed commonly among Serbs and, less prominently, among Bulgars, too. Tilling the land by individual family effort and selling a large part of the product on the best terms attainable gave Greek peasants a rigorous training in the skills of the marketplace, and encouraged development of personality traits that go with shrewd and successful bargaining. Not the village nor the kindred but the biological family itself was the in-group to which Greek peasants (and townsmen) alone were devoted: the rest of the world was there to be manipulated for private advantage insofar as a man's wits and skills allowed him to do so.

With such a rural pool of sharp-eyed buyers and sellers to draw upon, Greek commercial skills were rivaled only by the Armenians, whose rural base was not entirely dissimilar. Jews seem to have found Greek commercial competition impossible to withstand, after the leakage of especially talented and ambitious individuals from the Greek community into Turkish ranks came to a halt. At least this is a plausible explanation for the economic distress that beset the Jews of the Ottoman Empire in the course of the seventeenth century. For interesting sidelights on that decay see Itzhak Ben-Zvi, "Eretz Yisrael under Ottoman Rule, 1517–1917," Louis Finkelstein, ed., *The Jews: Their History, Culture and Religion* (3d ed.; New York, 1960), 1: 602–89.

121. Figures assembled by O. L. Barkan, "Essai sur les données statistiques des registres de recensement dans l'Empire Ottoman aux XVe et XVIe siècles," *Journal of the Economic and Social History of the Orient* 1 (1958): 9–36, show fewer Christians in many parts of Asia Minor than were there in the nineteenth century. It is not clear, however, when the expansion of Christian population took place nor whether natural increase or immigration from other parts of the Greek world account for what happened.

122. See Traian Stoianovich, "The Conquering Balkan Orthodox Merchant," *Journal of Economic History* 20 (1960): 234 ff.

123. See Nestor Camarino, *Alexandre Mavrocordato, Le Grand Drogman, son activité diplomatique, 1673–1709* (Thessalonika, 1970).

124. The Albanians transferred into urban context the attitudes developed in their native environment as a means of ending blood feud. The *besa*—verbal agreement to maintain peace—was endowed with sacrosanct quality; a man's honor depended on scrupulous observance of his word. The obvious survival value of such a principle in clan society explains the force the *besa* came to have among Albanians. In the seventeenth century (and perhaps before) its value in urban contexts was discovered by upper-class Moslems, who often badly needed someone in their household whom they could trust. Similar considerations in the sultan's household brought Albanians into high administrative posts, up to and including the grand vizierate, in proportions completely out of line with their numbers in Ottoman Moslem society as a whole.

Statistics are of course lacking and so is careful scholarship. But there is no doubt that the Albanians, both Moslem and Christian, expanded their territory and improved their status in Ottoman society *pari passu* with the Greeks throughout the eighteenth and into the nineteenth century. On Albanian *besa* and blood feud see M. Edith Durham, *Some Tribal Origins, Laws and Customs of the Balkans* (London, 1928), pp. 162–71.

125. Köprülü seems to have summoned ago-old ghazi traditions to life. This was easy for an Albanian to do, for ghazi and associated dervish traditions had retained vivacity in Albania uninterruptedly from the days of Scanderbeg. Moslem and Christian tribesmen lived cheek-by-jowl in Albania, and found frequent occasion to clothe tribal blood feud in the ideological garb of Holy War.

126. See Abraham Galanté, *Turcs et Juifs, études historiques, politiques* (Istanbul, 1932) p. 140. In the north, Jews also suffered a drastic setback, 1648–67. Anti-Jewish riots and wholesale slaughter

accompanied the Ukrainian popular revolt of 1648. Jews had often acted as agents for the Polish nobles in exploiting the peasantry, and suffered the brunt of peasant-Cossack anger. On Jewish disasters in the Ukraine see S. N. Dubnow, *History of the Jews in Russia and Poland from the earliest times until the present day* (Philadelphia, 1916–18), 1: 134–67.

127. On Sabbatai Zevi see Gershom G. Scholem, *Major Trends in Jewish Mysticism* (Jerusalem, 1941), pp. 283–320; John Evelyn, *The History of Sabatai Sevi, the Supposed Messiah of the Jews* [Augustan Reprint Society, Publication #131] (Los Angeles, 1968). Gershom Scholem, *Sabbatai Sevi, the Mystical Messiah* (Princeton, 1973), appeared too late to be consulted; but this magistral work will clearly supersede all earlier discussions of the subject.

Six—Venice becomes Archaic and Loses Influence Abroad, 1669–1797

1. Emmanuel Timonis (1669–1720), for instance, studied at Oxford, became a corresponding member of the Royal Society, and wrote on innoculation against smallpox and on the plague in Constantinople. He was personal physician to the sultan. His contemporary, Methodious Anthrakitis (d. ca. 1748), began teaching Cartesian science as elaborated by Malebranche in Janina in 1708. See Börje Knös, *L'Histoire de la littérature néo-grecque: La Période jusq'en 1821* (Stockholm, 1962), pp. 360, 473. Cartesianism had been taught as early as 1683 at Janina in cruder form. Cf. G. Chassiotes, *L'instruction publique chez les grecs* (Paris, 1881), p. 91.

2. See above, pp. 144–46.

3. The capture of Athens in that year involved the destruction of the Parthenon when a Venetian shot ignited stores of powder which the Turks had placed there for safekeeping.

4. Venetian stagecraft was grandiloquently mobilized to commemorate Morosini's victories and for the ceremonies surrounding his installation as doge and subsequent departure for the east. Roman triumphs of the age of Caesar and Augustus were the models. Cf. Pompeo Molmenti, *Vita Privata*, 3: 138–40.

5. Heinrich Kretschmayr, *Geschichte von Venedig* (3 vols.; Gotha and Stuttgart, 1905–34), 3: 341–53; Mario Nani Mocenigo, *Storia della marina Veneziana da Lepanto alla caduta della Repubblica* (Rome, 1935), pp. 262 ff. Venice also took possession of additional Dalmatian territories by the treaty terms.

6. The population of the Morea more than doubled in twenty

years of Venetian administration from a war-induced low of only 90,000 registered in 1688. Kretschmayr, *Venedig*, 3: 354. Moreover, as any modern visitor can testify, the fortifications of Nauplion and Corinth, built between 1695 and 1714, remain vast and impressive to this day.

7. In 1677 the Venetians acceded to papal wishes by installing a uniate archbishop over the Greek community in the city. The resulting quarrel was apparently resolved when the uniate prelate withdrew in favor of an "Orthodox" candidate who had secretly professed Catholicism; but when this deal was discovered in Constantinople, the pseudo-Orthodox archbishop was formally anathematized. As a result of this dispute, the post of ecclesiastical head of the Greek Orthodox community of Venice remained vacant, 1718–61. See Paul Pisani, "Les Chrétiens de rite orientale à Venise et dans les possessions vénitiennes, 1439–1791," *Revue d'histoire et de la littérature religieuse* 1 (1896): 215–17.

8. In addition to withdrawing from the mainland, Venice had to give up Tinos and two islets off Crete which had been salvaged from the wreck of their island empire in 1669.

9. It is ironical but not surprising to reflect on the fact that the crusading Roman Catholic enthusiasm which mobilized funds for Venice to use in the conquest of the Morea was also what made it impractical to retain what had been won since it systematically antagonized Orthodox Christians.

10. Ugo Tucci, "La Marina mercantile veneziana nel Settecento," *Bolletino dell'Istituto della Società e dello Stato veneziano* 2 (1960): 155–202.

11. In 1702, when navigation in the Mediterranean was much hampered by the War of the Spanish Succession, the Venetian Senate tried to revive the pattern of the Flanders galleys by sending a convoy of nine ships to London, loaded with currants, which had become a major export from the Ionian islands and adjacent regions of the mainland. This piece of sound mercantilist policy was literally shipwrecked. Only two vessels made the voyage successfully; five were lost at sea, one stopped for repairs; one was captured by the French! Ibid., p. 167.

12. In 1669 the Turks set Venetian tariff payments at 5 percent *ad valorem* as against 3 percent paid by the politically potent French, Dutch, and English. This was a crippling handicap. Venetian trade with the Ottoman Empire rapidly dwindled as a result. See Robert Mantran, "La navigation vénitienne et ses concurrents

en Méditerranée orientale au XVIIe et XVIIIe siècles," in Manlio Cortelazzo, ed., *Mediterraneo e Oceano Indiano* (Florence, 1970), p. 378.

13 Hermann Kellenbenz, "Le Déclin de Venise et les relations économiques de Venise avec les marchés au nord des Alpes," in *Aspetti e cause della decandenza economica veneziana nel secolo XVII* (Venice–Rome, 1961), pp. 108–83, points to a continuation of overland trade from Venice across the Alps into Austria and south Germany until well into the eighteenth century. As always, this was a luxury trade, since only valuable objects could bear the cost of trans-Alpine transport.

14. See Marino Berengo, "La crisi dell'arte della stampa veneziana alla fine del XVIII secolo," *Studi in Onore di Armando Sapori* (Milan, 1957), pp. 1321–38.

15. See Domenico Sella, *Commerci e Industrie a Venezia nel secolo XVII* (Venice-Rome, 1961).

16. Daniele Beltrami, *Saggio di storia dell'agricoltura nella Repubblica di Venezie durante l'era moderna* (Venice-Rome, 1955), calculated that towns over 10,000 in the Veneto accounted for 21.2 percent of the total population in 1548 but for only 14.3 percent at the end of the eighteenth century. Inasmuch as total population of the Veneto rose from 1.59 million in 1548 to 2.33 million in 1790, this did not require much actual shrinkage of town population, although Venice itself never did recover from its losses during the plague years 1630–31, as the following figures from Daniele Beltrami, *Storia della Popolazione di Venezia* (Padua, 1954), p. 59, show:

Year	Population of Venice
1563	168,627
1633	102,243
1696	138,067
1760	149,476
1797	137,240

17. Beltrami, *Saggio di storia dell'agricoltura*, pp. 11, 21–30.

18. Export of rice and of raw silk increased in the seventeenth century, but it is not clear how much this may have been due to decreased consumption of these products within Venice and how much to an increase in overall production. See Sella, *Commerci e Industrie a Venezia nel secolo XVII*, pp. 86–89.

19. The amount of land owned by Venetians almost doubled

between 1636 and 1740, according to Beltrami, *La Penetrazione economica dei veneziani in terrafirma: Forze di lavoro e proprietà fondiaria nelle campagne venete dei secoli XVII e XVIII* (Venice-Rome, 1961), p. 141. Cf. the summary and criticism of Beltrami's work in Stuart J. Woolf, "Venice and the terrafirma: Problems of the change from commercial to landed activities," *Bolletino dell' Istituto di Storia della Società e dello Stato Veneziano* 4 (1962): 415–44.

20. According to Hans von Zwiedineck-Sudenhorst, *Venedig als Weltmacht und Weltstadt* (Bielefeld and Leipzig, 1906), p. 201, in the eighteenth century as many as 30,000 visitors came to Venice at carnival time.

21. James Cushman Davis, *The Decline of the Venetian Nobility as a Ruling Class* (Baltimore, 1962), assembles much detailed data about the decay of the number of nobles, their percentage of the population as a whole, etc. In 1797 there were only 1,300 nobles as against 2,620 in 1527.

22. Jean Georgelin, "La noblesse vénitienne et le pouvoir," in an unpublished study (1970) identified exactly forty-two families which provided all the incumbents of the key offices of state in the seventeenth-eighteenth centuries. Fernand Braudel kindly allowed me to see this study in MS.

23. Cf. Brian Pullan, Review of J. C. Davis, *Decline of the Venetian Nobility as a Ruling Class* in *Bolletino dell'Istituto di Storia della Società e dello Stato Veneziano* 5–6 (1963–64): 506–25. Pullan's own book, *Rich and Poor in Renaissance Venice: The Social Institutions of a Catholic State, to 1620* (Cambridge, Mass., 1971), shows how skillfully the Venetian bureaucracy handled the first and sharpest phases of economic crisis, but I know of no similar study carrying the story beyond 1620. Marino Berengo, *La Società veneta alla fine del Settecento* (Florence, 1956), and the same author's "Il Problema politico-sociale di Venezia e della sua terraferma," in Centro Cultura e Civiltà della Fondazione Giorgio Cini, *La Civiltà veneziana del Settecento* (Florence, 1959), have little to say about administration within the city. Cf. also George B. McClellan, *Venice and Bonaparte* (Princeton, 1931), pp. 43–51.

24. Maize, the staple of peasant diet in the Veneto from the seventeenth century, cannot provide a satisfactory basis of human nourishment without meat, milk products, or some other source of protein. Without such supplements, a maize diet induces pellagra, because maize lacks certain amino acids which the human body requires. Long before starvation from inadequate calories becomes

apparent, and before the clinical signs of pellagra manifest themselves conspicuously, protein deficiency makes for lassitude and muscular weakness.

As rural population increased, pastures were plowed up, more land was put into cereal production, and the peasants ate more maize, less meat and milk. Such a pattern produced a miserable but meek peasant mass. Exactly the same evolution took place in the Rumanian provinces at the same time, with parallel results: for both in the Veneto and in the Rumanian provinces a rentier class was able to keep its power and position unchallenged, even amidst mounting rural distress, until outsiders injected new, revolutionary ideas into the situation. This happened in the Veneto in 1797 when Napoleon brought French revolutionary armies and rhetoric onto the scene; it almost happened in the Rumanian provinces a generation later, when Alexander Ypsilanti led his filibuster into Moldavia (1821) and started the Greek revolution; but the real breakdown of the Rumanian maize-based rural regime came only with World War I. Cf. David Mitrany, *The Land and the Peasant in Rumania: The War and Agrarian Reform (1917–21)* (London, 1930); Luigi Messedaglia, *Il Maïs e la vita rurale Italiana* (Piacenza, 1927), pp. 173–95, 261–82.

25. This may be unfair to Count Carlo Gozzi (1720–1806), who put a "romantic" challenge to Goldoni's "realistic" comedy before the Venetian public, beginning in 1761 when he staged a dramatized fairy story. But Gozzi ceased to write plays after 1765.

On this literary battle and its European echoes see H. C. Chatfield-Taylor, *Goldoni: A Biography* (New York, 1913), pp. 403–26. The protagonists can be consulted directly: *Useless Memoirs of Carlo Gozzi*, John Addington Symonds, trans. (abridged ed.; London, 1962); *Mémoires de M. Goldoni* (3 vols.; Paris, 1787).

26. Germany and Slavic Europe have been especially hospitable; between 1750 and 1800 a count turned up 303 translations of Goldoni's plays into a total of fourteen different languages; in the nineteenth century, 212 translations into twenty-two different languages, including Turkish, Armenian, and Georgian; and in the twentieth century 350 translations. Marxists of eastern Europe are particularly fond of the way Goldoni often portrays servants as morally superior to their masters. See Jaroslav Pokorny, *Goldoni und das venezianische Theater* (Berlin, 1968), pp. 106–9.

27. Chassiotis, *L'Instruction publique chez les Grecs*, pp. 83, 87. The names of 1,629 Greeks who studied at Padua between 1634 and 1797 are known; tabulation year by year between 1634–61

shows a gradual increase in numbers; then there is a break in surviving records until 1702, when the number of registered Greeks shows very little decline until almost the end of the eighteenth century. See G. E. Ploumides, "I Praxis Eggraphes ton Ellenon Spoudaston ton Panepistimion tis Padouis, 1634–1782," *Annuaire de l'Association d'Etudes Byzantines (Grèce),* (1969–70), pp. 260–321.

28. Berengo, *La Società veneta alla fine del Settecento,* pp. 288–89.

29. When a Venetian publisher undertook to print an Italian edition of the French *Encyclopédie* in 1782, articles touching on religion and other sensitive subjects were censored. See Guy Dumas, *La fin de la République de Venise: Aspects et reflets littéraires* (Paris, 1964), p. 174.

30. Berengo, *La Società veneta,* pp. 189–94; Dumas, *La Fin de la Republique de Venise,* pp. 182–88.

31. Sergio Bettini, *Il pittore Panajoti Doxarà, fondatore della pittora greca moderna* (Venice, 1942); A. Procopiou, *La peinture religieuse dans les îles ioniennes pendant le XVIIIe siècle* (Paris, 1939).

32. There seems to be no good study of Mavrocordato, but see Nestor Camariano, *Alexandre Mavrocordato, le Grand Drogman. Son Activité diplomatique, 1673–1709* (Thessalonika, 1970).

33. In 1667, for instance, Hospodar Serban Cantacuzene sent his brother to Padua. See A. A. Pallis, *Greek Miscellany: A Collection of Essays on Medieval and Modern Greece* (Athens, 1964), p. 116.

34. See *Istoria Artelor Plastice in Romania* 2 (Bucharest, 1970), with French summary, pp. 252–301; Paul Henry, *Les Eglises de la Moldavie du Nord, des origines à la fin du XVIe siècle* (2 vols.; Paris, 1930). These authorities equate periods of Rumanian independence with artistic greatness, and tend to denigrate Phanariot monuments in a way which the magnificent photographs of both works seem, at least to my eyes, not to sustain.

35. Early in his career as patriarch Dositheos quarreled with Roman Catholics in Jerusalem over control of the Holy Places. Having, on the whole, been discomfitted, he spent most of his subsequent career in Moldavia, where the patriarchate of Jerusalem owned important estates. See the article, "Dosithée" in *Dictionnaire de Théologie Catholique,* which, although disfigured by a strongly polemical tone, is magnificently learned and exact.

36. Emile Turdenau, *Le Livre roumain à travers les siècles* (Paris, 1959), pp. 16–18. Dositheos was consciously rivaling the *Propa-*

ganda Fide in this activity; publication of holy books in oriental languages was a regular part of Roman Catholic missionary effort.

37. As with earlier efforts to define Orthodox doctrine in brief compass, Dositheos' confession was also generated by western pressures; in this instance, arising from theological debate in France. In 1666 a Calvinist writer named Jean Claude claimed that Calvinist doctrines were also those of the Greek Orthodox church. He was relying, of course, on the creed published at Geneva in 1629 attributed to Cyril Lukaris. When this came to Dositheos' attention, he responded with a point by point rebuttal of Lukaris' creed. Earlier Orthodox credal definitions had not been published in western Europe; the later centrality of Dositheos' creed may in part depend on the fact that it was given great publicity by French Catholics as a way of showing how false and untrustworthy Calvinist propaganda was. Cf. Paul Trivier, *Cyrille Lucar, sa vie et son influence* (Paris, 1887), pp. 147 ff.

38. On Dositheos see P. A. Palmieri, *Dositeo, Patriarca greco di Gerusalemme* (Florence, 1909); Runciman, *The Great Church in Captivity*, pp. 347–52.

39. Karyophylles was compelled to withdraw to a monastery in Moldavia, directly under Dositheos' eye, where he soon died (1692). Cf. "Caryophylles, Jean" in *Dictionnaire de Théologie Catholique*; Cléobule Tsourkas, *Les Débuts de l'enseignement philosophique et de la libre pensée dans les Balans* (2d ed.; Thessaloniki, 1967), p. 85.

40. Jesuit schools existed at Constantinople, Smyrna, Chios, Naxos, Santorini, and Tinos. Some of them, especially the school of Chios, were flourishing institutions with scores or even hundreds of students. See G. Hofmann, "Apostolato dei Gesuiti nell oriente greco, 1583–1773," *Orientalia Christiana Periodica* 1 (1935): 139–63.

41. The title of one of his main works speaks for itself: *Ioannis Baptistae Van Helmont physices universalis doctrine et christianae fidei congrua et necessaria philosophia*. Van Helmont (1577–1644) was a Dutchman, most famous today for having invented the term "gas." What so impressed Cantemir was his posthumously published work *Ortus Medicinae* (1648), a mélange of chemical, physical, and medical information and ideas that struck Cantemir as being a clear advance upon the familiar doctrines and ideas of Paduan medicine. On Cantemir see Dan Badarau, *Filozofia lui Dimitrie Cantemir* (Bucharest, 1964), French summary, pp. 394–410; Nichola Iorga, *Byzance après Byzance* (Bucharest, 1935), pp.

208–11. Also the very impressive work, Demetrius Cantemir, *The History of the Growth and Decay of the Ottoman Empire*, trans. N. Tindall (London, 1734). This was the only part of Cantemir's writings that westerners were interested in.

42. Arsenios III first rallied to the Venetians, whose operations along the Dalmatian coast depended very much upon military aid from Montenegrin and other local fighting manpower. Only in 1689, when an imperial general penetrated as far as Peć itself and summoned Arsenios back to his see on threat of deposition if he persisted in preferring the Venetians, did the patriach accept Emperor Leopold's claims to exercise suzerainty over the Serbs by virtue of his title as king of Hungary. The withdrawal of 1690 shifted perhaps as many as 100,000 Serbs northward; it inaugurated a very significant series of population movements, allowing Albanians to take over the heartland of medieval Serbia, while Serbs undertook a large-scale pioneering enterprise in forested lands (previously almost uninhabited) lying to the northward in the valleys of the Sava and Morava rivers. For Arsenios III and his political entanglements cf. Ladislas Hadrovics, *Le peuple Serbe et son église sous la domination turque* (Paris, 1947), pp. 135–48.

43. Cf. the excellent discussion in Billington, *Icon and Axe*, pp. 163–205.

44. After a Catholic education in Poland and Rome, Prokopovich reacted against the indoctrination of his youth by becoming a follower of Christian Wolff, and it was this brand of "Enlightened" philosophy that he taught at Kiev Academy before Peter encountered him. Cf. Eduard Winter, *Byzanz und Rom im Kampf um die Ukraine* (Leipzig, 1942), pp. 108–12. This, of course, made Prokopovich doubly anathema to the Greeks!

45. In 1613 an Italian architect, Sebastiani Bracci, remodeled the Church of the Assumption in Kiev in baroque style. Cf. Ettore Lo Gatto, *Gli Artisti italiani in Russia* (Rome, 1934), 1: 97.

46. Arthur Voyce, *Art and Architecture of Medieval Russia* (Norman, Oklahoma, 1967), p. 210; Lo Gatto, *Gli Artisti italiani*, 2: 21–46. The two most important architects for Saint Petersburg were Domenico Trezzini (1670–1733) and Bartolemeo Bastelli (1700–1764). Peter hired Trezzini away from the king of Denmark's service; his fame prior to his arrival in Russia rested on the Copenhagen Stock Exchange building rather than on anything constructed in Italy.

47. For Peter's plans, which stirred response mainly in distant

Montenegro, see B. H. Sumner, *Peter the Great and the Ottoman Empire* (Oxford, 1949).

48. See Timothy Ware, *Eustratios Argenti, A Study of the Greek Church under Turkish Rule* (Oxford, 1964). The subtitle of this book is properly indicative of its contents, for the book is an opinionated and learned intellectual history of Greek Orthodoxy from 1453 to 1821. Ware appears to be a convert to Orthodoxy, and exhibits the usual traits associated with such a personal history.

His hero, Argenti (ca. 1685–1757), turned his back on the west where he had been trained (at Padua among other places) and devoted his mature years to defining and emphasizing theological differences between Orthodoxy and both Roman Catholic and Protestant doctrines.

49. Hadrovics, *Le peuple Serbe et son église*, pp. 152–54; Theodore H. Papadopoullos, *Studies and Documents relating to the History of the Greek Church and People under Turkish Domination* (Brussels, 1952), pp. 89–91.

50. In 1744, for instance, a revived and more inclusive code of canon law, the *Hexabiblios,* was published in *koine* (at Venice, incidentally), and this became thereafter the basis of most church-administered law. It remained officially in force in the kingdom of Greece until 1946. Cf. N. J. Pantazopoulos, *Church and Law in the Balkan Peninsula during the Ottoman Rule* (Thessalonika, 1967), p. 46. Between 1764 and 1768 Patriarch Samuel I made church property subject to the control of boards on which laymen served side by side with clerics. This prevented individual prelates from mortgaging church property for their personal purposes as had often happened before. Cf. N. Pantazopoulos, "Community laws and customs of Western Macedonia under Ottoman Rule," *Balkan Studies* 2 (1961): 1–22.

51. Pantazopoulos, *Church and Law*, p. 33.

52. In 1755 the œcumenical patriarch declared that converts from the Roman and Armenian obedience would have to be rebaptized. This was largely a riposte to recent Catholic missionary successes among Armenians and Arabic-speaking Christians of Syria. It amounted to a gratuitous insult; but popular sentiment in Constantinople supported the move, so that efforts to undo the ruling provoked popular riots. The principle therefore still stands. For details cf. Papadopoullos, *Church and Law*, pp. 159–247.

53. C. Th. Dimaras, *La Grèce au temps des lumières* (Geneva, 1969). G. P. Henderson, *The Revival of Greek Thought, 1620–1830* (Albany, N. Y., 1970), is disappointingly superficial.

54. See N. G. Svoronos, *Le Commerce de Salonique au XVIIIe siècle* (Paris, 1956), pp. 351–56 and passim.

55. The interest was mutual. In 1704 a translation of the *Thousand and One Nights* by Antoine Galland started a vogue for Ottoman exotica in France, which soon spread also to England and more widely in western Europe. See Norman Daniel, *Islam and the West: The Making of an Image* (Edinburgh, 1960), pp. 10–20. On Polish participation in this vogue see Jan Reychman, "A l'Epoque des 'Lumières': Les Influences orientales en Pologne et dans les pays limitrophes," *Annales: Economies, Sociétés, Civilisations* 22 (1965): 537–46. Among the English, Lady Mary Wortley Montagu's *Letters during Mr. Wortley's Embassy* (London, 1725) were largely responsible for initiating enthusiasm for things Turkish.

56. Niyazi Berkes, *The Development of Secularism in Turkey* (Montreal, 1964), pp. 25–50. Among the books Ibrahim printed were a history of America (written originally in 1583), a history of Tamerlane, and a chronology of universal history. A description of each may be seen in M. l'Abbé Toderini, *De la Littérature Turque*, (Paris, 1789), 3: 17–147; cf. also Abdulhak Adnan, *Le science chez les Turcs Ottomans* (Paris, 1939), pp. 74, 120 ff.

57. Celal Esad Arseven, *Les Arts décoratifs turcs* (Istanbul, n.d.), pp. 93–95.

58. Cf. Paul Masson, *Histoire du commerce français dans le Levant au XVIIIe siècle* (Paris, 1911).

59. Turkish victories over the Austrians were real enough; but the decisive factor was French diplomatic intervention, and the impending crisis for Hapsburg power involved in Maria Theresa's succession. The Turks were conscious of French aid, but were, not unnaturally, mainly impressed by their own victories. Cf. Lavender Cassels, *The Struggle for the Ottoman Empire, 1717–1740* (London, 1966).

60. Godfrey Goodwin, *A History of Ottoman Architecture* (Baltimore, 1971), pp. 334 ff. Mosques in baroque style are sometimes surprisingly successful, at least to my eyes, despite (or perhaps because of) fundamentally incongruous associations.

61. On Saint Nicodemus and the revival of hesychast styles of piety in nineteenth-century Russia see Timothy Ware, *The Orthodox Church* (Harmondsworth, 1963), pp. 110–11; 128–37; C. Papoulidis, "Portée œcumenique des renouveaux monastiques au XVIIIe siècle dans l'église orthodoxe," *Balkan Studies* 10 (1969): 105–12.

Register of Names and Places

Index

326

Index

Index

Index

Index

Index

Index

Index

Index